THE SUEZ–SINAI CRISIS 1956

Published in cooperation with
The Ben-Gurion Research Centre
Ben-Gurion University of the Negev
Sede Boqer

The Suez–Sinai Crisis 1956

RETROSPECTIVE AND REAPPRAISAL

Edited by

Selwyn Ilan Troen and Moshe Shemesh
Ben-Gurion University of the Negev

NEW YORK
COLUMBIA UNIVERSITY PRESS

Printed in Great Britain

c 10 9 8 7 6 5 4 3 2 1

Library of Congress Cataloging-in-Publication Data

The Suez–Sinai crisis, 1956 : retrospective and reappraisal / edited
by Selwyn Ilan Troen and Moshe Shemesh.
   p.   cm.
   Based on proceedings from an international conference held at Ben
Gurion Research Centre.
   Includes bibliographical references.
   ISBN 0-231-07292-9
   1. Egypt—History—Intervention, 1956—Congresses.   I. Troen
Selwyn Ilan.   II. Shemesh, Moshe.
DT107.83.S795   1990
962.05'3—dc20   89-25169
                                                            CIP

FOR OUR PARENTS

CONTENTS

PART THREE: THE SUPERPOWERS

CONTENTS

PART FOUR:
PARTICIPANTS RECORD THE EVENTS

MAPS AND ILLUSTRATIONS

PREFACE

The perspective of thirty years after the Suez and Sinai Campaigns offers a new and unique opportunity to reexamine one of the central events in contemporary history. By conventional wisdom, the crisis of 1956 was a turning point in international affairs and in the history of the Middle East. The inability of the British and French to recapture Suez after Nasser's nationalization of the Canal signaled the irrevocable decline of European imperialism. In the vacuum that emerged in the wake of the Suez and Sinai Campaigns, both Russia and the United States became far more directly active in the region. At the same time, the principles of Nasser's Arab nationalism spread rapidly throughout the region and Nasser emerged as the paramount leader of the Arab world. For Israel, the Sinai Campaign was a second war of independence and gained her recognition throughout the Third World and a decade of relative peace.

While each period offers its own opportunities for a perspective on historical events, the thirtieth anniversary of the Suez and Sinai Campaigns has special advantages. Since 1956, the region has undergone significant change in the light of which the events of Suez can now be more clearly understood – the union between Egypt and Syria and its disintegration, the continual changes in regimes and competition for primacy between them, the death of Nasser and the rise of Sadat and Assad, the Six Day War of June 1967 and the Yom Kippur War in 1973, the deepening Soviet penetration and the attempt by Sadat to reorient to the West, and the emergence of Israel as a significant pro-Western power in the region. In addition, many of the individuals who were involved in shaping the events of 1956 are still active and willing to share the benefits of their perspective and personal knowledge. Finally, new documentation from the period is available particularly through the opening of the Israeli and British archives under the 30-year rule that permits at least limited disclosure of official records.

In October 1986, the Ben-Gurion Research Centre and Archives organized an international conference to reexamine the events of 1956. There was, of course, an attempt to reconstruct with the benefit of hindsight as faithfully as possible the Suez–Sinai Crisis. Since many of the events leading to Suez and Sinai were shrouded in secrecy, much writing by statesmen, historians and journalists has been devoted to uncovering the facts and motivations of the co-operation or 'collusion' between France, Great Britain and Israel. Our concerns went well beyond reconstructing the past. We wished to examine central issues that have enduring value: (a) the military lessons that were drawn from the conflict, (b) the limits to power for regional states, the traditional imperialist states and the superpowers, and (c) the consequences of that conflict for the participants and the region.

As a result of these meetings, many of the participants prepared articles which developed the issues that were explored. In order to ensure that the book was comprehensive and balanced, other scholars were asked to contribute essays on designated topics. The final selection of contributors has favoured analyses of the belligerents with special emphasis placed on Israel, Britain and Egypt. In addition, the role of the superpowers has been incorporated, with emphasis being placed on the United States because of its crucial role in shaping the outcome of the war. The consequence is this book which blends the personal viewpoints of statesmen and military leaders who were involved in the war with the contributions of scholars who have established reputations for criticial analysis in international relations, military history and the history of the countries in the region. Our intention has been to provide an interdisciplinary book that has the qualities of balance, range and authority.

This book also makes an important contribution to our knowledge of Suez and Sinai through hitherto unavailable documentation. This documentation is biased towards Egypt and Israel since it appeared that the most interesting new materials were available from these sources. These include selections from Ben-Gurion's diary of 1956 which gives inside information on the decision-making process within Israel that led to the war as well as detailed testimony on the 'collusion' at Sèvres that produced the terms of agreement for a coordinated attack on Egypt. Although the official Protocol of Sèvres is not yet available for public examination, the Ben-Gurion diary covers more completely than any other document the principal points of the agreement by France, Britain and Israel for cooperation in a war against Nasser's Egypt. There are also selections from the memoirs of Nasser's Vice-President, Bughdadi, who was by Nasser's side during the war. He gives us an important picture of the Egyptian leadership's conduct during its most critical crisis since the Revolution in 1952. There are also selections from the diary of a high civilian official actively involved in politics, the Minister of Agrarian Reform, Sayyid Mar'i. Mar'i reports on government debates as well as popular reactions during the crisis. In addition, published here for the first time, is the captured Egyptian Army Operation Order of 1 September 1956 for the defence of Egypt, which sheds much light on Egypt's strategic, military and political assessments at that time.

Our intent, both in the body of the book and in the appendices, has been to present the events of 1956 from different viewpoints. This approach should provide scholars and students of military history, international relations and Middle Eastern history with a benchmark study that will enable them to reconstruct for themselves interpretations of the Suez–Sinai Crisis and its repercussions.

The creation of this volume is due to the efforts of many individuals. The first debt we wish to acknowledge is to the advisory committee which aided us in organizing the international symposium on the Suez and Sinai Campaigns that was held in Beer Sheva and Sede Boqer, Israel, in October 1986: Professors Shlomo Avineri and Yehoshafat Harkabi of the Hebrew University, Professor Itamar Rabinovich of Tel-Aviv University, and Professor Elie Kedourie of the London School of Economics. We also benefited from the assistance of Ambassador Asher Ben-Natan, Chairman of the Ben-Gurion Foundation, Mr. Haim Yisraeli, Director-General of the Office of Israel's Minister of Defence, Mr. Elhanan Yishai, Advisor to Prime Minister Shimon Peres, U.S. Ambassador to Israel Mr. Thomas Pickering and Mr. Stuart Eizenstaat of Washington.

Essential to the success of the project were the good offices and funds provided through Mr. Jack Spitzer of Seattle, Chairman of the David Ben-Gurion Centennial Committee of the United States. We are most grateful for grants from Mr. and Mrs. Leonard Shane of Newport Beach, California and Mr. Albert Bildner of New York. Special thanks are due Mrs. Mickey Katzman of Boston for support in translating the Ben-Gurion Diary and to Mr. and Mrs. Sidney Corob of London and to the Wolf Corob Foundation of Jerusalem for contributing to the publication of this book.

Professor Selwyn Troen wishes to express his deep appreciation to Lord Weidenfeld of Chelsea for the support he received from the Weidenfeld Fellowships as a Senior Associate Member at St. Antony's College, Oxford, in 1988–89 and through 1989–90. Dr

Moshe Shemesh would like to acknowledge Lord Weidenfeld in establishing the Weidenfeld Visiting Fellowship at St. Antony's College. Dr. Shemesh was the first and grateful recipient of this award in 1988–89. The editors had the opportunity to complete this book during their stay at Oxford.

We owe a special debt to our colleagues at the Ben-Gurion Research Centre in Sede Boqer for many and diverse services connected with the conference and the book. Mrs. Shulamit Amir-Zarmi produced the translation of the Ben-Gurion Diary and Abd al-Latif al-Bughdadi's memoirs. Benjamin Gil translated the article by Yonah Bandmann and the Operation Order of the Egyptian Army. Mr. Natan Aridan gave continual assistance from the early stages of the project through preparing the final text. Mr. Tuviya Freiling and Mrs. Yael Rosenfeld of the Ben-Gurion Archives provided essential services in preparing the text of Ben-Gurion's Diary. Dr Carol Troen afforded important editorial advice and assistance. Mr. Shaul Shragai of the Ben-Gurion Research Centre's Publications Unit faithfully organized the complex processes involved in turning the many articles in different languages into a manuscript. We benefited in numerous ways throughout the project from the efforts of Mrs. Ita Goldberg and Mrs. Shoshana Silberbush of the Ben-Gurion Centre's administration.

Selwyn Ilan Troen and Moshe Shemesh

Part I
INTRODUCTION

1

The Suez–Sinai Campaign: Background

Chaim Herzog

THE POLITICAL BACKGROUND

During the seven years following the signing of the Armistice Agreements, instead of peace treaties being achieved as envisaged in the preambles to the agreements, the rift between Israel and the Arab states widened, and the relations along Israel's borders (apart from that with Lebanon) deteriorated. The Arabs persisted in their policy of refusing to accept the fact that Israel existed as a sovereign state, a member of the international community and an independent entity. Whilst the War of Independence, as a war, had been fought and was, physically speaking, over, its causes and the motives behind the enmity of the Arab states against Israel continued to exist and to brew. Within months of the signing of the 1949 Armistice Agreements, border incursions, raids, economic warfare and other violations became the order of the day. By 1954, it was clear that the incursions of fidaiyyun murder groups were not isolated incidents, but, like the economic sanctions against Israeli commercial and maritime interests, were organized and implemented with the knowledge and co-operation of the Arab governments.

The major Arab defeat in 1948 exacerbated many of their internal problems, bringing to the fore the extreme elements and creating an atmosphere of unrest and near-revolution in many of the Arab countries. In July 1951, King Abdulla of Jordan, who had secretly initialled an agreement intended to lead to a peace accord with Israel, was assassinated, struck down by the agents of the Mufti of Jerusalem, Hajj Amin al-Husseini, on the steps of the al-Aqsa Mosque on the Temple Mount in Jerusalem. (His grandson Hussein, who was to be proclaimed King of Jordan a year later, was at his side.) In Egypt, the Egyptian Prime Minister, Nuqrashi Pasha, was assassinated in the aftermath of the war. The Syrian

3

Government was overthrown by General Husni al-Za'im in 1949, and he in turn was overthrown in 1951; thereafter, Syria was to be torn by frequent military revolutions until the advent in 1970 of President Asad. In Egypt, a group of so-called 'Free Officers' led by Lieutenant-Colonel Gamal Abd al-Nasser seized control of the government on 23 July 1952 and sent King Farouq into exile. For a period, the officers appointed as their leader General Muhammad Naguib, who had emerged from the 1948 war as a popular figure, but he was soon deposed and full authority over the new republic was assumed by Nasser. (One of the leading members of the Free Officers group who participated in the revolution was Lieutenant-Colonel Anwar al-Sadat, later to be the President of Egypt and the first Arab leader to sign a peace treaty with Israel.) In Jordan, moves made by the British government to induce the Kingdom to join the Western Middle East alliance known as the Baghdad Pact provoked riots in December 1955. This extreme reaction was brought about by an anti-Western, pro-Nasser change of direction in the Jordanian government: Glubb Pasha and the British officers serving in the Arab Legion were dismissed summarily, and thereafter armed incursions from Jordan by fidaiyyun groups frequently attacked objectives in Israel.

The rise of Nasser to power in Egypt was welcomed at first by Israel. Indeed the aims of the revolution and initial contacts with Nasser's regime inspired hope for the future. But Nasser's mixture of radicalism and extreme Arab nationalism, coupled with an ambition to achieve leadership in the Arab world, pre-eminence in the world of Islam and primacy in the so-called non-aligned group of nations (which, with Presidents Tito and Nehru, he founded), gradually came to expression in a bitter, blind antagonism to Israel. It was to lead Egypt to tragedy.

In late 1955, a massive arms transaction between Egypt and Czechoslovakia was concluded, whereby Egypt received modern weapons. This, as Nasser declared, constituted a major step toward the decisive battle for the destruction of Israel. Egypt received 530 armoured vehicles (230 tanks, 200 armoured troop carriers and 100 self-propelled guns), some 500 artillery pieces, and up to 200 fighter, bomber and transport aircraft, plus destroyers, motor torpedo-boats and submarines. Thus was established the first major Soviet foothold in the Middle East. This arms agreement with the Eastern bloc was a major boost to Nasser's ambitions. He was now establishing himself as the leading element hostile to 'Western imperialism' in the Middle East, and becoming a serious embarrassment to the British and French in the area. Besides supporting radical governments in Africa and backing the fidaiyyun raids on Israel, he was active in helping the FLN revolutionaries in Algeria against French rule. This, however, created a bond of common interest between Israel and France, as a result of which Shimon Peres (then the dynamic Director-General of Israel's Ministry of Defence) was able to promote various areas of co-operation between the two countries. Israel now began to receive shipments of arms from France (although sufficient only to prevent Egypt's superiority in weaponry from exceeding four to one on the eve of the Sinai Campaign).

Egypt meanwhile blocked the passage of Israeli vessels in the international waterways of the area in violation both of the 1949 Armistice Agreement and of international law. In order to reach the Red Sea and maintain commercial and maritime contacts with the Far East and Africa, Israeli vessels had to navigate through the Straits of Tiran, which Egypt had blocked by installing a coastal artillery battery at Ras Nasrani. Egypt had also barred all passage by Israeli vessels through the Suez Canal – despite a resolution of the United Nations Security Council in 1951 censuring Egypt's policy on this issue. But, even after this resolution, Egypt, aided politically by the Soviet Union, extended the maritime limitations, impounding Israeli vessels, cargo and crews.

In the course of negotiations with Great Britain, Nasser negotiated the withdrawal of British troops from the Suez Canal zone, where they had been stationed for over 80 years by treaty. He was also negotiating with the United States government and with the British government for a loan from the International Bank for reconstruction and development to finance the construction of a dam on the river Nile above Aswan. This would supply electricity, control the Nile floods and by irrigation increase considerably the area of arable land in Egypt. At the same time, he conducted parallel negotiations on this project with the Soviet Union. But his attempt to play off West against East on this issue aroused the wrath of the United States Secretary of State, John Foster Dulles, who in July 1956 withdrew the American offer to finance the dam. Infuriated, Nasser nationalized the Suez on 26 July 1956 by seizing control from the Suez Canal Company, in which the British government held a majority share, and abrogating the Anglo-Egyptian Treaty. Seeing the seizure of the canal as a threat to their strategic interests – including their oil-supply routes – the British and French began to prepare contingency plans. Forces were moved to Malta and Cyprus in the Mediterranean in preparation for the seizure of the Canal Zone and, indirectly, to bring about Nasser's downfall. Such a campaign, whilst objectively independent of the local Arab–Israeli problems, naturally had its implications – a factor that undoubtedly contributed to the decision-making process prior to the start of the campaign.

By this time, the Israeli leadership had reached the conclusion that Nasser was heading for an all-out war against Israel. This could be the only explanation for the joint military command established in October 1955 between Egypt and Syria (to be expanded in 1956 to include Jordan). The blockade of the Suez Canal and the Gulf of Aqaba was part of an all-out economic war against Israel, while the fidaiyyun incursions into Israel were becoming more frequent and exacting greater numbers of casualties – some 260 Israeli citizens being killed or wounded by the fidaiyyun in 1955. The Egyptians would very rapidly absorb the weapons supplied by the Soviet bloc. It was clear that Israel could not allow Nasser to develop his plans with impunity. Accordingly, in July 1956, David Ben-Gurion decided that he had no option but to take a pre-emptive move, and gave instructions to the Israeli General Staff to plan for war in the course of 1956, concentrating initially on the opening of the Straits of Tiran.

Israel meanwhile mounted diplomatic efforts to expedite the supply of arms from France. According to Moshe Dayan, the Chief of Staff at the time, the Israeli Military Attaché in Paris cabled on 1 September 1956, advising him of the Anglo-French plans against the Suez Canal and informing him that Admiral Pierre Barjot, who was to be Deputy Commander of the Combined Allied Forces, was of the opinion that Israel should be invited to take part in the operation. Ben-Gurion's instructions were to reply that in principle Israel was ready to co-operate. An exploratory meeting took place six days later between the Israeli Chief of Operations and French military representatives, while Shimon Peres continued talks in Paris with the French Minister of Defence, Maurice Bourgès-Maunoury. At the end of the month, an Israeli mission headed by Foreign Minister Golda Meir, and including Peres and Dayan, met a French mission that included the French Defence Minister and the French Foreign Minister, Christian Pineau. As the preparations were set afoot to strike at Egypt, Franco-Israeli meetings became more frequent. Then, on 21 October, at the invitation of the French, Ben-Gurion flew to Sèvres in France, accompanied by Shimon Peres and Moshe Dayan. At these negotiations, in which the French

Prime Minister, Guy Mollet, participated, they were joined by a British mission consisting of the British Foreign Minister Selwyn Lloyd and one senior official. After much discussion, during which Ben-Gurion was very hesitant because of his innate lack of trust in the British, the plan was arranged in such a way that Israel's first moves would not be interpreted as an invasion, and its forces could be withdrawn should the British and French allies not fulfil their part of the agreement.

A further factor affecting considerations was the way in which both the United States and the Soviet Union were preoccupied in such a manner (or so it was estimated) as to limit their freedom of action at the time. The United States was in the throes of a Presidential election, during which it was assumed that President Eisenhower would not take any vital international decision that might prejudice his chances of re-election. Similarly, the Soviet Union was busy during the three months prior to the campaign, quelling the national urge for liberalization that had begun to come to expression in Poland and Hungary.

By October 1956, the Egyptian threat to Israel had taken on an increasingly active form. Fidaiyyun raids reached an all-time high, in both intensity and violence, and the Israeli reprisal policy did not supply any final, secure or convincing answer. This and the prevailing global situation placed Israel in a position in which it had to take advantage of the circumstances in order to break the Egyptian stranglehold on its commercial sea routes and along its border areas. The aims were to be threefold: to remove the threat, wholly or partially, of the Egyptian Army in the Sinai; to destroy the framework of the fidaiyyun; and to secure the freedom of navigation through the Straits of Tiran. Only thus would Israel place itself in a comfortable bargaining position for the political struggle that would undoubtedly ensue.

The Israeli command had succeeded in creating an artificial tension with Jordan thus giving the impression that Israel's mobilization – as and when it would be noticed, as doubtless it would be – was in preparation for action against the Jordanians. Following the murder of two Israeli farm workers an attack was launched on 10 October on the frontier town of Qalqilia, and King Hussein invoked the Anglo-Jordanian Defence Treaty against Israel. This operation, costly to Israel, did however concentrate the area of tension along the Jordanian border and not Sinai.

7

INTRODUCTION

THE MILITARY BACKGROUND

The Sinai Peninsula is a parched desert area in the form of an inverted triangle, serving as both a connecting corridor and a dividing barrier between Egypt and Israel. It provides either side with an ideal jumping-off ground in an attack against the other. The northern side, on the Mediterranean coast, is 134 miles long; its western side, along the banks of the Suez Canal and the Gulf of Suez, is 311 miles long; and its eastern side, along the Gulf of Aqaba, is 155 miles long. Topography in the northern half ranges from undulating sand dunes and ridges, palm groves and salt flats along the coastal plain, to a central hilly area with a vertical range of ridges reaching heights of up to 3,500 feet. Here there are but limited axes for passage, through which Egypt had constructed main roads, utilizing the negotiable passes between the high ridges and the deep, powdery-sandy wadis. The lower half of the peninsula represents the most extreme forms of desert topography – steep, saw-tooth mountain ranges, deep powdery wadis devoid of water, greenery and negotiable roads. The only passable road built in this area by the Egyptians had been, in fact, the coastal road connecting Suez, Ras el-Sudar, el-Tur and Sharm el-Sheikh along the coast of the Gulf of Suez.

The nature of the territory dictated over the centuries the course of the warfare in the Sinai, a form of warfare concentrated on the negotiable routes and on the critically-strategic ridges overlooking such routes. In the Sinai, there are no rivers, forests or jungles: the conflict is predetermined by the demands of the desert, and this in fact is clear from the battles waged there in 1956.

On 29 October 1956, at 1700 hours, an Israeli parachute battalion under command of Lieutenant-Colonel Rafael ('Raful') Eitan, who was many years later to be Chief of Staff of the Israel Defence Forces, and part of the 202 Parachute Brigade commanded by Colonel Ariel Sharon, dropped in central Sinai at the eastern entrance to the Mitla Pass 156 miles from Israel and 45 miles from the Suez Canal. Two hours before the parachuting of the forces at the Mitla Pass, four Israeli piston-engined P-51 Mustang fighters carried out a hair-raising operation. Descending to 12 feet above the ground, they cut with their propellers and wings all the overhead telephone lines in the Sinai connecting the various Egyptian headquarters and units. The nature of this attack kept the Egyptians

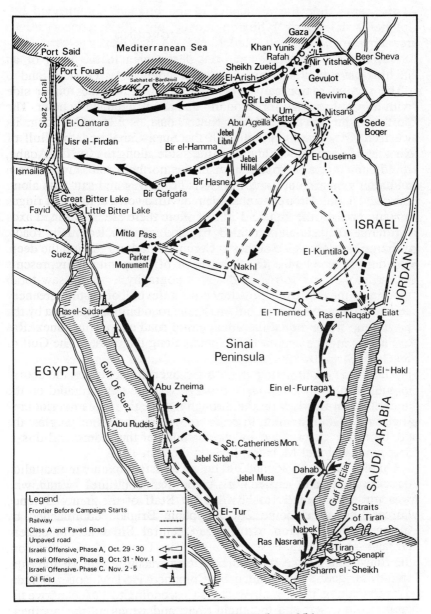

The Sinai Campaign 29.10–5.11.1956

guessing for some 24 hours as to the real purpose of the operation. At the same time the remainder of the brigade, commanded by Colonel Ariel ('Arik') Sharon moved out of its concentration area near the Jordanian border, crossed the Negev Desert and developed its drive across the Sinai, passing Kuntilla, Themed and Nakhl. Heavy fighting soon developed at the Mitla Pass.

The second major battle was that to neutralize the main concentration of Egyptian forces in the Sinai, the defended localities of Quseima/Abu Ageilla and Um Kattef, and to overrun the central axis from Quseima to Ismailia. This front blocked the main central axis that, if opened, would ensure the success of the campaign, as it would open up an alternative transport and supply route from Israel to Sharon's brigade at the Mitla Pass. The task was entrusted to the 38th Divisional Group commanded by Colonel Yehuda Wallach, and comprising the 4th and 10th Infantry Brigades and the 7th Armoured Brigade commanded by Colonel Uri Ben Ari. At a certain point G-o-C Southern Command Major-General Assaf Simhoni advanced the entry of the crack 7th Armoured Brigade into the battle.

By the morning of 2 November the Israelis had completed the assault on the Abu Ageilla/Um Kattef system of defence, thus opening up a good-quality supply route to the forces at the Mitla Pass and along the central axis, and cut off the Egyptian garrison in the Gaza Strip. A divisional task force under Brigadier-General Haim Laskov, comprising the 1st Golani Infantry Brigade under Colonel Benjamin Gibli, and the 27th Armoured Brigade under Colonel Haim Bar-Lev, broke through the Rafah camp area and the area of the Rafah junction in order to open up the route to el-Arish and northern Gaza. One of the battalions was commanded by Lieutenant-Colonel Meir Pa'il.

A major battle took place here, and on 2 November the 27th Armoured Brigade entered el-Arish and continued westward. Meanwhile the Israeli 11th Brigade under Colonel Aharon Doron was dealing with the 10,000 Egyptian troops, particularly the Palestinian 8th Division, in the Gaza Strip. By 3 November the area had been mopped up.

Perhaps one of the more dramatic moves was that of the 9th Infantry Brigade, commanded by Colonel Avraham Yoffe, which advanced along the rough west coast of the Gulf of Aqaba and negotiated a desert and mountain route nothing more than a camel route, over which no motorized unit had ever moved. The brigade negotiated the distance to Sharm el-Sheikh with 200 vehicles and 1800 men against sporadic resistance, but almost impossible physical ground conditions.

In the meantime the paratroopers had moved down from the north to Sharm el-Sheik, and on the morning of 5 November the 9th Brigade took control of the locality which was blocking the Straits of Tiran, and met up with units of Sharon's parachute brigade which had moved down along the Gulf of Suez.

In the initial air battles Israeli superiority was achieved in some 164 air encounters. Later, as French and British aircraft began to bomb Egypt, Egyptian air activity was reduced to a minimum. Thus by the morning of 5 November the Israeli forces had reached the Suez Canal and had opened the Straits of Tiran at Sharm el-Sheikh.

Meanwhile, the allied forces had planned an operation that obviously envisaged heavy opposition on the part of the Egyptians, and indicated their adherence to the set-piece type of battle they apparently anticipated. Consequently, the allied task force set sail only on 1 November from Valetta Harbour in Malta. There is no doubt that the results would have been completely different had the British Prime Minister, Anthony Eden, taken the advice of General Sir Charles Keightley and Lieutenant-General Sir Hugh Stockwell (who had command of British forces in Haifa in 1948 and was now commander of the Allied Land Forces) to effect the landing on 1 November as was originally planned. This would have changed the entire pattern of developments and would have avoided many of the subsequent political issues.

The British forces at sea included an infantry division, a parachute brigade group and a Royal Marine commando brigade, while the French forces included a parachute division, a parachute battalion and a light mechanized regiment. There were also the naval forces of both countries and air forces operating from the British and French aircraft carriers and from Cyprus. As this force was making its way slowly across the Mediterranean, to be joined en route by French units from Algeria and British units from Cyprus, political pressure from the Russians and in the United Nations increased, and the political limitations imposed on the British and French forces grew. They were hampered by a growing degree of hesitation on the part of the political leadership, particularly in Britain, where the government came under very heavy attack both from the opposition and from its own benches.

From 31 October, after the British and French governments delivered an ultimatum calling for a withdrawal of forces from both sides of the area of the Suez Canal, their air forces attacked air bases in Egypt, destroying many Egyptian aircraft. The attacks directed by the Allies were exclusively against Egyptian air bases; at no point did the French or British aircraft become involved in support of the Israeli Forces advancing in the Sinai.

Mounting efforts in the United Nations Security Council were being made to bring about a cease-fire, and twice the British and French vetoed such moves. Meanwhile, the Anglo-French Force was sailing slowly across the Mediterranean, but it was losing in the race against political pressure. Under the pressure of events, Stockwell advanced the dropping of the parachute Forces in the area of Port Said and Port Fouad by a day – to 5 November. Because of growing hostile public opinion in Britain and elsewhere, limitations were imposed on the types of guns that could be used by the naval vessels to shell the landing areas in support of the troops that were now sent in to land. On 6 November, the first British troops landed on the beaches of Port Said, while the French troops landed at Port Fouad. The Egyptian Commander of Port Said, Brigadier Mughi, who had been taken prisoner, refused to issue a general order to surrender. General Stockwell thereupon decided to advance his forces southwards by helicopter and by parachuting troops into Ismailia and Abu Suweir. But, just as these operations were about to be mounted, the British government caved in under international political pressure, and agreed to a cease-fire at midnight on 6/7 November. The French were left with no alternative but reluctantly to follow the British. Thus ended the Sinai–Suez War of 1956.

THE AFTERMATH

There now began protracted negotiations, in which Israel attempted to obtain guarantees in respect of the two major developments that had brought about the war – the blockade of the Straits of Tiran and the fidaiyyun operations into Israel from Egyptian-controlled territory. The creation of a United Nations Emergency Force was proposed by the Canadian government and accepted by the United Nations. Although Israel attempted to hold on to the essential areas of Sharm el-Sheikh and the Gaza Strip, United States pressure forced her to withdraw from these positions in return for 'real guarantees' of passage through the Straits and United Nations participation in the administration of the Gaza Strip. Both the Gaza Strip and Sharm el-Sheikh were to be placed in the control of United

Nations Emergency Forces. Israeli withdrawal was carried out in stages.

In Gaza, the withdrawal of the Israeli forces led to a period of violence in which those who had allegedly 'co-operated' with the Israeli occupying forces, from November 1956 until the Israeli withdrawal in March 1957, were summarily executed. The United Nations soldiers in the Strip lost all control of the roaming fidaiyyun gangs and, indeed, of the entire situation. Within two days of Gaza being transferred to the United Nations, Nasser had nominated a Military Governor for the Strip who, without asking the UN, moved in with his headquarters – the United Nations did not even demur, and this weakness sowed the seeds for future problems in the area. Within a short time, the UN, under pressure of the Egyptians, ordered its forces to vacate the Strip and only to patrol its borders. The UN Emergency Force took up positions along the borders between Israel and Egypt, and at Sharm el-Sheikh.

Israeli shipping did, at last, move freely through the Straits of Tiran to and from Africa and Asia. A comparative lull set in along the Israel–Egyptian border, until ten years later when the 'real guarantees' of passage through the Straits were to be forgotten as Nasser ordered the United Nations forces out of Sinai. As they departed, the threat of war was to loom again.

To conclude, the Sinai Campaign was in many ways a classic. The opening phase was a brilliant application of the strategy of the indirect approach. Captain Sir Basil Liddell Hart, who coined this strategy, characterized the opening moves in the Sinai as one of the most brilliant applications of such an approach in the history of warfare – he considered the Sinai Plan to have been 'a work of art'. It was also the first opportunity accorded to the Israel Defence Forces to prove that what it had built since the War of Independence was an effective fighting force retaining the originality of movement and thought that had prevailed in the Israeli forces as they fought for the establishment of Israel in 1948–49. A marked degree of flexibility also characterized the main decisions in battle, with commanders proving themselves capable of adapting rapidly to changing conditions. This was particularly evident in the manner in which the task forces of the 7th Armoured Brigade were handled during the breakthrough at Abu Ageilla. The Israeli reserve system, which had been mobilized for operations against Egypt in Sinai while managing to keep the objectives of the operation secret, had proved itself. Israel succeeded at the same time in maintaining command of the air, before it became evident to the Egyptians that the British and French Air Forces were likely to become involved. But perhaps the most important point to note was that the tradition established in the War of Independence — whereby the officers invariably led and set a personal example in battle — was implemented in this campaign. A very high percentage of the casualties were incurred by the officers and NCOs and, in all phases of the battle, senior officers were to be seen leading their men under fire.

The Egyptians, who by and large had suffered many reverses during the operations against the Israelis, could maintain that they had not been defeated by the Israelis because they had been obliged to withdraw under the Anglo-French threat. Indeed, Nasser's stand against the onslaught gained for him considerable political prestige, which he portrayed as a highly successful outcome in the final analysis of the war.

The Sinai Campaign also marked the inauguration of the United Nations Emergency Force for peace-keeping purposes. For ten years, the Force performed a valuable task. The failure in 1967 was not that of the Force on the ground, but rather that of the Secretary-General of the United Nations and of that organization itself. A new and important element, which was to become part of the Middle East scene, had been introduced.

Part II
THE BELLIGERENTS

2

Military Lessons:
The British Perspective

J.A. Sellers

The purpose of this paper is to examine the military aspects of the 1956 Suez Crisis from the British perspective to see what lessons can be drawn from it. First, it is important to understand what we and others thought were the aims of the campaign, and how and to what extent they were carried through into the planning and execution of the operation. Next, a brief glance at the structure of our armed forces at the time is necessary to see how well it was suited to the task. Last, the knotty problems of command and relations between allies also merit some attention. The lessons can only be seen in perspective against a short summary of the political and military aspects of the operation.

NATIONAL AIMS

Eden's aim is unequivocally stated in the record of the meeting of the Egypt Committee, a group of five Cabinet Ministers under the Prime Minister's chairmanship, on 30 July. It stated, 'While our ultimate purpose was to place the Canal under international control, our immediate aim was to bring about the downfall of the present Egyptian Government'.[1] It reflected the decision the Cabinet had taken three days earlier, when it met to review Nasser's seizure of the Canal the day before, that HMG should seek to secure, by the use of force if necessary, the reversal of the Egyptian Government's action to nationalize the Suez Canal Company.[2]

Since we had only just left the Canal Zone, a reoccupation posed political and military problems. Two Ministers, Macmillan, Chancellor of the Exchequer, and Lord Salisbury, Lord President of the Council, were tasked to examine the political aspects on the basis of a temporary occupation, after the installation of a more

17

congenial government while an international Canal authority was established.[3] The Chiefs of Staff were to spell out the implications of tying up our theatre and strategic reserves again, plus a division from Germany.[4] Six years later Montgomery was to relate to the House of Lords that when Eden called on him for advice he asked, 'What is your object?' When Eden replied, 'To knock Nasser off his perch', the Field Marshal observed that such an aim would not do and went on to explain that he would need to know what the political object was when Nasser had been knocked off his perch as this would determine how the operation should be carried out.[5]

While the problem of what to do next was a serious one, the criticism that the future had not been considered was unfounded. However, Mountbatten, First Sea Lord, who had advocated the seizure of Port Said by an *attaque brusque* using the Mediterranean Fleet and 3 Commando Brigade in Cyprus, soon changed his mind to become an opponent of the plan but never to the point of resignation.[6]

However, there was a contradiction between the avowed aim of reoccupying the Canal and the main, but more covert, aim of bringing down Nasser. This ambivalence led to a number of problems:

a. How to start the war.
b. The choice of objective: The Canal or Cairo or both?
c. Because the military aim, used by the Joint Planning Staff, was to reoccupy the Canal the operational level of command was not entirely sure what the real aim was.
d. We could neither take advantage of Macmillan's suggestion of an alliance with Israel nor avoid a charge of collusion.[7]

As it was, each of the three participants viewed the situation from different perspectives:

a. Israel, threatened on all sides, and faced with the delivery of Soviet weapons to Egypt, her most powerful neighbour, felt compelled to launch a pre-emptive strike at Egypt's growing power. In particular, Ben-Gurion was intent on breaking the Egyptian blockade of the Straits of Tiran to open up the port of Eilat so that the Negev could be developed. Bringing down Nasser was not an indispensable aim.
b. France, with her interests in the Suez Canal and a guerrilla war in Algeria vociferously supported by Cairo Radio, agreed with Eden that the aim was the removal of Nasser.

18

c. As I mentioned earlier, the British had an overt and a covert aim. Furthermore, open cooperation with Israel would risk straining relations with friendly Arab States, particularly Jordan, with whom we had a treaty, the oil producers and the members of the Baghdad Pact.[8]

COMMAND STRUCTURE

Before looking at the planning it is necessary to take a quick glance at the command structure which had to cope with it (see fig.1). Because the British were to provide nearly two thirds of the Anglo-French forces the Allies agreed that the commanders at the theatre and operational levels would be British and their deputies French. At the theatre level, General Keightley wore two hats. He doubled as Supreme Allied Commander and Commander-in-Chief British Middle East Land Forces. General Beaufre was critical of this arrangement because it insulated the Task Force Commanders from the political requirements, factors and nuances which influence military planning and operations. This was, perhaps, a failure in communication rather than organization. The British Commanders-in-Chief controlled the logistic facilities in Malta and Cyprus and the communications back to the UK. With the need to keep the Task Force Headquarters small so that it could work in Cyprus during the planning stage, afloat during the assault and ashore afterwards, it would have been difficult to cater for the radio facilities to work back to London and Paris, forwards to the subordinate commanders, and sideways to the naval and air task forces and the national theatre force headquarters. The Task Force commanders might have been even more harassed than they were. *Tyne*, our headquarters ship, proved too small to take Beaufre and his staff who had to use the *Gustave-Zédé*.

The diagram, which shows a monolithic structure with the reins of command firmly in British hands, is a little misleading. Although the concept was that the two Governments were to agree on a common policy which would be passed on in directives to General Keightley, there were many matters of national concern over which the French Government had to deal with Admiral Barjot direct. Similarly, at Task Force level, the Allies were supported by their own national logistic systems. Some measure of national command was inevitable. At sea, the Allied Naval Task Forces operated in concert but separately in support of their own land forces. On land, the French assault echelon, known as Force A (10 Parachute

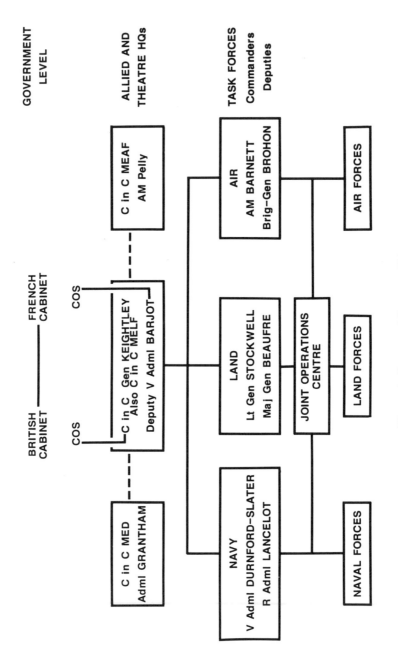

Figure 1. Command Structure Diagram

Division, 7 DMR and three commandos), was tacitly commanded by General Beaufre, although this was never officially recognized. Indeed, General Beaufre's Chief of Staff, Colonel Prieur, was even excluded from a planning conference at General Stockwell's headquarters in Cyprus.

As far as personalities were concerned, Admirals Durnford-Slater and Lancelot got on well together with their pragmatic arrangement. In the air, Air Marshal Barnett, a quiet and workmanlike New Zealander, stayed in the JOC afloat in *Tyne*, tying up air support with the land and sea elements, leaving General Brohon to act as a true deputy ashore, tasking the French and British wings and, incidentally, the French Air Force squadrons supporting the Israelis. One gets the impression that the land force command arrangements did not work quite so smoothly. The charismatic, intuitive, volatile Stockwell and the cool, lucid, intellectual Beaufre did not achieve quite such a close rapport.

INITIAL PLANNING

To return to the planning. The British Joint Planning Staff (JPS) do not appear to have had an outline plan for the reoccupation of the Canal Zone and its base and so the Chiefs of Staff were asked for their advice at the initial Cabinet meeting on 27 July. The Chiefs faced some serious problems.

a. First, the opposition. The Egyptian Army consisted of one armoured and three infantry divisions split between Sinai, the Canal Zone and the Delta backed by a large National Guard and the Police, many of whom were to fight stubbornly. 300 or so Russian tanks had been delivered to Egypt. The Air Force was thought to have had about 200 aircraft in squadron service, including about 45 Mig 15s and 24 Il 28s, whose pilots were still under training. In fact, there were probably no more than 70 operational aircraft.[9] There were some 600–800 Iron Curtain pilots and technicians in Egypt but what their orders would be in the event of an attack, no one knew. Nevertheless, the call on our available resources would be considerable.

b. In spite of having some 750,000 men under arms in all three Services, our defence posture was geared to deterring war in Europe and dealing with minor insurgencies in our colonies. There was no provision for projecting a force overseas for a limited war without calling up reservists and much specialist

21

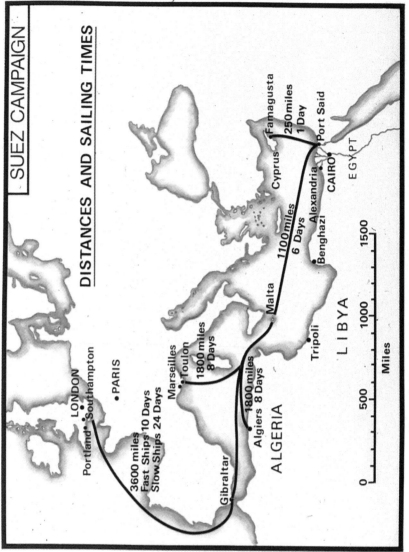

Figure 2. The Suez Campaign – Distance and Sailing Times

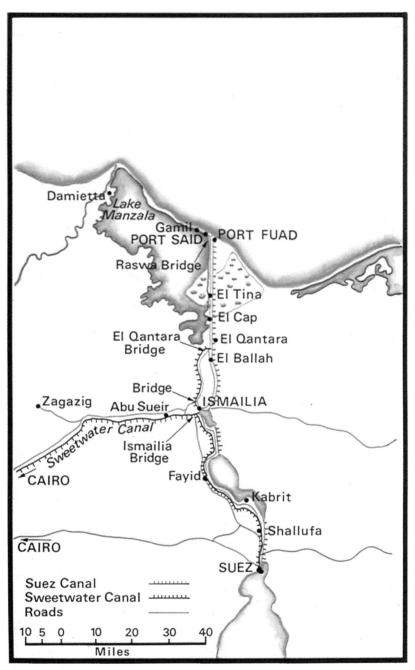

Figure 3. The Canal Zone

training. Nasser appreciated that it would be three or four months before we could mount an attack but reckoned that the political risk of one would fade as time wore on and world opinion mobilized behind him. His estimate of the risk was 90 per cent up to 10 August, 80 per cent to the end of August, 60 per cent in September, 40 per cent in the first half of October and 20 per cent in the second half; thereafter he considered that the risk would evaporate.[10]

c. Our forces in Libya, where we had two armoured regiments, could not be used against another Arab state, however keen our Chancellor of the Exchequer, Harold Macmillan, was about using them.

d. Cyprus had no deep water harbours with alongside loading facilities. The nearest good port was Valetta, Malta, over 1,000 miles away.

e. Our air bases in Cyprus and Malta needed much work to handle the large number of British and French squadrons.

Against this background the Chiefs of Staff considered that a force of some three divisions would be needed to enter Egypt and control the Canal Zone afterwards. They would have recollected that to protect the former base from guerrilla activity after the abrogation of the 1936 Anglo-Egyptian Treaty in 1951 it was necessary to commit to the Canal Zone 1 Infantry Division from the Middle East Land Forces theatre reserve, and two brigades of 3 Infantry Division, 3 Commando Brigade, RM and 16 Independent Parachute Brigade from the UK Strategic Reserve. It would take five to six weeks to requisition the shipping and move the forces to the Mediterranean. Some idea of distances and sailing times may be seen in figure 2. The plan was to land an air and seaborne force at Port Said under cover of a heavy air and naval bombardment while a feint was made at Alexandria. Subsequently, it might be necessary to reoccupy the whole of the Canal Zone but not indefinitely. Eden pressed for a quick airborne attack but the Chiefs of Staff ruled it out as impracticable, emphasizing that such a complicated operation would have to be carefully planned and the assault forces re-trained in their specialist roles.

When General Stockwell was shown the plan in London on 3 August he did not like it. Port Said, at the end of a 27-mile causeway, he said, 'was like a cork in a bottle with a very long neck'[11] (see fig.3). Furthermore, it was on an island. The bridges at Raswa and over the Sweetwater Canal near Qantara were obvious targets for demolition. The port had a limited capacity. The force build-up would be slow. The small airport at Gamil was thought to be unsuitable for anything larger than a Dakota and the nearest major airfield was at Abu Sueir, 50 miles away.

So Stockwell prepared a new plan, HAMILCAR, for a landing at Alexandria, a port with three times the capacity of Port Said and a good airfield close by (see fig.4). He enumerated eight principles:

1. We could neither afford to lose nor risk a setback.
2. The destruction of the Egyptian Air Force was a prerequisite for the protection of sea convoys and the landings.
3. The port and harbour would have to be taken by direct assault supported by naval gunfire. Damage to the town was inevitable.
4. The causeways leading south across Lake Maryut to the airfield would have to be secured by airborne forces.
5. There must be a quick link-up between the seaborne and airborne forces.
6. The follow-up forces must disembark rapidly to destroy the Egyptian army.
7. We must be ready by 15 September.
8. We would not enter Cairo.

The first, second and fifth principles led to over-caution. Provided the Allies had not declared war, the convoys could be sailed from Malta and Algiers with safety. The rapid link-up was the ghost of Arnhem when, faced with a first class enemy, we had tried to capture the bridges over eight water obstacles in a row with insufficient logistic support.[12]

He said that his aim was to occupy the Canal and restore it to international control. It was neither to overthrow Nasser, nor occupy Egypt, nor capture Cairo.[13] Hopefully, the operation could be accomplished in eight days:

2 days to win the air superiority battle.
1 day to establish the force ashore.
2 days to meet and defeat the Egyptian Army.
3 days to reach the Canal.

These timings were optimistic but at least they showed an encouraging concern for speed. The British forces allotted are shown below:

Land Forces:
   3 Commando Brigade

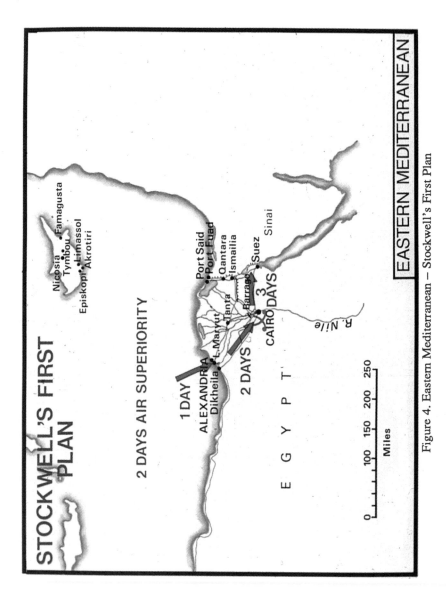

Figure 4. Eastern Mediterranean – Stockwell's First Plan

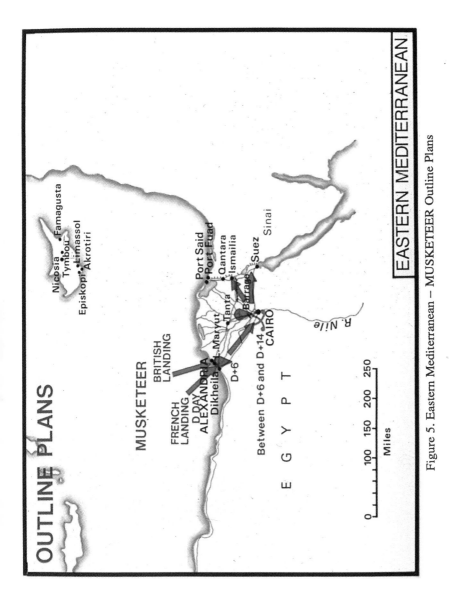

Figure 5. Eastern Mediterranean – MUSKETEER Outline Plans

16 Parachute Brigade
3 Infantry Division, including two armoured regiments
Naval Forces: three carriers with embarked:
  13 fighter-ground attack squadrons
  1 airborne early warning squadron
  2 carriers, troop lift
  Amphibious Warfare Squadron
  Escorts
Air Forces:
  Bomber squadrons: 4 Valiant; 14 Canberra
  Fighter-ground attack squadrons: 2 Hunter; 4 Venom; 1 Meteor,
    night fighter
  Reconnaissance squadrons: 1 Shackleton, maritime reconnais-
    sance; 1 Valiant, photographic reconnaissance; 1 Canberra,
    photographic reconnaissance
  Transport Squadrons: 3 Hastings; 3 Valetta

Two thirds of the Commando and Parachute Brigades were tied up on anti-guerrilla operations in Cyprus. Neither they nor the Amphibious Warfare Squadron had trained in their specialist roles for a year. R.A.F. Transport Command had no recent practice in dropping parachutists and its few Hastings and Valettas, with side-loading doors, could not drop a stick in less than 1,000 yards. 3 Infantry Division was to absorb a couple of armoured regiments whose squadrons were split up all over the UK on every task except training themselves for war.

The Royal Navy's three carrier air groups and the R.A.F. provided some 20 fighter-ground attack, 18 bomber and 4 reconnaissance squadrons. The plan, considered to be the best of four options,[14] was agreed by the British Chiefs of Staff and presented to the Prime Minister by 10 August. Initially, it is said, Eden had some qualms because of the political difficulty of justifying going to the Canal via Alexandria and Cairo.[15]

The same day Beaufre arrived in London. Stockwell explained the plan to him and Eden's objections. Naturally, Beaufre was not pleased about being presented with a *fait accompli* and returned to Paris to tell General Ely what the British had proposed.

Four days later Beaufre returned to London to discuss the plan again with Stockwell and to arrive at some rather more realistic timings (see fig.5):

28

a. The air superiority battle was still to last two days.
b. The amphibious and airborne assault on D Day would be followed by a six to seven day build-up at Alexandria before the advance on Cairo started on D + 6.
c. The decisive battle would be fought outside the capital by D + 14, followed by the
d. Capture of the Nile barrage or the Cairo bridges to allow the
e. Exploitation eastwards to occupy the Canal.

Eden agreed the plan on 15 August and D Day was to be a month later, 15 September. The operation was renamed MUSKETEER because HAMILCAR is AMILCAR in French and while the British were busily painting a large white air recognition 'H' on the canopies of their vehicles, the French were painting an 'A' on theirs!

Ten days later (25 August), at a conference chaired by Keightley in Cyprus, Barjot revived the original Port Said proposal. His Chief of Staff, Gazin, an engineer with an inventive mind, had some novel ideas for landing vehicles on the Canal bank. Barjot may have been anticipating an Israeli advance into Sinai. While Keightley agreed that it would be useful to have such a plan in his pocket he confirmed the Alexandria plan but with a two day postponement, the first of many. The critical decisions were those to concentrate the forces on 2 September and to launch the operation on the 10th to achieve a landing on the 17th:

31 August: Call-up of reservists for 3 Division.
2 September: Decision in principle to launch MUSKETEER.
3 September: British transports sail from UK with vehicles and equipment.
5 September: 3 Infantry Division sails from UK.
5–6 September: Naval forces concentrate at Malta.
8 September: 10 French Parachute Division leaves Algiers for Cyprus.
10 September: Final decision on date of landing to meet D Day on 17 September.
11 September: French transports with 7 DMR sail from Algiers.
15 September: Air superiority operation starts.
17 September: D Day, landing.

The dates were not far removed from a time appreciation submitted to the Egypt Committee by Norman Brook, Secretary to the Cabinet, on 14 August prior to the meeting of the International Maritime Conference on 16 August:

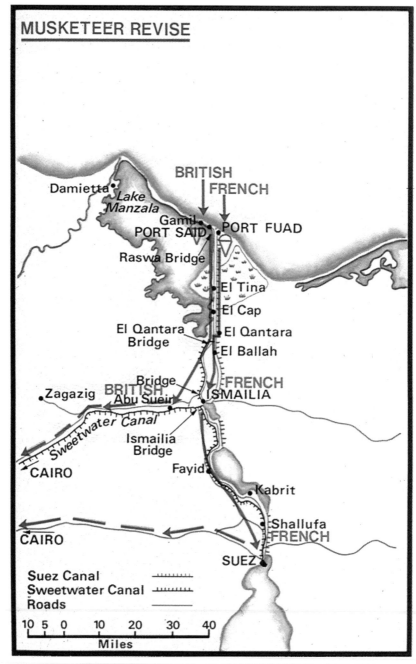

Figure 6. The Canal Zone – MUSKETEER Revise

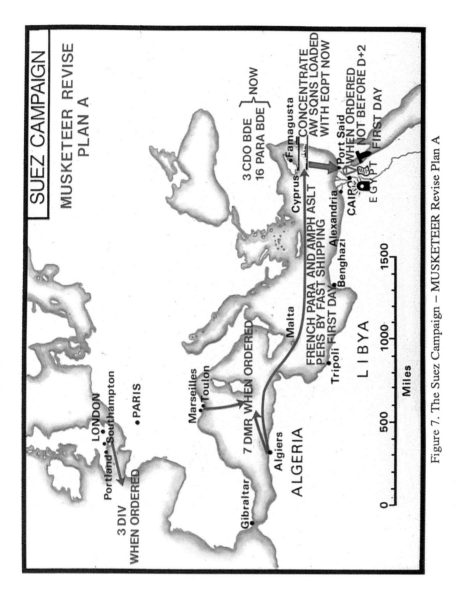

Figure 7. The Suez Campaign – MUSKETEER Revise Plan A

31

5 September: Estimated date Nasser would reject its proposals.
7 September: British forces sail from UK.
17 September: Air Campaign begins.
20 September: Landing.[16]

On 2 September, as a result of a decision taken by the Egypt Committee five days before, the troops were told that the landing was postponed eight days until the 25th, to await the result of the Menzies mission to Nasser. Between 2 and 9 September Menzies unsuccessfully tried to persuade Nasser to accept the principles proposed by the eighteen Maritime Nations in London (16–23 August). An air of unreality was creeping into the operation. The new critical dates for making the decisions were:

Completed: Call-up of reservists for 3 Infantry Division.
10 September: Decision in principle to launch MUSKETEER.
11 September: British transports sail from UK with vehicles and equipment.
13 September: 3 Infantry Division sails from UK.
13–14 September: Naval forces concentrate on Malta.
16 September: 10 French Parachute Division leaves Algiers for Cyprus.
18 September: Final decision on date of landing to meet D Day on 25 September.
19 September: French transports with 7 DMR sail from Algiers.
23 September: Air superiority operation starts.
25 September: D Day, landing.

Because of the practical difficulties of holding the forces in suspense Stockwell advised that 6 October would be the last date a landing could take place.

ASSEMBLY OF THE FORCE

While the staffs got down to work on the operation orders the forces began to assemble and train. The two parachute battalions in Cyprus were scraped off the Troodos Mountains and sent home for refresher parachute training with the Hastings and Valetta air-crews.[17] 3 Commando Brigade concentrated in Malta from Cyprus and the UK to work up with the Amphibious Warfare Squadron and practise street fighting.

The move of the two armoured regiments[18] from Salisbury Plain to Portland and Southampton was bedevilled by a lack of Army tank transporters. So Pickfords, a civilian removals firm, was engaged in much the same way as the Federal Government in the American Civil War contracted intelligence out to the Pinkerton Detective Agency. What with trade union rules and road safety regulations the move took a month. Once the tanks were embarked the roles of the two regiments were switched but the tanks had to stay where they were. Two old carriers, *Ocean* and *Theseus*, were used to ship troops out to Malta in great discomfort. On their return home towards the end of September they were fitted out with metal tiered bunks, just in time to have them ripped out again to refit *Ocean* as a hospital ship and *Theseus* as a helicopter carrier. A few days later the hospital fittings were torn out of *Ocean* to refit her as a helicopter carrier as well. In spite of all the trouble the final conversions were fortunate. It was to be the first time helicopters were used to lift troops into an operation.

But the troops who suffered most were those of 3 Division. Their equipment was all embarked and the units had nothing to train with while their vehicle batteries slowly ran down. The machinery for STUFT, ships taken up from trade, had withered away, causing endless delays. Meanwhile, the first 2,700 men of the French 10 Parachute Division started concentrating in Cyprus where the airstrip at Tymbou was being enlarged.

MUSKETEER REVISE

To return to the planning, MUSKETEER did not last long. On 7 September, Eden was amazed to see a Chiefs of Staff paper recommending a reversion to Port Said, just three days before 3 Division was due to sail from the UK. Although the whole story of this change of plan has yet to be fully explained, Mountbatten claimed that he had the support of the Chiefs of Staff and Keightley to abandon a plan which risked heavy civilian casualties in Alexandria.[19] Eden could not persuade the Chiefs of Staff to drop the new plan and he felt unable to overrule their professional opinion.[20]

However, as a silver lining to a rather black cloud there were some military arguments:

a. The beaches off Alexandria were being mined, suggesting a security leak. If there had been one, Alexandria would make a good cover plan.
b. The problem of securing a crossing over the Nile, either through Cairo or over the Barrage and of

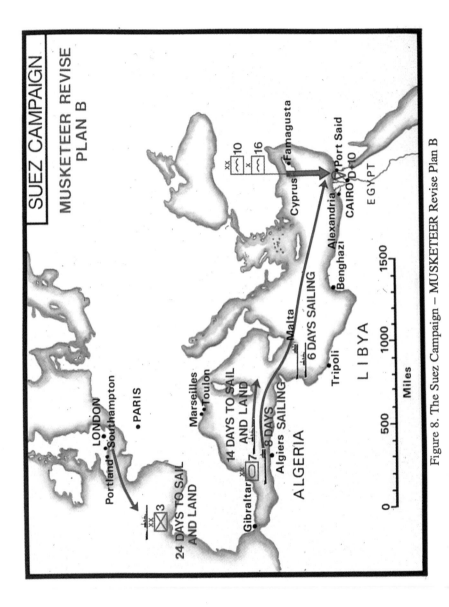

Figure 8. The Suez Campaign – MUSKETEER Revise Plan B

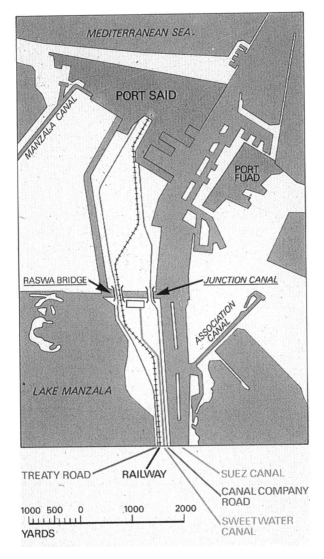

Figure 9. The Exits from Port Said

c. Supplying a force at Suez, 215 miles from Alexandria, with a possibly hostile Cairo behind us, would be difficult until we could open Port Said.

d. Port Said to Suez is only about 110 miles and

e. Photographic reconnaissance showed no defensive preparations on the beaches.

f. Provided that it was not blocked the Canal could be used to move and supply our forces. At least small craft and lighters might get past any obstructions.

The change caused some friction between the Allies. Stockwell thought Beaufre was behind it but Beaufre blamed Barjot. Perhaps Keightley had pulled Barjot's and Gazin's Port Said plan out of his pocket and turned it into a major proposition for the Chiefs of Staff. Just four days later (12 September) came the third postponement, from 25 September to 1 October. This was necessary to adjust the plan although the pre-loading of the ships imposed severe restrictions. The equipment would just be disembarked at Port Said instead of Alexandria, hence the revamped plan's name, MUSKETEER REVISE (see fig.6).

The idea was that the Allies would make a combined parachute and seaborne landing, the British at Port Said, the French at Port Fouad. While the British advanced down the west bank to Abu Sueir airfield, the French would use the east bank, cross at Qantara, take Ismailia and advance to Suez. Then, if necessary, both would be prepared to converge on Cairo.

Now another complication crept into the plan; the idea that the Egyptians would collapse under a combination of air attacks and psychological warfare. The air superiority battle would be followed by a six to ten day attack on targets which would damage the Egyptian economy and prevent the movement of its Army but not harm the civilian population.

An air marshal[21] was put in charge of the targetting while Brigadier Bernard Fergusson,[22] one of Orde Wingate's Chindit brigade commanders in Burma, was pulled off the night train to Perth to plan the psychological aspects. Only when we were sure that there would be no or negligible opposition would the ground forces occupy the Canal. The problem was to know when this state had been reached.

Two contingencies were drawn up for MUSKETEER REVISE:

a. Plan A (fig.7) provided for an early collapse.

(1) The amphibious shipping, loaded with vehicles and equipment, would concentrate off Cyprus.

(2) Because of the submarine risk the French assault troops would remain in Algeria together with the rest of 10 Parachute Division.

(3) 3 Commando Brigade would join 16 Parachute Brigade in Cyprus.

(4) Directly the air battle began the French assault troops would be moved rapidly to Cyprus in the Jean Bart and the parachutists would concentrate at Tymbou.

(5) When Egyptian resistance was judged to have weakened:
   (a) The air and seaborne landing would take place at Port Said, and
   (b) The follow-up forces would sail from Algiers and the UK.

b. Plan B (Fig.8) provided for opposition and a more relaxed state of readiness:

(1) No forward concentration of amphibious shipping off Cyprus.

(2) The air and seaborne assault forces from Cyprus, Malta and Algiers would land simultaneously.

(3) Eight days notice would be needed to sail the convoys.

(4) The follow-up forces would take even longer to complete loading, sail and unload, 14 days for the French and 24 for the British.

The problems were:

a. The decisive battle would be fought with only 100 tanks and less than the equivalent of two divisions but would enjoy excellent air support.

b. The need to capture intact the bridges at Raswa and Qantara by the night of D Day or early the next morning.

On 19 September the target date for the landings was put back from 1 to 8 October. The Suez Canal Users Association (SCUA) was meeting between 19 and 22 September and Eden was contemplating taking the political case to the Security Council.

It was then that photographic reconnaissance revealed that there was no road on the east bank of the Canal and no bridge connecting Port Fouad to the causeway (see fig.9). The French forces would have to move with the British down the west bank, adding immeasurably to the traffic control problem. Only two roads led south from Port Said, the Canal Company road along the bank itself, only capable of taking light traffic, and the old Treaty Road, less than 200 yards to the west. Between them ran the Sweetwater Canal and the railway. Fortunately, the Treaty Road crossed the Junction Canal on the same bridge as the railway. It was strong enough to take tanks but needed engineer effort to widen it.

But MUSKETEER REVISE seemed to have stalled. The Security Council was about to meet (5 October) and so on 1 October the staffs got to work on a Winter Plan which could be held indefinitely. This was the fifth postponement. You will not be surprised to learn that the plan was cancelled a fortnight later. By now everyone was becoming exasperated. In early October the reservists, bored and uncomfortable, staged demonstrations in Cyprus, Malta, Germany and the UK. More ominously, the French were getting impatient.

MORE PLANNING

It was on 14 October that Albert Gazier and General Challe visited Eden in London to propose a plan for starting the operation. If the Israelis were to advance into Sinai, posing a threat to the Canal, the Allies could call on Israel and Egypt to withdraw 10 miles from the waterway to allow an Allied force to secure it.

From the purely military point of view the main points were that Ben-Gurion's anxiety for the safety of Israel's cities could only be allayed by early Allied air attacks on the Egyptian airfields. Eden, concerned to provide a reason for such early intervention, insisted on a credible Israeli threat to the Canal. Dayan, the Israeli Chief of Staff, came up with the suggestion of a parachute drop east of the Mitla Pass on the first day.[23]

Stockwell and the other Task Force Commanders were kept in the dark. Consequently we were now doubly committed to an aero-psychological operation which would go on for days while the amphibious forces sailed down the Mediterranean. The attacks on the Egyptian airfields were originally planned to start 72 hours after the Israeli drop at the Mitla. A compromise was reached on a 36 hour delay to give a period for the delivery and consideration of the Allied proposals. In the event, the bombing was delayed for military reasons until after dark on the 31 October, 48 hours after the Mitla drop.

It was not until the 17th that Stockwell began to wonder what was going on between the French and the Israelis and it was another nine days before he got an inkling that the French knew more about

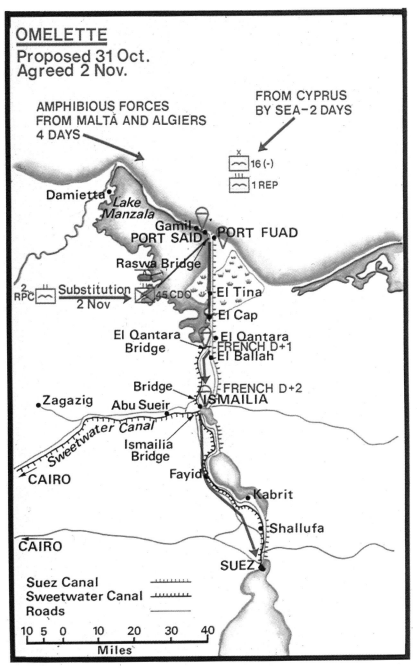

Figure 10. The Canal Zone – OMELETTE Plan

Israeli plans than he did. If a government keeps its soldiers in the dark when it depends on them to carry out its policy, it is likely to be disappointed later. More immediately it led to friction between Stockwell and Beaufre over the need for urgency.

Anyway, MUSKETEER REVISE, Plan B, the slow plan, was revived. A restriction on embarking the troops before the 29th, both because the Security Council was scheduled to meet towards the end of the month and to avoid charges of collusion, delayed the response time still further. Meanwhile, Stockwell's staff put the final touches to MUSKETEER REVISE and, on 24 October, what was confidently expected to be the last operation order was issued. The next day, Eden obtained the agreement in principle of his Cabinet to occupy the Canal if Israel took the expected action, possibly on 29 October.[24]

On the following day, the 26th, Stockwell flew from London to Malta to watch Exercise BOATHOOK, an amphibious forces work-up. On the way he landed at Villacoublay to meet Beaufre from whom he gathered that the French were preparing for MUSKETEER rather than BOATHOOK. Beaufre's anxiety to impress a sense of urgency on him led Stockwell to believe that an Israeli attack was imminent, although he never said as much.[25]

When Stockwell met Admiral Grantham, C in C Mediterranean Fleet, that evening they put Beaufre's hints in the context of information coming in from London and news of the French embarkation at Algiers. They decided to use Exercise BOATHOOK as a cover to load and sail the Amphibious Warfare Squadron and Admiral Power's Fast Carrier Group (*Eagle, Bulwark* and *Albion*) the next day. The helicopter carriers, *Ocean* and *Theseus*, with 45 Commando on board were able to delay sailing until 31 October on account of their speed. Some time had been saved at the expense of two problems:

a. The final orders had to be given out at sea so that the commanding officers had to be collected from round the Fleet by helicopter.

b. Because BOATHOOK was just an exercise, units left some valuable kit, such as spare radio batteries, behind in Malta.

It was only on the 29th, the day of the Israeli parachute drop at the Mitla, that the 3rd Battalion, The Parachute Regiment, the unit earmarked for the drop at Gamil, was hurriedly withdrawn from operations against EOKA in the Troodos Mountains to pack and prepare for action.

The political decision to keep the military in the dark now backfired. When a quick operation to secure the Canal was essential politically, militarily it was not feasible. The carriers and the amphibious shipping might have been sailed earlier under cover of another exercise.[26] One of the useful characteristics of naval forces is their ability to loiter below the horizon. While committing no act of aggression their presence provides a warning and keeps the other side guessing.

THE WAR BEGINS, IMPROVISATION

The Task Force Commanders and their Deputies next met in Cyprus on the evening of 30 October just after the withdrawal appeal had been delivered to Israel and Egypt. Alarming but inaccurate reports were coming in that the Egyptians were reinforcing the Canal and digging positions every 50 yards down the causeway, reports which were to be exaggerated and misinterpreted when Nasser ordered the withdrawal of his troops from Sinai at the start of the Allied bombing the next night (31 October).

Stockwell's plan was to wait until the seaborne forces arrived on the morning of 6 November and to land them 35 minutes after sunrise after a short bombardment by the light guns of the Fleet. Nothing heavier than 4.5 inch guns were to be used for fear of the material and political damage the ships' main armaments might do to Port Said. The parachutists would start dropping half an hour after the landing. Beaufre, pressed by Barjot and Paris, urged a parachute drop before the convoys arrived in order to establish a presence before the 'diplomatic clock' ran out. It is of interest that Major General Massu, GOC 10 Parachute Division, suggested a series of drops to secure the entire Canal Zone called Operation VERDICT.

Over the next three days a plan called OMELETTE, later dubbed SIMPLEX, evolved (see fig.10). It provided for a British drop on Gamil airfield, a French drop south of Port Fouad and a *coup de main* operation to seize the Raswa bridges over the Junction Canal intact. Originally, 45 Commando was to be landed by helicopter from *Ocean* and *Theseus* but the task was transferred to a battalion of 2e Régiment de Parachutistes Coloniaux (2 RPC) because there was no experience of the effect of small arms fire on helicopters. Further French parachute drops were envisaged to reinforce Gamil on D Day, if necessary, and at Qantara and Ismailia on the two following days. The rest of 16 Parachute Brigade would be shipped

41

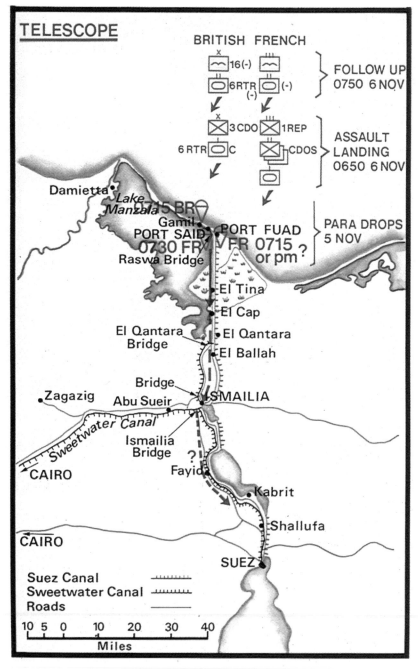

Figure 11. The Canal Zone — TELESCOPE Plan

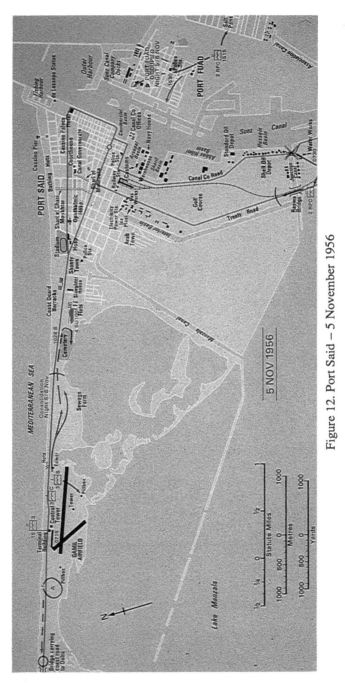

Figure 12. Port Said – 5 November 1956

in from Cyprus over a two day period to hold Port Said until the convoys arrived from Malta and Algiers.

There was one proviso. Because the withdrawal of the Egyptian Army was misinterpreted as a build-up in the Canal Zone, Stockwell insisted on the insertion of a 'no effective resistance' stipulation in the operation order.[27] This reflected the Chiefs of Staff anxiety about the concentration of disorganised Egyptian troops in the Canal Zone from Sinai.[28] It also led to some heated argument between the Allied commanders, with the French contemplating an operation without the British.[29] Eventually, Plan TELESCOPE was produced on 3 November (see fig.11). The parachute operation was to be advanced a day to the morning of 5 November. The Port Fouad drop was to be left open for another 24 hours but was finally confirmed for mid-afternoon. The only worry was the near certainty that 'overs' from the naval guns aimed at Port Said would fall on the French in Port Fouad. The reason Eden pressed for the earlier drop was that the 'diplomatic clock' was running out at the United Nations and the French Government was contemplating unilateral action if the British held back.[30] The go-ahead was given on the evening of 3 November. Meanwhile the aero-psychological operation was in full swing. The Egyptian Air Force was knocked out in 36 hours. The high level bombing did little damage on the first night, more on the second. The real damage was caused by fighter-ground attack aircraft in daylight. However, the attacks caused Nasser to fly his Russian aircraft with their Iron Curtain pilots to safety, to recall his troops from Sinai and to block the Canal.[31]

The psychological campaign was less successful. The radio announcers were Palestinian Arabs who were mistaken for Israelis. It was not until the following morning that London came through with a signal to say that our announcers had been putting out anti-British propaganda all night! Radio Cairo was not attacked until 2 November, by which time it had served Nasser's purposes well. The delay was due to a misunderstanding in London where it was thought that the transmitters were located alongside the broadcasting studios in Cairo, whereas they were 15 miles away in the desert.[32] Damaged, but not destroyed, it was back on the air two days later.

THE ANGLO-FRENCH OPERATION

At 0715,[33] 3 PARA dropped on Gamil Airport (see fig.12). Securing it by 8 o'clock, and supported by accurate close air support from the Fleet Air Arm, who maintained a continuous air alert, they pressed on to secure the Sewage Farm and Cemetery by 1030. Patrols were pushed forward to the Coast Guard Barracks and some blocks of flats where two of the four SU 100 SP guns deployed there were destroyed by an air strike. The patrols were now entering the danger area for the next morning's naval bombardment, so they withdrew that evening back to the Sewage Farm.

A quarter of an hour after the British jump a battalion of French Chasseurs Parachutistes made a brilliant jump into a small DZ south of the Water Works to secure the Raswa road and rail bridge over the Junction Canal by 1030. Unfortunately, the Canal Road bridge had been blown. A British patrol, which landed with the French, pressed on down the Treaty Road for 6 miles without meeting any opposition. The French used an airborne command post to immense advantage. After a consultation between Stockwell and Beaufre afloat and Gilles in his airborne command post, the order was given to drop a second French parachute battalion from 2 RPC (2e Régiment de Parachutistes Coloniaux) south of Port Fouad at 3 p.m. A cease-fire, to arrange the surrender of Port Said that afternoon, came to nothing but wasted valuable time.

The next morning, 6 November, the amphibious assault went in (see fig.13). Luckily, news that Port Fouad was in French hands came through in time to stop the naval bombardment. West of the Canal, 3 Commando Brigade landed at 0650 after a 10 minute strafing by the Fleet Air Arm and a 30 minute bombardment by the guns of the destroyers. On the right, 42 Commando, with a couple of troops of tanks (C Squadron, 6th Royal Tank Regiment) fought their way through the town to reach their objective, the Gas Works by the Interior Basin, by 10 o'clock. On the left, 40 Commando had a much tougher fight on their hands. They were to clear the harbour front with Abbas Hilmi Quay as their final objective. However, by 11 o'clock they had only reached the Commercial Basin after a stiff battle for the Police Station.

Meanwhile, 45 Commando flew in by helicopter from *Ocean* and *Theseus*. The Commanding Officer and his reconnaissance party came in ahead of the main body to confirm the landing zone near 3 Commando Brigade Headquarters in the area of the Cassino Pier. It was obscured by smoke and obstructed by high tension cables. So they tried the new Sports Stadium. No sooner had the party alighted than the Egyptians opened fire. Luckily, the pilot realized something was wrong when a bullet nicked his finger. With some presence of mind he touched down to pick up the party and find a new landing zone near the de Lesseps statue. Because the heli-

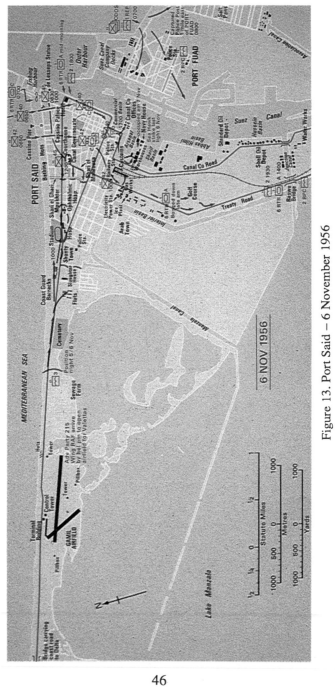

Figure 13. Port Said – 6 November 1956

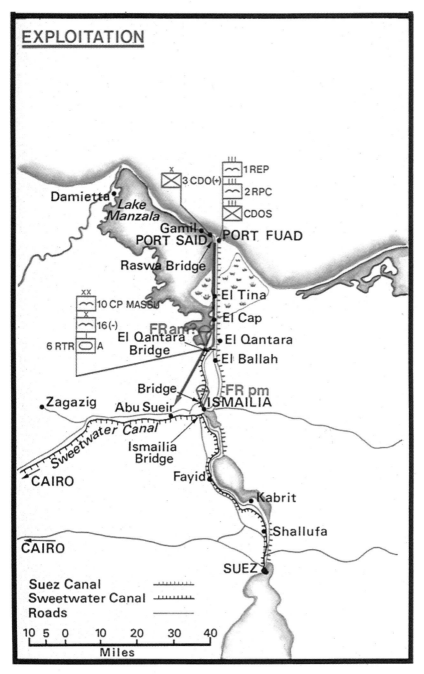

Figure 14. The Canal Zone – Exploitation

copters were so small it took an hour and a half to land 45 Commando, another good reason for not giving them the Raswa Bridge task. Forming up soon after 10 o'clock they moved across the tracks of 40 and 42 Commandos to take the Canal Governorate by midday. As they were advancing down the Shari al-Mahrusa a Fleet Air Arm Wyvern attacked their command post. The Commanding Officer was among the 16 casualties. Reorganizing under a major, 45 Commando pressed on against heavy opposition to reach the Shari al-Ghazi Mukhtar by 6 p.m. There was no sign of 3 PARA.

3 PARA had supported the landing with medium machine-gun fire and reoccupied the Cemetery and Coast Guard Barracks by 10 o'clock. Pressing on they took the Ophthalmic Hospital but a patrol sent into Shanty Town met fierce resistance from the Police Station and took 100 per cent casualties. The supporting anti-tank and naval gunfire set Shanty Town ablaze which prevented a link-up with 45 Commando.

An advance party from 215 Wing, R.A.F. was helicoptered ashore to Gamil in the morning to clear the runway of obstructions to allow four Valettas to land that afternoon.

The Task Force Commanders and Beaufre decided to come ashore. Beaufre was in radio contact with his own people but Stockwell had no communications, so that when their launch approached the Canal Company offices it ran unexpectedly into small arms fire. The Admiral, with customary naval understatement, observed, 'I don't think, General, they are quite ready to receive us yet.' Diverting their launch to Fishermen's Harbour they walked to the Commando Brigade Headquarters at Cassino Pier where they heard that the Italian consul was trying to organize a cease-fire. It turned out to be unfounded but an hour was wasted investigating it. Returning to the Brigade headquarters, where they were in communication with their forces again, they heard that another squadron of tanks (A Squadron, 6th Royal Tank Regiment) had come ashore and married up with the French at Raswa at 2 o'clock. The Admiral and the Air Marshal returned to *Tyne* while Stockwell gave out orders (see fig.14).

a. 3 Commando Brigade was to clear Port Said.

b. When 2 PARA came ashore it was to pick up the armoured squadron (A Squadron, 6th Royal Tank Regiment) at Raswa Bridge and press on to Abu Sueir, starting that night.

c. Massu was to organize parachute drops at Qantara tomorrow morning, if necessary, and at Ismailia in the afternoon. He was also to command the advance.

Beaufre left to pass on the orders to Massu and Chateau-Jobert (2e Régiment de Parachutistes Coloniaux) and, much later, Stockwell took a launch back to *Tyne* at last light. Lost in the dark, he found his Headquarter Ship by sheer luck to be told that a cease-fire had been ordered for 0200 (0001Z).

40 Commando had a hard fight round Arsenal Basin to take the Customs Warehouses. The 130 defenders of Navy House proved as stout as the building. An air strike destroyed it[34] at last light but there the Commando stopped, well short of its objective, Abbas Hilmi Quay. Consequently, 2 PARA had to disembark from a troopship down scrambling nets into lighters and did not reach Raswa until 1930, after dark.

A quarter of an hour later, the squadron of tanks there (A Squadron, 6th Royal Tank Regiment) set out with some French parachutists (2 RPC) down the Treaty Road to reach El Tina by 0200. There they were ordered to stop. The 'diplomatic clock' had run out (see fig.15).

LESSONS LEARNED

Many of the lessons learned had a familiar ring:

a. Selection of the Aim

The three combatants against Egypt formed an uneasy and equivocal alliance. Their aims were different. Consequently, there was some confusion as to the choice of objective. The British Task Force Commanders were not taken into their Government's confidence. The operation was postponed five times and there were seven changes of plan. 'For if the trumpet give an uncertain sound, who shall prepare himself to the battle?'[35]

b. Command, Control and Communications

(1) Although the preponderance of British forces may have justi-fied the appointment of British officers as commanders and French as deputies, when one ally is in such a subordinate position it leads to resentment. In one respect the French had a preponderance in a vital capability, airborne assault.

(2) Stockwell and Beaufre were not very compatible and they faced appalling difficulties. Beaufre had one of the most brilliant

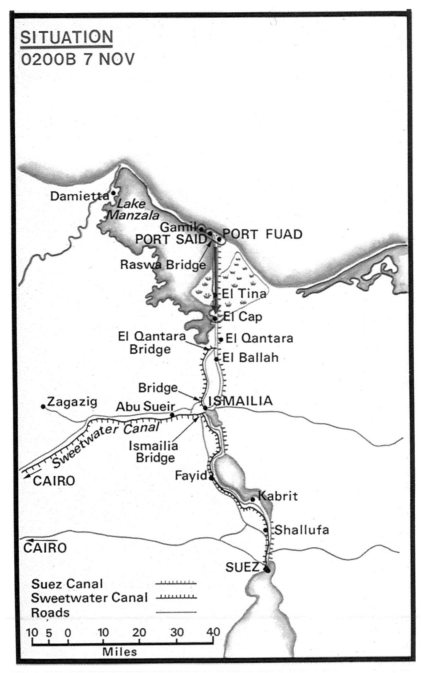

Figure 15. The Canal Zone – Situation 7 November

military minds of his generation and one wonders whether the best use was made of him.

(3) It is a pity that there was not a headquarters ship large enough to accommodate Beaufre and his staff together with the Task Force Commanders.

(4) Commanders must always be in touch with their subordinates and their own headquarters.

c. Military Preparedness

(1) Defence is a seamless garment. Unfortunately we had a large gap in our limited war capability to meet the unexpected and, because the expected is well prepared for, it is the unexpected which usually happens. Nasser had spotted the chink in our armour.

(2) Sufficient reserves, essential for any quick intervention, parachutists, commandos, transport aircrews and amphibious shipping, must always be kept trained for their primary role.

(3) Our dependence on reservists for a comparatively small war was unwise.

(4) The machinery for requisitioning merchant shipping was rusty.

d. Flexibility

The campaign showed a lack of flexibility in every respect, except in the production of paper plans and postponements:

(1) Once the shipping was loaded the margin for changing the operational plan was limited.

(2) Reliance on civil contractors and port facilities in the UK caused unacceptable delays.

(3) We lacked a sense of urgency and willingness to take risks.

(4) We failed to exploit one of sea power's greatest assets, the ability to loiter below the horizon.

(5) Did we make the best use of our parachutists, helicopters and landing craft to exploit or switch reserves? Could not the squadron of British tanks and French paratroopers have started down the Treaty Road from Raswa by 3 p.m.?

e. Pyschological warfare

This is treated with a healthy suspicion in a peacetime democracy. In any case, it is difficult to prepare for a sudden operation. It takes time to find the right people and the appropriate tools to run a successful psychological warfare campaign. As it was known that we

51

were not prepared to bomb cities our empty threats to do so were ignored.

LESSONS APPLIED

By the time of the 1961 Kuwait emergency we had put some of these shortcomings right. By the Falklands Campaign (1982) we had applied them sufficiently to win a small war over 8,000 miles from home:

a. The aim was clear because the political direction was clear and consistent.
b. We had developed a suitable command structure.
c. Our amphibious forces were well equipped and trained.
d. STUFT had been overhauled.
e. The campaign demonstrated flexibility in choice of landing sites, restricted only by the loss of the Chinook helicopters in *Atlantic Conveyor*.

NOTES

1. Rhodes James, Robert, *Anthony Eden* (London, 1986), p.469.
2. *Ibid.*, p.461.
3. *Ibid.*, p.470.
4. *Ibid.*, pp.460, 534, 535.
5. *Hansard*, Lords, Vol.238, col 1002–3, 16 March 1962.
6. Ziegler, Philip, *Mountbatten* (London, 1985), pp.537–547.
7. Rhodes James, *op. cit.*, p.484.
8. Nutting, Anthony, *No End of a Lesson* (London, 1967), pp.47–8.
9. Dayan, Moshe, *Diary of the Sinai Campaign* (London, 1966), note to Apndx 3, p.218.
10. Extract from Mohamed Heikal, Cutting the Lion's Tail (London, 1986) in *Sunday Telegraph Supplement*, 12 Oct. 1986.
11. Stockwell, General Sir Hugh, 'Suez from the Inside', *Sunday Telegraph*, 30 Oct. 1966, p.6.
12. *Ibid.*
13. *Ibid.*
14. The others were (a) A landing at Port Said; (b) A landing at Alexandria with a feint at Port Said; (c) A landing at Port Said with a feint at Alexandria. Rhodes James, *op. cit.*, p.490.
15. Fullick, Roy and Geoffrey Powell, *Suez: The Double War* (London, 1979), pp.21–2.
16. Rhodes James, *op. cit.*, p.499.
17. 1 and 3 PARA. 2 PARA, in UK, was sent out to relieve them having completed refresher training.
18. 1st and 6th Royal Tank Regiments.
19. Ziegler, *Mountbatten, op. cit.*, p.543.
20. Until Robert Rhodes James examined the Eden papers in detail, it was assumed that the decision was a political one. See Fullick and Powell, *Suez: The Double War* (London, 1979), pp.56–7 and Rhodes James, *Anthony Eden, op. cit.* pp.507–9.
21. Air Marshal Huddleston.
22. Later Lord Ballantrae.
23. Fullick and Powell, *op. cit.*, pp.81–6; Carlton, David, *Anthony Eden* (London, 1981), pp.435–41; Thomas, Hugh, *The Suez Affair* (London, 1976), pp.177–94; Eden, Sir Anthony, *Full Circle* (London, 1960), p.523; Rhodes James, *op. cit.*, pp.527–32.
24. Rhodes James, *op. cit.*, pp.535–8.
25. Stockwell, 'Suez from the Inside', *Sunday Telegraph*, 30 Oct. 1966, p.7.
26. Stockwell, 'Suez from the Inside', *Sunday Telegraph*, 6 and 13 Nov. 1966.
27. Beaufre, André, *The Suez Expedition, 1956* (London, 1969), p.85.
28. Rhodes James, *op. cit.*, pp.564–5.
29. Fullick and Powell, *op. cit.*, pp.106–7.
30. Rhodes James, *op. cit.*, pp.564–5.
31. 20 Mig 15s and 20 Il 28s due for delivery to Syria were flown there via Saudi Arabia. 10 Mig 15s and 10 Il 14s of the EAF were flown to Saudi Arabia and 20 EAF Il 28s were flown to Luxor, where they were destroyed by FAF F84Fs operating from Lod on 4 Nov. Jackson, Robert, *Suez 1956, Operation MUSKETEER* (London, 1980), p.60.
32. For other problems connected with the psychological operations see Fergusson, Bernard, *Trumpet in the Hall* (London, 1970), pp.263–75.
33. All times are local, B Time Zone.
34. The next morning 20 survivors emerged from the wrecked building, leaving 30 dead. The rest had escaped in the dark.
35. 1 Corinthians, XIV, 8.

3

The Military and Political
Contradictions of the Suez Affair:
A French Perspective

André Martin

The Suez Crisis is an example of the significance of Karl von Clausewitz's maxim: 'War is a continuation of politics by other means.'

What can one say about the Suez Affair after thirty years? The media, getting their opinion in ahead of the judgment of history, is convinced that this military victory turned into a political fiasco. Although everything seems to have already been said, I would like to try to reply to the question on everyone's lips: why did the Suez Affair turn out as it did? In doing so, I should also like to draw the main lesson in a dispassionate fashion.

My presentation will focus on the main contradictions which explain the abortive conclusion of Suez. I shall first discuss the purely military aspects and then turn to the politico-military side of things, which I call the politico-military dialogue. I do not intend, however, to describe in detail the military events or the diplomatic ones. I shall attempt only to identify the main military points which appear to have been responsible for the final defeat.

Immediately after the nationalization of the Canal, the British and French governments reached an agreement that they would deliberately seek a military confrontation. On the French side, the situation was extremely clear-cut. Prime Minister Guy Mollet's government was struggling with the Algerian War. The decision was taken to emerge from it victorious even though the previous year had been a bad one with the spread of the rebellion. The main reason for this unfortunate turn of events was Cairo's material and psychological support. The French knew from experience that in order to be successful a rebellion needed external support. The Egyptian radio programme, 'Voice of the Arabs', had begun to awaken in young people an Arab nationalism which had never before existed.

Nationalization provided the opportunity for justifying doing away with Nasser, the prime mover in encouraging rebellious ferment. It was expected that he could be brought down by wiping out the Egyptian army. French opinion was in favour of removing Nasser even as it showed considerable pro-Israeli sympathies.

For geographical and political reasons, France required a partner, and the only possible choice was Britain which was an ally and a friend. The British situation was the reverse of the French. British public opinion had become accustomed to decolonization and British troops had just satisfied Nasser by withdrawing from the Canal Zone. Nevertheless, although the British were no longer masters of the Middle East, they were still obliged to protect their friends who were threatened by the subversion that was being preached by Cairo.

British public opinion, although perhaps less unanimously than French, agreed that something had to be done to make the Egyptian dictator see reason. However, only the Prime Minister, Anthony Eden, had a clear idea of the danger represented by the new Hitler of the Arab world. Eden was traumatized by the memory of Munich. He shared with Guy Mollet the conviction that Nasser had to be brought down.

Eden was primarily a brilliant diplomat, and what could be called an honest man. He was to concentrate all his powers on the art which had brought him to the top – diplomacy. He invested a great deal of energy to make public opinion accept war against Nasser as an honourable act, but, in the exhausting weeks which followed, he failed to inspire in his military leaders the desire to bring Nasser down at all costs.

In Israel there had been ever increasing attacks on frontier settlements, and it was believed that Nasser was fomenting a coalition with Syria and Jordan in order to be able to slip a noose over Israel's neck. It was therefore natural that there developed an overwhelming need among Israelis to take military action, and every fighter burned for victory.

Against this background, Admiral Nomy, the Chief of the Naval Staff, and I arrived on July 29 in London for a meeting with the British Chiefs of Staff. The British permitted some amazement to show despite their outward phlegm and courtesy. However, the considerable military resources we were prepared to use, despite our Algerian commitments, convinced them that we were perfectly serious. In fact, the French contributed 34,000 men, including 2,900 pilots, 3 fighter escorts and fighter-bombers (150 aircraft), an air transport group, 10,000 vehicles, 25,000 metric tons of equipment and the Mediterranean fleet.

A combined NATO-style general staff was established as a consequence of these meetings. In the planning of 'Musketeer', the general staff did excellent technical work but, when the time came to make adjustments in their plans, they were unable to do so. France accepted British leadership in both the political and military spheres and control was passed to the hands of a friendly nation which was less motivated and whose troops were less highly trained. It was understood that without Malta and Cyprus, we could do nothing, and we really wanted this war! I did discuss this state of affairs with General Paul Ely, the Chief of Staff, but he saw no alternative.

The planning was complicated and took much time. Before initiating operations, for example, some items that were manufactured in the United States and acquired under the Marshall Plan had to be restocked — which the Americans did very willingly. The most delicate point and the one which generated the greatest problems involved drawing up the timetable for the entire landing operation. Plans were drawn up for a real mini-'Overlord' (the code-name given to the landings at Normandy by the Allies in the Second World War). Attention had to be paid to the major distances to be covered at sea, particularly the 900 miles between Malta and Port Said. Indeed, this emerged as a real problem during the course of the fighting. In addition, movements on Cyprus were kept a close-guarded secret, and generally speaking, things were entirely satisfactory in the all-important area of maintaining secrecy. However, despite our efforts, the seeds of defeat were already present in the fruit. It took seven days to sail from embarkation points to the British coast at Port Said. This cumbersome aspect of the operation was to prove fatal.

What was actually accomplished was a resounding success, and those involved in the operations could be proud of their achievements. When the ultimatum addressed to Nasser expired on October 31, an air raid began, followed by airborne operations. On November 5, Gamil, Port Said and Port Fouad were in our hands. On November 5, just one 'push' was needed to bring the whole scrum down!

This is where another of the errors in our approach became

manifest. We had been wrong in our assessment of the enemy. He had been overestimated – as grave an error as underestimating the enemy. The British had an excellent opinion of the Egyptian Army, which they had trained in earlier days. The Egyptian air force, equipped and trained by the Russians, was thought to be a formidable fighting force. The assessment had been that seven days would be needed to neutralize it. In fact, we had wrapped everything up by the evening of November 2. The plan could have been put into operation without wasting these extra three days which were to prove fatal.

Finally, we were faced by the last contradiction, which was by no means the least – the search for a diplomatic result which would be honourable. In my judgment, we were in a situation in which political leaders were trying to achieve both one thing and its opposite. Political and military objectives did not coincide. If they had, I have no doubt that the affair could have ended differently.

We were in a situation in which there was fear of being criticized for having acted in collusion with Israel. There was especially a quasi-morbid hostility to the Israelis in the British High Command on Cyprus. These factors inhibited making the only logical decision: putting aside the prepared plan in order to respond to the unstoppable Israeli advance towards the Canal. The headlong flight of 45,000 Egyptian troops from Sinai had completely demoralized the rest of the Egyptian army. On the evening of November 3 we could have been in Ismailia, but the operations plan, concocted so scientifically, had not taken into account the difficulties of the diplomatic situation and the limited room for manoeuvre. The frustration was expressed in a joke that went the rounds among the participants who were bitter after the November 6 ceasefire: if Churchill had been in Eden's shoes, and Leclerc in Beaufre's, the fate of the Suez expedition would have been different. This was, however, a somewhat simplistic view of things. Nevertheless, on the French side, such bitterness would continue and was again expressed over the events in Algiers on 13 May 1958.

On reflection, it becomes clear that the military powers set up an expedition which ran completely counter to the policy which the allies wanted to pursue and that overall responsibility for failure must lie with the political side. A vital cog seems to have been missing from this coalition: a real defence council between political and military leaders. At the beginning of October, after my colleagues and I returned from Israel, such a meeting should have been held. We had become convinced of Israel's future success.

Collusion or no collusion, this was a prime fact which made it vital to reconsider the military plan.

Clemenceau used to say that war was too serious a matter to be left to the generals. *Au contraire*, one can argue that the running of a war cannot be determined exclusively by politicians. In his work *On War* Clausewitz demonstrated this point in his fundamental contribution to military-political thinking. Many historical examples teach us that success goes to the side which has managed to adapt and execute military operations that suit the aims pursued by its policy. Alexander the Great, Julius Caesar, Ghengis Khan, Frederick II, even Bonaparte before he became Napoleon, all reflect the same principle. They were 'politicians' who also had military power. Later, great statesmen knew how to choose a military commander who could integrate the political aspects and suggest appropriate ways of running military operations. This was the case of Roosevelt and Marshall, and of Ben-Gurion and Moshe Dayan. In my view, this is what can be called establishing a politico-military dialogue. The man in power must have read and reflected on Julius Caesar, Machiavelli and, obviously, Karl von Clausewitz.

Eden did not have such a military chief working with him. Although his role and behaviour in the Suez Affair is still subject to question, Britain's great admiral, Lord Mountbatten, could have acted in this capacity. Moreover, there should have been meetings at the highest level between French and British leaders where military plans could have been adapted as necessary.

It is possible that the affair would have terminated differently if the British and French had dealt with Nasser without Israeli participation. In the secret negotiations at Sèvres, it had been difficult to persuade Ben-Gurion to play the role we expected from him. However, once Israel's role was accepted, as a result of French pressure, it could have been exploited for more than merely as an alibi for British and French intervention. It could have allowed for the kind of lightning success achieved by Moshe Dayan.

What we did not fully appreciate was that the real danger was not the Egyptian army but the United States, the United Nations and public opinion. What we should have done – forgive the expression – was to 'circumvent' the State Department and Eisenhower and to catch the United Nations unawares. The Americans came to understand the Middle East only after Suez. In addition, the British, who were still the guardians of portions of the Middle East, had to convince the moderate Arab countries that her brief collaboration with Israel was in their interest. Sadat was to appreciate this later.

For the reasons outlined above, the military head should have been made party to the head of the government's innermost thoughts. In a democracy, the norm is to keep the military chief on a tight leash, but this concept is now outmoded. Moreover, it must be accepted that it is very difficult to choose a commander to head a country's army in peacetime. The French experience from 1870 to 1940 illustrates this well. The military chief must be able to say 'no' if the operation is not a feasible one or if the proposal is unwise politically or not properly prepared.

The consequences of Suez were disastrous for the whole of Europe. For the French it led later to the Fifth Republic. As for the British, they were to tie their skiff to the American ship and they were not to raise their heads again until the Falklands. In the end, the only country to benefit was Israel. The upshot was the consecration of the Israel Defence Forces as the guarantor of future security. The conflict also gained Israel greater freedom of movement on the high seas.

It is my deeply-held belief that intelligence should dominate force and that political power should be pre-eminent. I believe that the complex nature of the modern world will always require a full and trusting dialogue between political and military leaders. Nevertheless, the motto which Louis XIV had engraved on his cannon – *Ultima Ratio Regum* – continued to prevail for a considerable time. In the world of Star Wars the possibility of such a dialogue is a subject for serious speculation.

4

The Military Lessons of the Sinai Campaign: The Israeli Perspective

Rechavam Zeevy

This article studies the performance of the Israeli army in the Sinai campaign and the lessons that can be derived from this war. There will be no attempt to deal with the political background which influenced events on the battlefield. Although during the campaign I served as the Chief of Staff of the Southern Command, the following reflects my personal views, not those of the IDF.

PREVENTIVE WAR OR PRE-EMPTIVE STRIKE

In order to approach the question whether the Sinai campaign is to be considered a preventive war or a pre-emptive strike, we must recall that the major Powers during the mid-1950s vied for influence in the Middle East. One of the means they used was the massive supply of arms. On the one side, the Western Powers intensified the flow of arms to Iraq, Jordan and Saudi Arabia. On the other, the Soviets brought vast amounts of armaments into Egypt through the Czechs. Nevertheless, the campaign started before the Egyptians could absorb and digest Soviet largesse.

While arms poured freely into the Arab countries from East and West, Israel was subjected to closed markets due to embargoes, both overt and covert. For the small amounts which Israel managed to purchase, she was forced to pay fully and in cash, while the Arabs obtained weapons practically at no cost, or on especially favourable terms such as long-term repayments or in barter deals.

Israel was faced with the dilemma of how to respond to this intensive military build-up – whether to wait till her enemies, especially Egypt, decided on a military confrontation at a time of their choosing or to launch a pre-emptive strike to break up the growing military power which threatened Israel's existence.

Towards the second half of 1956, the evaluation of the situation was as follows:

a. The Egyptian army had received large quantities of weapons, but had not as yet managed to absorb them into its service.
b. The Egyptian army was still partitioned on both sides of the Canal.
c. Even though it joined a military alliance, there was no certainty Jordan would go to war, for various reasons including the danger of Iraqi forces coming into her territory.
d. The Syrian army had not fully absorbed the large quantities of arms supplied by the Eastern bloc.
e. An international juncture focused the Soviets' and the world's attention on events in Hungary, while the Americans were occupied with the Presidential elections.
f. The British and the French sought to teach Nasser a lesson, and wished to bring him down for having nationalized the Canal and becoming involved in the revolt in Algeria.
g. A victorious strike against Egypt would impress and restrain the other Arab states.

Against the background of this evaluation the decision was taken to initiate a preventive war, and an alliance was therefore formed with the British and the French. The Sinai campaign broke down the Arab build-up, and militarily weakened the Egyptian dictator who had been enhancing his power and influence in the region. On the eve of the Sinai campaign, the Egyptian Chief of Staff General Amir said, 'The Egyptian army has the capability to liberate every inch of Arab soil from its defilement by the conquerors.' He added that 'the Egyptian army can wipe Israel out in 48 hours'. However, it can be said now that, as a result of the Sinai campaign, Israel won 11 years of non-belligerence along the Egyptian border, until the Six Day War in 1967.

ISRAEL'S WAR AIMS

Israeli aims were formulated or defined over time and in conjunction with political developments, including consultations with her allies. These aims can be summarized as follows:

a. Eradicating fidaiyyun activity against Israel.

b. Ensuring free navigation (in the Gulf of Eilat and the Suez Canal).
c. Ensuring free air traffic.
d. Breaking the Egyptian war machine – a preventive war.

STRATEGIC AND TACTICAL SURPRISE

The Sinai campaign was a strategic surprise. Due to the deliberate deception and disinformation by the Israeli GHQ the Arab states, particularly Egypt and Jordan, expected an Israeli attack on Jordan. The Israeli deception benefited from a series of clashes and skirmishes along the Jordanian border in the months prior to the campaign. The Arab Legion itself encouraged increased infiltration from Jordan during this period, which further contributed to the tension between Israel and Jordan. Israel reacted with a series of retaliatory raids against military and government objectives, which resulted in yet further escalation. In response to an anticipated massive Israeli operation, Jordan and Iraq had planned for the entry of Iraqi troops into Jordanian territory.

Against the background of the tensions along the Israeli–Jordanian border, it was easy to explain the covert mobilization of the reserves which began on the night of the 24–25 October 1956. It was apparent that it would be impossible to conceal a mobilization of such large scope, but the explanation that Israel was worried about the entry of Iraqi troops into Jordan seemed reasonable to foreign observers and media representatives. The fact that Jordan and Iraq took defensive measures against a possible Israeli attack, and that the Egyptian Minister of War visited Jordan and Syria to coordinate positions, further strengthened speculation concerning the possibility of Israeli intentions against Jordan. Furthermore, the staging and concentration areas of the Israeli forces in the northern Negev were suitable for an attack on either Egypt or Jordan. The Soviet intervention in Hungary also contributed to diverting attention from Israel's real intentions.

Senior field commanders did not know the real objectives until D-day. The IDF always plans operations in various sectors of the border with varying options. The deception was so effective that officers who were prepared for combat in Sinai expected to operate against Jordan.

Deception was carried on up to the first phases of the fighting. During the early stages of the fighting, the Israeli General Staff endeavoured to convey the impression that only an extended 'retaliatory raid' was in progress. This was achieved by the following activities:

- Gradual entry by their forces and avoidance of using armour during the opening phase.
- Throughout the opening phase, the major positions of the Egyptian army in Sinai were not attacked, and the attack during the second phase was to be done mainly by infantry.
- The Air Force was instructed to defend Israeli air space only, and provide close tactical support to the ground forces. (During the Six Day War in the following decade, the Air Force was given the task of first destroying the Egyptian Air Force.)
- No blackout was imposed in the cities of Israel, so as to give the impression that this was no war.
- An IDF spokesman stated that 'the IDF went in and attacked fidaiyyun units in Ras el-Naqab and Kuntilla and seized positions west of the Nakhl junction near the Suez Canal. This action was taken following Egyptian military attacks on Israeli transportation.'

Thus, strategic surprise was achieved; the enemy was surprised by an attack and by its location and timing. This plan of diversion and deception was conceived by the then Chief of Staff, General Moshe Dayan, who cleverly exploited the international and regional configuration of events.

The tension between Israel and the Arab states and the extensive mobilization of the reservists indicated that a war was soon to start. Nevertheless, the IDF took steps to achieve surprise in order to avoid an enemy concentration of forces at the points of confrontation, and to countermand international pressure which might seek to prevent the impending conflict, or to quench it at its beginning. In addition to the strategic surprise in the timing (D-day) and in the location (Egypt), the IDF achieved tactical surprise by battle methods such as airborne operations deep in enemy territory, bypassing positions and junctions, and attack from unexpected axes of advance.

THE CHARACTERISTICS OF WARFARE AND THEIR LESSONS

The following principles guided the planners of Kadesh:

a. A short quick war before superpower intervention.
b. Reliance on the British and French air forces.

c. Control of the entire Sinai Peninsula.
d. Neglecting the Gaza Strip during the first phase of the operation.
e. Gradual entry into attack within the strategic deception and diversion plan.
f. Seizure of targets deep in enemy territory by airborne units and linking up with them.
g. Bypassing enemy positions and advancing.
h. Taking positions which could not be bypassed or taking them at a later stage, when isolated and cut-off.

The Indirect Approach

The Sinai Campaign was based on the doctrine of indirect approach. This applied both to the command level (e.g., sending the Ninth Brigade along an uncharted route to the Straits of Tiran, or leaving enemy positions in order to attack them from the rear later), and to the tactical level, whereby every unit attempted to attack its objectives from the rear or from the flanks (e.g., the Seventh Brigade attacking the positions at Abu Ageilla from an unexpected direction). In evaluating this operation, the noted military historian, B.H. Liddell Hart, noted: 'Qualitatively speaking, the Sinai campaign is one of the outstanding examples of the strategic quality of the oblique approach in the modern era and possibly throughout world history. The strategic plan of the IDF was a work of art.'

Familiarity with the Terrain

The IDF was acquainted with the eastern part of Sinai well before the Sinai campaign, having operated there at the end of the 1948 War of Independence. The crossing point at the border was reconnoitred for years. The deeper areas were studied theoretically, mainly from maps on a scale of 1:100,000 for northern Sinai, and on a scale of 1:250,000 for the southern part of the peninsula, and from aerial photos. Only one reconnaissance mission was made before the war along the Eilat–Sharm el-Sheikh axis. Nevertheless the forces operated in the Sinai expanses as in familiar terrain, thanks to map exercises and operational planning carried out for years. Indeed, the first trip to Mount Sinai and the St. Catherina Monastery was made with a Baedeker guide dating from the nineteenth century.

Terrain Trafficability

The Sinai Peninsula embraces vast areas of sand dunes and mountains. These areas were considered impassable to motorized transport. At that time there were only two asphalt-covered roads – the northern and the central routes. All other roads were poor dirt roads, whose condition further deteriorated as vehicles, in particular tanks, travelled over them, making them impassable. The Ninth Brigade advancing from Eilat to Sharm el-Sheikh along paths never traversed by motorized transport, almost literally carried the vehicles on its back. The men pushed and pulled the vehicles stuck in the sand of the wadis more than they rode in them. The reconnaissance troops were the Brigade's advance parties to discover routes and axes uncharted in the maps.

The lessons from this experience were that even in the expanse of desert sands and mountainous areas it was possible to find routes, and that forces needed vehicles with front-wheel drive.

Vertical Outflanking (Parachuting in Rear of the Enemy)

During the Sinai campaign the IDF twice parachuted troops to seize objectives in the enemy's rear area: one battalion at the Parker Monument in front of the Mitla Pass, and one at el-Tur on the western coast of the peninsula. Despite the superiority of the Egyptian air force, it did not intervene during the air drop or while the paratroops were in the forming-up stage.

The dropping of these troops deep in enemy territory strongly motivated the force designed to link up with them to accomplish it as soon as possible. The brigade to which these paratroopers belonged crossed the international border with vehicles which had no front-wheel drive. Only four AMX 13 tanks were seconded to it. It had to overcome problems of terrain, and take two enemy positions in Nakhl and el-Themed which blocked its advance, crossing a distance of 300 km – 100 in Israel, 200 in Sinai. The brigade linked up with the paratrooper unit in 28 hours instead of 48, as expected.

The maintenance and supply of a brigade in the enemy's rear area necessitated the planning and implementation of supply operations by air-lift, which had never been carried out by the IDF except during manoeuvres. Supplies included anti-tank weapons – recoilless artillery which, together with the four AMX 13 tanks, gave the minimum anti-tank defence. When the brigade entered combat in the Mitla pass, it was necessary to evacuate casualties through the use of light aircraft and transport airplanes taking off from an improvised air strip, laid out by paratroopers.

From this vertical outflanking operation, the following lessons were learned: the possibility of utilizing an airborne force to seize objectives deep in enemy territory; the need for rapid linking with the parachuted force; the use of airborne forces only where air superiority was certain.

Deployment of Armour

Prior to the Sinai campaign, there was a serious dispute in the IDF as to objectives and methods of the deployment of armour. Whereas the Chief of Staff thought that the main use of the tank was to support the infantry, Gen. Chaim Laskov maintained that the armoured corps should be an assault force with practically independent missions. In the end, Dayan adopted the viewpoint of the armoured corps and from then to this day the armoured corps took primacy over the infantry in the ground forces. The armoured corps was deployed in the framework of a brigade with practically independent tasks. It proved its high mobility and manoeuvrability, as well as its capacity for breakthrough assault and overpowering. During the Sinai campaign the IDF operated merely three armoured brigades which represented its entire armoured strength. These brigades operated as an armoured corps, and successfully executed their tasks.

Speed in Combat

In the words of Moshe Dayan, 'The speed of advance was of major importance to us, for thus we could exploit our principal advantage over the Egyptian army. The Egyptians operated schematically, and their commanders sat in the rear, far from the front. I judged that any change in the disposition of their forces would require some time. We, on the other hand, were able to act with greater flexibility and with less military routine.'

Speed in combat was crucial in the Sinai campaign (and in other wars) in order to reach the objectives before superpower intervention. Taking into account that the enemy tends to be put off by any changes in pre-planned drills, whereas IDF commanders and units are flexible and skilled at improvising, speed in combat is an asset. Since the Sinai campaign speed in combat has been adopted in the IDF as a guideline; there were even those who advocated its incorporation in the principles of war.

Speed in combat can be obtained by correct operational planning, but a necessary condition for this is the mobility of the fighting echelons in vehicles with front-wheel drive. Still, speed in combat causes situations of uncertainty when commanders have no precise up-to-date pictures of the disposition of forces. Consequently, there is a danger of clashes with one's own forces, which actually did happen during the campaign. It can be prevented by such measures as common code maps, continuous reporting, vehicle marking for aircraft, etc.

Another negative aspect of speed in combat is that commanders get drawn into unnecessary skirmishes because of their over-independence. One can try to eliminate this liability through proper training of the commanders, as well as enforcement of immediate control levels.

Divisional Organization

Up to a short time before the Sinai campaign, the IDF ground forces were a combination of reinforced infantry and armoured brigades. Prior to the campaign and in its aftermath, a fierce controversy took place in the army concerning the correct organizational framework above brigade level: either a 'division' with permanent brigades or a 'division' consisting only in a permanent headquarters plus an unfixed number of infantry or armoured brigades, according to assignment. The IDF started the Sinai campaign with the latter framework – two divisional headquarters with armoured and infantry forces attached according to mission. This organizational form proved suitable to the battles of the Sinai campaign.

Inter-Corps and Inter-Arm Cooperation

The Sinai campaign was the first war in which formations from different corps operated against common objectives. We quickly learned that one must have the infantry cooperate with the armoured corps, supported by artillery and engineering corps. This cooperation is mandatory on the battlefield, and since the Sinai campaign the battle doctrine of inter-corps and inter-arms cooperation has been consolidated, eventually leading to the establishment of the Ground Forces Command in 1983. During the Sinai campaign there was close cooperation between the air and ground forces, with the Air Force giving close support to ground formations. Close cooperation also existed between naval and air forces.

Air Supremacy

The open desert and lack of cover made it very difficult to conceal troop movement and concentration. They were exposed to air attacks. The Sinai campaign taught us the importance of air supremacy. In air combat not one Israeli plane was destroyed, while nine Egyptian aircraft were downed and others damaged. Moreover, the Israeli Air Force secured our ground forces. This was made possible thanks to the attacks on the Egyptian airfields by the allies. When the Egyptians dared to bring in armoured reinforcements without air cover, their tanks were prey to our air attacks (as on the Ismailia–Abu Ageilla route).

The Air Force engaged in strafing duties, bombarded positions, cut off Egyptian communication, intelligence, liaison and transportation of commanders. It participated in the attack against the Egyptian destroyer in Haifa Bay, the evacuation of casualties, and executed airdrops of men and supplies. Even though it was still a small force, it successfully carried out all these tasks. In the aftermath of the Sinai campaign, the IDF resolved to create a strong and powerful air force that would ensure 'friendly skies' in future wars.

The Navy

Naval participation was limited to assistance from the sea during the capture of the Rafah position, assistance to the Ninth brigade in the movement of forces and supplies, and the subduing and capture of the Egyptian destroyer in Haifa Bay.

Fighting Spirit

The lack of sophisticated arms, the lack of suitable transport, air inferiority, defective equipment, etc. were compensated for by the magnificent fighting spirit of the troops – regulars and reserves – who gave momentum to plans and orders through devoted and enthusiastic execution. In addition to sophisticated equipment and weaponry, the campaign demonstrated the military significance of scouts who searched for routes in the desert, of soldiers who pushed vehicles through sand dunes, of paratroops who stormed the clefts of the Mitla Pass, of pilots who cut telephone wires with propeller blades, of tank personnel who did not sleep for four days and fought continuously, and of the aggressive spirit of the commanders. This spirit was determined in large measure by the commanders, who set an example through their behaviour, actually leading their troops in combat, which explains the high casualty rate among the commanders.

Logistics

Egypt's weaponry originated mainly in the Eastern Bloc, consequently it was not possible to use captured ammunition dumps. Vehicles or familiar weapons were put into operation immediately upon their seizure, as were the fuel dumps. It was not possible to use the captured food supplies since they were not up to the standard, quality and tastes of Israeli soldiers.

The problem of water in the desert was solved by prior planning of the water supply and use of local resources. The Israeli logistical set-up was challenged for the first time by the need to supply fighters on the move. Until the Sinai campaign this capability had been tested only in exercises; the echelons attached to the troops provided partial supplies, during the advance, but soon the need arose for supply by unit distribution. Therefore the high command ordered a quicker opening of the axes. In other words, logistical requirements influenced the operation of the campaign. Air and naval forces also took part in carrying supplies, such as to the troop brigade at the Parker Monument and to the Ninth Brigade on its way to the Straits of Tiran from Eilat.

Mobilization of Reservists

It is no secret that most of the IDF strength lies in its reserves and its power depends on their mobilization. The IDF mobilizes its reserves by two methods: the public call-up and the 'quiet' one. Even a 'quiet' mobilization is hard to conceal, but the constant exercising of this method creates a cloud of uncertainty and confuses foreign intelligence monitoring this activity.

The IDF used the quiet call-up method in the Sinai campaign. Even had mobilization been identified by foreign quarters, they would have associated it with the tension with Jordan, as a function of the strategic deception plan already mentioned. Initially, the mobilization did not succeed, and it was necessary to proceed using emergency methods. Subsequently, it did succeed, and the units entered the staging areas with full manpower strength.

The mobilization of the entire fighting echelons a week before the war would have undermined secrecy and minimized surprise, and therefore the GHQ decided that the commanding officers of the reserves would be called up several days before D-day, the armoured units on D-day minus three, and the other units on D-day minus two.

In an emergency, IDF also relied on civilian vehicles: trucks, pickups and heavy engineering equipment. Thus the columns breaking through into Sinai contained vehicles bearing the signs and trademarks of commercial firms. The call-up of these vehicles also encountered many difficulties due to their poor mechanical condition. To quote Moshe Dayan on this topic: 'When I said in Paris that the IDF relies mainly on an army of reserves and that we do not have sufficient equipment for it, and that our soldiers will have to use civilian transportation and wear their own winter clothes – there appeared before them [the audience] a picture of a people's army in eighteenth century style, capable of storming barricades, but unable to wage desert warfare with armoured vehicles and to ensure supply along the routes.'

BALANCE OF POWER BETWEEN ISRAEL AND EGYPT

Egyptian forces were numerically superior. In weaponry the proportion was 1:4 in their favour. In Infantry it was 1:15 for the Egyptians. In armour there was almost an equilibrium. In the air, Israeli had 140 planes, half of them propeller-engined, while the Egyptians had 250 planes, all of which were jet-engined. In the sea, Egyptian superiority came to 1:7. The IDF solved its numerical inferiority by qualitative superiority at the place and time it chose to operate. Yitzhak Rabin has commented: 'The quality of IDF teaches us that one does not necessarily have to position against each and every enemy plane, tank and soldier the same number of Israeli soldiers and weapons.'

The Egyptian Army knew the terrain and prepared it properly for defence: all junctions, axes and vital areas were ready for manning or were already manned. The positions were already dug-in, fenced and mined; units from nearby camps were used to taking up defence dispositions at short notice; the logistical system was deployed, the taking of positions was repeatedly drilled, and each soldier knew his position.

The Egyptians prepared brigade-sized reserves on each one of the three main routes: on the northern route a motorized infantry brigade; on the central, an armoured brigade; on the southern, an infantry brigade. These units were familiar with their tasks, rehearsed prior to the war. In war, too, they executed their tasks with speed and efficiency. All Egyptians were in position before the battle started, or before IDF units arrived on the scene. But the Egyptian army carried out its defensive tasks so long as the fighting proceeded as foreseen and drilled. Whenever change occurred, and the need arose for improvising or for a change in plans, its weakness was exposed. (This was also true of the Egyptian army during the Yom Kippur War.)

President Nasser aspired to a system of military treaties with the Arab countries. After having signed such a treaty with Syria he expanded it to include Jordan, and Israel found herself facing a belligerent continental belt which was to pounce in coordination. In fact, the Unified Arab Command had no operational significance. The IDF fought against Egypt alone.

THE ROLE OF OUTSIDE POWERS

Israel aspired to cooperate with France and Britain in this campaign because of political and military considerations. This cooperation assured the supply of French arms to the IDF, which was then short of heavy weapons and aircraft. Israel placed great hopes on the pinning down of Egyptian air power by the Powers. (One must remember that Israeli leaders worried about air attacks on civilian targets in Israel.) The preparations for military intervention by the Powers forced the Egyptians to hold back forces and thereby facilitated the advance of the IDF.

The joint Israeli–French–British preparation for the campaign had its ups and downs, with crises erupting during the campaign itself. With hindsight it can be said that the IDF could have undertaken this war without the belated and intermittent operational involvement of the British and French in the Canal Zone. In this event, the IDF would have paid a higher price in casualties and in time, but would have achieved all its military objectives, and Israel would not have been accused of collusion with the forces of imperialism (an issue of great importance in the Third World, which Israel aimed to reach out to) as a consequence of the Sinai campaign.

The validity of the war principle 'unity of command' was proved again. The only sectors in which there was combined action (apart from overall planning) were:

(a) The artillery bombardment by French warships of the Rafah camps as a preparation for their storming by the IDF. We set great store by this bombardment, but the forces which broke through were somewhat disappointed with its scope and effect;

(b) The bombardment of airfields in Egypt by the Powers, which was carried out at a later stage in the campaign.

The main advantage of joint action was in obtaining weaponry. From the operational aspect, it would have been possible to achieve the operational targets without his partnership. It is not pleasant to accuse partners, but it appears that the Powers did not give sufficient thought to space and time, hesitated too long, and missed the opportunity to do what they wished.

71

At the opening phase of the campaign, the Soviets were tied up with the uprising in Hungary. A few days elapsed before they reacted to events. In my estimation, the Soviets were unable to substantiate their pressure and threats, therefore they were allowed unjustified weight in evaluating the political situation. The upshot was that the IDF was given the order to withdraw from the Sinai.

CONCLUSION

Before assessing the accomplishments of the Sinai campaign, the advantages which the IDF enjoyed should be acknowledged:

1. The IDF fought on one front only and could concentrate its efforts and forces on this front.
2. Israel initiated the war.
3. The strategic surprise overwhelmed the enemy.
4. The Sinai campaign caught the Egyptians at a period of transition from Western to Soviet arms, necessitating a period of familiarization and absorption which had not yet run its course.
5. The war took place away from the civilian centres and did not affect them.

The achievements of the Sinai campaign were:

1. The strengthening of the deterrent power of Israel, which continued to be effective for over ten years.
2. Reinforcement of its sense of security, based on military prowess, which bolstered IDF self-confidence.
3. Eradication of the fidaiyyun based in the Gaza Strip.
4. Opening the Tiran Straits to free navigation, thus facilitating economic ties with Africa and Asia, and the development of the port of Eilat.
5. Annihilation of the offensive formation in the Sinai.
6. Crystallization of the combat doctrine, organization and structure of the IDF.

The Sinai campaign was the first war initiated by the IDF after the War of Independence in 1948. The lessons learned in the Sinai were incorporated in IDF battle doctrine, which guided the four wars to follow. The IDF proved yet again the role of the human factor and the importance of fighting spirit over overwhelming numbers. As it is written in the book of Exodus:

For they were departed from Rephidim and were come to the

desert of Sinai, and had pitched in the wilderness; and there Israel camped before the Mount, and Moses went up unto God, and the Lord called unto him out of the mountain, saying, 'Thus shalt thou say to the house of Jacob and tell the children of Israel; Ye have seen what I did unto the Egyptians and how I bore you on eagles' wings'.

5

The Egyptian Armed Forces during the Kadesh Campaign

Yonah Bandmann*

On the eve of the Kadesh Campaign, the Egyptian armed forces had reached a turning point. Only two years earlier, on 19 October 1954, the Egyptian and British governments had signed an agreement according to which the British forces would vacate the bases they still held in the Suez Canal region within 20 months. Thus for the first time since 1882, the sole responsibility for Egypt's defence lay with her armed forces. At about that time, towards the end of 1954, Egypt and the USSR signed the first arms deal, known as 'the Czech Deal', to which the Egyptian president, Gamal Abd al-Nasser, first referred in public in his speech on 27 September 1955.[1]

On the outbreak of the Kadesh campaign, Egypt had received under the terms of this deal more than 500 tracked A.F.V.s – some 200 tanks, mainly the T-34 medium tank with 85 mm gun, some 100 SU self-propelled guns (100mm A/Tk guns mounted on the chassis of T-34 tanks) and more than 200 armoured troop carriers of the types BTR-40 and BTR-152; some 500 artillery pieces of various sizes; approximately 200 jet planes – some 120 MIG-15 fighters, some 50 IL-28 medium bombers and 20 IL-14 transport aircraft – and various naval vessels, including 2 'Skory' type destroyers and 12 MTBs (motor torpedo boats).[2]

This was without doubt an extremely significant addition, both qualitatively and quantitatively, to the arsenal of the Egyptian armed forces and produced a drastic change in Egypt's favour in the relative strength of the military forces in the Middle East,

---

* This article deals only with that part of the Egyptian armed forces which fought against the IDF during Kadesh Campaign. The main part of the discussion concentrates on the fighting of the Egyptian land forces. I would like to express my deep appreciation to my former colleagues in the Department of Military History of the IDF for their kind assistance in locating some of the material which aided me in preparing this article.

74

particularly with regard to Israel. However, by October 1956 this equipment had not all been absorbed on an operational level in formations and field units and only a small number of the aircraft had joined operational squadrons. Furthermore, in the case of armaments that had actually been absorbed, this was only on a technical level, without any accompanying changes yet, in the structure and organization of the field and air formation units or in combat doctrine. These continued to be based mainly on British models from the Second World War – testimony to the many years during which the Egyptian armed forces were subjected to solely British training and influence.

Parallel with the military links that had just been forged with the USSR, arms sales and military aid from the Western powers were maintained. The land forces absorbed British-made Archer tank destroyers (17 lb anti-tank guns mounted on the chassis of Valentine tanks), as well as cannons and vehicles, whilst the air force continued to acquire Meteor and Vampire jet fighters. France supplied AMX-13 light tanks with 75 mm guns, 155 mm medium-range guns, etc.

Also at this period a group of about 80 German military experts was operating in Egypt, consisting of officers who had served in the Wehrmacht in the Second World War, and headed by the retired artillery commander General Wilhelm Frambecher. On the recommendation and under the guidance of these experts one of the infantry brigades was converted in the summer of 1956 to a mechanized brigade along the lines of the German formations in the Second World War (this unit was known as the 'experimental brigade').

This juxtaposition of British instructors, Soviet technicians and weapons experts and German advisers, as well as the acquisition of weapons systems from different sources and of different types, are clear evidence that the Egyptian armed forces had by this time reached a stage of reorganization and reorientation. This situation was resolved in the way it was only after the Kadesh and Musketeer Campaigns and as a direct result of them.

On the eve of the outbreak of the Kadesh Campaign, the Egyptian armed forces included about 100,000 regular troops and about the same number of conscripts in the National Guard. The regular army service were divided among the three services as follows:[3]

(a) Land Forces

approximately 88,000 regular army service (and a further 100,000 conscripts in the National Guard) organized in the following formations (main formations only):

3 Egyptian infantry divisions (nos. 1,2,3)
1 Palestinian infantry division (no. 8)
1 armoured division (no.4; only 2 armoured brigade teams)

The land forces were equipped with the following principal weapons systems:

approximately 430 medium tanks (half of which were Soviet T 34s and the rest were of Western manufacture, mainly Sherman Mk 3 with 75 mm short barrel)
several hundred armoured troop carriers (some 150 of which were Soviet BTR-152s)
approximately 100 self-propelled SU-100 guns
approximately 200 Archer tank destroyers
over 800 artillery pieces of various types

(b) Air Forces

6,000–8,000 men in active service, with some 400 aircraft at their disposal, organized in the following squadrons (not including training and communications squadrons):[4]

3 fighter squadrons equipped with MIG 15s
5 fighter squadrons equipped with Meteors and Vampires
3 medium bomber squadrons equipped with IL-28s
3 transport squadrons equipped with IL-14s, Commandos and Dakotas

Out of these squadrons, only the following were operational at the start of the campaign:

2 squadrons of MIG 15s – 30 aircraft
1 squadron of Vampires – 15 aircraft
1 squadron of Meteors – 12 aircraft
1 squadron of IL-28s – 12 aircraft
3 transport squadrons – 60 aircraft

(c) Naval Forces (vessels in operational condition only)

5 destroyers, 4 corvettes-minesweepers
3 frigates, 18 MTBs

SINAI PENINSULA IN EGYPTIAN STRATEGIC THINKING
TO JULY 1956

Whilst British forces were stationed in the canal area the Egyptian General Staff assumed that the territorial objectives of the 'aggressor' Israel in Sinai would be restricted to certain areas around Rafah and perhaps the demilitarized zone at Nitsana.[5] On the basis of this assumption the planners at General Staff gave highest priority to the defence of the Rafah–el-Arish sector, since the capture of el-Arish by Israel could force them to retreat from Northern Sinai and thus place the area under Israeli control. They believed that the defence of that sector would have to be based on the vital Quseima–Abu Ageilla sector because they feared that a deep flanking operation through Abu Ageilla to el-Arish by the IDF would outflank their defence layout in the Rafah area as was done towards the end of the War of Independence in Operation Horev (22 December 1948 – 6 January 1949).[6]

The signing by Great Britain of the agreement of 19 October 1954 concerning the evacuation of the military presence that she had maintained in the Suez Canal region created a new situation for Egypt. The Egyptian High Command altered its previous evaluation of Israel's possible operational objectives, which in turn produced a re-assessment of Sinai as a future theatre of war. The new defence plan viewed Northern Sinai as an area of defence in depth, with the purpose of its deployment to prevent Israel from achieving her possible vital strategic objectives in the Canal area. According to this plan the Egyptian Armed forces were to conduct their defensive campaign in four operative areas, extending across Northern Sinai from east to west, as follows:

(a) the international border zone with its vital areas: Rafah–al-Giradi; Nitsana–Quseima–Abu Ageilla; Kuntilla–Ras al-Naqab–Themed;
(b) the region extending from both sides of the axis el-Arish–Jebel Libni–Nakhl with the vital areas: el-Arish, Jebel Libni, Bir Hasne and Nakhl;
(c) the mountain pass between Bir el-Hamma and Bir Gafgafa (the central road axis) and the one between the Parker Monument and Mitla (the southern axis);
(d) the western sector of the Suez Canal.

In this plan the Egyptian High Command adopted, at least in

principle and along general lines, the recommendations that had been made by the German General Frambecher in the spring of 1951, when he had been asked by the Egyptian General Staff to make a survey of the defence of Sinai. However, almost no appropriate preparations had been made on the terrain to make a defensive campaign in the depth of northern Sinai possible, as was required by the new concept of Sinai as a theatre of war and as had been proposed by General Frambecher.

On the other hand the strength of the forces deployed in Sinai had been increasing since the spring of 1955 as a consequence of the marked deterioration in the security situation along the border with Israel, both in the Gaza Strip and the demilitarized zone at Nitsana. This deterioration was marked, inter alia, by a series of increasingly large-scale operations carried out by units of the IDF against Egyptian military objectives.[7]

By the beginning of the summer of 1956 the Egyptian land forces in Sinai amounted to three divisions, as compared with one division that was stationed in Sinai up to the end of 1954. These were deployed as follows:

(a) one reinforced infantry division in the Rafah–el-Arish sector (divisional HQ in Rafah);
(b) one reinforced infantry division in the Quseima–Abu Ageilla sector (divisional HQ in Abu Ageilla);
(c) an armoured brigade combat team and a reserve infantry brigade at Bir Gafgafa;
(d) an armoured brigade combat team at Bir el-Hamma;
(e) an infantry brigade at Jebel Libni.

The forces in Sinai came under the command of the Eastern Command, which maintained a forward HQ in el-Arish and a tactical forward HQ at the Jebel Libni crossroad, the last one to be manned only in an emergency. The Eastern Command held in Sinai two armoured brigade teams and two infantry brigades in reserve (see above, c-e). The forward command post of the HQ General Staff was located at Bir el-Hasne.

THE DEPLOYMENT OF FORCES IN SINAI
ON THE EVE OF THE KADESH CAMPAIGN

By the end of June or beginning of July 1956 there began a reduction in the military deployment in Sinai due to a combination of at least three considerations:

(a) Fear of the possibility of an immediate war initiated by Israel had largely disappeared. The Egyptian intelligence services estimated that Israel was likely to create tension along the border and even initiate large-scale incidents but would *not* launch a general offensive.

(b) There was a desire to establish a tougher training programme in order to absorb the new weapons systems, especially those acquired through the 'Czech Deal'.

(c) Budgetary difficulties necessitated a reduction in military spending (maintaining units and formations in temporary camps in Sinai involved large expenditures).

Following President Nasser's declaration of the nationalization of the Suez Canal Company (26 July 1956), there were far-reaching changes in the Egyptian leadership's assessment of the dangers facing their country. Military action by Britain and France was seen as a real possibility. Cairo estimated that Israel was likely to exploit the situation that would occur during an attack by 'some Western powers' in order to initiate military action. Furthermore they even saw the probability that 'Britain and France might push Israel into launching military action in the Gaza Strip and the central sector [the Nitsana area] in order to achieve a rapid victory and to *force the Egyptian army to fight on two fronts*'. However, as we have mentioned above, the fear of a large-scale attack initiated by Israel, which was current before the declaration of nationalization, had by this time diminished.[8]

In this context it should be pointed out that the Egyptian government tried very hard to reduce the tension and not to provide Israel with an excuse to act against her. The activities of the fidaiyyun were stopped; the Palestinian Division, which held the line in the Gaza Strip, was placed under strict control and the state-controlled media ran an extensive propaganda campaign aimed at placating Israel and emphasizing the objective of peace with her.

The new evaluation of the situation caused the emphasis on defence to be shifted from Sinai to Egypt proper, as was illustrated by the orders issued to the forces. The operation order for the defence of Egypt from 1 September 1956 read: 'We must expect that forces of the Western countries will carry out hostile action against Egypt as a result of the nationalization of the Suez Canal.' The authors of this order assumed that their objectives would be:[9]

(a) capture of the Suez Canal Zone by air and naval action;
(b) capture of the base at Alexandria by air and naval action;

(c) attack on the Cairo area after one of the first two objectives had been achieved – all the more so if both of them were achieved;

(d) action in the Delta region by paratroopers and/or by landing forces from the sea.

As for Israel, the assessment concluded: 'We should not ignore what action Israel might carry out in such circumstances.'

The order dealt in detail with the defence of the vital objectives in the Canal Zone, Alexandria and Cairo areas. It also determined that 'in the light of the current conditions the authority of the eastern command will [also] be extended to the Canal and Eastern Delta front'. The extension of this command's area of operational responsibility demonstrates in the clearest possible manner the evaluation of the High Command, according to which the danger of a large-scale offensive by Israel had diminished to a large extent. It is therefore not surprising to learn that the Northern Sinai and the Gulf of Aqaba sectors were not even mentioned in that operational order, apart from one sentence which determined that the forces in these two fronts would act 'in accordance with instructions that had already been promulgated'. The following forces were allocated in the defence of these two sectors:[10]

(a) 3rd Infantry Division – Qidmat Sinai;
(b) the Palestinian Infantry Division – the Gaza Strip;
(c) 2nd Border Battalion (Motorized) – Southern Sinai;
(d) 21st reinforced Infantry Battalion – Gulf of Aqaba

All the other forces deployed in Sinai at the beginning of summer – one infantry division, the two armoured brigade teams, etc. – were withdrawn during the months of August–October 1956 and redeployed in the Suez Canal Zone.

QIDMAT SINAI*

Responsibility for the defence of Qidmat Sinai was with the 3rd Infantry Division. The detailed orders of the divisional commander, Brigadier-General Abd al-Wahab al-Qadi, stated: 'The division and the forces attached to it will defend Rafah, el-Arish and Abu Ageilla to the end.' These forces and their assignments, as determined by the orders, were as follows (see map no.1):[11]

---

*Qidmat Sinai is a Hebrew geographical-military term, aimed to differentiate the eastern part of North Sinai from the rear part of the peninsula. For a very general bordering of Qidmat Sinai see map no.1.

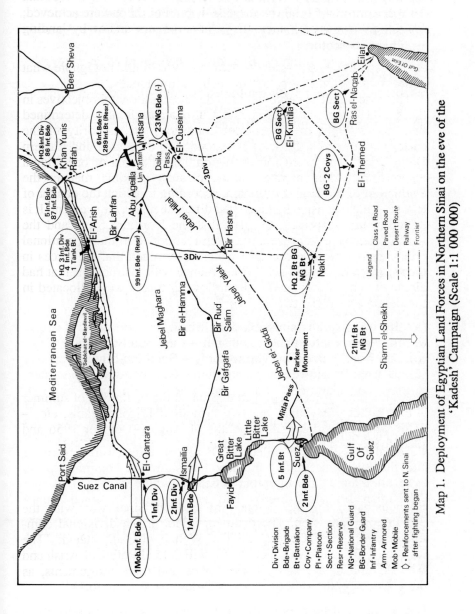

Map 1. Deployment of Egyptian Land Forces in Northern Sinai on the eve of the 'Kadesh' Campaign (Scale 1:1 000 000)

(a) HQ 3rd Infantry Division – el-Arish;
(b) 5th reinforced Infantry Brigade – defence of Rafah sector;
(c) 6th reinforced Infantry Brigade – defence of Abu Ageilla–Quseima sector;
(d) 99th reserve Infantry Brigade – concentrated in the Abu Ageilla–Jebel Libni area;
(e) battalion from the 4th reinforced Infantry Brigade – defence of the eastern approaches to el-Arish;
(f) 4th reinforced Infantry Brigade (less one battalion), together with a tank battalion and an artillery brigade (incomplete), concentrated in el-Arish and forming the reserve force of the divisional commander.

In addition to the 3rd Infantry Division, which bore the main responsibility for the defence of Qidmat Sinai, there were three additional sector HQs in Sinai and the Gaza Strip, responsible for the defence of the secondary sectors:

(a) The Gaza Strip Sector

From a geographical point of view the Gaza Strip was not part of Sinai. Moreover, the Egyptian leadership was clearly aware of the fact that it was quite impossible to defend it, or in President Nasser's words, 'We are always aware that from the purely military viewpoint it was easy to cut off that sector [the Gaza Sector] from the rest of the front.'[12] However, due to internal, inter-Arab and international considerations, the Egyptian leadership could not risk forgoing the sector without demonstrating at least determined resistance. Thus, the plan for the defence of the Gaza Strip was based on a delaying battle, to be fought mainly by conscripts from the local Palestinian population. These conscripts were organised into the 8th [Palestinian] Infantry Division (the command posts were all manned by Egyptian officers), which consisted of two Palestinian brigades (86,87) and an Egyptian National Guard brigade (no.26) under command.[13] The 8th Division was subordinated to HQ Eastern Command and not to HQ 3rd Infantry Division which was, as already mentioned, in charge of the defence of Qidmat Sinai.

(b) Southern Sinai

The operational borders of the sector were Ras el-Naqab–Kuntilla in the south, the Mitla Pass in the west, and an imaginary line joining Bir el-Hasne and somewhere south of Quseima in the north. The

2nd Border (Motorized) Battalion, to which a National Guard Battalion was attached under command, was stationed in the sector. Its units were patrolling in the area from firm bases at Ras el-Naqab, Kuntilla, Themed, Nakhl, and Bir el-Hasne. The HQ of the Sector, which was identical to HQ 2nd Border Battalion, was based at Nakhl and subordinated to HQ Eastern Command. The tasks of the Battalion, as were defined by the Eastern Command were: (a) to prevent infiltration of small Israeli units; (b) to warn in case of penetration of large scale forces into the region and to conduct a delaying battle with them; (c) to conduct an active defence of the two vital areas in the sector – Themed and Nakhl.[14] However, it was quite clear from the very beginning that in case of war, the units of the 2nd Border Battalion could carry out only a symbolic resistance and it is doubtful if the Eastern Command expected more from them.

(c) The Gulf of Aqaba

The HQ Sector was responsible for the blockade of the Straits of Tiran to shipping sailing to the port of Eilat, as well as protecting the eastern shore of the Suez Gulf up to el-Tur. The defence of the Sharm el-Sheikh area proper was planned against the possibility of attack by an airborne paratroop force or of a naval landing. (The possibility of a land attack from the East was ruled out since the Egyptian planners considered the terrain impassable for motorized forces of any size.) The HQ Sector was located at Sharm el-Sheikh (because of the port and the airfield that were built there) and was under the direct command of the General Staff in Cairo. The forces in the sector were the 21st Infantry Battalion, a National Guard Battalion, anti-aircraft and other artillery units, and 3–4 camel-mounted platoons ('Hajjana').[15]

THE EGYPTIAN LAND FORCES IN THE KADESH CAMPAIGN

The Kadesh Campaign came as a complete surprise to the Egyptian leadership. The two weeks prior to the campaign saw an easing of the tension that had arisen from the fear of military action by Britain and France in the wake of the nationalization of the company operating the Suez Canal. The possibility of action to capture the Canal had almost been ruled out. (It must be remembered that discussions between representatives of Egypt, France and Britain were due to begin in Geneva on 29 October 1956 under the auspices of the UN in order to reach a settlement of the Suez Canal crisis.)[16]

The Egyptian leadership did not totally exclude the possibility of military action by Israel but all the evidence shows that they were not ready for the date when the IDF opened the offensive. This was in spite of the fact that the Egyptian military intelligence had accumulated considerable information from Arab and other sources indicating an extensive mobilization of the reserves and a bellicose atmosphere throughout Israel. However, the military intelligence explained this atmosphere in terms of the increased tension which had developed on the Israeli–Jordanian border and the entrance into Jordan of Iraqi troops.[17] An indication of the Egyptian leadership's appreciation that the target of a possible forthcoming Israeli attack would be Jordan rather than Egypt was the departure for an official visit to Jordan and Syria on the 25th of October of a highranking military delegation, headed by Marshal Abd al-Hakim Amir, the Commander-in-Chief of the armed forces.

On 27 October the commander of the 3rd Infantry Division HQ reported IDF troop concentrations in the Negev region, and in particular in the Nitsana area. Despite this report and the accumulation of additional information on what was happening on the Israeli side of the border, Marshal Amir returned to Egypt only on the morning of 29 October.

ACTIVITIES OF THE GENERAL STAFF

In the course of 29 October the Egyptian General Staff received information from various sources on the intention of the IDF to start a war. On the same day towards midday the air force was put on alert and during the ensuing hours the army and navy, too, were placed in a state of high alert.

In the early evening the first reports reached Cairo that IDF forces had parachuted near to the Parker Monument (890 Battalion) and later that they had captured Ras al-Naqab and Kuntilla (202 Brigade). In the evaluation of the situation, which took place at the HQ General Staff with the participation of Nasser, the view was taken that Israel was acting alone. This was because 'Britain has terrific interests in the Middle East and any rash action of a military nature [by her] would destroy these interests'.[18]

On the basis of this appraisal the General Staff ordered the officer commanding Eastern Command to send without delay the 1st Armoured Brigade team ('the main striking force' in Nasser's words), which was part of the command reserves and stationed at Camp Fanara, along the Ismailia–Nitsana longitudinal route in the direction of Abu Ageilla (their place at Fanara was to be taken by armoured forces from General Staff reserves) and to send 2nd Infantry Brigade (stationed at Camp Shalufa) against the paratroop force at the Parker Monument. It also gave orders to reinforce the 3rd Infantry Division by the 1st motorized Infantry Brigade, which was part of the General Staff reserves.[19]

From early morning on 30 October the Egyptian General Staff started to receive the first reports from the field on the advance of IDF troops along the Kuntilla–Nakhl route and on the capture of Quseima and the outposts in the Um Kattef sector. On the strength of these reports a view of the situation emerged in Cairo according to which the actions of the IDF went beyond a limited invasion both in terms of objectives and the troops involved (as was the style of the official announcement broadcast on the Israeli radio station, Kol Yisrael). It further appears that the Egyptian General Staff was unable on that occasion to estimate the composition and strength of the attacking forces and even less to locate the operational targets assigned to the IDF.

In the afternoon of the same day (1600 GMT, 1800 local time) the Egyptian (as well as the Israeli) ambassadors in London and Paris were handed the Anglo-French ultimatum, which demanded that within 12 hours:[20]

(a) belligerent activities should cease on land, sea and air;
(b) the armed forces of both sides should withdraw 10 miles from either side of the Suez Canal;
(c) the Egyptian government should 'accept the temporary occupation by Anglo-French forces of key positions at Port Said, Ismailia and Suez';
(d) 'if at the expiration of that time one or both Governments have not undertaken to comply with the above requirements, United Kingdom and French forces will intervene in whatever strength may be necessary to secure compliance.'

The Egyptian government, at a meeting headed by the President, rejected the ultimatum the same night. President Nasser explained later that the reason for this decision was 'that British invasion was only a possibility, although we reckoned that the possibility was then 70 per cent'.[21] Forces in Sinai were ordered to continue their resistance to the IDF offensive.

During the afternoon of 31 October 1956, the Anglo-French air forces began to attack airfields throughout Egypt. Following this, Nasser called a meeting of the Army High Command later that evening to discuss the new situation. It was decided to withdraw the forces from Sinai and concentrate them in the defence of mainland Egypt against the Anglo-French invasion. The withdrawal from Sinai was to take place under cover of darkness and to be completed within 48 hours, up to the morning of 2 November.[22] However, the order for withdrawal only reached HQ Eastern Command at midday on 1 November and the forces fighting in Sinai several hours later still.

WARFARE BY SECTORS AND FORMATIONS

It is not intended to discuss operational moves in detail and certainly not to examine the warfare in the Kadesh Campaign on a tactical level. These have been exhaustively covered in the dozens of publications that have appeared during the 30 years that have elapsed since that time. Instead we have chosen to discuss in general terms some of the main points that characterized the fighting of the Egyptian land forces in Kadesh in the principal sectors.[23]

The Abu Ageilla–Um Kattef Sector

On 31 October and during the night of 31 October–1st November the units of the 6th reinforced Infantry Brigade, holding the Um Kattef locality, repulsed at least two attacks by IDF forces from the east (10 Infantry Brigade and 37 Armoured Brigade) and one from the south (7 Armoured Brigade). However, once an armoured force of the IDF (7 Armoured Brigade) succeeded on the night of 30–31 October to cross the Daika Pass and to capture Abu Ageilla the following morning, the 6th Brigade found itself cut off from its rear. On 011600 November (local time) the HQ 3rd Infantry Division ordered the sector commander to evacuate Um Kattef and withdraw to el-Arish. Under cover of darkness the regular troops of the 6th Brigade succeeded in reaching el-Arish in orderly manner (prior to its capture by IDF forces on the early morning of 2 November) and from there returned to Egypt. The reserve Battalion's withdrawal was held up in the sand and soon became a disorganized escape.

The Central longitudinal route (Ismailia–Abu Ageilla Sector)

On this route the 1st Armoured Brigade Team ('the main striking force' in President Nasser's words) failed to fulfil the mission it received on the late evening of 29 October, prior to crossing the Suez Canal and entering Sinai – namely, to proceed from its staging area

86

at Bir Gafgafa towards Jebel Libni, to re-conquer the Abu Aweigila junction and thus rescue the 6th Brigade from its encirclement. On 31 October the main body of the Brigade team remained stuck between Bir Gafgafa and Bir Rud Salim under attack by the Israeli Air Force. In the early morning of 1 November the IDF Air Force renewed its attack on the armoured units. During that morning contact was also made, for the first time, near Bir Rud Salim between the tank Battalion of the Brigade team and the advance party of IDF's 7th Armoured Brigade that had come from the direction of Bir el-Hamma. Under these circumstances the officer commanding the Brigade team notified HQ Eastern Command that he was organizing his units for withdrawal. Thus, on the night of 1–2 November the main body of the Brigade team crossed the Canal to the west.[24]

Rafah Sector

In the early hours of 1 November HQ 3rd Division ordered the officer commanding the 5th reinforced Infantry Brigade, which was in charge of defending the sector, to evacuate the Rafah zone and withdraw to el-Arish. However, because of unknown reasons the Brigade HQ only transmitted the order for withdrawal to its units some hours later, when the IDF attack (involving 1st Infantry Brigade 'Golani' and 27 Armoured Brigade) was already at its height. (Until they received the order, the units put up quite a strong resistance.) However, the greater part of the Brigade succeeded in withdrawing to el-Arish prior to the take-over by the IDF forces of the Rafah junction at about 010830 November (local time).

El-Arish Sector

The defence of el-Arish from an attack from the east was mainly based on the el-Giradi locality, which was captured by IDF forces in the afternoon on 1 November. During the night of 1–2 November el-Arish was evacuated by its combat units, who were assisted with the retreat by two trains sent that night by HQ Eastern Command.

The Gaza Strip Sector

When Rafah was captured on the morning of 1 November, the Gaza Strip was actually cut off and its fall, even without fighting, was merely a question of time. Although the order for general withdrawal from Sinai by the Egyptian forces had already been issued by the General Staff towards midday on 1 November and although Rafah, el-Arish and Um Kattef had already fallen, the officer commanding the 8th Palestinian Division, Maj.-Gen. Yusuf Abdulla al-Agrudi (who also served as the chief military commander and Military Governor of the Gaza Strip), received on 2 November firm orders to hold on and 'to fight for every inch' by street fighting in Gaza and Khan Yunis. These orders were without any military significance whatsoever and primarily based on political considerations of Egyptian leadership; it appears that the cost in human lives (Palestinians!) did not play any part in those considerations. However, the desire to spare losses among the civilian population guided the senior commanding officers of the Gaza Strip – the administrative governor Maj.-Gen. Mahmud al-Digwi and the military governor Agrudi (both Egyptian officers) – to submit their surrender during the morning of 2 November.

South Sinai Sector

The IDF forces who penetrated the sector (mainly the 202 Paratroop Brigade) did not encounter any significant opposition from the units of the 2nd Motorized Border Battalion. That said, there was one exception – the force at Themed (about two companies) holding dominating ground to the west of the village, resisted strongly. However, once that resistance was overcome, the way westward became practically open. And thus, at about 301800 October (local time) the advance party of 202 Brigade linked up with 890 Paratroop Battalion near the Parker Monument.

The Mitla Pass

As already mentioned, on the late evening of 29 October the HQ Eastern Command ordered the 2nd Infantry Brigade, which was stationed at Camp Shalufa, to cross the Canal and to advance eastwards: on the first phase to seize the Mitla Pass and thereafter to proceed towards the Parker Monument (information about the dropping of Israeli paratroops nearby the Monument had already reached Cairo). On 30 October the 5th Infantry Battalion of the Brigade crossed the Canal and sent ahead an advance guard which stopped west of the Monument and conducted fire contact with soldiers of the 890 Paratroop Battalion. Next morning, 31 October the main body of the 5th Battalion (reinforced by at least one company of the 6th Battalion) continued its advance and seized positions on both sides of the Mitla Pass. From about midday onwards, this force fought with stubborn resistance against the paratroopers of the 202 Brigade, who tried to break their way through westwards. However, the resistance of the 5th Battalion's soldiers weakened on the following day.

The Gulf of Aqaba Sector

When the battles started, the Egyptian High Command estimated that one of Israel's objectives might be to break off the blockade of the Straits of Tiran. Since no reinforcing forces could be allocated for the defence of the sector, the General Staff ordered, at midday on 1 November, the evacuation of the force stationed in the sector (the 21st reinforced Infantry Battalion) and its regrouping in the Canal Zone. However, the Sector Commander objected to the order, claiming the lack of sufficient transport facilities. Therefore, a few hours later the General Staff abolished the order for the withdrawal. It simultaneously ordered a transport unit to be sent to Sharm el-Sheikh to ensure the evacuation of the forces at a later date, if the developing situation required it.

On the 3 November the officer commanding the sector received reports on the fall of Dahab and the advance of IDF vehicles (the 9th Infantry Brigade) towards Ras Nasrani. On the basis of this information he decided to evacuate Ras Nasrani and to concentrate all the force at Sharm el-Sheikh. This was done during the night of 3–4 November (see map 2). On 5 November Sharm el-Sheikh was occupied in the face of quite firm resistance by the defending units.

THE EGYPTIAN AIR FORCE

Air force activity in Sinai was restricted to the two days 30 and 31 October since in the late afternoon of 31 October the Anglo-French air forces commenced action against the Egyptian airfields. Despite the general state of readiness in which the air force had been kept due to the Suez crisis, it was not prepared for action when the Kadesh Campaign broke out. This is the reason for its low level of activity on 30 October (only 40 operational sorties), which increased only on the following day (90 operational sorties).

The activity of the air force in Sinai consisted mainly of observation and patrol sorties, although it did carry out a small number of attacks on IDF ground forces (for example, on 30 and 31 October in the Mitla Pass area). Requests by the ground forces for air support were nearly all unanswered. The Egyptians lost four Vampires, and four MIGS were damaged in air combat with the Israeli air force.

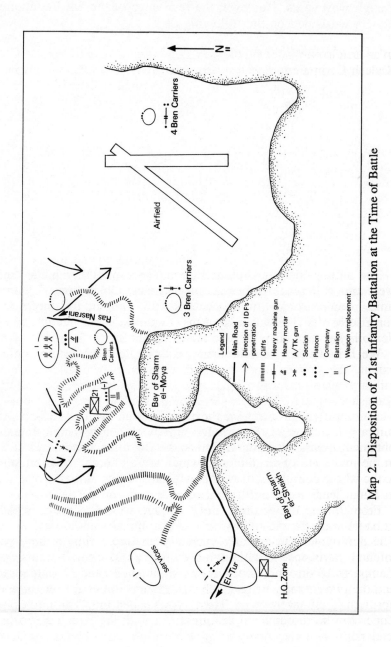

Map 2. Disposition of 21st Infantry Battalion at the Time of Battle

DISCUSSION AND CONCLUSION

In an article published on the occasion of the 10th anniversary of the Kadesh Campaign, it was stated, *inter alia*:

> It would not be an exaggeration to say that there was not one vital area of terrain that was not held by the Egyptians and there was not one access to these vital areas that was not blocked by a planned defence layout. The possibilities of manoeuvre in this 'vast desert region' were extremely restricted. Where the Egyptian defensive plan had determined that the danger of attack on a certain position could come from two directions, it was certain that there was no possibility of a third direction. In every case where the plan had determined the probable direction of *the main attack*, that was the direction from which the attack was mounted.[25]

The author continues to say that in the Kadesh Campaign there were almost '*no surprises on the tactical–operational level*, neither in time, place, strength or means'.[26] In his opinion the Egyptians' surprise by the IDF was related to 'the pace of the fighting and the flexibility and fluidity [of] the attacking force'.[27]

We have quoted these remarks because they reflect, to a great extent, the conventional assessment of many Israeli and other military historians, who have studied the military aspects of the Kadesh Campaign. If the Kadesh Campaign had taken place during May–June 1956 instead of at the end of October and had ended with military achievements for the IDF similar to those that were actually obtained, it would be possible to accept the above analysis, at least in the main. However, a closer examination of Kadesh with regard to the whole complex situation in which the Egyptian army operated in Sinai, leads us to a different conclusion.

From July to the beginning of October 1956, the Egyptian order of battle in northern Sinai was cut back as has been discussed above. The deployment in Qidmat Sinai, which had formerly been two infantry divisions, had been reduced by the time of the Kadesh Campaign to one division, whilst the two armoured brigade teams and the two infantry brigades that had been stationed in the rear of northern Sinai were withdrawn and concentrated in the Canal Zone. Furthermore the operational attention of both the civilian leadership and the Army High Command were distracted away from Sinai and drawn to the Canal Zone and the Delta because of the fear of Anglo-French military action over the nationalization of the Suez Canal Company.

These facts, in our opinion, must lead to the first conclusion: *the defence plan* that had been drawn up in the summer of 1955 and which was aimed at countering an attempt by the IDF to capture Sinai *was not put to the test at all in Kadesh.* It follows that the strength, composition and defensive deployment of the forces in Sinai on 29 October, combined with the simple fact that the IDF enjoyed an absolute advantage in terms of relative strength on the operational level, as well as in each individual sector, ensured *in advance* that the Egyptian order of battle could not produce a suitable response to the IDF's operational plan.[28]

This plan called for the activation, in stages, of four operational efforts: along the northern axis (77 Divisional Combat Team), the central axis (38 Divisional Combat Team), the southern axis (202 Brigade) and the independent effort to capture Sharm el-Sheikh (9th Brigade). Furthermore, even if the forces in northern Sinai had been deployed exactly according to the defence plan and at full strength, the movement of 9th Brigade would have come as a complete surprise at operational level.

The general operational concept of the Egyptian General Staff as regards the defence of the Sinai region was not therefore applied at all in Kadesh. The operational–tactical planning of the 3rd Infantry Division, which was responsible for the defence of Qidmat Sinai and which fought against the IDF, still has to be examined. The divisional defensive plan is evidence that the planners assumed that the IDF was likely to direct its main effort along the central axis (Nitsana–Ismailia), with the intention of breaking through the deployment at Um Kattef and advancing through Abu Ageilla north towards el-Arish.

The detailed plans of the commander of the 6th Infantry Brigade for the defence of Um Kattef confirm this assumption and also attest that the defence disposition was organized to face only a frontal attack from the east. The brigade reserve was also expected to operate in this direction. On the other hand the planners did not estimate that the IDF might use relatively large forces to take Quseima in order to outflank the deployment at Um Kattef and to mass in its rear. For this reason only secondary forces were deployed at Quseima – units of the National Guard which were inferior to the regular infantry forces in terms of their composition, weaponry and standard of fighting – and their sole mission was delay and warning (see maps 3 and 4). Thus the troops in the Um Kattef area successfully withstood repeated IDF frontal attacks (by the 10th Infantry Brigade and the 37th Armoured Brigade) and evacuated, in orderly manner, when they received the order to withdraw.[29]

On the other hand, however, the direct result of this operational concept was that even in the central axis sector the Egyptians could not find a suitable response to the IDF's moves. After the 4th Infantry Brigade had taken Quseima the 7th Armoured Brigade passed through it, advanced in a northerly direction through the Daika Pass and formed up at the Abu Ageilla crossroads to the rear of the Um Kattef deployment (the 6th brigade at Um Kattef found itself trapped and cut off!). After the Abu Ageilla crossroads the main effort of the 7th Brigade continued west towards the Suez Canal whilst a secondary effort turned south in the direction of Bir el-Hasne. The 4th Infantry Brigade, which had captured Quseima almost without opposition, was able on D-day +1 (i.e., 30 October) to send one of its battalions to Nakhl to join up on the following day with the 202nd Paratroop Brigade, advancing along the southern axis towards the Mitla Pass.

In conclusion it seems that the 3rd Division assumed, as a basic premise, that the IDF would repeat the operational moves that it had carried out at the end of the War of Independence, during Operation Horev. On the basis of this appraisal its forces were deployed in a manner that in terms of strength and method of their deployment did not enable them to respond to the IDF's operational plan.

Beyond the question, important in itself, as to whether the Egyptian disposition in Qidmat Sinai was or was not a proper answer to the offensive plan of the IDF on the operational level, the Kadesh Campaign highlighted two additional central issues:

(a) In conditions of modern warfare, where the fighting ability of the land forces is centred on its armour and the high mobility of all forces, no defensive plan based solely on a static disposition in Qidmat Sinai, whilst neglecting the centre and rear of the peninsula, could be expected to succeed. In such a situation, if the attacker succeeded in breaking through this deployment, or outflanking it in even one sector, this would lead to a collapse of the whole defensive plan and the way to the Suez Canal would be open. (It should be noted that as early as 1951 General Frambecher emphasized exactly this topic in his survey of Sinai, commissioned by the Egyptian General Staff.) This is exactly what happened in the Kadesh Campaign when the 7th Brigade succeeded in outflanking Um

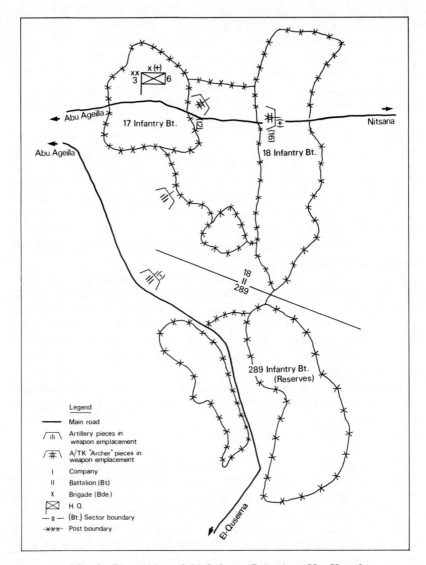

Map 3. Disposition of 6th Infantry Brigade at Um Kattef

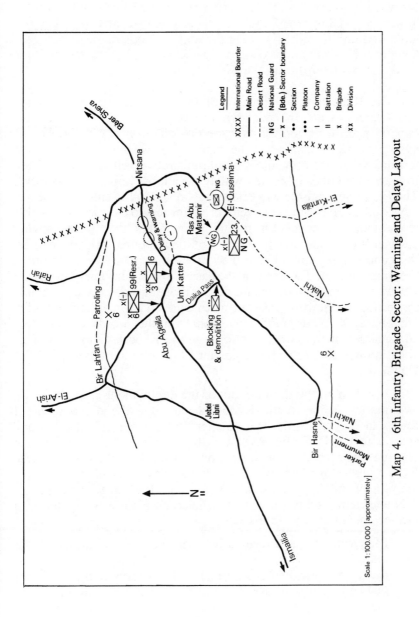

Map 4. 6th Infantry Brigade Sector: Warning and Delay Layout

Kattef and continued to the west whilst the 77 Divisional Combat Team, after taking the Rafah crossroads and overcoming el-Arish, advanced uninterruptedly along the northern axis in the direction of Qantara. This situation was in a general fashion to repeat itself eleven years later during the Six Day War.

(b) The Kadesh Campaign highlighted for the first time in the Arab–Israeli wars the decisive importance of air superiority in general and of air control over the battlefield in particular. This is even more significant when the campaign is waged over bare desert terrain, where the movement of administrative vehicles is restricted to a small number of routes which are almost impossible to leave. The Egyptian air force was effectively in action for only the first two days of the campaign. Yet even during these two days it was not able to provide air cover for the reinforcements that were moving eastwards (for example, in the case of the armoured brigade team on the central longitudinal route) or give air support for units under pressure from the IDF, as was the case of the 6th Infantry Brigade at Um Kattef. On the other hand, during those two days 'we were able to permit freedom of movement to our land forces and interdict the enemy's freedom of movement', in the words of the then commander of the Israeli air force in the Kadesh Campaign. This situation was also to be repeated along the same lines during the Six Day War.

In conclusion, the thinning out of the deployment in Sinai during two months prior to the Kadesh Campaign, the deployment of forces in Qidmat Sinai in a manner that did not afford them any answer to the IDF offensive, and the inability of the air force to provide air cover for the formations on the battlefield – all these factors taken together constitute, in our view, the main reason for the rout of the Egyptian land forces in the Kadesh Campaign.

Nasser admitted to the defeat inflicted on his forces, but added a further consideration. In his words:

> I felt when I was informed of the successful withdrawal of the main Egyptian forces from Sinai that we had won the battle, as the enemy plan had been foiled ... The enemy [Anglo-French] manoeuvre was to use Israel to draw our forces to a battle in the open in Sinai so that they might be isolated and easily destroyed. Had the withdrawal been delayed for 24 hours, the enemy would have succeeded in carrying out the sinister plan.

He then pointed out that in the course of the war 'we suffered some losses. We lost, for instance, 30 tanks of the Czech T-34 type which were destroyed by enemy aircraft bombing ... the same being the case with armoured cars, 50 of which had been lost.' However, continued the Egyptian president, 'it was easy for us to have the 30 destroyed tanks replaced by others of the same type' and new armoured cars, too.[30]

In our opinion these remarks should not be rejected out of hand, or merely viewed as an attempt to sweeten the bitterness of military defeat, or as an exercise in simple self-deception. In fact, the major part of the regular combat formations actually *succeeded* in withdrawing from Sinai, some of them with their supporting arms (the 1st, 4th, 5th, 6th Infantry Brigades and the 1st Armoured Brigade Team managed to withdraw with relatively small losses). No less important from the Egyptian point of view is the fact that, thanks to Soviet military aid, they were able to rebuild their armed forces within a fairly short time and to equip them with weaponry that was more advanced and sophisticated than they had possessed and lost in Kadesh.

Taking this consideration further, it is possible to look ahead and see what was to happen following the Six Day War. Within a year after the end of this war, in which the Egyptian armed forces suffered a far greater defeat than in Kadesh and their losses in equipment and arms were many times heavier, they were able, thanks to the massive military aid extended by the USSR, to make good all their losses in materiel and to reconstruct their smashed units, even if only at a technical level. As a result of this they felt themselves to be sufficiently strong and self-confident on 8 September 1968 to launch a heavy artillery bombardment on the IDF forces on the east bank of the Suez Canal. Thus began the 'War of Attrition', as it was termed by Nasser, only one year and three months after the end of the Six Day War.

NOTES

1. The Egyptian version of the circumstances leading to the signing of the deal, as well as its publication, in Mohamed Heikal, *Nasser, – The Cairo Documents* (London, 1972), pp.57–60 (henceforth *Cairo Documents*). See also Mohamed Heikal, *The Sphinx and the Commissar – The Rise and Fall of Soviet Influence in the Arab World* (New York, 1978), pp.57–62.
2. Nadav Safran, *From War to War – The Arab–Israeli Confrontation 1948–1967* (New York, 1969), p.209 (henceforth Safran).
3. Safran, pp.209–10 and the table on p.217, col.2. See also Colonel Yehuda Wallach and Moshe Lissak (eds.), *Carta's Atlas of Israel – The first years 1948–1961* (Jerusalem, 1978) [Hebrew], table on p.126 (henceforth *Carta's Atlas*).
4. Moshe Dayan, *Diary of the Sinai Campaign* (London, 1966) Appendix 3, pp. 218–19 (henceforth *The Sinai Campaign Diary*). It should be noted that all the data in Dayan's book were taken from a study completed by the MI Branch IDF at the beginning of 1957. The study was based on Egyptian documents captured in Sinai, interrogation of Egyptian POWs and information from various sources obtained during the campaign.
5. For the extent of the demilitarized zone in the Nitsana area, as defined in the Egypt–Israel armistice agreement (24 Feb. 1949), see *Carta's Atlas*, map no.134, p.68.
6. See *ibid.*, map no.120, p.62.
7. IDF's most prominent actions include Gaza–'Hetz Shachor' ('Black Arrow' – on the night of 28 Feb.–1 March 1955), Khan Yunis (night of 31 Aug.–1 Sept. 1955), Kuntilla (night of 27–28 Oct. 1955), Hatzabcha and the positions at Wadi Siram (night 2–3 Nov. 1955) and the artillery bombardment of Gaza following which the Egyptians used fidaiyyun units on a large scale against targets in Israel (1–7 April 1956). For a concise description of the actions and the security background immediately preceding them, see *Carta's Atlas*, pp.116–18 and 120–1.
8. It should be noted that on 27 August 1956 intelligence staff once again gave warning about the possibility 'that Israel might try to provoke our forces, perhaps *with the agreement of the western countries'* (our emphasis).
9. GHQ, Operations and Planning Branch, 'Army Operation Order No. 50, for the year 1956' (1 September 1956), p.1 (Arabic). For the entire text of the order see Appendix.
10. *Ibid.*, p.2.
11. HQ 3rd Infantry Division, 'Operation Order No. 1' (14 Aug. 1956), pp.2–4 (Arabic). For a detailed deployment of the divisional units and designation of the areas of responsibility of each of the units see also *Diary of the Sinai Campaign*, Appendix 3, pp.211–13.
12. 'Nasser reveals the story of operations and secrets behind the Sinai attack', *The Egyptian Gazette* (6 Dec. 1956), p.4, col.2 (henceforth 'Nasser Reveals'). [This is an edited translation into English of an original Arabic version that was published in the Cairo weekly *Akhir Sa'a*; publication date of the original version was not mentioned.]
13. The 8th Palestinian Division was an integral part of the Egyptian order of battle and not by chance. This was a political symbolic act aimed to demonstrate the direct link existing between mainland Egypt and the Gaza Strip. For a detailed deployment of the forces in the Gaza Strip sector see *The Sinai Campaign Diary*, Appendix 3, pp.213–15.
14. HQ Eastern Command/Operation Section, 'Operation Order No. [missing]' (23 Aug. 1956), pp.1–3 (Arabic); see also *The Sinai Campaign Diary*, pp.215–17.
15. HQ Gulf of Aqaba Sector, 'Operation Order for the Gulf of Aqaba No. 2' (16 Sept. 1956) (Arabic); *The Sinai Campaign Diary*, pp.217–18.
16. 'Nasser Reveals', p.4, col.1.

17. Because of the increased tension that developed on the Israeli–Jordanian border, King Hussein asked King Faysal II of Iraq in September 1956 to station an infantry division in Jordan. On October 14 the advanced party of the division entered Jordan even though Israel repeatedly declared that it would regard the entrance of Iraqi troops as a *casus belli*.
18. 'Nasser Reveals', p.4, col.6.
19. For the appreciation of the situation as it was formed in Cairo, and the decision to reinforce the forces in Sinai by using the reserves, see 'Nasser Reveals', p.4, col.5. See also Heikal, *Cairo Documents,* p.106.
20. *Cairo Documents,* p.108.
21. 'Nasser Reveals', p.4, col.6.
22. *Ibid.,* p.5, col.1. According to Heikal, Nasser had to overcome bitter opposition to withdrawal from Marshal Abd al-Hakim Amir, *Cairo Documents,* p.109.
23. For President Nasser's version see 'Nasser Reveals' as follows: (a) Abu Ageilla–Um Kattef Sector: p.4, col.5 and p.5, col.2,3; (b) Rafah Sector: p.5, col.1–2; (c) el-Arish Sector: p.5, col.2; (d) Sharm El-Sheikh Sector: p.5, col.3.
24. President Nasser described the events that happened in the Bir Rud Salim area in the following words:

    November 2 arrived. It was the last day of the withdrawal plan. The air force of the enemy was in control of the sky ... [but] I do not mean the Israelis. The enemy in Sinai that day were the British whose planes struck with fury at the withdrawing forces ... and tried to inflict the maximum amount of damage with the second part of the principal forces which were returning from the Bir Rud Salim assembly point. (*ibid.,* p.5, col.2–3)

25. Segan Aluf (Lt.-Col.) M. Ilan, 'Nitzul Ha-Hafta'a Bemivza' Kadesh' ('Utilization of Surprise during the Kadesh Campaign'), *Ma'arakhot* 178–9 (Oct. 1966) [Hebrew], p.24.
26. *Ibid.,* p.23 (emphasis added).
27. *Ibid.,* p.27.
28. *Carta's Atlas,* table on p.126, showing the relative strength of forces of both sides. For the order of battle of the IDF see *The Sinai Campaign Diary,* Appendix. 4, pp.220–1.
29. See also *The Sinai Campaign Diary.*
30. 'Nasser Reveals', p.5, col.3. For the Egyptian losses in military equipment, captured by the IDF in Sinai, see *The Sinai Campaign Diary,* Appendix 6, pp.227–9.

6

Eden

Robert Rhodes James

For an Englishman of my generation, born in 1933 under the shadow of war and whose childhood was spent in the reality, and the son and brother of professional soldiers, the life and career of Anthony Eden has a very special poignancy and attraction. He was of my father's generation, although ten years younger. Both were brought up in an England and a world in which the internal combustion engine had only just been invented and the mere idea of manned flight the prerogative of madmen and novelists. Britain's wealth, her empire and her power were incontestable. As Sir Winston Churchill, born twelve years before my father, later wrote nostalgically in his autobiography *My Early Life*:

> In those days the dominant forces in Great Britain were very sure of themselves and of their doctrines. They thought they could teach the world the art of government and the science of economics. They were sure they were supreme at sea and consequently safe at home. They rested therefore sedately under the convictions of power and security.

When, in the last year of his long life, Anthony Eden wrote his account of his childhood and young manhood as a young officer on the Western Front between 1916 and 1918, he titled it 'Another World'. As he wrote of that period in the last year of his life, 'It all seemed so permanent.' So it did. Like my father, he was to serve in the First World War and with great distinction and courage, and to feel himself lucky to be one of the survivors of that catastrophe in which a million of his generation in Britain and the Empire died, countless others were injured physically or mentally, and all was changed. To give some idea of the carnage of that generation, of Eden's contemporaries at his small preparatory school 72 – including his younger brother Nicholas – were killed, and of his Eton contemporaries 1,157 died. There are no statistics of the grievously injured, but we know that they were very large indeed. Eden lost two of his three brothers. These terrible experiences did not make Eden a pacifist, any more than they did my father, but they left a very deep mark.

Eden and my father then had to go through the whole ghastly experience again between 1939 and 1945. Both died in the 1970s, having seen not only war but change that was unimaginable – they went, in one lifetime, from a world in which the motor car was an amazing rarity and the horse and cart was the method of locomotion in the English countryside to that of the atomic age and supersonic aircraft. Sarajevo in 1914 was considerably further away from England than the Gulf of Iran is today. In my childhood it took three weeks from London to Bombay. Today, it takes seven hours. When the young Eden and his wife in the nineteen twenties travelled round the world it took six months. I have recently done it in less than a week. When Eden first visited the Middle East in the 1920s he took a rather amazing route. He went by train to Marseilles, by sea to Alexandria, then by car to Jerusalem, by boat from Haifa to Beirut, then by car to Damascus and thence to Baghdad, which was his objective. Why this devious route? The reason was the absence of roads – and the ones he took were almost apologies for roads – in this largely deserted and uninhabited area. He found some exploratory oil research at Abadan, and took snapshots, which have survived, of these very modest and tentative drillings in the empty desert. It is not only England that has changed!

Because Eden was born into an aristocratic family and was brought up in a fine house, with beautiful pictures and furniture, and surrounded with lovely sweeping park and farmland and educated at Eton, some false assumptions have been made. His childhood in reality was a turbulent and difficult one: whether or not Sir William Eden was in fact Anthony's father is seriously in doubt, and Sir William himself was an extraordinary and often impossible man. Eden's mother was feckless about money to such an extraordinary degree that through her depredations and follies everything – Windlestone Hall, the farms and parkland that had been in the Eden family for five centuries – had to be sold. Until late in his life Eden had money troubles and these were a constant concern. Those who saw the dapper and charmingly handsome exterior had no idea of the inner tensions, unhappiness, variable health and nervous energy behind the façade. What always amazed those who got to know him well – and these were sadly very few – was how Eden lacked true self-confidence. He carried honour and integrity to an extent that was politically unwise. He certainly totally lacked the ruthlessness and fire of a Churchill or a Ben-Gurion. In a way one would not have it otherwise, and this factor, his absolute integrity, sincerity and kindness, is the so-called 'secret' of his astonishing popularity and following in my country among people of all parties and of none.

This did not add up to weakness or irresolution. He demonstrated great physical courage in the Great War. Having become the youngest Foreign Secretary since the eighteenth century, he demonstrated great moral and political courage in resigning in protest against the myopic and self-deluding and perilous fantasies of Neville Chamberlain. At that moment, early in 1938, he was, in Churchill's words, 'the one strong young figure standing up against long, dismal, drawling tides of drift and surrender, of wrong measurements and feeble impulses'. He thought he had ended his political career. He thought very seriously of not standing again as a Conservative. When Churchill said to him in 10 Downing Street in the terrible days of 1940 'if it were not for Hitler neither of us would be here' it was only too true.

There was no irresolution when he became Churchill's War Minister at the hour of shattering defeat in 1940. Knowing what we know of the appalling position of the British after Dunkirk, when many men were saved but not their equipment, we can fully realise that Churchill and Eden undertook one of the most remarkable confidence tricks in history. By Churchill's eloquence and growling defiance and Eden's sunny confidence they persuaded the British, the remaining fragments of the free world, and above all the Germans, that Britain was bristling with weaponry, when the reality was very different. Eden was by no means a ruthless man, but at that hour niceties had to be dispensed with. Officers who had failed were removed – characteristically, Eden did the sacking himself and in person. He had been a soldier himself, was always happiest in the company of soldiers, and knew what it means to have a career ended.

Eden was the lynch-pin of the wartime coalition. As a Foreign Secretary he was the best-equipped, through intellect, experience, and sensitivity, Britain has had this century. He had not been fooled, as had so many others, by Hitler and Mussolini, nor was he by Stalin, who had a profound respect for him. As a negotiator he was in a class of his own, and it would have been better for history if his advice had been taken more often than it was. His deep mistrust of ill-prepared 'Big Three' summits was abundantly, and tragically, justified. At times Churchill and Roosevelt seemed mesmerised by Stalin: Eden never was. If he was the pacifier in the coalition, as Foreign Secretary he was ever the realist, and never afraid to stand up to Churchill.

This extraordinary political career must be seen in the context of constant worries about money, the disintegration of his marriage, which had gone wrong from a sadly early date, and the shattering blow of the death of his elder son Simon in the last weeks of the war in Burma. His health temporarily collapsed, and in 1945 he very nearly became the first Secretary-General of the United Nations, a post he coveted as an escape from partisan politics which he hated, and private sadnesses. He was denied the solace of a happy home, so crucial for everyone, but especially in politics, and he had very few real friends in politics. He was an exceptionally shy man, only truly self-confident in foreign affairs, where his touch was so sure and his skills so formidable.

These were never seen to better advantage than in his third period as Foreign Secretary between 1951 and 1955. Indeed, it was virtually a series of glittering triumphs. Politically, the bravest act of all was to negotiate the withdrawal of British forces from the Suez Canal Zone, and firmness with the new regime in Egypt resulted in Sudanese independence rather than Egyptian colonisation. Neither Churchill nor a significant minority in the Conservative party liked this at all, but Eden had as his purpose the creation of what he called 'a Middle East NATO' to resist Soviet penetration, the Baghdad Pact. By moving the British bases to Cyprus Eden was not appeasing the Egyptians, but removing an element that not only daily inflamed Anglo-Egyptian relations, but also those with much of the Arab world. His relations with Neguib had been good, and for a time he hoped to have the same with Nasser.

Eden saw British foreign policy as based upon three pillars – the Empire and Commonwealth, the Atlantic Alliance, and Western Europe. The list of priorities was indeed significant. Eden was all for European unity and cooperation but not with British involvement. Harold Macmillan's enthusiasm for the fledgling Common Market was not at all shared by Eden. Also, both Churchill and Macmillan were themselves half-American, a fact that definitely – and often beneficially – affected their judgements and decisions. Eden never really felt at home in the United States, as he did in Canada or Australia and New Zealand. He often found himself in sharp clashes with the Americans, and particularly Foster Dulles, over Indo-China. Here, Eden was absolutely right, but the Americans were resentful and angry. I also think they believed that he did not have a high opinion of American diplomatic skills and grasp of world realities. In this, their suspicions were fully merited.

American policy in the Middle East was simultaneously anti-colonialist and anti-communist. This fatal dichotomy was explained by Dulles to the National Security Council on 1 November 1956:

> For many years now the United States has been walking a tightrope between the effort to maintain our old and valued relations with our British and French allies on the one hand, and on the other trying to assure ourselves of the friendship and understanding of the newly independent countries who have escaped from colonialism.

It was this ambivalence that lay at the heart of what happened.

The new element that made Eden concentrate so hard on the Baghdad Pact was the arrival of the Soviet Union in the area, a fact that Eden took very seriously, but the Americans did not – at least not to the same extent. Addressing both houses of the U.S. Congress, Eden said in January 1956:

> Brought to a halt in Europe, Soviet expansion now feels its way South and probes the other lands. There is nothing particularly new in this. You can read it all in Russian imperialist history. But the emphasis has changed, and the symbols and method, too.
>
> This is a struggle for men's minds, once expressed in these regions in conflicting faiths, but now in rival ideologies. From the Kremlin streams forth into the lands of what we call the Middle East, and into all Asia, a mixture of blandishment and threat, offers of arms and menaces to individuals, all couched in terms of fierce hostility for Western ideals.

The Americans applauded politely, but the deadly ambiguity remained.

The other new element was Nasser. To depict this ruthless, megalomaniacal, and conspiratorial man, with his vast ambitions, as a kind of misguided but essentially genial Third World leader, standing up to the tides of colonialism is simply to accept his own very skilful propaganda. Eden genuinely wanted to get on terms with him, ideally for him to join the Baghdad Pact but, if that was not possible, to tolerate it. Nasser saw it – or claimed to see it – as an anti-Egyptian conspiracy. It certainly formed no part of his constant work to destabilize those Arab governments whose sympathies lay with the West and to eliminate the strong British presence in the area. All Eden got for his pains and for the withdrawal of the British forces from the Canal Zone was more virulent abuse from Radio Cairo and an escalation of the destabilizing process. Also, having turned to Moscow for arms, aircraft, and pilots, a regular and honoured visitor to Eastern Europe, and the hero of the Non-Aligned Conference, he had aroused Dulles' distrust. Uneasiness in Tel-Aviv was now moving to something more, and hostility was arising in the United States Congress as the evidence of Soviet involvement in Egypt steadily grew.

It was to counteract this influence that Eden was so keen on the West building Nasser's cherished project, the Aswan High Dam. As Eden emphasized again and again to the Americans, this was a political dam. But as Nasser's excesses grew, American enthusiasm faded. What has been under-appreciated until now is that the British, and notably the new Foreign Secretary Selwyn Lloyd, also lost their first zeal. When Dulles abruptly withdrew the American offer the British acquiesced easily enough. Indeed, they had several days' warning and made no protest. On this, both Eden's accounts and Lloyd's are wrong, and unfair to Dulles who also had to cope with a Congress that, for varying reasons, was now becoming very hostile indeed to Nasser and all his works.

One of Eden's nightmares as he put together the pact was an outbreak of war between Israel and Jordan, towards whom we had such strong obligations that in 1955 the Chiefs of Staff were instructed to draw up plans for a British invasion of Israel. Apart from any other factor, the domestic political reactions in Britain, Western Europe, and America to such an action would have been appalling. A major part of Eden's strategy was to do everything possible to avert a major conflict between the two countries.

Anglo-Israeli relations can best be described as cool. The circumstances of the end of the Mandate were only too well remembered on both sides, and in addition to the residue of bitterness British national interests lay exclusively in the Arab countries. Eden did not share the actual hostility to Israel felt by many Foreign Office Arabists – he was far too knowledgeable and shrewd to fall into that trap – but his eyes were fixed on his pact, and any overt closeness to Israel would have wrecked its chances. From the Iraqis in particular this warning was constant. With Nasser's agents hard at work and with a never-ending stream of vitriol from Radio Cairo, King Faysal and Nuri had difficulties enough without being accused of being involved, however remotely, with an alliance that had an Israeli element. This did not make for closeness, indeed it caused consider-able mutual suspicion.

To the British, the Suez Canal was absolutely vital, and it is today often not realized just how vital it was. The oil that passed through it represented two-thirds (sixty million tons) of the fuel requirements of Western Europe. Britain was virtually wholly dependent for its oil through the Canal from the Gulf. In 1955, 14,666 ships had passed through it, one third of them British, and three quarters belonging to Nato countries. In those far-off days the economies of Britain, Australia and New Zealand were closely intermingled, and British trading interests in the East were vast. The Canal, from which their ships were debarred by Nasser, did not concern the Israelis as much as the position of the Straits of Tiran. It did not concern the Americans at all. Here again, there was another fundamental difference about priorities. The British would not have lost much sleep if the Panama Canal had been closed.

There was also an emotional element that Nasser totally mis-judged when on 26 July in response to the Aswan Dam decision, but in fact planned long beforehand, he seized the Canal by force and seized all the assets of the Suez Canal Company. Tens of thousands of young men from Britain, Australia and New Zealand had fought for the Canal in two world wars and too many lay in war cemeteries for that fact to be forgotten. Large numbers of French people had shares in the Company. Also, after bitter defeat in Indo-China and with a harsh war on their hands in Algeria, they had no reason to have anything but loathing and fear for Nasser and his regime. The seizure of the Canal thus brought the British and the French closer together than at any time since 1945.

These common concerns had also brought Paris and Tel-Aviv closer together, but not London and Tel-Aviv. One of the most interesting of my discoveries when I was the first to have access to the 1956 archives and the British Suez Papers was that it was at the first meeting of the newly formed Egypt Committee that was planning the response to Nasser's action that Macmillan raised the possibility of involving the Israelis in the military operation, which Eden totally rejected. Macmillan came back with memoranda pressing the point but with no response. When the French, despair-ing of American procrastination and Dulles' deliberate tactics of stalling any military action while also making hostile remarks about Nasser, turned to talk to the Israelis, the British had no knowledge of this.

The personal element in Eden's attitude towards Nasser has

been exaggerated by many commentators and historians, and it is important to note that it was Hugh Gaitskell and not Eden who first publicly compared Nasser to Hitler and Mussolini. As Eden told Eisenhower, the comparison with Hitler was absurd, but that with Mussolini was more valid. Like Mussolini, he was a menace to Western interests. He had an element in him both of the calculating and the wildly reckless. Their powers as orators were formidable, not least because their populism was xenophobic and also dwelt heavily on ancient days of glory. Both were erratic, but had constant and clear purpose. Thus, while it is not true that Eden was re-living the 1930s, it would be wrong to deny that there was a personal element in Eden's approach. Eisenhower was consistent that the Canal was not worth a war. Eden was consistent that it was – as he had told Bulganin and Khrushchev during their discussions at Chequers earlier in the year (a fact that goes some way to explain the remarkable Russian docility throughout the crisis) – and he was determined to bring Nasser down, preferably by diplomatic pressure, but by military if not.

As I have emphasized, Eden believed deeply in the sanctity and honour of agreements in international affairs. Mussolini had been a great one, as had Hitler, for tearing up treaties and agreements when it suited him that he himself signed, and Nasser had done the same. International jurists might muse about whether Nasser was technically in breach of international law, but in Eden's eyes the key fact was that he had signed agreements only weeks before his annexation that confirmed the 1888 Constantinople Convention and the position of the Suez Canal Company. When Nasser gave assurances that there would be complete freedom of passage through the Canal in all circumstances Eden did not believe him. Nor, given Nasser's record, was this surprising. Nasser, like Mussolini, was essentially amoral. It is impossible to quarrel with Eden's valuation of this man, but it was not seen so clearly elsewhere, particularly in Washington, and in Britain, after the first fury, the Labour Party and others began to change their line. One of Eden's greatest mistakes – and one we were very careful not to repeat over the Falklands – was not to take the opposition parties with him. It might not have been possible, but he did not really try.

We now move to other personal factors. Eden had very nearly died in 1953 when a gall-bladder operation went dreadfully wrong and his biliary duct was cut. His life was saved and his health restored by a brilliant operation by Dr. Richard Cattell in Boston but there was always the chance of a recurrence, which in fact happened early in October, when Eden suffered a severe fever. It quickly subsided, but an ominous bell had sounded. It is entirely wrong to claim that Eden was a sick man during the Suez Crisis, or that his famous temper got the better of him. He was in fact remarkably calm, as he always was in a major crisis – trivialities enraged him, never the big things – but the mental and physical strain was immense by October. So was the domestic political pressure.

Everything was ready for military action, except that the military planners kept changing their minds and their plans, and the restiveness of the British forces was becoming a source of serious concern. It is very difficult to keep troops and airmen in a high state of readiness and tension for over two months, particularly when they do not know whether there will be action. The British press was becoming impatient, and even derisive. Winter was approaching. The restiveness of the British armed forces was being detected within the Conservative Party.

I am convinced that the combination of these factors led Eden, after initial strong reluctance, to go along with the French–Israeli stratagem to provide a legally valid pretext – and this was Eden's own description of it in the crucial cabinet meeting, when he also used the word 'collusion'. His uneasiness at what happened at Sèvres was demonstrated by his desperate attempts to have all records of the agreement – or protocol – destroyed. But again he was let down by his military advisers, who did not believe that the Israelis could possibly get to the Canal as quickly as they said they could. As it would take the Anglo-French armada six days to reach Port Said from Malta, it was time and not the Egyptians that destroyed him. For in those six days, and particularly after the R.A.F.'s bombing of Egyptian airfields, the storm broke nationally and internationally. With victory assured, the American pressure broke Macmillan and the Eden cabinet. All was then dismal aftermath.

No one has written more wisely about Eden's role in the Suez Crisis than my late friend Martin Wight:

> Eden's moral dilemma has a lasting significance. In trying to preserve the political conditions of international life, he allowed himself to become unscrupulous ... He explored the region of the moral universe of politics, with high-mindedness and self-righteousness, blindness and clear-sightedness, misjudgement and courage.

Time is not only a healer, it brings perspective. We can certainly now see Nasser in a clearer and colder light than many did in 1956.

His memorial is the Middle East of today. If Eden got many things wrong in the conduct of the Suez Crisis he did not get that wrong. And this is why, in Britain and Israel and in Egypt, he is regarded much more highly than seemed possible in the dark night of January 1957 when his premiership and his long political career ended.

When one looks on this long and ultimately tragic life, one is vividly reminded of the words used by Winston Churchill on George Curzon:

These heavy reverses were supported after the initial shocks, with goodwill and dignity, but undoubtedly they invested the long and strenous career with ultimate disappointment. The morning had been golden; the noonday was bronze; and the evening lead; but all were solid, and each was polished till it shone after its fashion.

The Suez Group:
A Retrospective on Suez

Julian Amery*

I suppose the first meeting of significance of the Suez Group was a chance encounter between Captain Charles Waterhouse and myself in Cape Town in January of 1953. Captain Waterhouse was a senior member of the Conservative Party, a former Minister and a Privy Councillor. I was a backbencher with only three years' service in the House. Waterhouse had just been on a visit to the Sudan, Uganda and Kenya and was very disturbed by reports that the British Foreign Office was working towards an agreement with Egypt which might lead to an Egyptian takeover of the Sudan.

In discussion I put to him the point that any decision over the Sudan depended on Britain. As Britain was in control of the Suez Canal Zone, we were in a position to apply a veto to any Egyptian policy towards the Sudan which we could not accept. I added, however, that I was myself concerned by rumours which had already reached me that Mr. Eden was beginning, under American pressure, to consider a British withdrawal from the Suez Canal Zone. Waterhouse and I discussed these questions for an hour or so before dinner. We separated for different dinner engagements but met again later that night and decided we should meet again as soon as we got back to London.

Back in London, Waterhouse and I sounded out different people about the increasing prospect of a British attempt to reach agreement with Neguib and Nasser. Such an agreement would have involved a British withdrawal from the Sudan in favour of Egypt and some modification of the Suez Canal Zone base. We soon found a

---

* Mr Amery has requested that the editors note that his contribution to our symposium was made from notes and not a prepared text, and accordingly takes account of what other contributors had said in earlier proceedings. He hopes that this explains occasional repetitions of an argument and any shortcomings in logical presentation.

number of significant supporters. Among senior Members these included Ralph Assheton, a Privy Councillor and former Chairman of the Conservative Party, Major John Morrison, deputy chairman of the 1922 Committee, Christopher Holland-Martin, the Treasurer of the Conservative Party. At the younger end were Fitzroy Maclean who had led the British Mission to Tito during the war, Enoch Powell and, later, Angus Maude. In the House of Lords we had the support of Lord Hankey who had been secretary to the War Cabinet in World War I and a member of Neville Chamberlain's Government, and Lord Killearn, former Ambassador to Egypt.

Waterhouse emerged, naturally, as the chairman of the Group. In the first phase, Enoch Powell and I acted more or less as secretaries. It would be wrong to call the Group right-wing or left-wing. It was principally concerned with maintaining the British Commonwealth as a military and political entity.

Like most British groups of this kind, it was essentially informal. There were conversations both private and by telephone between members of the Group. There were social occasions such as lunches in my father's house. But, from time to time, Captain Waterhouse would call us together in a Committee room and, after hearing our different views, would write to the Prime Minister, the Foreign Secretary or the Chief Whip, reporting the views of the Group. Very occasionally those who were present added their signatures to his letter. As a general rule, however, the letter began: 'Some of us ...'. Waterhouse usually invited one of the Party Whips to attend our meetings so that he could see for himself what views were held and by whom. In addition, individual Members took it upon themselves to ask questions, to make speeches in defence or foreign affairs debates and to express their views in the ordinary Party committees, particularly the foreign affairs committee and the defence committee of the Conservative Party.

The importance of the Group, looking back, was that their assessment of the situation was proved to be right. They can be compared, though it was on a smaller stage, with the group of Conservative Members who opposed Chamberlain's policy of appeasement of the Axis Powers before the Second World War. We did not have much open support from the Opposition Parties though Stanley Evans was a notable exception as a former Labour Minister giving his whole-hearted support at every stage; Aneurin Bevan also was very careful to avoid condemning us. British public opinion after the nationalization of the Canal became very strong in support of the Group. Something like two to three million British people had been through the Canal either as members of the armed forces or in the course of trade and business and had a strong appreciation of its importance. I would add that even when I was quarrelling with the Government over the 1953–4 policy, I was strongly supported by my own constituency party, and other members of the Group had the same experience. Indeed, even after the defeat of British policy in 1956 and Anthony Eden's resignation, I believe that the Conservative Party would have had little difficulty in winning an election, so strong was public support for the policy we had attempted to pursue and so strong was the disapproval of the Labour Party for 'sabotaging' that policy.

We knew that, after the British withdrawal from India, Palestine and Malta, it was only the Suez Canal Zone base which could enable Britain to exert influence westward in the Mediterranean, including North Africa and eastward into the Middle East, the Indian Ocean and southward into Africa. We did not represent any particular economic or social interest, nor any particular political element. It is significant that while the Group was mainly concerned with Anthony Eden's wish to come to an agreement with Cairo over the Sudan and the Suez Canal base, his Prime Minister, Winston Churchill, was by no means in sympathy with his own Foreign Secretary and gave a surprising amount of encouragement to individuals like myself who were active in the Suez Group.

After the conclusion of the 1954 Agreement with Egypt, which the Group as a whole opposed, the situation changed. Some Members, like Enoch Powell, fell away. Powell concluded that the abandonment of the base meant the end of the Commonwealth as a military and political force in the world and ceased to join our activities. Some others followed his example. Most of us, however, remained convinced that we had been right in our assessment of the consequences of abandoning the base and believed that it would still be possible to retrieve the ground that had been lost. In this we were supported by a number of new Members who came into the House of Commons either at by-elections or in the General election of 1955. These included John Biggs-Davison, Patrick Maitland (later Lord Lauderdale), and John Eden (himself a nephew of Anthony Eden).

It is difficult to assess how strong was our support in the Party. When the decisive vote came in July of 1954, only twenty-six Members were found prepared to vote against the Government. It must be remembered, however, that this number followed Churchill's decision, taken extremely reluctantly, to support the

Treaty which Anthony Eden advocated. Until that time, however, I suspect that fifty or sixty members felt strongly in the same way as those of us who actually voted against the treaty. We were not so very far from the wartime years. There was a high proportion of Conservative Members with military experience.

The goals of the Group have to be seen in three phases. The first was to prevent a sell-out of the Sudan to Egypt and here I recall very clearly a lunch which my father, Leo Amery, gave for Sir Abd al-Rahman al-Mahdi, then the head of the Umma Party, attended by Charles Waterhouse and myself. Al-Mahdi made it very plain to us that he had no intention of accepting the restoration of Cairo's sovereignty over the Sudan and gave us plenty of ammunition with which to fire questions and write letters to members of the Government. This undoubtedly had some effect on the events leading to the independence of the Sudan, though it would be only fair to say that local forces had more to do with this than our own pressures in London.

The next and most vital phase was concerned with the maintenance of the base in the Suez Canal Zone. I do not think we can understand the Suez crisis without seeing in perspective the importance Britain attached to the Suez Canal Zone.

Before the Second World War, the order of the battle of the British Commonwealth and Empire was based on two strategic reserves: one was stationed in Britain, the other in India. Communications between them were assured partly by the Royal Air Force (air power was not yet fully developed), with air-fields in Palestine and Iraq, but above all by the Royal Navy, which had a series of stations at most of the choke-points in the Mediterranean, as well as at Simon's Town in South Africa. Particularly important was the choke-point of the Suez Canal which was owned jointly by Britain and France and was garrisoned by a small English force, backed up by a force between a brigade and a division before the Second World War in Palestine.

During the Second World War the situation was changed dramatically. Communications between Britain and Egypt were virtually interrupted by the Axis powers. But the Suez Canal Zone then became the main base from which British influence and power were exercised in North Africa, in the Middle East and the Horn of Africa, down to Ethiopia. Air-fields, workshops and port facilities were developed on an unprecedented scale, it thus became the hub of British military power in the Middle East in the Second World War.

113

After that war, when we withdrew first from India and then from Palestine, the bulk of the forces were withdrawn and their equipment was concentrated in the Suez Canal Zone. This meant, of course, stationing in Egypt more than the ten thousand men we were entitled to station under the 1936 Treaty. Egyptian reactions were at first mainly verbal. But then, in 1950, Britain, under American pressure it must be said, accepted Dr. Mossadegh's seizure of the oil refinery at Abadan and the nationalization of the Anglo-Iranian oil company assets there. This encouraged the Egyptians to pass from verbal objections to attempt terrorist attacks on the base. These began while King Farouq was still in power. But when Colonel Nasser and the Free Officers took over in Cairo, these terrorist attacks assumed much more serious proportions, up to a point where, for a time, the British forces in the Canal Zone base were virtually besieged. Opinion in Britain was very divided about what to do to face this problem. Many military advisers wanted to withdraw our forces to Britain, so as to strengthen our strategic reserve against what was then perceived to be the growing threat of a Soviet attack on Western Europe. Many Foreign Office officials favoured withdrawal so as to enable us to come to terms with the new Egyptian regime. It was clear that the base in the Suez Canal Zone was the last remaining fulcrum of continuing British power effective both east of Suez and west of Suez. There was no alternative. Neither Cyprus nor Aden could be developed in short order. Even if they had been, they would not have had communications between them if there had been a hostile air barrier between them, between Cyprus and Aden.

The argument raged from 1951 onward. Sir Anthony Eden, then Foreign Secretary, judged that we should withdraw from the Suez Canal Zone altogether, if necessary. He did his best to keep something but he was prepared to go altogether. He believed this to be the condition of achieving an understanding with Nasser and, more important in his eyes, of securing American support for the defence of the Middle East. He was to be proved wrong on both counts. He underestimated altogether the extent of Nasser's ambitions to lead the whole Arab world and to base his leadership on a crusade against British, and indeed, French imperialism. More seriously, he underestimated altogether the determination of the United States, good allies of Britain as they had been in the World War, to eliminate the influence of the European imperial powers from the Middle East and North Africa, as they had already begun to do in South-East Asia with the Dutch in Indonesia. Even he was persuaded by Washington that if Britain withdrew from the Canal Zone, the Americans would defend British interests in the Middle East, including the security of the Canal.

The question was, should Britain retain any forces in the Canal or withdraw from it altogether? Prime Minister Nuri al-Sa'id of Iraq urged us to stay. So did Prime Minister Ben-Gurion of Israel. The Australian, New Zealand and South African governments urged us to stay. The Indian General Staff in an interesting message, which they sent to me for some reason, said that while their government would urge us to go, they, the Indian General Staff, would cease to have any regard for us, as a force east of Suez, if we left. At this stage, our French friends were still largely unconcerned in spite of Nasser's initial support for the fidaiyyun of the FLN in Algeria.

The question of the Suez base led to a very serious difference between Churchill, still Prime Minister, and Eden. One morning, after I had made a strong, and perhaps excessive attack on Eden in the House of Commons, I received a call from No. 10 Downing Street. One of the Prime Minister's secretaries was on the line. I expected to be ticked off for what I had said. Instead, the private secretary said: 'Sir Winston asked me to tell you that he has read your speech and very much agrees with you.' There were to be two or three subsequent occasions while Eden was pressing the case for withdrawal when Churchill encouraged me to keep up a protest against it!

Encouraged by his attitude, a number of us formed what was later to become known as the Suez Group. But to vote against the government, to mobilize opposition to the government, Churchill's government, was a very difficult operation. And then Churchill gave up his resistance to Eden. He was in his eightieth year and his main preoccupation was to secure a summit meeting with the new Soviet leadership. As I indicated previously, only 26 of us voted against the proposed Anglo-Egyptian treaty. Eden thus had a free hand to commit Britain to withdraw all its troops from the zone within two years. We were to leave only civilian technicians to maintain our facilities and equipment. His decision to withdraw was a catastrophic gamble. Had we stayed Nasser could never have nationalized the Canal and could never have attacked Israel again. It can be quite difficult to stay put, but a damned sight more difficult to get back. Events were to prove Eden's decision disastrous.

It is important to reflect on the argument he had been conducting between 1951 and 1954. He had been telling the House of Commons and his colleagues in the government, and indeed public opinion and the press, that we could get on with Nasser. He had developed the case for appeasing Nasser. Here was perhaps a more solid government than the previous monarchist governments; here was the tide of history in the Middle East. We really ought to try to get on with it. And of course, in committing himself to friendship with Nasser, he inevitably committed himself to cooling off still further, relations with Israel. But as Nasser was all the time broadcasting his hatred of Israel, we could not very well pursue a pro-Israel policy if we were going to secure the advantages of co-operation with Nasser.

Nasser himself, knowing of my opposition to the agreement, very politely invited me to call on him. I found an opportunity to do this on the way back from a journey to South Africa. He spoke good English. After some exchange of views I said to him, 'Your Excellency, would you agree to free elections?' 'No,' he said, 'The Wafd would win and that would never do.' I found his frankness endearing and asked why he was opposed to the Baghdad Pact and Prime Minister Nuri al-Sa'id. 'Nuri', he said, 'is a dictator. He censors the press; he imprisons his political opponents ...' 'More than you do?' I intervened. 'No,' he said, 'not more, but less efficiently.' At the end of our talk he was kind enough to say, 'I enjoyed this talk. I must say, I think if you had been an Egyptian you would have been with me. But I have to say that if I'd been an Englishman I would have been very tempted to join the Suez Group.' Perhaps we were both unreconstructed nationalists; though I am bound to say that I think Nasser destroyed the Egypt which could have been the financial, industrial and air traffic centre of the Middle East.

The Suez Group had warned that if Britain withdrew from the Canal, there would be a rapid decline of our influence in the Middle East. We were convinced that the 1954 agreement would lead to an active policy on Colonel Nasser's part to destroy British influence in the Middle East and French influence in north Africa. The event confirmed our views. Our warnings were fulfilled much quicker than even I expected. In Jordan, Field-Marshal Templer's attempt to bring Jordan into the Baghdad Pact was rebuffed. General Glubb was dismissed. Selwyn Lloyd, by this time Foreign Secretary, was stoned in Bahrein. Meanwhile, Egypt was taking increasing deliveries of arms from the Soviet bloc, and the 'Voice of the Arabs' never ceased to pour out a stream of vitriolic attacks aimed at British and French imperialism. When a few days after the withdrawal of the last British soldiers from the Canal base Nasser nationalized the

Canal, our view became the view of the vast majority of the Conservative Party and indeed of Anthony Eden himself.

In his speech after the nationalization of the Canal, Eden admitted that perhaps he had been insufficiently appreciative of the views expressed to him by the Suez Group. Aneurin Bevan tapped me on the shoulder as we were waiting to enter the Chamber to say, 'I'm sorry to say, Julian, you've been right after all.' Our hope, therefore, was that since the bankruptcy of Eden's former policy had been proved, he would now take steps, which he had outlined in the original agreement for withdrawal from the Zone, to resume control of it. We were, therefore, pressing for action to take back the Canal Zone and reach a new agreement with an Egyptian government – not led by Nasser – for a future regime of the Canal. The Group accordingly supported Eden's co-operation with France to take military measures against Nasser. We pressed increasingly for action in the long period of delay that ensued. We strongly supported the action when it was taken and equally strongly condemned the decision to cease fire, to halt the action and later to withdraw.

In the final critical phase in 1956 I have little doubt that it was the firmness of Guy Mollet, with whom I was myself in regular contact both before he became Prime Minister and after, which enabled me to persuade the Suez Group to force through a particular resolution at the Llandudno conference of the Conservative Party. This made it virtually inevitable that the Conservative government should give the go-ahead to the military operation which ensued.

To my dismay, in this deteriorating situation, nothing had been done to take precautions so that we could, if necessary, reoccupy the Suez Canal Zone. No hard standings had been built in Cyprus from which tanks could have been loaded onto transport. Nothing had been done at all; there had been no contingency planning begun. There was still the prevailing mood that Nasser had become our friend and we must work with him. But within days of the withdrawal of the last soldier, in July 1956, Nasser grabbed the Canal and took over all of our installations.

Eden's policy was thus in ruins. I would compare his situation with that of Neville Chamberlain in 1939. Chamberlain had tried, sincerely, to reach an arrangement with Hitler and believed that it would stick. He was rewarded by seeing only a few months later Hitler march into Czechoslovakia, and the Czech defence line thus finally dismantled. Like Chamberlain with Hitler, Eden thought that he could settle with Nasser in 1954. He now saw the fruits of his

117

decision. The Americans, delighted by his decision to withdraw had brought him into a situation which was disastrous nationally and threatened his political life as well. Would they bail him out? Our friends in France had by this time been alerted by my good friend M. Bourgès-Maunoury, and his very efficient office and by Prime Minister Mollet, and Mr. Lacoste in Algeria, as to the extent of the danger that Nasser represented to them. So we had at last a potential ally in sight.

Eden was now determined to recover the Suez Force and bring down Nasser. But he was a prisoner of his past. He had been the man of the League of Nations, the man of the United Nations; he had inspired the foundation of the Arab League. He was even stronger for the American Alliance than Churchill himself. He had cold-shouldered Europe. He was never keen on the concept of Europe. Indeed, I had great difficulty in persuading him to meet with Guy Mollet, still in the Opposition, when he, Eden, came to Strasbourg. All the arguments that he had developed for doing a deal with Nasser were now a boomerang. However, the British and French governments encouraged by many Arab voices decided that Nasser must be persuaded to disgorge, if necessary, by force.

But a military operation would take time to mount. Meanwhile, the United States got in on the act. President Eisenhower and his Secretary of State, while expressing sympathy for the British position, were determined to prevent a military solution. Dulles, I think, sometimes hesitated on this. Eisenhower was even more opposed to the use of force against Egypt. But while London hesitated and the United States procrastinated, local events took charge.

Israel was itself in danger of being strangled. It had to break out of the siege if it was to survive. Jordan was an easy target, but Britain could not afford to let down King Hussein without threatening the very existence of the Baghdad Pact. On the other hand, if Israel attacked Egypt, no such problem would arise. Here our French allies saw an unexpected opportunity to bring matters to a head. But Prime Minister Ben-Gurion argued very sensibly that he could not risk an attack unless Egypt and the Egyptian air force were taken out first. And only the Royal Air Force could do this. Agreement was reached for Israel to launch Operation Kadesh while Britain and France would launch Operation Musketeer. Eden has been criticized for the collusion with Israel and subsequent denial of it. The denial we can dismiss as routine diplomatic expediency. After all what are diplomats for, as Francis Bacon said many centuries ago, except to lie in the interest of their country. My only criticism of the collusion is that it did not go far enough. If we had had better coordination between the three allies, the Anglo-French Armada could have sailed earlier from Malta. Two days would have made a big difference; we might have then attained our objectives in Egypt before the American and international pressures had time to build up against us. There is also the possibility that with closer coordination, men like Dayan would have fed new ideas into our strategy which could have been advantageous.

Eden has also been criticized for not consulting or informing President Eisenhower in advance. But he knew that by then the Americans were not going to support him and indeed were implacably opposed to the operation. There is not much sense in consulting even with your friends if you know that they will advise against what you propose to do. Britain and France, however, went ahead hoping that Eisenhower, in the heat of the presidential election, would hesitate to turn against his two principal allies in the world and alienate the Jewish vote as well. We were wrong.

I think all of us who were involved came reluctantly to the conclusion that while the United States regarded Britain as a major ally in Europe against the threat of Soviet expansion, they were equally concerned to destroy the British Commonwealth and Empire, not least in the Middle East. Our opinions, therefore, became increasingly anti-American, extending even to informal contact with the representatives of the Soviet Union. We tried to persuade Moscow that a British or French presence in the Middle East or North Africa was preferable to an American takeover of these areas.

Public opinion in France and to a lesser extent in Britain was very strong in its support of the operation. I said to a lesser extent in Britain because the Labour Opposition which in July had strongly supported the government had come very much under the United States' influence in the summer. Mr. Gaitskell was a frequent visitor to the United States Embassy and was changing his tune. Nevertheless the successful landing in Port Said was greeted with widespread enthusiasm, not I would say among the chattering classes, but among the ordinary people, Labour as well as Conservative. But once the operation began, American opposition became public and clear. It was not just expressed through the diplomatic channel, but in the Security Council where we had to veto two resolutions promoted by the Americans and afterwards in the General Assembly. This can only be explained by Washington's

119

determination to break the British predominance in the Middle East and the French predominance in North Africa.

The United States was favourable to the idea of a united Europe based on an understanding between France and Germany; they did not want an alliance between the French and the British Empires. They meant to take over the French and British positions in the Third World. The Soviet threat to intervene was not taken seriously in London, nor I think, in Paris. But it was a diplomatic embarrassment. With no nuclear weapons of our own we had to rely on the American nuclear umbrella to protect us from the consequences of an operation to which Washington was strongly opposed. The key at this point was the willpower of the British government in power. French willpower was not in doubt. Even the French Communist party kept pretty quiet. Here Eden made a critical mistake. At Gaitskell's demand he kept the House of Commons sitting on a Saturday. Members of Parliament, therefore, had very little opportunity to visit their constituencies. Had they done so, I believe, they would have found a ground swell of opinion urging them to support the government. In the absence of this pressure, the rift between the parties widened, and even some Conservatives began to waver.

Eisenhower called repeatedly for a cease-fire. Dulles encouraged the banks to sell sterling. Faced with a devaluation of the pound, critical by the standards of those days, though much smaller than devaluations that we have endured since, Ministers lost their nerve. Strong supporters of the operation in Eden's Cabinet changed their mind. Two junior Ministers resigned. Something like a panic spread to Whitehall. Eisenhower, just re-elected President, persuaded Eden that if Britain and France ceased-fire he would receive Eden and Mollet at the White House and work out with them a new regime for the Canal. Eden, isolated now in his Cabinet with only three or four Ministers supporting him, and physically exhausted, grasped at this straw. But straw it was. He accepted what he thought was Eisenhower's genuine offer. Mollet had no choice but to comply. The cease-fire was ordered; the invitation to the White House was cancelled.

Britain and France were in possession of one end of the Canal, and within 48 hours could have the whole of it. There might have been a tank battle outside Cairo, but with the Soviet instructors departed this seems unlikely. Nasser would probably have left Cairo. A shadow Egyptian government was waiting in the wings in Cairo. Its leaders proposed to come out to parley with us once

Nasser had gone. They would have offered to negotiate a new treaty over the Canal, and the whole question of the base would have been up for discussion again. No doubt the United States would have had a considerable say in it and so might have had the Soviets. But we were in a strong position; we were in possession, or would have been, and possession is nine-tenths of the law. American banks seeing our victory would have soon been buying up the pound as quickly as they had sold it. Instead, Britain, France and Israel were forced into a humiliating withdrawal from the battle-fields that they had conquered.

I was never able to see any justification for the cease fire. Another 48 hours and we would, in my judgement, have toppled Nasser and seen the emergence of a new Egyptian regime. This would have asked the British not to enter Cairo or Alexandria and would have offered to negotiate a new agreement, a new regime for the future of the Canal Zone. Had we acquired full control of the Canal and been in a position to threaten Cairo I believe Nasser would have withdrawn to the Sudan and probably to the Soviet Union. International negotiations would have followed.

I had personally been in touch with a number of Egyptian personalities including the former Prime Minister, Nahhas Pasha, who were only too anxious to achieve such a solution both on its merits and to get rid of the increasingly pro-socialist government of Nasser. Along with other members of the Group, therefore, I was strongly opposed to the withdrawal from Port Said and spoke to that effect both at home and at a meeting of the Independent Members of the French Parliament in Versailles.

It would, of course be naive to believe that we could have restored the status quo exactly as it had existed before the advent of the Nasser regime. No doubt the United States and the Soviet Union would have wanted to take part in whatever international conference followed the end of the hostilities. I believe, however, that the British and French, being in possession, would have been able to make satisfactory terms both for a future regime of the Canal and for the establishment of an international or, better still, Anglo-French base to police the area. This would in effect have prevented any further hostilities between Israel and Egypt and thus probably any further Arab–Israel wars. It might also have enabled the development in Cairo of a generally pro-Western regime as happened after the British intervention against Araby Pasha's revolt in the latter part of the last century.

The failure was one of politics, not one of strategy. It was one of willpower. Eden was sincere and determined in his resolve, but he failed to communicate his intentions and purpose to the Cabinet at large, still less to the opposition. Churchill had mobilized British opinion in 1940 very largely because his record showed that he had been implacably opposed to the German danger for several years. Eden did not have this advantage.

Two verdicts on the operation are perhaps worth repeating. Churchill's only known comment was, 'I don't know if I would have dared to start. I would have never dared to stop.' Foster Dulles was visited in hospital by Selwyn Lloyd some weeks after the operation and according to Lloyd, Dulles said to him, 'I don't understand why you didn't go on.'

The operation itself was very slow. The French have since argued that our operation was too heavy in the sense that we were not prepared to attempt the landing until we could bring enough armour ashore to face up to the Egyptian armour. In retrospect the French are probably right. But we could not be sure at the time that the Egyptian tanks would not be manned by Soviet personnel. Had they been we might well have faced a humiliating setback comparable to that suffered by the Tsarist empire in the Russo-Japanese War. I do not know whether it would have been possible to have attempted an earlier attack either against Alexandria or against the Canal. I think it doubtful in view of the lack of rapid naval transport.

In Eden's absence in Jamaica, however, the Conservative government decided to withdraw from Port Said, and when Macmillan formed his government I accepted that the Suez venture was a lost cause and agreed to become a Minister in his Administration. In that capacity I was entrusted with undertaking the post-mortem inquiry six weeks or so after the operation. This led me to interview both General Keightley who had been in overall command, General Stockwell who had commanded the operations on the ground, Air Marshal Barnett who had commanded the air force and some of the leading French military figures, in particular General André Beaufre, the senior French Commander.

The British General Staff believed that there were between two to three hundred Soviet tanks with the Egyptian army. They were understood to have Soviet instructors with them. Would these instructors man the tanks in battle? If so, we would be at a great disadvantage unless we had landed forces capable of meeting such a challenge. But our tanks had to sail from Malta, in the absence of any hard standings in Cyprus, in old and slow landing crafts. This imposed an inescapable delay of some six days. As it happened the

Soviet tank crews left hurriedly for the Sudan as soon as the RAF began to bomb the Egyptian air fields. But of course we couldn't know this. We were haunted by the spectre of the Russo-Japanese War of 1904 and the Gallipoli Campaign when the general staffs had underestimated, both on the Czarist side and on our own side in World War I, the capability of the enemy. So the operation went ahead more slowly than it should have done.

It has also sometimes been argued that we might have left it all to the Israelis. But here again it is quite clear that Ben-Gurion would never have authorised Operation Kadesh unless the RAF had first taken out the Egyptian Air Force.

The really disastrous error was the failure to recognize, after the withdrawal from the Canal Zone in 1954, that it might be necessary to reoccupy the Canal Zone base. For this purpose it would have been necessary to have hard standings in Famagusta harbour from which British armour could have sailed to Egypt with only 24 hours' delay. There was equally a failure to plan the parachute operations which would have been necessary.

In advocating the withdrawal from the Canal Zone, Eden fell into the same trap that Neville Chamberlain fell into after the Munich Agreement. Since his policy was based upon trust in the goodwill of Nasser, it became important to him not to take any steps which suggested a lack of faith in Nasser's goodwill. As a result nothing was done to insure against the danger – against which the Suez Group had always warned – that Nasser would take over the Canal and, once the British had gone, declare open hostility towards their interests in the whole Middle East.

The failure of the British and French to succeed in what should have been a relatively minor effort of gunboat diplomacy was psychologically disastrous for their prestige in the rest of the Middle East and Africa.

It was equally disastrous in relation to their own public opinion. Both countries had been accustomed to seeing themselves as great powers. After Suez, both subsequently felt themselves cut down to size.

A third disastrous consequence was the undermining of Britain's entente with the French. Our failure at Suez led directly to the collapse of French policy in Algeria, to the rise of General de Gaulle and thus to his decision to exclude Britain, for a time, from the European Community.

A fourth consequence was that the failure of the Anglo-French operation made it inevitable that Egypt would resume hostilities with Israel as soon as opportunity offered. Without Egypt an Arab–Israeli war was impossible. The 1967 and 1973 Arab–Israeli wars may make a further Arab–Israeli war unlikely. But in 1956 a final decision could have been taken.

A fifth consequence was the withdrawal of Britain and France from the rest of their responsibilities in Africa with catastrophic consequences which we have witnessed in the Sudan, Uganda, the Congo, Tanzania, right down to South Africa itself.

The consequences of our failure at Suez were tragic for Europe, for the Middle East, for Black Africa, and indeed for the world international order. Tragic for Europe, Anthony Eden had not been a convinced supporter of European union. But Guy Mollet told me a few days before the operation that he regarded an Anglo-French victory over Nasser as of even greater importance for Europe than for Britain and France alone. If we prevailed in the face of American and Soviet opposition, Eden, he believed, would be converted to Europe, and Europe would be built on an Anglo-French axis. This would have been an outward-looking Europe, embracing those states associated with us in the Middle East and Africa. Instead, by deciding for the cease-fire our French allies felt let down, almost betrayed. A French withdrawal from Algeria became almost inevitable. The withdrawal from Algeria, or the Algerian crisis, brought General de Gaulle to power with his concept of a Carolingian Europe based on a Franco-German axis. Britain was condemned by his veto to be out in the cold for almost fifteen years.

In both Britain and France our defeat produced a collapse of the will to rule. Within a few years Britain had withdrawn from the Middle East and France from North Africa. Predictably they proceeded to the decolonisation of the rest of the African continent. A vacuum was created in the Middle East with disastrous results. These included two Arab–Israeli wars, the murder of Nuri al-Sa'id and King Faysal in Baghdad, and a series of Iraqi revolutions, the destabilisation of the Lebanon, the Egyptian invasion of Yemen, the rise of Qadhafi, the Soviet takeover of Aden and Ethiopia, and the emergence of Palestinian terrorism. None of these things were inevitable. They might never have happened had Britain and France prevailed at Suez. They might even have been prevented after our failure if the Americans had taken over the imperial responsibilities they had been at such pains to destroy. They did make one or two feeble efforts. One was the landing of the American troops in Lebanon, in 1958, but they scarcely got beyond the beaches, hardly even to the brothel quarter. The other attempt was the attempt to build up the Shah of Iran, as the gendarme of the Gulf. But this put too heavy a burden on him; and so it contributed to the Iranian revolution and thus to the Iran–Iraq War. Now thirty years after Suez, the United States is, and rightly so, seeking to rebuild some stability in the area on the basis of the Camp David understanding between Israel and Egypt. But the burden is very heavy for the Americans alone. We could have had Camp David and much more if the Americans had supported Britain and France in 1956 instead of acting as they did.

Several years ago I had a letter from former President Nixon, who was Vice-President at the time of the Suez Operation. In this he said,

In retrospect I believe the U.S. role in restraining Britain, France and Israel at the time was a major foreign policy mistake. When I talked to Eisenhower several years after he had left the Presidency, I found that he shared this view. Allowing Nasser to continue to play the role of spoiler in the Mid-East was bad enough, but far worse was the profound effect our action had in discouraging Britain and France in playing a major foreign policy role not only in the Middle East, but in other parts of world.

The consequences for Black Africa have been no less serious than those for the Middle East. Idi Amin is one of the children of our defeat of Suez. Had the United States supported us the situation in Eastern Europe also might have been different. Sir Orme Sargent, one of our cleverest diplomats, remarked at a lunch party in 1956, 'so the satellites are revolting on both sides of the Iron Curtain'. Had the United States supported Britain and France would Khrushchev have dared to invade Hungary? The Soviets were certainly worried about American reaction to the situation in Eastern Europe. As it was, the action of the United States in disciplining its British and French allies rather than giving priority to Hungary, gave Moscow a green light for its own actions against Budapest. You could say, a cynic could say, that the Americans were the first to impose a Brezhnev doctrine on their allies. In doing so they inevitably consolidated the spheres of influence of the two superpowers.

What of the future? Europe can only play a small part in the solution of the Middle Eastern problem today, whether looked upon as the Arab–Israel confrontation, or the Gulf War between Iran and Iraq, or the Soviet occupation of Afghanistan. It is possible that in the long run, as Europe recovers, Europe will play a more important part. We are after all only a rocky extension of the Euro-Asian continent. All through our history, the Roman Empire, the Crusades, the great Colonial expansion, all these things arose from the scarcity of raw materials and indigenous resources in Europe itself. Will the pattern of history repeat itself, or will we relax like the Vikings in Scandinavia into a comfortable social democratic decline? I don't pretend to know the answer. Well before the Suez Crisis two World Wars had greatly weakened the strength of Europe. A Franco-British victory at Suez might just have begun to reverse the trend. As it was our defeat finally marked the end of Europe as the arbiter of international affairs. Suez was indeed Europe's Waterloo.

I have described the Suez operation as a minor gunboat operation. Historians, however, will I believe judge it as one of the decisive battles of modern history. The casualties were few in terms of human lives, but the withdrawal from Port Said marked the end of a particular phase of European influence in the world. Europe, under the Roman Empire, had been a major centre of world power. This had declined until Europe's revival at the end of the seventeenth and the beginning of the eighteenth century. Thereafter it became a kind of collective superpower in the second half of the nineteenth and the first half of the twentieth century. Suez marked the end of this development. Whether Europe can recover from it remains to be seen.

8

Guy Mollet, the French Government and the SFIO

Jean-Paul Cointet

Suez has imprinted in the collective French memory a heterogeneous legacy which, thirty years later, reflects the diversity of French temperaments. For some, the episode was a courageous page in the book of French history; for others, it reflects a shameful incident in an outdated and decadent history of French colonialism. But in order to understand the full impact of Suez, it is necessary to analyse the inner workings of political groups. In this sense, Suez – together with the Algerian war – represents a watershed in the transformation of the non-Communist Left from the end of the 1950s.

Our analysis therefore has a double focus. One is to consider how the ruling Government perceived and analysed the events and undertook to act, relative to the state of public opinion. The second is to show how Suez stood for a stage in the transformation of the French Left and also, in general terms, of French political life.

Given the various issues involved, we shall also consider the changes in French foreign policy as a result of Suez.

THE CONTEXT: INITIAL REACTIONS
(26 JULY–3 AUGUST 1956)

Guy Mollet's Government

The French electorate went to the polls on 2 January 1956. The record turnout of these elections led to a Centre-Left success, combined with the problem of creating a majority Government. The success was a result of the excellent showing of Guy Mollet's Section Française de l'Internationale Ouvrière (SFIO) and Pierre Mendès-France's Radicals (Mouvement Républicain Populaire – MRP) in an alliance with François Mitterand's Union Démocratique et Socialiste de la Résistance (UDSR). The major losers in

127

the coalition were the Gaullists and the MRP. Despite their apparent success, the Republican Front found it difficult to produce a solid majority in the Assembly, as they had only one quarter of the total number of seats (172). Instead, Guy Mollet, having stated publicly that he was prepared to head a responsible left-wing Government, was called upon to form a Cabinet. His Government was installed on 31 January 1956. It commanded a wide-ranging majority, extending from the extreme left to the centre right. Nevertheless, this was a highly artificial majority, which explained the Government's anxiety at being confronted by an insoluble crisis.

At the outset, however, the Government benefited from a double set of advantages: on the one hand, the serious and pressing nature of the Algerian problem, to which we shall return, and on the other hand, the combination in the person of Guy Mollet of a head of Government as well as the leader of the Socialist Party apparatus which was well under control.

Guy Mollet's Government: Context and Tendencies

At the beginning of 1956, French public opinion was divided over three major issues. On the eve of the elections,[1] the various political parties expressed divergent attitudes on the following issues:

– The first was the Algerian crisis. This had become increasingly grave since the fall of 1955, both in Algeria and in the international arena, with the growing representation at the UN of the Afro-Asian group (the FLN was set up in April 1955). In his policy statement, even as he spoke of the indissoluble link between France and Algeria, Guy Mollet undertook to adopt a peaceful approach to the problem, based on dialogue.
– The second issue of concern to public opinion was the quest for and organization of world peace during this period of the emergence of international detente. This concern was taken up by the new President of the Council, who added, however, a reminder of the need for France to remain well within the structure of the Atlantic Alliance.[2]
– The third issue was the establishment of a unified Europe. Since the failure in 1954 of the European Defence Community, European integration had come to a halt. Guy Mollet's intention was to revive and pursue it.[3] This concern was to play a considerable role in Suez involvement.

In practice, this wide range of initiatives on the part of the President of the Council was subject, nevertheless, to various constraints and influences, because in order to survive, the President was obliged to maintain a balance among the opposing forces within the Government.

Policies up to 26 July 1956

Thirty years later, with the benefit of hindsight on the French Government's attitude the day after the 'coup' of July 26 (the nationalization of the Suez Canal by Egypt), it is extremely tempting to imagine that the positions adopted were marked by continuity and coherence. The truth of the matter is less clear-cut.

Until the end of July, as the real inspiration behind Government policy, Guy Mollet had had little to do with the problems of the Middle East with which he was not particularly familiar. However, from the end of 1955 onwards, the tempo of events in this area accelerated, with arms supply agreements between Czechoslovakia and Egypt, escalation in the number of incidents on the borders of the State of Israel, and the Great Powers taking up policy positions. It is true that from the end of 1954 on, and particularly from 1955 onwards, there was some rapprochement between France and Israel in the area of military supplies. There were, nevertheless, still many stumbling blocks, and French diplomacy remained pro-Arab, a tendency no head of Government was able to radically amend.

Guy Mollet was particularly desirous of seeing France make a contribution to international detente in two areas: that of East–West relations as evinced by a visit to Moscow in the first half of May 1956 by a large SFIO delegation; and that of links with the countries of the 'non-aligned' movement as reflected by the trip of the Socialist Minister of Foreign Affairs, Christian Pineau, to India and Egypt (March 1956). The latter did, in fact, have some relation to the Algerian crisis, but it also highlights France's desire to play a peacemaking role in the Middle East and to pursue its own policy there, independently of that of the United States.

In the weeks leading up to 26 July 1956, therefore, nothing seemed to indicate that France might come to play a leading role in Middle East affairs. Some commentators have, however, identified the seeds of the French Government's future attitude in the aftermath of the events of 6 February in Algiers. That was the day that Guy Mollet, who had come to see the situation for himself, was pelted by various objects at the war memorial. The upshot of this incident was the resignation of General Catroux, the Resident Minister, who had a reputation for liberalism, and his replacement by Robert Lacoste, considered to be more understanding of the unease of the Europeans. The events of 6 February and their consequences may indeed have been the prelude to something of a shift on the Algerian issue. Furthermore, on the eve of 26 July Guy Mollet was 'dropped' by some of those who had previously supported his Algerian policy from within the Government. At the same time, the Socialist delegation returned from Moscow, the Communist Party withdrew its support, and Pierre Mendès-France submitted his resignation. Prior to these developments, Guy Mollet had had the support of a very wide-ranging coalition with a Centre-Left axis. From now on, he would have to rely on a Centrist majority, subject to the growing pressure of the Right of the Assembly.

Thus, the weight of the Algerian issue and the loss of some political support combined to play a decisive role in French attitudes after 26 July.

It is nevertheless our contention, albeit without ignoring these factors, that the analysis must be extended. In fact, as we shall show, French policy was not unwavering throughout the three-month period between 26 July and 30 October. The exclusively Algerian argument fails to hold water, because it cannot on its own explain the various attitudes adopted by and the analyses made by Government circles.

Initial Reactions, 26 July to 3 August 1956

The first effect of the decision of 26 July on the French parliament was to facilitate Government actions, which had been restrained for the past few weeks. Guy Mollet's Government, whose position had been weakened a few days earlier, received a fairly large majority in a vote of confidence in the National Assembly on July 28. On 1 August, Guy Mollet addressed a tense, extremely 'heated' Assembly. The result was that the Government decided on a 'hard-line forceful response'.[4]

On 3 August, Maurice Schumann, representative of the Foreign Affairs Committee, presented a draft resolution containing an extra paragraph which considerably augmented the hard-line approach. This paragraph, presented by Pierre Montel (Independent), was insisted upon by the Socialist group, which stipulated the wording. The text states:

> The National Assembly notes that Colonel Nasser, by discriminating between Canal users, has violated his undertakings and the rules of international law; that he has declared his

intention of establishing his hegemony over the Arab world; and that by his behaviour he thus represents a permanent threat to peace.[5]

Let us at this stage in the events summarize the situation.

The first reaction, shared by Guy Mollet, the Socialist group and the entire Government, was that of an anti-Munich reflex. In Guy Mollet's own words,

> We had one single overriding concern: no compromises with a dictator's expansionism. Violation of international law presented to the free world as a challenge, must not be allowed to pay off. This was the basis of collective security. Before 1939, this rule was neglected. One name stands for the policy of concessions, of successive capitulations to Hitler: Munich. It is true, our instinctive reaction to the Suez coup was an anti-Munich reflex: and it was the right reaction.[6]

This line was also that of the left-wing parties in opposition to Guy Mollet's Government, whose entire position centred on a negotiated solution in Algeria. Thus Maurice Duverger wrote in *L'Express*: 'The fate not only of all the shipping which uses the Suez Canal, but also of the whole of Western influence on the Middle East, depends on the reply to this question: "Are Western democracies less spineless today than they were twenty years ago, on March 7, 1936?"'[7] Jean Daniel, the editor of *L'Express*, wrote: 'Everything which helps make Nasser a great man makes it impossible for Bourguiba and the Sultan of Morocco to turn their backs on the Arab League and associate closely with France'.[8]

Very early on, this anti-Munich reflex was supplemented by a desire to protect the State of Israel which, without help from the West, might be wiped out. Concerning Israel, a Western enclave in the Orient and a Socialist country, Guy Mollet wrote: 'When my Government came to power, Israel asked for French assistance; I did my duty as a democrat and a Frenchman by supplying this endangered country with the arms it needed to survive'.[9]

Lastly, the question of Algeria was the third issue of concern to play a role at this initial stage of the affair – but only at this stage. The first reference, during the debate of August 2 and 3, came not from a Socialist speaker, but from a representative of the MRP group, Pierre de Chevigné: 'If we bow before these strong-arm tactics, the fellaheen will realize that they have chosen the right camp and will be sure of their inevitable victory in the long term ...'[10] It should be noted that in his self-vindicating book, *Bilan et perspectives socialistes*, Guy Mollet repudiated this line of reasoning.

At the end of the debates of 1–3 August, the position of Guy Mollet's Government was approved by an overwhelming majority. The only dissenting voice came from the Communist group. François Mitterand acted as spokesman in presenting the Government's approach to the Council of the Republic. However, it was then that talks started (in London on July 29) between Christian Pineau, Selwyn Lloyd and Robert Murphy (Deputy U.S. Secretary of State, replaced on 1 August by John Foster Dulles).

These talks were not imposed on Guy Mollet. Rather, they were something he had hoped for from the outset. In his 1 August speech, in the same breath as his wish for a 'hard-line forceful' response, he specified that this should 'take the form of joint action by the Western Allies'. As for the dismissal of the resolution submitted by the Foreign Affairs Committee, the addition in the shape of the extra paragraph, referred to above, was specifically designed to exert pressure on the United States, reluctant as it was to make any external commitments; the reference to a policy of discrimination in the Canal, the allusion to Nasser's desire to dominate the Middle East, were in fact arguments targeted at American public opinion.

Since the Americans continued to be allergic to any intervention, at the beginning of August the British and French were forced, under American influence, to accept the option of negotiations. However, when he spoke to the Assembly of 3 August, Christian Pineau very clearly considered what would happen if efforts to negotiate came to naught, and stressed the link between events in the Middle East and those in North Africa. There is an implied reference to the possibility of action separate from any by the United States: 'In the last six months, all of Egypt's strength has derived from deplorable divisions ... If it maintains its current attitude, there is no question but that Egypt will bear the entire responsibility for any events which might occur.'

Before concluding this first section, it should be stressed that these parliamentary debates and stances were set against an almost total consensus both in French public opinion and in political circles. The only discordant notes were struck by the Communist Party and also, in part, by the 'New Left'. The latter, however, while supporting the Government in its hard-line attitude towards Nasser, took exception to the effort to connect the events on the Nile with those in North Africa. On 3 August, *L'Express* wrote: 'It would be deplorable if the action called for on the international level were to be used as a pretext for maintaining the status quo in Algeria.' There is also a rejection of any idea of strong-arm tactics: 'To wish to force Egypt into abandoning this nationalization of the Canal would be to take serious risks.'[11] However, these discordant notes are simply the precursors of future breaches.

ONE STEP FORWARD, TWO STEPS BACK: DIPLOMATIC RETREAT AND FAILURE OF THE FRENCH GOVERNMENT (4 AUGUST–28 OCTOBER 1956)

In terms of the Socialist attitude, the period between 4 August and 28 October can be divided into two distinct phases of unequal length: from the beginning to 22 October, a phase of diplomatic deadlock and gradual involvement between France, Great Britain and Israel; and from October 22 to 29, the phase of direct preparation for joint involvement. How were these two phases expressed at the level of the French Government?

In practice, any distinction between these two phases is artificial. They were closely intertwined in two developments: one where the French and British were finally, reluctantly, forced to recognize that the Americans would never agree to associate themselves with an inter-Allied operation; and the second, in which the French and Israelis, joined later by the British, set up an operation which, up to the end, was beset by formidable problems in the allocation of roles and issues of timing.

We shall not deal in detail with the various stages of these preparations, which were cancelled several times; nor shall we discuss the difficulties resulting from the form of British involvement and the interconnections between each side's aims. Clearly, in addition to a common aim – the overthrow of Nasser or his decisive loss of prestige – each of the protagonists had their own specific aims: France had Algeria in mind; Great Britain wished to maintain a degree of influence in the Middle East; and Israel wanted to safeguard its security. These aspects have now become common knowledge since the publication of various authoritative books by participants in the events, journalists and historians.[12] In this paper, we shall limit our considerations to the French side: those involved, their motivations, and their problems.

Actors and Motivations

It is necessary to set French involvement alongside with Israel in its proper perspective. In the aftermath of 26 July, no one appears to have envisaged military action. It is true that at the time, the French High Command drew up plans, but at all times in all countries that is the *raison d' être* for High Commands, who have no implementing powers of their own, let alone the power to decide on any involvement. The reasons are easily grasped: initially, it was hoped that the United States would become involved in the conflict (particularly if Egypt were unable to operate the Canal); secondly, no direct Israeli intervention in the conflict was thought likely.

Looking at the Israeli angle – still from a French analytical perspective – there would appear to be considerable variation in viewpoints, depending on the period and on the observer. At the outset, Israel showed no basic hostility to the nationalization of the Canal, just as in 1955 it showed no vigorous response to the Baghdad Pact. Military contacts with France were indeed strengthened following 26 July, but not with any immediate operational intentions. Some observers have been able to determine two clear positions: an absence of any Israeli unanimity as to the advantages of joint action, and the desire to combine non-intervention by the Allies with air cover for Israeli towns.

Second, there is the question of divergent opinion within the French Government. Jacob Tsur, the Israeli Ambassador to France, believed that he had identified such differences, as he noted in his diary on April 17: 'I have the impression that there are differences of opinion in the Government.' If there were differences of opinion, did they continue after July 26? Sometimes French involvement in Suez has been presented as the outcome of a conspiracy inspired and led by a small group of men acting in concert: Maurice Bourgès-Maunoury and his principal private secretary, Abel Thomas; Emile Noel, Guy Mollet's principal private secretary; Louis Mangin, Abel Thomas' colleague. According to this version, Christian Pineau was not entirely in on the secret, and Guy Mollet himself was often presented with a *fait accompli*.

However, this hypothesis is contradicted by various sources. In his diary, Jacob Tsur, with his outstanding connection with French Government personnel, stresses Guy Mollet's personal interest in Israel, as well as his many assurances as to his concern with seeing Israel's security guaranteed. Nor does the picture of Guy Mollet being confronted by a *fait accompli* and forced to cover up for his colleagues stand up to closer scrutiny. From July on, the head of Government kept an eye on the details of the military talks. He always maintained control of operations.

134

Guy Mollet in the Crisis

What is most striking about Guy Mollet's behaviour throughout the long Suez crisis is his restrained, responsible attitude to the risks of any hasty, rash involvement. American reservations and British hesitations certainly had something to do with this, but his attitude was certainly in striking contrast to public opinion and an Assembly which were in favour of swift, forceful action, and none more so than the SFIO.

Under these circumstances, what were the reasons behind the meeting at Villacoublay on 21 October and the Sèvres talks of 22–24 October?

At this stage, Guy Mollet was still convinced that his original analysis was correct: the need to stand up to Nasser's action, and to refuse to give in to the violation of agreements; the conviction that Israel's existence was subject to a deadly threat; the fear that the balance of power in the Middle East might be disturbed in a way fatal to the West; and the existence of links between Nasserism and the Algerian situation. His outlook reflects the qualities of the rigid moralist and former member of the Resistance.

Did he take the American factor into consideration? There can be no doubt that Guy Mollet deliberately took into account the risk of a serious disagreement with the United States. He was often candid about his disappointment with American hesitations and weaknesses, as well as with interference in French affairs involving the Algerian question. As for the choice of a date, the forthcoming Presidential elections on November 6 may well have influenced Mollet's calculations, by convincing him that this timing would effectively tie the United States' hands, as he could not imagine its voice being added to a condemnation of the USSR.

One further factor must be taken into account. As a committed European, Guy Mollet wished to provide tangible proof of the desire and ability of Europeans to act on their own. The fact that one of these European countries was Great Britain further reinforced the symbolic value of this involvement, which was to take place as a demonstration of overall Western solidarity, but would be left up to two European partners to implement.

Any reference to considering the Soviet 'risk' can obviously only be made for the record. Russian intervention in Hungary might be a handicap, and in any case the French Government did not believe in any actual direct threat. Moreover, Guy Mollet's Government would appear to have shown considerable patience and caution. Until the end of September, he went along – unless he did so in a spirit of resignation – with the interminable diplomatic processes initiated by the United States, which were doubtless designed more to postpone any Franco-British intervention indefinitely, than to come up with a suitable solution to the crisis.

As late as 27 September, at a meeting of the Socialist Party Executive, in reply to a speaker calling for military intervention, Guy Mollet said, 'I cannot see a Socialist Government turning itself into the world's policeman'.[13] At that date, he was still favourably inclined towards the American lend-lease offer and a loan from the Import Export Bank if the Canal were to be closed.

But the determining factor was the threats which Mollet saw as hanging over Israel. After intervention, he stated, 'Israel wanted to act before the American elections. If we had let it act on its own, it would have been wiped off the face of the earth.'[14]

THE TEST OF STRENGTH AND THE ISOLATION OF THE MOLLET GOVERNMENT (29 OCTOBER–22 DECEMBER 1956)

After the 29 October parachute drop of the first Israeli airborne brigade into Egypt, the die was cast. The next day, 30 October, the French national Assembly approved French involvement by 368 votes to 182. Only a few isolated votes came from the Communist group. François Mitterand, Senior Minister and Lord Chancellor, spoke out firmly for the armed operation in Egypt:

> Whatever the consequences of our decision ... , we trust with all our heart that these consequences will be such that our generation of French men and women, who have lived through the upheaval of two major wars, will benefit from the peace which is the greatest good of all. It may well be that this peace is better served by what we are doing than if we were to allow things to drift; it is possible that our action is safeguarding peace better than any inaction on our part.[15]

It does not appear necessary to us here to recap the events of the crisis, from 29 October to 22 December – at which point Franco-British forces withdrew completely from Egypt – which, for Guy Mollet's Government, was nothing but a series of trials and tribulations, as well as disillusionment. We shall concentrate on an analysis of the French Government's reactions.

The Government and Its Ordeal

When he addressed the Assembly on 7 November, Guy Mollet first referred to the aims of the operation, and the decision to accept a cease-fire. He then drew the first lessons from the French–British involvement: the collapse of Egyptian military power; the end of Nasser's dreams of hegemony over the Arab world; the real situation in the Middle East in the spotlight of world opinion, together with Soviet ambitions; and the 'demonstration of the vital necessity for the three great Western powers to make their policy in this region in concert'.

For his part, Christian Pineau hesitated about referring to the attitude of the United States, which presented itself as 'a mediator and defender of international morality, but which voted against us when it came to Suez, while not daring to vote against Russia when it came to Hungary'.[16] Such sentiments logically led the Minister of Foreign Affairs to express the wish that Europe would act for itself.

Under the circumstances, the Government should have been defeated. Having reiterated on each vote of confidence its programme of non-involvement in a war, it eventually became involved in one without obtaining any particularly decisive results. However, it was not defeated. It received a vote of confidence of 325 votes to 210. Half of the Poujadist members and some 15 Radicals (out of 46) added their votes to those of the Communists. Clearly, behind this majority lay a great deal of criticism directed at the Government. However, the Assembly did not think it should topple the Mollet Government, not only because of the problems of forming a new Cabinet, but also because of French public opinion. In December 1956, 42 per cent of the French population was in favour of the Suez operation.[17]

However, while Guy Mollet had managed to avert disaster in Parliament, within the SFIO differences grew as the opposition's numbers swelled.

Socialist Crisis of Conscience[18]

We have already indicated how, initially, internal opposition in the SFIO was offset by indignation immediately after the 'Suez coup', so that preparations for involvement were approved. Later, however, opponents did try to sever the link between the Algerian question and the threats of intervention.

In the light of the diplomatic retreat before the UN, the view-

137

points of the United States and the Soviet Union were radically different. On 12 November, André Philip spoke out in vigorous criticism of Guy Mollet's policy. On 24 November 1956, 15 Socialist deputies addressed a critical letter to Pierre Commin, acting SFIO Secretary-General. After pointing out that France had intervened in Egypt (the text did stress 'against the dictator, Nasser') without a mandate from the United Nations, the signatories emphasized what they saw as the disastrous consequences for France: isolation in the international arena, less close ties with NATO and the United States, opening up of the Middle East to the USSR, closure of the Canal and oil reprisals.[19] Paradoxically, the Soviet repression of the Hungarian revolt seemed to them to confirm their views: the Soviet Union might have hesitated about intervening in Budapest had it not had the requisite pretext in the shape of Franco-British intervention in Egypt.

Thus, the Suez Affair helped to speed up the transformation occurring in the French Socialist Party. However, actual events show an extremely unexpected blend of a 'colonial' affair with a foreign policy event reduced to the dimensions of an ongoing ideological debate. For the Socialist Left, those in power sought a success in Egypt which had eluded them in Algeria.

There can be almost no doubt, contrary to the oft-heard argument, that for Guy Mollet and his closest ministerial associates Israel's survival was a far-reaching motivation. They never regretted their decision. As Guy Mollet said: 'I have only one regret: not to have been able to go all the way – but this was not determined by France ... As far as I am concerned, I accept the entire responsibility of the Suez Operation, and I am convinced that I did my international duty'.[20]

NOTES

1. L'Année Politique, 1956.
2. Journal Officiel, Assemblée Nationale, 10 February, 1956.
3. Journal Officiel, Assemblée Nationale, 10 February, 1956.
4. Journal Officiel, 2 Aug. 1956.
5. This text was amended on the request of Daniel Mayer, Chairman of the Foreign Affairs Committee.
6. Guy Mollet, *Bilan et perspectives socialistes* (Paris, 1960), p.31.
7. *L'Express*, 3 Aug. 1956.
8. *France Observateur*, 10 Aug. 1956.
9. Op.cit., p.33.
10. Journal Officiel, 3 Aug. 1956.
11. Gilles Martinet, *L'Express*, 2 Aug. 1956.
12. For example, Michel Bar Zohar, *Suez, Ultra Secret* (Paris, 1964); Abel Thomas, *Comment Israel fut sauvé* (Paris, 1978); Christian Pineau, *Suez* (Paris, 1976).
13. Minutes, Executive, Socialist Party.
14. Executive, 28 Nov. 1956.
15. Journal Officiel, 8 Nov. 1956.
16. Ibid.
17. Sondages, Jan. 1957.
18. The term is taken from Roger Quilliot, *La SFIO et l'exercice du pouvoir* (Paris, 1976), p.650.
19. Roger Quilliot, *op. cit.*, pp.649–50.
20. *Op. cit.*, pp.33–4.

139

9

The Road to Sèvres:
Franco-Israeli Strategic Cooperation

Shimon Peres

On 22 October 1956, David Ben-Gurion, Moshe Dayan, and I flew to Paris on a plane sent by Guy Mollet. In the car on the way to the airport (Ben-Gurion, wearing a hat, Dayan, wearing heavy eyeglasses to camouflage himself, and I, squeezed in the middle), we were almost 'hiding' from each other, because all three of us were fully aware who we were, and in what direction we were heading. Actually, to be precise, only two of us knew where we wanted to go, and neither knew what the third person, Ben-Gurion – the one who had to decide – really intended to do.

Ben-Gurion was in an undecided mood. He would often say, 'When I appear stormy, I am actually quiet, but when I am quiet, I am actually stormy.' He was quiet, and we knew that there was a storm behind the calm. As we approached the military airfield from which we were going to take off, he turned to me angrily, and said, 'Does Guy Mollet know for sure that there is no commitment on our part to go to war or to participate in a war?'

Ben-Gurion had decided to go to France in order to maintain the good and very close relations which existed between that country and Israel, and not in order to take part in a war. Ben-Gurion had begun to appreciate the relations between our two nations only with great reluctance. In the wake of the Second World War, he had become sceptical. He did not know de Gaulle well enough. However, once the relations were established, he considered it Israel's most important political achievement of that time. Ben-Gurion was very sophisticated, but he could sometimes also be very innocent, and when he had a friendship, he took it very seriously and sincerely. He was quite afraid that if he did not accept Mollet's invitation, he might endanger relations between France and Israel. That is why he went to Paris.

140

Dayan and I had other ideas. It was easier for the two of us to talk and converse between ourselves than it was to bring Ben-Gurion into our fast-paced conversation. Therefore, we could only guess his intentions.

There were at least two dates which forced Israel to make a decision. The first was October 1955, when Nasser decided to close the Straits of Tiran. At the time, I was convinced that Ben-Gurion would go straight ahead and try all that he could to open the Straits of Tiran – if possible by diplomacy, and if not, by force. He said so, he meant it, and he was decided on it. As a matter of fact, in January 1956, he brought before the Cabinet a proposal to open the Straits of Tiran by force. In his mind, the choice was between keeping the Straits open and closing the conflict, or allowing the Straits to remain closed and keeping the conflict open. I know for sure that once Ben-Gurion said something, he meant it; he would do it sooner or later. The blockade was clearly and decisively a *casus belli*. What remained, therefore, was just a matter of opportunity and time.

A second date, a much later one, that was also decisive was 11 October 1956. On that day, a heavy clash took place between units of the Jordanian army and the Israel Defence Forces in the vicinity of Qalqilia. An atmosphere of tension and concern prevailed, and this encounter was on the verge of turning into a war. Eighteen Israeli soldiers lost their lives, and four were wounded; the Jordanians lost 70 soldiers. While the battle was going on, we were considering bringing in the air force: if the armoured corps couldn't save the rest of our encircled boys, we would use even greater force. As for the Jordanians, they approached the British, reminding them that Britain had a military agreement with Jordan, and that since the Jordanians were in danger, the British must intervene on their side. On the morning of the battle, the British Chargé d'Affaires knocked on Ben-Gurion's door, and told him: (1) that within three days, an Iraqi division would cross the frontier and join the Jordanians; (2) that Britain was obliged to stand by Jordan. We smelled war. It was no longer a matter of having a war or not having one; it was no longer a matter of having a choice or not having one – it was just a matter of time.

Thus, Nasser's blockade of the Straits of Tiran and the clash with the Jordanians were very much on our minds.

I heard about the Musketeer Operation for the first time in July 1956. I was approached by Maurice Bourgès-Maunoury, then the Defence Minister of France, and in confidence he asked me two questions. First of all, he asked how long it would take the Israeli

141

army to cross the Sinai Peninsula. I told him that we estimated about six or seven days. He was astounded. He said, 'Impossible! We estimate that it is a matter of three to four weeks minimum.' Then he said: 'Speaking as friends, may I ask you, do you intend to conduct an Israeli operation southward?' I said, 'Yes.' He asked, 'What is the intention − what is the purpose of that operation?' I said immediately, 'to open the Straits of Tiran. We shall not agree to the Straits remaining closed. So sooner or later we shall do it.' Things quieted down after that conversation, but we continued to meet quite often.

Between the 18th and 25th of September I had a very busy and difficult week. On my way to the United States, I stopped in Paris, where I again met with Bourgès-Maunoury. We talked about Musketeer, and he said that the chances did not look too good − the British were reluctant. He told me, 'Apparently, your timing is closer to the British timing than our own.' I cabled this back to Ben-Gurion and received a reply, 'Tell the French that the French timetable fits us as well as the British one.' Thus, I already had a hint. Since I saw that there was still a great deal of reluctance and misunderstanding between the French and the British, I proceeded to the United States.

After arriving in the United States, Yosef Nachmias, our defence procurement representative in Paris at the time, cabled me that Bourgès-Maunoury wanted to see me immediately. So I flew back and arrived in Paris on 22 September, a Sunday. We went to the headquarters of the French Defence Ministry on Rue St. Dominique; it was empty. We then called a friend of ours and were told that Bourgès-Maunoury was at a hunting club somewhere, four hours from Paris. We met him that night, and he told us that, in spite of what we had been told previously, the French and the British were coming closer together. He asked if Israel would participate.

I decided that very same night to return home. I arrived early in the morning, on 25 September, and I was met at the airport by Dayan, who gave me a short summary of the events that had taken place. The situation in Israel had become exceedingly complicated: there were many victims, many people who were being killed all over the country − students at Sodom, archaeologists at Ramat Rachel, a couple of people in Ashkelon. The whole country was drenched with blood.

We left Lod airport for a small airfield in Ramle. Ben-Gurion arrived there on a Piper Cub from Sede Boqer. The three of us continued on to Jerusalem and, on the way, Dayan and Ben-Gurion discussed possible retaliation against the Jordanians. Ben-Gurion turned to me and asked, 'What's new with your French friends?' I told him. He said, 'Well, this changes the situation completely. We are not going to deal with retaliation; we are going to deal with the new French proposal.' On our way to Jerusalem, we agreed that a delegation would go to France. We discussed who the members of the delegation would be, and decided that it would consist of Golda Meir (then the Foreign Minister), Moshe Carmel (the Transport Minister, fluent in French), Dayan, and myself.

The delegation arrived in Paris on 28 September, and we met at the house of Louis Mangin; Christian Pineau, Bourgès-Maunoury, Abel Thomas and General Challe were also there. Golda Meir, who was not a great admirer of mine, and probably did not take my assessment at face value, had some reservations, and, therefore, sought to catch me on some vulnerable point. When we arrived in Paris, I was already in the middle of a complication, because initially I was told that a meeting would take place with Mollet, Bourgès-Maunoury, and Pineau, but Mollet was not there. There was a good reason for his absence, because on the 22nd, the French had intercepted a plane carrying Ben-Bella and Mohammad Haydar, and that day Mollet was replying to some questions in the French Parliament. Therefore, he couldn't attend the meeting. Nevertheless, it appeared to be a bit of a bluff on my part that here we were invited to meet the Prime Minister of France, and he was not present. Consequently, I went to Mollet afterwards and explained to him the trouble I was in; he finally met with Golda Meir in private.

Pineau, a real intellectual and a man of honesty, said at the meeting, 'Look, we don't know where we are. In America, they are on the eve of elections; there won't be an American government before January 1957, because the President, even if he is elected, as you know, doesn't take office officially until January – they are in the middle of a campaign. Even if Eisenhower is re-elected, we don't know which direction he will take. It will probably be to reach a consensus with the Russians, and the Russians are very tense'. (At the time, trouble was starting up in Poland with Gomulka.) Pineau added that the British were very reluctant, and all that had been achieved with the British so far had been to reduce a complete misunderstanding down to a partial misunderstanding. Pineau's picture was quite bleak, and I looked from time to time at Golda to see her reaction. I could see that she felt that I had been completely misleading.

Bourgès-Maunoury was a man of great wisdom and strong character. He and Chaban Delmas, now the President of the Parliament, were young generals in the French Resistance at the time of the German occupation. Both were men of great courage, and both had emerged from the war determined that there should never be another Hitler, neither great nor small; no longer should there be support for any 'pan' movement, be it pan-Germanism or pan-Islam. 'There must be an end to it: we are not going to surrender; we are not going to give in,' he said, with a keen admiration for Israel. He continued, 'I know that all of us are very experienced, mature people, occasionally cynical. I tend to believe, in spite of all my experiences, that sentiments play a great role, not only in human relations, but also in political relations. I can't describe France without a deep feeling for the Jewish people and for Israel.'

I shall never forget that once we were hosted by France's Chief of Staff, Ely. I was sitting at the right of Madame Ely, and she told me, 'Look, you don't have to tell me anything. I was myself in a concentration camp with Jewish people. What more can you tell me?' I remember meeting André Malraux, an intellectual, and he told me that were he a young man again, he would join the Israeli forces. These were the sentiments that existed in France. Traditionally divided between rich and poor, between Catholics and Protestants, between Parisians and provincials, France found itself divided after the Second World War in a different way: between the Maquis and the collaborators, between the people who fought against the Germans and the people who had accepted the German iron fist. The Maquis completely sided with Israel.

The most that we were able to agree on, at that meeting in Paris, was the need to obtain more arms. Upon returning home, Golda reported that there was no chance whatsoever of France co-operating with us. I, however – being too young and inexperienced – remained as optimistic as I was before the whole thing started.

In reaching his decision to take military action, Ben-Gurion was guided by a number of taboos and constraints. First of all, he was interested in preventing war. In the Knesset, the Herut Party demanded on several occasions in 1956 that the Straits of Tiran be opened by force, and some Knesset members made speeches calling for a preventive war. Ben-Gurion responded very strongly against that idea. Given a choice between a preventive war or preventing a war, he preferred the latter. When he finally agreed to the Sinai Campaign, as strange as this may sound, he did so not in terms of a preventive war; it was to be a limited operation instead of a full-scale war. In his view this was preventing a war.

Ben-Gurion was a born strategist. However, before thinking about strategy, he thought about history. He felt very strongly that every war is fought twice: once on the battlefield where it takes place, and afterwards in the history books where posterity judges the rights or wrongs of a military action. Before looking at a military plan, he tried to imagine its historical significance. He was very careful not to become involved in a war that did not have moral justification, and that included the existence (i.e., self-defence) of the Jewish people. On occasion Ben-Gurion would say, 'If I have to weigh on one scale all the moral values, and on the other scale the existence of my people, I have to deal first with the existence of my people.' He noted, 'Einstein was a genius, but a very small bullet could put an end to his life; what can you do with his mind, if his body is insecure?'

Therefore, Ben-Gurion was still reluctant. Although some now describe the Sinai Campaign as a preventive war, that was not his intention.

He set parameters to limit the operation: Israel was not going to occupy a land; it was going to alter a situation, not a map. He told the Cabinet beforehand that Israel was not going to remain in the Sinai. Later statements to the contrary that he made were for negotiating purposes. I was with him when he was asked at a Hashomer Hatza'ir kibbutz, after we had withdrawn from the Sinai, why he had spoken about the Third Kingdom of Israel; did that mean that we were going to remain in Sharm el-Sheikh? He said, 'What did you want me to say? That we are going to withdraw? Who would negotiate with us?' Therefore, one must distinguish between these statements and the commitment which he clearly made beforehand in the Cabinet. Great leaders are those who are able to compromise without compromising themselves. If Ben-Gurion compromised by withdrawing, he did not compromise himself, since, in the first place, he had not intended to remain in the Sinai.

Another taboo that Ben-Gurion had – one which Dayan also had an important hand in implementing – was to avoid as many casualties as possible in the upcoming operation, not only on our side, but also on the Egyptian side. The objective was to destroy arms, not armies. That is the reason why so few Israeli soldiers lost their lives, and why so many Egyptians, 4,000, were taken prisoners-of-war (the Egyptians took four Israeli prisoners-of-war).

Had the operation been a bloodbath, who knows how many of the 4,000 Egyptian POWs would have remained alive.

Moreover, civilian lives were not to be endangered. Cities and other civilian locations were not to be bombed. In spite of some attempts by the Egyptians to bomb some cities in Israel – attempts that fortunately failed – we did not seek to retaliate by striking at the Egyptian civilian population.

Another principle also guided us. While we were willing to co-operate with others, we were not going to serve their interests. I must note, in favour of the French, that when Mollet, Pineau, and Bourgès-Maunoury proposed to us that we co-operate, they began by saying, 'We do not expect you to solve French or British problems. If you have in mind the solution of Israeli problems, go ahead.' All of us, in fact, insisted that everyone serve his own purpose (Churchill once said that when you have a coalition of different nations, each country's army should fight for its own purpose, at its own time and place – if this were possible).

When we went to Paris, we did not have any assurances beforehand that these limitations and qualifications would be met. However, had they not been met, there would not have been co-operation in the Sinai Campaign.

War is not a goal for its own sake. Moreover, war seldom brings about anything, except victims. Consequently, one can ask, what were the reasons for Israel's operation?

The first was the opening of the Straits of Tiran. The second was to bring an end to the terrorist activities. In that order, these were Ben-Gurion's priorities. Had it been up to Dayan and me, our priorities would have been ranked differently. The situation had become impossible: our first priority would probably have been to put an end to the terrorist attacks; our second would have been to open the Straits of Tiran.

On 25 September, when Dayan and I left Jerusalem, Dayan told me that a retaliatory operation (by a paratrooper unit commanded by Arik Sharon) was being carried out that night at a place called Hussan, and he suggested that we visit the soldiers. By the time we arrived – either the middle of the night or close to morning – the fighting was already quite heavy. Upon reaching the place, Dayan, his driver, and I had to take cover on the ground. A minute after we did so, the driver was wounded just a metre away from me. In the morning, when the operation was over, we found out that ten Israeli soldiers had been killed, and about twenty or so were wounded. We knew the name of almost each one of the boys. When you read in the papers about an attack or retaliatory response, it is one thing; but, when you feel it in the middle of the night, it is another. The entire country was being hit by a wave of attacks: during the day, at night, in gardens, in homes, on the roads, young and old, men and women.

Unlike the situation today, the fidaiyyun then maintained their headquarters under Egyptian auspices, in the Gaza Strip. Furthermore, the archaeologists who were killed at Ramat Rachel were shot by Jordanian troops – not terrorists. It was the Jordanian army, on the one hand, and the Egyptian army, on the other, that were attacking us. We knew for sure where they were located, who the responsible people were, and who were issuing the orders. We knew how to stop them, and, deep in our hearts, we knew that a point of no return had been reached – that we were on the verge of a full-scale war.

Developments in October 1956 also greatly influenced our course. October 1956 was one of the craziest months in history. On 11 October, the Qalqilia operation took place. The next day, 12 October, the British Chargé d'Affaires came to Ben-Gurion to warn him about possible British intervention and the Iraqi division that was joining up with the Jordanians. Seven days later, on 19 October, a joint command was established by Jordan and Egypt. Four days later, on 23 October, elections were held in Jordan, and the pro-Egyptian candidates won (this at a time when Egypt was openly threatening our existence). Then, two days later, on 25 October, military talks started between Jordan, Egypt, and this time also Syria: they announced their decision to form a joint command and unite the fronts. Again there were threats, even as the Iraqi division was getting ready to move in at any moment.

Israel found itself facing a terrible situation. The Russians were supplying the Arab countries with modern arms, and three countries – Egypt, Jordan, Syria – were uniting themselves militarily, backed by Britain and Iraq; all this, just four days before the Suez operation.

As for the French and British, several important events were taking place as well. On 20 October, a ship was caught transporting arms from Egypt to Algeria, thus providing evidence that Egypt was actually helping the Algerian rebels. Two days later, on 22 October, France recalled its ambassador from Egypt. Earlier, on 14 October, the British (who had an agreement with Egypt to operate the Suez Canal) tried to diplomatically resolve the crisis over the Canal; actually, they were determined to take military measures, and their two diplomatic attempts were misleading. First, they had attended a conference of the Sinai Canal Users Association; the meeting was initiated by U.S. Secretary of State John Foster Dulles, who was trying to convince the French and the British that the United States was on their side. Nothing, however, came out of that conference, and the issue was then brought before the Security Council on October 14. The Security Council was considering a proposal to place the Suez Canal under international control, but the Russians vetoed it. So nothing came out of either the conference or the Security Council. From every side, every development appeared frustrating, dangerous, or frightening.

Upon arriving in Sèvres on 22 October, we found the atmosphere already heavy with disappointment and danger. Ben-Gurion was going to co-operate with the French and the British – to co-ordinate timing, not joint military action. This was because our political objective was different from theirs. We considered the Suez Canal to be Egyptian, and we were not going to use force to open it. We were not a party to the Anglo-Egyptian agreement; neither were we a party to the Algerian war. We had problems of our own. The only things, therefore, that could really be co-ordinated were timing and participation.

Frankly, Ben-Gurion was exceedingly suspicious when it came to the British, particularly Anthony Eden. The British warning about possible intervention was considered by Ben-Gurion to be additional evidence of Great Britain's and Anthony Eden's hostility. We looked upon Anthony Eden as the builder of the Arab League, as the supporter of Iraq, as a man who was looking for an opportunity to join the Arab side at the last minute, and thereby gain an advantage. Today, I know that we were wrong; we were overly suspicious and did not read Eden's intentions correctly. However, that was how we perceived matters at the time.

We succeeded in co-ordinating the timetable, and each of us had a role to fulfil. What we achieved was beneficial. In spite of all the criticism, what Britain and France prevented must also be taken into consideration. Had Nasser been left a free hand, who can say what kind of a Middle East we would be living in today? We would probably be talking about Red Africa, not Black Africa. Aggression and war would have continued for many more years, leading to increased Russian involvement, especially as the era of the British and French empires was drawing to a close, and the superpowers were beginning to become more and more involved in the Middle East. The superpower presence would have become virtually one-sided, with all attendant dangers. As for Israel: we got rid of the fidaiyyun; we had eleven years of tranquillity; the Straits of Tiran were opened; the brilliance of the Israeli army and of Dayan emerged and received world recognition as an army that could move fast and a commander who was capable of translating political talk into military action. The success of the Sinai operations was not a matter of luck, but a result of wise handling. Our relations with France remained very close until late in 1967. Later on, we also straightened out our relations with Great Britain. These were the results of the Sinai Campaign, an operation in which Israel's moral considerations were equal to her strategic needs.

10

Egypt: From Military Defeat to Political Victory

Moshe Shemesh

The nationalization of the Suez Canal Company on 26 July 1956 symbolized for the Egyptians and the Arab world the independence of Egyptian decision-making and the liberation of Egypt from foreign political and economic influence. Sayyid Mar'i, then Minister for Agrarian Reform, wrote in his memoirs: 'The nationalization gave rise to a feeling of euphoria. It was as if Egypt, in this manner, settled a long account which had accumulated over 70 years.'[1] Abu Iyyad (Salah Khalaf), a leader and founder of Fatah who then resided in Egypt, well expressed the reaction of the Arab world by writing,

> Nasser has now become the leader of the struggle against imperialism. The daring of the act and the challenge it posed to England and France made a strong and deep impression on all the Arabs. Nasser restored to the Arabs and to all the peoples of the Third World their honour and self-confidence. Everything is now possible, even the liberation of Filastin.[2]

This achievement had been the dream of every Egyptian leader since the British occupation. It is no wonder that Nasser described the nationalization as 'the peak of the national struggle of Egypt for political independence'.[3] He presented the nationalization as a step in the 'sacred march'[4] towards achieving Egypt's national aims. Later on, Nasser described the Suez crisis as a 'war of independence'. 'For the first time in 600 years the country enjoyed full independence without any foreign or English control', Nasser declared. He continued: 'The campaign for independence developed into a war of independence.'[5]

Nasser achieved, as a result of nationalization, an unprecedented popularity in Egypt and the Arab world. Thus, under these circumstances, Nasser could not retract this decision even at the price of war.

The most striking phenomenon in Nasser's evaluation of the situation during the Suez crisis was the fact that he was entrapped by a strategic concept which he did not abandon until the evening of 31 October 1956, when he was completely surprised by the British and French air attacks. This concept and its ensuing surprise recalls, in its component elements, the concept and surprise of the Israeli intelligence in the Yom Kippur War. Nasser was imbued with his perception that military action by the French and British to force a solution to the crisis was very improbable. Nasser's assessment on deciding to nationalize the Canal (26 July 1956) was:

> Peak danger time ... 80 per cent at beginning of August, decreasing each week through political activities. How can we make the political situation swim? Fawzi [Foreign Minister] can do that. Second week in August, danger 60 per cent. Third week, 50 per cent. Fourth week 40 per cent. End of September danger 20 per cent. If we succeed in gaining two months by politics, we shall be safe.[6]

Nasser's aim after nationalization was to gain time and to try to prevent a confrontation in particular with England, and with France and the USA. Bughdadi, the State Minister for Planning, writes in his Memoirs:

> Our evaluation was that time would be in our favour, so long as world public opinion was convinced of our right to nationalize the Canal. Our belief was that Britain, who more than any other country would use military force against us, would need time in order to organize the force it would require for such an operation. In order to avoid any clash with those forces [of Israel] Nasser ordered that all the Egyptian fidaiyyun units in the Gaza Strip be taken out and to halt all their sabotage activities in Israel ... Mahmud Yunis [Managing Director, Egyptian Suez Canal Authority] was instructed to make every possible effort in order not to prevent the passage of any ship ... through the Canal.[7]

Nasser estimated that he needed a month, after which the chances of Anglo-French military action would decrease. By then, Egypt would convince world opinion of the justness of its position. Nasser expected that the Canal crisis would be resolved in the framework of the UN or under its umbrella. 'This would be the ideal settlement of the crisis' from Egypt's point of view.[8]

Nasser completely ruled out the possibility of 'collusion' between Britain, France and Israel. In his opinion, collusion between Britain and Israel would be political suicide for Britain in the Arab world. His estimation was that, at most, Israel would attack in the Sinai, but that an all-out attack was not probable at the time. This evaluation was strengthened as time passed, despite information of military preparation by France and Britain. By the middle of October 1956, Nasser's assessment continued to be that a military attack was unlikely.

The Egyptian command, on the other hand, did not rule out the possibility of a British–French attack, but they did not believe that an all-out war in the Sinai at the initiative of Israel was likely. A military report issued by the Egyptian General Command of the Armed Forces in early September 1956, as well as the Egyptian Army Operation Order 1 September 1956 for the Defence of Egypt, stated that Britain and France were liable to attack Egypt with the purpose of occupying Alexandria and the Canal Zone, and from there to advance along two axes towards Cairo. The General Command assumed that during an attack by France and Britain, Israel might make provocative attacks on the Eastern Front to seize forward military positions or to cut off the Gaza Strip. According to Nasser, 'If Israel's aim was to perpetuate incidents or raids, then it would direct them either at the Gaza sector or at our advanced positions on the border.' All this was supposed to be by agreement on the part of France and England.[9]

However, since the Egyptian Command did not expect an overall Israeli attack, half the forces based in the Sinai in June 1956 were withdrawn during the months of August–September to the Canal Zone. During the Sinai war, in addition to the Palestinian division in the Gaza Strip, one infantry division faced the Israel Defence Forces in the north and the centre of Sinai, instead of more than two which had been there in June 1956. Reports received during October 1956 as to the French–Israeli connection were discounted by Nasser and Amir, the Minister of War and Commander-in-Chief, and the Military Intelligence. A part of these reports was thought to have been leaked for the purpose of concentrating Egyptian forces in the Sinai and abandoning the Alexandria area.

When Khalid Muhi al-Din (who resigned from the Revolutionary Command Council [RCC] in 1954, and was nicknamed the 'Red Major') informed Nasser of the reports that he had received from one of his friends in Paris in October 1956, which stated that France would co-operate with Israel in attacking Egypt, Nasser did not take this information seriously. Nasser, as well as Amir, the Minister of War and Commander-in-Chief, believed that this information was intentionally leaked in order to induce the Egyptian leadership to concentrate Egypt's defence forces in Sinai, 'thereby abandoning Alexandria and Rashid which were on the expected route for the British troops to take'.[10]

On 6 October 1956, Colonel Zakariya al-Adli Imam, the Egyptian Military Attaché in Istanbul, despatched to the Military Intelligence in Cairo his conclusion, based on information gathered by him and his agents, to the effect that 'England and France will present a final ultimatum to Egypt; this will be followed by a tripartite attack (England, France and Israel) in the middle of November'. According to Imam, shortly after that he reported: 'All the signs indicate that the attack will take place before the end of October.' Imam complained that the Head of the Military Intelligence discounted his reports saying that 'there is information about expected attack through Libya ...'[11]

Moreover, ten days before the war Colonel Tharwat Okasha, the Egyptian Military Attaché in Paris, sent to Nasser a special report which included 'details of the tripartite attack on Egypt', which he gathered from his 'high level' sources in Paris. 'But Nasser did not believe that such an attack might occur.'[12]

It is significant that on 25 October 1956 Amir began a visit to Jordan and Syria, accompanied by a high level military delegation. On 27 October 1956, Nasser urged him to visit Lebanon also. Amir's visit took place while the preparations for war in Israel were discernible. The mobilization of the reserves was already in full swing. Amir's visit should be seen in light of the Egyptian Military Intelligence assessment that these preparations were being conducted against the background of the rising tension on the Israel–Jordan border and the entry of Iraqi army units into Jordan.

The basic appraisal of the situation did not change even during the evening of 29 October 1956 when the first reports were received of IDF activity. The conclusion drawn was that only a 'limited operation' was in progress. Later on during the night, the leadership concluded that the operations were more extensive. Orders were then sent out to reinforce the units in the Sinai with armoured forces.[13] The original assessment remained the same through 30 October. The Anglo-French ultimatum on the evening of 30 October 1956 was judged by Nasser as an empty threat.

Against this background, the surprise and shock of Nasser and the leadership when they heard the reports of British and French air

153

attacks on the evening of 31 October can be understood. Now, Nasser thought that the purpose of Britain and France was to push the Egyptian army into Sinai and then, by conquering the Canal Zone, to isolate and destroy it. Nasser immediately dictated a plan of retreat from Sinai to the Egyptian High Command. He claimed that the purpose of this retreat was to preserve the strength of the Egyptian army, and thus to foil the aims of the 'tripartite aggression'.[14] From his point of view, this was the lesser of two evils. According to Heikal:

> Nasser had a heated discussion with Amir. Amir had started to push his armor into the Sinai to meet the Israeli threat. He wanted to maintain this movement to fight off the Israelis from the Canal. But Nasser insisted that the tanks be brought back to defend the Canal against the British and the French. 'If they land at Port Said', he argued, 'all the armor will be cut off in the desert. I prefer to evacuate the Sinai ...' Amir protested that the Egyptian army would never retreat. Amir had unfortunately lost his nerve. He went on arguing with Nasser ...[15]

Eventually, Amir succumbed. But Nasser's aim was not achieved, as evidenced by almost 6,000 prisoners and large amounts of military equipment captured by the IDF and the hundreds of Egyptian soldiers wandering around in the sands of Sinai with every soldier 'looking out to save himself', as Heikal relates.

Despite this, Nasser believed in the wisdom and correctness of his decision to retreat from Sinai. He tried to imbue the army, the Egyptian people and the entire Arab world with his faith. He presented the retreat as the 'primary factor of the victory' in the war.[16] Thus, Nasser transformed the retreat into an operable norm and, indeed, this norm was activated again in June 1967 by the same leaders and commanders.

Nasser had no difficulty in transforming military defeat into political victory. The researcher of the Israeli–Arab wars easily discerns the astounding phenomenon of the absence of reliable Arab reportage on the war's progress or its results. Criticism of this lack of reliable reporting during the war was not lacking, but this criticism had no effect.

Of no less interest is the fact that the public believed the stories of victories and bravery, which had no connection at all with reality. Unlike in Western society, lies expressed by an Arab regime are not considered negatively, especially when these lies coincide with the outlook of the individual and meet his hopes and aspirations. The lie, on this occasion, becomes the norm, even among the leaders themselves, when they wish to meet the people's expectations and to safeguard their own prestige and position.

A vivid example of this phenomenon is to be found in the conversation intercepted and taped by Israeli intelligence between Nasser and King Hussein on the morning of 5 June 1967 and made public by the Defence Ministry on 8 June 1967. In this conversation, Nasser arranged with Hussein to accuse the USA and Britain of participation in the Six Day War, even though both knew that this was not true. Nasser even informed Hussein that his planes had been attacking Israeli airfields since morning, even though most of the Egyptian aircraft had already been destroyed on the ground.[17]

As to the propaganda machine during the Sinai war, Sayyid Mar'i was to write, 'It was clear in those days that we suffered a military defeat, which was covered up by Egyptian propaganda. This propaganda created out of thin air imaginary battles [in Sinai] and tales of courage by the popular resistance in Port Said.'[18] Egyptian propaganda created the impression on the public mind that, if the war had been only between Israel and Egypt, then Egyptian victory would have been ensured. Brigadier General Kamal Abd al-Hamid, Commander of Civil Mobilization during the war, went so far as to write, in his semi-official book published in 1959 on the Sinai and Port Said battles, that as a result of the British and French surprise 'Egypt was forced to change her plans during the critical moments of the war, just when Egypt was about to finish off Israel. Egypt was compelled [to change its plans] in order to confront a new dangerous situation imposed on her by the Anglo-French ultimatum.'[19] Research carried out among Egyptian officers captured in Sinai revealed that they believed the official propaganda. All the officers believed that Egypt had not been defeated in Sinai. In their opinion, the main effort was in Suez, and Sinai was not important. One officer even claimed that the Gaza Strip was occupied by British forces. (He, himself, was captured in Gaza.) They were convinced that, if not for Western intervention, the Egyptian army would have reached Tel-Aviv, although not within 48 hours.[20]

In the wake of the French and British attack on the eve of 31 October 1956, a leadership crisis emerged. Two figures played a major part in the war drama: Nasser, as President, and Abd al-Hakim Amir, as War Minister and Commander-in-Chief. Three members of the Revolutionary Command Council acted with them: Abd al-Latif al-Bughdadi (State Minister for Planning), Zakariya

Muhi al-Din (Minister of the Interior), and Salah Salim, the editor of the daily *al-Sha'b*.

In June 1956, the regime in Egypt was at the beginning of a new era of civilian rule after the ratification of a new constitution and the election of Nasser as President on 22 June. Nasser began his period of one-man rule. Amir, who was his best friend from the time of the founding of the Free Officers Organisation, had the rank of Major at the outbreak of the Revolution in July 1952, and he still held this rank in June 1953, when he was appointed by Nasser as Commander-in-Chief and elevated to the rank of Major General. The purpose of this appointment was to ensure control over and loyalty of the army, even though his military experience was, at most, that of battalion commander. Amir was also re-appointed War Minister on 26 June 1956.

This, then, was the leadership that was faced with a deep crisis during 2 and 3 November 1956, when it realized that Britain and France together with Israel were at war with Egypt. The air attacks on the night of 31 October shook the leadership and, in the words of Bughdadi, 'many of us were paralysed'. The assessment was that Egypt could not win against the two Powers and Israel together. On 4 November, Nasser admitted before Bughdadi in English, 'I was defeated by my army.'[21] An important discussion took place within the leadership on 2 November. The question on the agenda was whether to surrender or to fight to the end. Amir opened the discussion with the announcement that 'the continuation of the war means the destruction of the country and the killing of many civilians. To prevent this, it is preferable to ask for a cease-fire.' Salah Salim supported him and suggested that Nasser go to the British ambassador and submit his surrender so as to save the country from disaster. Of course, these proposals were rejected by Nasser. The conclusion arrived at was that Egyptian honour demanded a continuation of the fighting until Cairo fell. It was also concluded that, should this happen, the government would go underground and conduct a popular resistance against the conquerors.[22] This issue was never raised again for discussion because of the unexpected political and military developments in Egypt's favour.

From the military aspect, the difficulty was how to wage war when, at the apex of the pyramid, stood a Major dressed up as a General. He was a political officer, not a military one. As a consequence, Amir was very dependent on the commanders of the three branches of the armed forces, but these had failed in their undertaking. 'Amir was very nervous, confused, gave orders on issues large and small, and his mental condition was very poor.'[23] Amir might have been the commander of a battalion, but not of an army. The ineffectuality of Mahmud Sidqi, the Commander of the Air Force, was particularly blatant. When it was decided, on the night of 29 October, to bomb the forces at the Mitla and, on the following morning, the Israeli air fields, he replied that it could not be done as there was insufficient fuel at the bomber base. After the crisis, Nasser wished to dismiss the heads of the three branches, especially Sidqi. Amir objected, claiming there were reasons for the mishaps. He argued: 'If they made mistakes, consider me responsible, and it is best that I also resign.'[24] Nasser gave in, and they all stayed at their posts. There is no doubt that Nasser's personality and fortitude prevented the collapse of the leadership during those critical days.

The Suez crisis had two important results arising from the political success of Nasser. One was his massive emergence onto the Arab scene; and the other was increased Arab awareness of the Palestinian problem. Nasser decided to exploit his political success in order to establish his position as leader of the Arab world after having emerged as the undisputed leader of Egypt. He captured the Arab world politically by endorsing the idea of Arab nationalism. This idea appeared on several occasions in his speeches in 1955, but without any explanation of its significance. In his speech of 7 November 1956, he initiated his drive for this idea.[25]

The period between 1956 and 1961 was the glorious period of Arab nationalism. The contents of this nationalism made up the essence of Nasserism. An entire generation of Arab political leaders was brought up on this doctrine. Nasser preached a militant and active Arab nationalism, using all means, including force, to achieve its aims. He believed that in so doing he, more than any other Arab leader of his time, expressed the aspirations of the Arab nations. Nasser defined a number of the aims of Arab nationalism. First, the political, social and economic liberation of the Arab world, and the elimination of imperialism and reactionary Arab attitudes. Pan-Arabism was destined to fill the void created in the Arab world by the elimination of Western influence. He presented this as a strong weapon in the hands of the Arab world and a guarantee of its security. Arab nationalism meant Arab solidarity (later he added Arab unity), based on the independence of the Arab countries. As time passed, he added further content, such as positive neutralism – non-alignment – as well as social justice and true democratic life. In one of his speeches, he defined Arab nationalism as a spiritual and historical movement, without explaining these terms.[26] He threatened to use force to defend Arab nationalism and, indeed, did so in the Yemen with 50,000 – 70,000 Egyptian soldiers fighting for five years. Thus, he divided the Arab world into his allies and his enemies, nationalists and agents of imperialism, reactionaries and the forward-minded. On this basis, he undermined the regimes which did not follow his line. The break-up of the union between Egypt and Syria in September 1961 marked the beginning of the decline of Arab nationalism according to the Nasser formula. The defeat of June 1967 was a further serious blow.

As stated above, the second result of the political victory was the increased Arab awareness of the Palestinian problem. The problem of 'Filastin' in the widest sense was central to the political outlook of Nasser. This centrality began gaining expression after the Sinai war and reached its peak when, after the Six Day War, the Israeli–Arab conflict became the substance and aim of Arab nationalism. The lessons of 1948 were, for Nasser, the starting point for establishing his strategy vis-à-vis the conflict. The Sinai campaign caused a change in his strategy as to the manner in which to solve the Palestinian problem. For Nasser, the Palestinian problem was an integral part of his concept of Arab nationalism. Nasser presented the struggle against Zionism as the second aim of Arab nationalism and equal in importance to the battle against imperialism. He emphasized that the call to Arab nationalism was to be interpreted in the fact that the Arab nation did not recognize the existence of Israel.

As part of his drive to encourage Arab nationalism and as a lesson from the Sinai war, Nasser started a campaign to deepen Arab awareness of the Palestinian problem; he tried to instil into the Arab public the sense of danger to Arab nationalism deriving from the existence of Israel and the danger of her aim to expand, in his opinion, from the Nile to the Euphrates. Nasser believed, or tried to convince his audience, that only he expressed the feeling of every Arab. Immediately after the war, Nasser started to attack Israel in his speeches to a degree unheard of from him before, and he laid much more emphasis on the liberation of Filastin. In his opinion, 'the Arab stand on the rights of the Palestinians became, after the aggression of 1956, the main motivating force in events in the Arab world'.[27]

An important lesson learned by Nasser from the Sinai war was the need to prepare well for the next round against Israel, which, in his opinion, was inevitable. He claimed that he must prepare for war, not only against Israel, but against her backers. As a result of the war in Sinai, Nasser was convinced that the Arab world must be mobilized to fight Israel on more than one front. He was of the opinion that it would be easier to wage war against Israel if the Syrian and Egyptian armies were under one command.[28] Unlike in the Sinai war, Nasser endeavoured to determine for himself the moment to start the next war.

Intensive preoccupation with the Palestinian problem led Nasser in 1959 to try to make the Palestinians a party to the conflict, to establish representative bodies for the Palestinians, and to present the problem as a national political issue, rather than as a humanitarian one concerning refugees. Thus, he endowed the Palestinian problem with a new political dimension.[29]

CONCLUSION

There was a basic error in the assessment of Britain and France and in that of Egypt. The West, and in particular Britain, did not grasp the significance to Egypt and to the Arab world of the decision to nationalize the Suez Canal. They could not understand that it was impossible for Nasser to rescind his decision, even though it might lead to war. They neither appreciated nor understood the new political processes taking place in the Arab world as a result of the revolution in Egypt and the emergence of Nasser. They still looked upon Nasser and the region from the perspective of an era when Britain had a decisive influence on Egyptian policy.

Nasser, on the other hand, judged the British position through Arab eyes, and not without a bit of wishful thinking.[30] He did not understand that he had very seriously wounded British Imperial pride, and also the power of France, just as they were in the process of decline. He did not realize the strength of Eden's hatred towards him for his attempt to undermine Britain's standing in the area. The gap between Eden and Nasser was historical. In this situation, armed confrontation was inevitable.

The political victory of Nasser was apparent to all the Arabs, and there is no better proof than the facts themselves: the evacuation of the British and French forces by 22 December, without achieving any tangible result, the resignation of Eden (and Guy Mollet), and the withdrawal of the IDF from Sinai and the Gaza Strip with conditions not affecting the sovereignty of Egypt. For Nasser, the crisis was a test of the legitimacy of his leadership and his decision to nationalize the Canal. He emerged from the crisis as the charismatic leader of Egypt and the Arab world. His concept of Arab nationalism, in all its aspects, became the cornerstone of Arab politics. The period after the Suez crisis was witness to the flowering of Arab nationalism, whose peak was the union between Egypt and Syria in February 1958.

For Nasser, the Sinai war was not a military defeat. He did not see it as a true expression of the balance of power between Egypt and Israel. He saw only the political victory. The glory of victory in Sinai and Port Said, which lasted throughout the Nasser period, declined during the rule of Sadat to such a point that in 1976 Heikal was complaining that the victory was not being celebrated on its 20th anniversary.[31] Sadat, on the other hand, saw the military defeat and not the political victory.[32] Later on, when he was president, he strongly criticized Nasser for not dismissing Amir from his position immediately after the war and not even after Amir's failure in Syria (the dissolution of the UAR, September 1961), when the decision was in Nasser's hands.[33] Nasser paid the price. There is no doubt that the retention of Amir and the high command officers, in particular the commanders of the three branches, in their positions was one of the reasons for the defeat of June 1967.

NOTES

1. Sayyid Mar'i, *Awraq Siyasiyya* (Political Papers), Vol.2 (Cairo, 1978), p.351.
2. Abu Iyad (Salah Khalaf), *Filastini Bila Hawiyya* (Palestinian Without Identity) (Kuweit, n.d.), p.52.
3. See Nasser, *Cairo Radio* (or *al-Ahram* issue of the following day), 26 July 1957, 5 Dec. 1957.
4. Nasser, *Cairo Radio*, 25 June 1956.
5. Nasser, *Cairo Radio*, 5 Dec. 1957.
6. Muhamed Hassanein Heikal, *The Cairo Documents* (New York, 1973), pp.88–9, *Cutting the Lion's Tail, Suez through Egyptian Eyes* (London, 1986), p.119.
7. Abd al-Latif al-Bughdadi, *Mudhakkirat* (Memoirs), Vol. 1 (Cairo, 1977), p.327.
8. Mar'i, *op. cit.*, p.355.
9. Nasser, *The Egyptian Gazette*, 6 Dec. 1956; See also Appendix; Amin Hewedy, *Hurub Abd al-Nasser* (Nasser's Wars) (Beirut, 1977), pp.90–1.
10. Bughdadi, *op. cit.*, pp.327–8.
11. Zakariya al-Adly Imam, in Ahmad Hamrush, *Qissat Thawrat 23 Yuliu* (the Story of the 23rd July Revolution) Vol. 4 (Beirut, June 1977), pp.163–5, also Vol. 2, pp.99–101.
12. Tharwat Okasha, *Mudhakkirati fi al-Siyasa wa al-Thaqafa* (Memoirs), vol.1 (Cairo, 1987), pp.209–15, also in Hamrush, *ibid*, Vol.4, pp.105–6, Vol.2, *loc. cit*; Muhammad al-Tawil, *Lu'bat al-Umam wa Abd al-Nasser* (The Game of the Nations and Abd al-Nasser) (Cairo, 1986), pp.285–6, 296–7.
13. See Heikal, *The Cairo Documents*, p.106, *Cutting the Lion's Tail*, pp.177–78,

Milaffat al-Suweis (the Suez Files) (Cairo, 1986), pp.530–3; Hewedy, *op. cit.*, p.92.
14. See Bughdadi, *op. cit.*, p.339; Nasser, *Cairo Radio*, 1 Nov. 1956, 26 July 1957, 23 Dec. 1957; Heikal, *The Cairo Documents*, p.109, *Milaffat al-Suweis*, pp.535–6. On the Operation Order given following the decision to retreat, see Hewedy, *op. cit.*, pp.94–6; Heikal, *Qissat al-Suweis* (The Story of Suez) (Beirut, 1974), pp.233–5.
15. Heikal, *loc. cit.*, pp.180–1; see also Tawil, *op. cit.*, pp.288–9.
16. Nasser, *Cairo Radio*, 26 July 1957.
17. For the wording of the conversation see Dan Hofstadter, ed., *Egypt and Nasser*, Vol.3, 1967–72, Facts on File (New York, 1973), p.35.
18. Mar'i, *op. cit.*, p.360.
19. Muhammad Kamal Abd al-Hamid, Brigadier General, *Ma'rakat Sinai wa Qanat al-Suweis* (The Sinai and the Suez Canal Campaign) (Cairo, n.d., 1959 ?), p.7.
20. 'Choker' (Researcher), 'Haksinim Hamisrim Shevuye Kadesh' (Hebrew) (The Egyptian Officers Captured in Kadesh), *Ma'rakhot*, Tel-Aviv, No. 155, Nov. 1963.
21. Bughdadi, *op. cit.*, pp.340, 352, 354.
22. *Ibid*, 344–5; for Heikal version on this discussion see *The Cairo Documents*, pp.110–14, *Cutting the Lion's Tail*, pp.179–80, *Milaffat al-Suweis*, p.535; Tawil, op. cit., pp.289–90.
23. Bughdadi, *op. cit.*, p.337.
24. Ibid. p.361; Hamrush, *op. cit.*, Vol. 2, pp.105–6.
25. Nasser, *Cairo Radio*, 7 Nov. 1956.
26. Nasser, *Cairo Radio*, 7 Nov. 1956, 17 Jan. 1957, 11 Feb. 1957, 26 July 1957, 5 Dec. 1957, 20 March 1958, 3 Sept. 1958, 23 Dec. 1958, 25 Dec. 1960, 5 March 1961.
27. See Nasser, *Cairo Radio*, 24,27 July 1957, 15 May 1958, 3 Sept. 1958, 23 Dec. 1958, 17 Feb. 1960, 25 Dec. 1960.
28. Fouad Matar, *Bisaraha An Abd al-Nasser, Hiwar Ma'a Muhammad Hassanein Heikal* (Frankly About Abd al-Nasser, a Dialogue With Muhammad Hassanein Heikal) (Beirut, Jan. 1975), p.126.
29. See Moshe Shemesh, *The Palestinian Entity 1959–1974; Arab Politics and the PLO* (London, 1988), pp.1–40.
30. On the Egyptian view of the diplomatic history of the Suez crisis see Mahmoud Fawzi, *Suez 1956; An Egyptian Perspective* (London, 1986).
31. Heikal, *al-Anwar* (Beirut), 10–13 Oct. 1976, *Qissat al-Suweis*, pp.7–11.
32. Anwar el-Sadat, *In Search of Identity* (London, 1978), p.158–60.
33. Musa Sabri, *al-Sadat: al-Haqiqa wa al-Ustura* (al Sadat: The Truth and the Legend) (Cairo, 1985), pp.245–7.

11

The Suez–Sinai Campaign: The Regional Dimension

Itamar Rabinovich*

As a war waged on two levels, by two declining colonial powers and by a Middle Eastern state, the Suez–Sinai campaign and its relationship to the regional politics of the Middle East should be examined in two contexts. The British–French campaign sought not only to unseat Nasser, but, by so doing, to restructure the political complexion of the Middle East. This raises a question as to what that complexion was in 1956 and in what ways it was altered by the campaign. Israel's aims were more limited and focused on its leaders' quest for a swift military victory over Egypt. The failure of Egypt's Arab allies to join the war facilitated their task. An examination of that failure affords significant insights into the interplay between the Arab–Israeli conflict and the system of inter-Arab relations.

ARAB REGIONAL POLITICS IN THE MID-1950s

The single most important development in Arab politics in the 1950s was the emergence of Nasser as Egypt's leader and as the centre of a millenarian movement.[1] It was a gradual development. Nasser was the leader of the Free Officers' movement and of the July 1952 revolution, but his supremacy had not been established before 1954. Even then he was not accepted by the Arab Left as a genuine revolutionary.[2] It was only in 1955 and 1956 that his successful challenges to the Western powers and his role on the international stage were turning him into an Arab hero. It would be erroneous to project the impact of Nasserism as a full-blown movement in, say,

* This paper was written during my stay at the Wilson Center as a Fellow in the International Securities Studies Program. I am grateful to the Center and the Program for their help and support.

1959 back into the mid-1950s, but some of its elements were already having their effect then.

This effect will now be examined with regard to three distinct but inter-related issues: inter-Arab relations, Western policies in the region and the Arab–Israeli Conflict.

The years 1945–1954 can best be defined as the dynastic phase in the evolution of inter-Arab relations.[3] The quest for Arab unity was translated through the formation of the Arab League into a mundane pursuit of political ends. Political competition was governed by the rivalry between the two Hashemite states (Iraq and Jordan) and the rival Egyptian–Saudi axis. The Palestine question and the future of Syria were the two main issues and Lebanon and Yemen the two peripheral actors.

The rise of Nasser and Nasserism ended this phase and transformed inter-Arab relations in a number of ways. Like his more conservative predecessors, Nasser wanted regional hegemony for Egypt, but he was better equipped to obtain it. For one thing, by establishing a stable and effective regime he could make use of the considerable resources of the Egyptian state and bring them to bear on the other, weaker, Arab states. His charisma and the introduction of novel techniques (primarily the use of the radio) projected his personality and leadership to other parts of the Arab world. As an idea, pan-Arab nationalism had taken hold in the aftermath of World War I but until the appearance of Nasser there had not been a leader who came to embody it in such a fashion.

In addition to his own charisma and to the effective mobilization of Egypt's resources, Nasser also placed Egypt more firmly in the Arab fold. King Farouk, Nahhas Pasha and Azzam Pasha had all sought preeminence for Egypt in the Arab world, but in their day Egypt's relationship to Arabism was ambivalent.[4] Nasser ended that ambivalence. Of the three circles he mentioned in *The Philosophy of the Revolution* as the national spheres for Egyptian influence (Arab, African and Islamic), he took the first most seriously. He also understood that in order to become the effective leader of the Arabs, Egypt had to be unquestionably Arab. He launched an effort to fully Arabize Egypt that culminated a few years later in the disappearance of the name Egypt from the official appellation of his state. This process had a considerable impact both on Egypt and on her Arab environment.[5]

Finally, Nasser served to turn revolutionary Arab nationalism into the dominant brand of Arab nationalism. In earlier decades revolutionary Arab nationalism, as distinct from its conservative brands, was in the main a matter of ideological writings or a message borne by small and ineffective political movements. This changed in the 1950s as a different generation was gaining political influence and as movements like the Ba'th were moving towards the centre of the political stage. The trend was accelerated by the gradual radicalization of Nasser and his regime through the first half of the 1950s. When they became the advocates and leaders of pan-Arab nationalism they preached a revolutionary version of that idea, quite different from the conservative Hashemite versions of pan-Arabism. Put together, Nasser's leadership, Egypt's mobilized power and full commitment to Arabism and the revolutionary dimension of its creed and policies completely transformed the nature of inter-Arab politics.

A series of errors by the Western powers contributed to this process. In a regional context the Cold War has often been conducted indirectly, by proxy. It is rather rare that one of the protagonists should affect the course of events by a bold direct intervention. More often it is through their local allies and proxies that the protagonists gain or lose ground. In the Middle East of the early 1950s the three Western powers, pursuing divergent aims, failed in their efforts to organize the Arab world in a pro-Western pact. By 1955 Britain had abandoned hope of including Egypt in any pro-Western structure. It therefore implemented the Baghdad Pact in which Iraq joined the pro-Western Muslim states of the Northern Tier.[6] The United States endorsed the Baghdad Pact without losing all hopes of maintaining a good relationship with Nasser's Egypt.[7]

It was the worst of all possible worlds. By turning Baghdad into the lynchpin of its Middle Eastern policy, the West was promoting Egypt's traditional Arab rival. Old and new elements were fused together. One familiar theme was the ancient rivalry between Egypt and Iraq, played out in the territory of Geographic Syria. Another was Saudi Arabia's support of Egypt against the spectre of a fortified Iraq. New were the ideology and the imagery. Nasser was depicted in this conflict as the symbol of a fresh Arab force, standing for Arab independence and autonomous power reinforced by social reform. Nuri al-Sa'id, his chief protagonist, was depicted as the epitome of an old order fighting a rearguard action against these aims and in league with the Western powers.[8]

Syria and Jordan, invited to join the Baghdad Pact in order to swing the regional balance, were the battleground and by 1956 Nasser was clearly winning. Syria was marching toward the 1958 union, with Nasser's civilian and military allies enhancing their

164

political power. In Jordan, young King Hussein was bending in an effort to save his throne. In 1956 he experimented with fairly free elections. The nationalists headed by Sulayman al-Nabulsi won and the King entrusted Nabulsi with the formation of a government.

By October 1956 Nasser had military pacts with Syria, Jordan and Saudi Arabia. On paper, at least, Egypt, Syria and Jordan had a joint military command headed by an Egyptian general. Iraq was isolated and on the defensive. Nasser felt that the assets he had acquired in the Arab world gave him greater power. Clearly when he calculated the risks involved in nationalizing the Suez Canal, he was encouraged by his ability to mobilize much of the Arab world in his support.

Closely related to these developments was the evolution of Egypt's conflict with Israel. It is still impossible to determine whether that conflict could have been solved or at least attenuated in the 1950s. Even when archives are opened, historians are likely to continue the debate, one school arguing that a compromise formula was feasible, the other holding that the collision between the leader of revolutionary pan-Arabism, championing the cause of Palestine and seeking regional hegemony, and the State of Israel was inevitable.[9]

In the event Egypt and Israel were caught in a vicious spiral which in turn became part of the larger regional picture. Nasser radicalized the Arab–Israeli conflict and was radicalized by it. His support of the fidaiyyun was anti-Jordanian as well as anti-Israeli and the Gaza Raid that Israel launched in the Israeli–Egyptian context acquired an additional dimension in the development of the Soviet–Egyptian security relationship.

Enmity to Israel became an important component of the revolutionary brand of Arab nationalism that Nasser's Egypt expounded. Solidarity with the Palestinian Arabs and resistance to Zionism were not new elements, but they were now integrated into a new ideological formulation and infused with a new potency. Arabism, according to that view, had three mutual enemies – Imperialism, Zionism and local Reaction. They were allied and mutually reinforcing. Nuri al-Sa'id was allied with the West and the West was allied with Israel and so Nuri al-Sa'id, too, was seen and depicted as an ally of Israel.

In the summer of 1956 as Arab–Israeli tensions grew and as he feared a European hostile reaction to the nationalization of the Suez Canal, Nasser's view of the external threat was telescoped further, though not to the point of actually anticipating the October col-

165

lusion. Nasser's own strategy was manifold. Arab opinion was mobilized so as to make the threat of disrupting the flow of oil credible and effective.[10] Military co-operation and co-ordination were enhanced both in order to bolster Egypt's posture and to increase its influence over its Arab allies.

The Israeli government, for one, was impressed by the apparent success of these preparations. When planning the Sinai Campaign, its chief Israeli architect, Moshe Dayan, assumed that Syria and Jordan would join the war on Egypt's side. He subsequently noted in his diary on 31 October 1956 that 'so far there is no sign of a Syrian or Jordanian attack. I must admit that I was wrong when I assumed that they will come to Egypt's aid. It's all for the better.'[11] The Israeli Chief of Staff's frame of mind makes the question 'why was the Arab world's reaction to the campaign so mild?' all the more intriguing.

ARAB ACTIONS AND INACTIONS

Part of the answer to the question derives from an obvious fact. The two superpowers, the U.S. more significantly so than the Soviet Union, denounced the campaign and the U.S. took it upon itself to undo its consequences. This defused much of the tension.

Two other aspects should be dealt with briefly. The Arab world's relative passivity became an issue with which their critics tried to denigrate both Arab nationalism and Abd al-Nasser. Nasser himself was sensitive to the criticism and made a deliberate effort to deflate the argument.[12] This secondary aspect will not be dealt with in any detail in this paper. Nor is it necessary to devote much space to the conduct of Nasser's Arab enemies. It can be surmised, and in some cases substantiated by evidence, that some of Nasser's Arab rivals were delighted by the prospect of his downfall and subsequently dismayed by his survival and political victory.[13] In an Arab world still governed by notions of unity and solidarity they had to go through the motions of expressing their identification and support.

The question that was posed above in general terms should be perused now in more specific ones: why did Syria and Jordan, Egypt's actual and formal military allies, respectively fail to join the battle in support of Egypt? The answer is that both, each in its own way and for its own reasons, offered to do so and both were restrained by Nasser.

In Syria it was the military who exerted pressure on the Egyptians to let them join the battle. Syria, as has been mentioned, was well on its way to the eventual union with Egypt. It was formally governed by a coalition government in which the Ba'th was an important partner. President Quwatli and Prime Minister Asali were seasoned and cautious politicians, but they did not fully control the government and in any event ultimate power resided in the military. Among the latter the unionists, independents and Ba'this were the strongest factions. Nasser and Amir were the true leaders of these officers and Mahmud Riad, Egypt's ambassador in Damascus, had an unusual influence over them. But this influence was used in this case rather in order to restrain them.[14]

In early November the pumping stations of the I.P.C. oil pipelines crossing Syrian territory to the Mediterranean were blown up. According to one version this was the action of volunteers who did not have to be told what their duty was.[15] But another version arguing that the pumping stations were blown up by ordinary units of the Syrian army was subsequently substantiated by Mahmud Riad who described in his memoirs how he and a group of officers headed by Syria's Director of Military Intelligence, Abd al-Hamid al-Sarraj, made the decision in the ambassador's office.[16]

Jordan's conduct was more complex. There is no disputing the fact that King Hussein offered his military aid to Nasser and ordered his Prime Minister to stage an attack on Israel. The version offered by the King's biographer is worth quoting in full:

> The moment Hussein heard of the British involvement, he telephoned President Nasser and told him that Jordan would attack Israel. His fury at Israel, Britain and France was in striking contrast to the caution of his new Prime Minister who was too new to power and too concerned with the consolidation of his internal position to regard a military adventure with any enthusiasm. Nabulsi told the author that Hussein ordered him to attack Israel, but he refused.

'The idea was ridiculous,' Nabulsi recalls. 'We were no match for the Israelis, particularly with the British and French involved on their side.'[17]

This was an intriguing turn of events: the controversial and beleaguered Hashemite monarch acting with reckless nationalist chivalry while his Arab nationalist Prime Minister plays the role of the responsible and cautious statesman resorting to the arguments and language of *raison d'état*. This version could presumably be accepted at face value. The King's conduct in June 1967 would, in that case, be a re-enactment of the same pattern but without the restraining influence of a nationalist Prime Minister.

But another version seems more credible. It is suggested by the speech Hussein delivered in April 1957 justifying his decision to fire Nabulsi. In his speech Hussein said that:

> During the violent attack on Egypt, I was determined from the first moment to enter the battle alongside our sister Egypt before the Franco-British ultimatum, but I encountered resistance by Mr. Nabulsi and some of his cabinet members, as well as the then Chief of Staff. They had sent to me the ambassador of one of the Great Powers to dissuade me. Had I encountered real determination among those ministers before the ultimatum and had we joined the battle at the outset we might have altered its shape and outcome ...[18]

It may very well be, then, that in November 1956 the King, though young and inexperienced, was more calculating and less carried away than one may have thought. If this interpretation is correct, he understood Nabulsi's predicament and took full advantage of it.

A question now remains as to why Nasser and his associates took such pains to restrain the Syrians and the Jordanians. Several explanations are offered by various sources. Nasser wanted to regain his bearings and clarify the new situation before engulfing the region in a larger war. He was worried that Jordanian and Syrian participation in the war would provide his attackers with new opportunities.[19] But perhaps the most important consideration developed later when he ordered his forces to withdraw from the Sinai. It would have been awkward and embarrassing if the Jordanian and Syrian armies had begun their operations in the aftermath of an Egyptian withdrawal.[20]

While Egypt had prepared the ground, well before November 1956, for the disruption of the flow of Iraqi oil to the Mediterranean and then encouraged the Syrian military's decision to destroy the pumping stations, it pursued an entirely different policy toward Saudi Arabia's oil which flowed through the Tapline to the same Mediterranean coastline. It is quite easy to account for the difference in policies. The I.P.C.'s pipeline concerned Britain and Iraq, Egypt's arch-rival in the Arab world. Tapline concerned the U.S. and Saudi Arabia.[21] The U.S. was busy salvaging Nasser and Saudi Arabia, which, despite growing unease, was still, for traditional dynastic considerations, his ally in inter-Arab affairs.[22] There is no positive evidence to confirm it but it can be reasonably assumed that Nasser invested efforts to ensure that the Tapline would not be hurt.

THE CONSEQUENCES

The failure of the Suez Campaign and Nasser's political victory contributed in the short run to reinforcement and acceleration of the very trends that Britain and France set out to arrest. Nasserism as a movement reached its full bloom in the late 1950s, Syria immersed itself in a union with Egypt, and the Iraqi monarchy was toppled by a military revolution that seemed to draw its inspiration from Nasser's revolution. The impact of Suez was apparent in these developments. Nasser emerged from the crisis bolder and more confident and other Arabs, too, thought that his forward march could not be stopped. It is impossible to measure the precise role that the Suez crisis played in the downfall of the Hashemite monarchy in Iraq, but it certainly contributed to the undermining of its position.

But there were other developments and consequences, too, as well as contradictory forces at work. Saudi Arabia's partnership and Jordan's rapprochement with Nasser's Egypt had been difficult and problematic before November 1956; they then became impossible in its aftermath.

The United States, in turn, came to view the efforts to maintain a good relationship with Nasser as futile and came out with the Eisenhower Doctrine. The Arab world became sharply divided into a revolutionary camp allied with the Soviet Union and a pro-Western conservative camp. This remained essentially the situation until the early 1970s.

Nasser's very success had other dialectical consequences. His Iraqi arch-enemies were defeated and replaced by a nationalist revolutionary regime. But the Egyptian–Iraqi rivalry did not end. It was soon manifested in a different and equally bitter form of rivalry between two kindred regimes. In Syria the culmination of the unionist dream led to disappointment and failure whose impact on the vision of Arab unity is still being felt.[23]

For Israel which had launched its campaign with a very narrow political objective, the political consequences were far-reaching. On the negative side of the ledger was the fact that its image, in the Arab world and in parts of the Third World, as a European extension into the Middle East was reinforced. But this was more than balanced by the consolidation of its position in the region. Its military performance impressed Nasser and also impressed Turkey, Iran and Ethiopia whose tacit co-operation enabled Israel in the late 1950s to pursue its orientation on the periphery, the strategy seeking to overcome Arab hostility through co-operation with the pro-Western powers in the region's external perimeter. Israel's role in that tacit alliance was also instrumental in the gradual phasing out of official Washington's view of Israel's place in the Middle East.[24]

In the Arab–Israeli conflict the Sinai campaign produced eleven years of relative calm. The security regime established in the Sinai had significant merits. But still more significant was Nasser's conclusion that he must not be drawn into another war with Israel before Egypt was ready for it. It is a curious and ironic fact that he still held this view in early May 1967 when forces beyond his control were pulling him toward another, still more disastrous, war with Israel.

NOTES

1. See Shimon Shamir's introductory essay in S. Shamir (ed.), *The Decline of Nasserism 1965–1970* (Tel Aviv, 1978, in Hebrew) and P.J. Vatikiotis, *Nasser and his Generation* (New York, 1978).
2. The initial scepticism displayed toward Nasser by the Ba'th and its gradual transformation is well documented in the pages of *Nidal al-Ba'th*, the series of volumes published by the party itself.
3. See P.J. Vatikiotis, 'Inter-Arab Relations' in idem., *Arab and Regional Politics in the Middle East* (London and N.Y. 1984), pp. 77–156.
4. See Elie Kedourie, 'Pan Arabism and British Policy' in his *The Chatham House Version* (London, 1970), pp. 231–6 and Israel Gershoni, *The Emergence of Pan Arabism in Egypt* (Tel Aviv, 1981).
5. See Y. Oron, 'The Nationalist Myth in Contemporary Egypt', *Hamizrah Hehadash* (in Hebrew), Vol. X, No. 3, 1960, pp. 153–77.
6. J. Campbell, *Defence of the Middle East* (N.Y., 1960), pp. 39 ff. and Roger Louis, *The British Empire in the Middle East, 1945–1951* (Oxford, 1951), Chapter III.
7. Steven L. Spiegel, *The Other Arab–Israeli Conflict* (Chicago and London, 1985), p.62.
8. Patrick Seale, *The Struggle for Syria* (Oxford, 1965) provides both an excellent analysis and a vivid depiction of these periods and issues.
9. See for instance, Avi Shlaim, 'Conflicting Approaches to Israel's Relations with the Arabs: Ben Gurion and Sharett 1953–1956', *Middle East Journal*, Spring 1983, pp. 180–201.
10. Shmuel Ya'ari, 'The Arab Oil Weapon and the International Oil Trade 1945–1970', Ph.D. dissertation, Tel Aviv University, 1975. Ya'ari's dissertation provides an excellent description of the ineffective efforts to use Arab oil as a political weapon prior to the 1970s.
11. Moshe Dayan, *Milestones* (Hebrew original version) (Jerusalem and Tel Aviv, 1976), p. 276. Dayan erroneously writes in the same passage that Egypt urged the other Arab states to open war against Israel.
12. In his public speeches during the crisis, he expressed gratitude to the other Arabs.

The material provided by his government for Kenneth Love, *Suez the Twice Fought War* (N.Y. and Toronto, 1969) reflects the same tendency. See in particular pp. 482–3, 514–15 and 532–33.

13. Thus, the Syrian politician Khalid al-Azm in his memoirs *The Memoirs of Khalid al-Azm* (three volumes, in Arabic, Beirut, 1972) describes Syrian parliament members who did not try to conceal their pleasure at Nasser's distress (p. 481). For Nuri al-Sa'id's outlook see W.J. Gallman, *Iraq under General Nuri* (Baltimore, 1964).

14. This is attested to by several sources but most authoritatively by Mahmud Riad himself in Mahmud Riad, *The Struggle for Peace in the Middle East* (London, 1981), pp. 9–10.

15. P. Seale, pp.258–62. For a detailed account of the same episode, see Mohammed H. Heikal, *Cutting the Lion's Tail; Suez through Egyptian Eyes* (London, 1986), pp. 187–91.

16. Gordon Torrey, Syrian Politics and the Military (Columbus, Ohio, 1964), pp.323–325 and Riad, ibid. See also Hazza' al-Majali, *Mudhakkirati* (Jerusalem, 1970), p. 205 and Charles Johnston, *The Brink of Jordan* (London, 1972), p.21.

17. Peter Snow, *Hussein* (N.Y., 1972), p.100.

18. See the text of the King's speech in *Filastin*, April 25, 1957.

19. Love, pp. 482–483; Riad, ibid.

20. Seale, p.262; Heikal, ibid., describes the difficulty the Egyptians had in explaining the blowing up of oil stations in Syria to their American interlocutor, Kermit Roosevelt.

21. Ya'ari, passim. By September 1956 several observers had noticed the change in Saudi–Egyptian relations, see Humphrey Trevelyan, *The Middle East in Revolution* (London, 1970), p. 101 and several documents released by the Israeli Foreign Office. Israel's State Archive, File 2450/3 and 2593/18.

22. Nadav Safran, *Saudi Arabia, The Ceaseless Quest for Security* (Cambridge, Mass., and London, 1985), pp. 77–81.

23. See Malcolm H. Kerr, *The Arab Cold War* (London, 1971).

24. I. Rabinovich and J. Reinharz, *Israel in the Middle East* (N.Y. and Oxford,1986), pp. 165 ff.

12

The Suez War in Arabic Literature

Sasson Somekh

Literary scholarship has long ceased treating literature as a mirror of reality. A literary portrayal of events, individuals and social environments is, at best, partial and subjective. Literature, however, often provides a powerful indication of the way in which a given culture views itself and creates the myths through which reality is perceived by its members. Contemporary Arabic literature is no exception, and it is from this premise that I shall discuss a number of literary works written by Egyptian authors in conjunction with the Suez war.

At the outset, however, it would be useful to outline briefly some major trends in Arabic literature in the years under consideration, namely the late 1950s. It would be safe to say that the Suez war not only heralded a new era in Arab politics, one of intense nationalism and growing radicalization, but also marked a new period in Arabic literature: one of engagement and greater identification with national causes.[1] In previous decades authors in Egypt, Lebanon, Iraq and other Arabic-speaking regions had been gradually shedding the age-hallowed declamatory poetry and didactic prose in favour of a more individualized mode in verse and a realistic style in prose fiction and drama. Western genres and styles were increasingly overshadowing the classical Arabic literary tradition. The Suez war and the subsequent tide of Nasserism effected a radical change in the course of literature in the 1950s and 1960s. Admittedly, the flow of Western literary models into Arabic literature did not subside; but the literature produced in these decades exhibits a marked shift from individual and social issues to commitment to militant nationalism. Many of the new authors were infinitely more vociferous than their predecessors. Poetry, which had been developing softer and more intimate tones as compared with classical Arabic qasidas, now reverted to the old, familiar bombastic cadence, this time under the guise of a modernized language and a rejuvenated prosodic scheme. Let me quote, in translation, the opening lines of a well-known poem written by Salah Abd al-Sabur (1931–1981), a young Egyptian who in subsequent years emerged as the most prominent poet of the Suez generation. The poem is entitled 'I Shall Kill You', and is addressed to the aggressors in the Suez war:

> I shall kill you
> Before you kill me I shall kill you
> Before you plunge into my blood
> I shall plunge into yours
> Nothing but arms is between us
> Let arms, then, adjudge between us.
> The resounding hoofs of our forefathers' horses
> Reverberate in the memory of the ages
> And their light radiates on History's forehead.[2]

These lines, blunt and declamatory as they are, amply reflect the major themes that pervade the myriad *qasidas* and *divans* produced by Egyptian poets in the wake of the Suez war: the utter shock at the brutality of the aggressors; the militant, defiant Egyptian stance; the invocation of the valiant forefathers, Arab and Egyptian alike. At times a mythical dimension is present in these poems: the eternal Egyptian, the guileless but heroic *fellah* of the Nile valley, once again defeating the modern-day Hyksos and driving them away from the sacred land.[3]

Poetry can conceivably fulfil its mission by sheer expression of emotions and attitudes. Prose, on the other hand, and especially realistic prose-fiction and drama, presents its practitioner with a different set of artistic demands. The realistic novelist and dramatist are required to tell a plausible story based on the interaction between characters, as well as between them and their environment. Whether these 'realistic' characters present an accurate picture of a society at a given moment is open to question. But the selection of characters, events and settings is definitely an indication of the aspects of reality to which literature (or author) is attentive, and very often it reveals the basic perceptions of a society vis-à-vis a particular event. These generalizations are true of all literatures: but they are doubly applicable to authors operating within an atmosphere of intense ideological and nationalistic fervour, and, indeed, such was the atmosphere in Egypt during the late 1950s and most of the 1960s. As we shall see, not all Egyptian authors were willing to abide by the guidelines – overt or implied – of the Nasserite regime. In fact, many Egyptian authors of distinction resisted the call to put their talents 'in the service of the revolution'. But we will also discover that certain basic assumptions regarding the Suez war persist even in the works of such writers as may be aptly described as nonconformists.

In the following I shall discuss a play and three novels by four different Egyptian authors. It is worth noting that the political and cultural leanings of these authors represent all or most of the different shades of the Egyptian political spectrum. The first author, Yusuf Idris (b.1927), was at the time a Marxist who occasionally clashed with and suffered from the Nasserite regime. The second, Abd al-Hamid al-Sahhar (1913–1974), was a novelist with a marked Islamic bent (among other things, al-Sahhar co-operated with Sayyid Qutb, the well-known author and leader of the Muslim Brothers, in writing a series of didactic novels on the history of Islam). The third, Latifa al-Zayyat (b.192?), was (as evidenced by the novel in question) in near-total harmony with the 'revolution'. Finally, Naguib Mahfuz (b.1911), the foremost novelist of modern Egypt, represents the pre-revolutionary school of Egyptian liberalism and secularism.

Yusuf Idris' play *The Critical Moment (Al-Lahza al-Harija)*, written shortly after the Suez events, was first published in 1958.[4] The plot is set in a 'front-line city', presumably Port Said, during the war and shortly before it. The protagonist is Sa'd, a young engineering student and an ardent patriot. He is striving to assert the values of his generation, which are sharply in contrast to those of the old middle class represented by his father. Sa'd is certain that war is imminent, and along with his friends he engages in para-military training. His father is averse to Sa'd's 'war games' because he is unaware of the malicious intentions of the Western powers. When the war finally breaks out, the father locks Sa'd in a room lest he be exposed to danger. It transpires that Sa'd could probably break out of his confinement if he wanted to, but at the critical moment he flinches. Before long, however, danger bursts into the house, personified by a group of British soldiers searching for guerrillas and arms. A confused soldier by the name of George kills the father while the latter is praying, because he misinterprets his ritual prostrations. Consequently, George goes mad, mistaking Sa'd's young sister for his daughter Shirley, whom he left behind in Southampton. Finally Sa'd emerges from his room and kills George. He then dashes out to the battlefield, stouthearted and vengeful, intent on dipping his hands in the aggressors' blood and

174

accompanied by his mother's blessings. But before leaving the house he addresses his father's dead body with the following question: 'Dear, dear father! Was it necessary for you to die so that I can rid myself of fear?' (p.140).

The didactic message of Idris' play is crystal clear. Those who were naive or unaware of the designs of the imperialist powers were not immune to the lethal effects of the tripartite aggression; those who were hesitant or frightened at the outset turned into potential heroes by dint of the war. But it is significant that not only the Egyptians are viewed as victims. George, the British soldier, also belongs to this category. He was brought from his distant country to fight an unjust war, and paid dearly for it.

The second work to be discussed here is a bulky novel entitled *White Plains (Al-Suhul al-Bid)* written by Abd al Hamid al-Sahhar and published in 1965, nine years after the events which it relates. This is a 'panoramic' novel whose plot takes place during the Suez crisis. It portrays the life and struggle of a group of residents of the Arab quarter of Port Said, as well as the fates of a few 'outsiders', mostly British. In al-Sahhar's novel we find a detailed account of the events that led to the war, the Israeli invasion of Sinai, the Anglo-French attack, the heroic resistance of the people of Port Said, and the final victory of Egypt. There is extensive reportage of several crucial battles in Sinai and the Canal zone, and the author duly acknowledges his personal indebtedness to no less an authority than Marshal Abd al-Hakim Amir, with whom he apparently consulted on military points. Admittedly, the author and his reader are not unaware of the role of international pressures in precipitating the Anglo-French withdrawal. The names of Dulles and Bulganin are very much in evidence in the text of the novel, as are the names of lesser characters in the Suez drama, including Gaitskell and other Labour MPs. But the novel also makes it clear that none of these would have lent a helping hand had it not been for the Egyptian soldiers and civilians who thwarted the aggressors' blueprint by delaying the Israeli advance in Sinai, and then fighting heroically against the British and French in Port Said.

Among the scores of characters that make their appearance in al-Sahhar's novel, I would like to single out four:

* Abdu, a young Port Saidian workman who is employed at the salt plant in Port Fouad. He hates wars and violence and dreams of a life of peace and quiet; but the aggressors cause the death of his wife

175

and infant son. Subsequently, he turns into a dauntless fighter, a true hero of Egypt.

* Sheikh Hasan, another young worker at the Port Fouad plant. He is a devout Muslim and a believer in Islamic activism. He views the current struggle of the Arabs against Western incursions as a *jihad*. Similarly, he sees a clear analogy between the godless acts of the State of Israel and those of the Jewish tribe of Qurayza in the days of Muhammad. To underline this analogy, the author opens his novel with a prologue in which he points out the similarity in the pattern of perfidy between the Jews of Muhammad's time and those of today.

* Janet, a British woman who is married to an Egyptian engineer and who lives in Port Said. She whole-heartedly identifies with the Egyptian and Arab causes and discovers that Eden is 'the greatest criminal of our century'. She meets her death during an air-raid (British planes!) while trying to rescue an Egyptian child.

* Rasim, a Palestinian refugee who is fighting with the Egyptians in Sinai. Having witnessed the killing of many members of his family in Dir Yasin, his native village, he vows to avenge himself and his nation by hurling the despicable Zionists into the sea and ridding the holy land of their filth.

The novel, especially its first half, is studded with rabidly anti-semitic statements, coming as a rule from the mouth of Rasim, the Palestinian, or of Hasan, the Muslim fundamentalist. The preoccupation with Israel and the Jews in *White Plains* is truly obsessive. This can be ascribed first and foremost to the author's personal inclination. But there is more to it than that. It is to be remembered that the novel was published in 1965, at the peak of the Nasserite era, when violent anti-Israeli propaganda had become an essential ingredient in the Nasserist creed. Throughout al-Sahhar's novel, the Israelis are depicted not only as treacherous and deceitful, but also as weak and cowardly.[5] The Israeli army in Sinai was totally incompetent and, in fact, it lost all the battles in which it engaged. The hordes of Jewish soldiers were repeatedly defeated by Egyptian garrisons which were numerically far inferior, just as the infidel armies were defeated by the much smaller band of the followers of the prophet of Islam.[6] The myth about Jewish feebleness on the battlefield, which is so well reflected in our novel, was, two years after its publication, probably one of the sources of Nasser's miscalculation on the eve of the Six Day War.

In the two works I have discussed so far, the Suez crisis serves as the background against which the whole plot unfolds. Two other novels will be of interest to us in the context of our topic, although the 1956 events occupy only a minor portion of their entire texts. But as we shall presently see, these events play a decisive role in transforming the protagonists of both novels.

Latifa al-Zayyat's novel *The Open Door (Al-Bab al-Maftuh,* 1960)[7] is in a way a feminist *Bildungsroman* whose protagonist is Layla, a sensitive young Cairene woman (again of a middle-class background) who finds the family atmosphere and customs stifling. Equally unsavoury are the young men with whom she is allowed to associate by her conservative family. At one point she agrees to get engaged to one of her university professors, but he too proves to be an old fashioned reactionary. Finally, the Suez crisis provides her with an opportunity not only to express her patriotic sentiments, but also to declare her rebellion against her oppressive society: in September 1956 she goes to Port Said, purportedly to take up a teaching position. When hostilities break out in the Canal Zone, Layla refuses to be evacuated and stays on as a hospital auxiliary. She witnesses the barbaric Anglo-French air raids, as well as the courage and resourcefulness of the defenders of Port Said. Among the fighters she finds Hussein, an acquaintance of old, whose love she had turned down in the past. Her final rebellion takes shape when the war is over. She then casts away her engagement ring, and, hand in hand with Hussein, she jubilantly observes the demolition of the statue of Ferdinand de Lesseps. Layla is finally a liberated woman, a proud daughter of a liberated nation.

The last text is *Autumn Quail (Al-Summan wa al-Kharif)*, a novel by Naguib Mahfuz, which was published in 1962.[8] This is the story of the 1952 revolution and its impact on a group of Wafd activists whose careers were frustrated in the wake of the Free Officers' revolution. Its plot spans the years 1952–1958, and its main protagonist is Isa al-Dabbagh, a promising Wafdist whom the 1952 events take by surprise, leaving him jobless and alienated. He feels that the revolution has shattered his life and ambition. Like many other prominent Wafdists, he is jealous of the new regime which is, in effect, implementing those ideals for which the Wafd party stood, but which it never dared implement. When the British troops finally evacuate the Canal zone, and when the Canal is nationalized, Isa feels at once elated and bitter. However, when Egypt is attacked in October 1956, he comes out of his shell for a while and discovers that 'the barrier which stood between him and the revolution was dissolving at a rate which he would never have thought possible before'.[9] Yet no sooner does danger pass than he returns to his former posture of alienation.

In Mahfuz's novel we find no description of battles and fighters – Egyptian or otherwise. The relevant chapters take place not in Port Said, as in the aforementioned works, but in the relatively safe capital. Only distant echoes of the actual fighting are recorded:

> The Cairo sky was criss-crossed with planes day and night. The incredible thing was that daily life in houses, offices, shops and markets carried on as usual, even though planes were screaming incessantly overhead and explosions kept going off. People kept thinking that the bombs were not falling indiscriminately, but there were many rumors of casualties. They carried on as usual, but death was looking on them from a nearby window; its harbingers flew into their ears and it intruded into their innermost thoughts. The city was turned into an army camp; convoys of armored vehicles and trucks moved along the streets, and normal life was drowned in a sea of thoughts and misgivings.[10]

There are no heroes or martyrs in *Autumn Quail* as there are in other war novels; nor does its author engage in enumerating the atrocities committed by the aggressors. In fact, Mahfuz's special brand of humour does not fail him even here. Consider the following scene, taking place shortly after the Israeli attack in Sinai, in which Isa and his unsophisticated wife, Qadriyya, discuss the news:

> 'War and raids again?!' asks Qadriyya scornfully.
> Isa treated the whole thing as a joke and wanted to tease her and calm his nerves.
> 'You're very concerned about getting food ready,' he said. 'Tell me, how would the world be if everyone behaved like you?'
> 'Wars would stop!' she replied simply. In spite of his anxiety he managed to laugh.
> 'Qadriyya, you're not worried about public affairs,' he said, feeling the urge to make a joke. 'I mean things involving the people and our country.'
> 'It's enough for me to look after you and your home.'
> 'Don't you love Egypt?'
> 'Of course!'
> 'Don't you want our army to win?'
> 'Of course. Then we'll have some peace again.'

'But don't you even want to think about it?'
'I've got enough to worry about.'
'Tell me how would you feel if the Jews intended to take over your mother's property?'
'What a terrible thought,' she replied with a laugh. 'What has my family ever done to them?'
He found it all amusing, and it helped relieve his tense feelings.[11]

It is possible that the emotional experience which Isa underwent during the Suez war was instrumental in the change of heart that took place in him some time later, as we discover in the final chapters of the novel. But such causation is a matter of literary interpretation rather than a fact which the novel expressly indicates. Whatever the case may be, *Autumn Quail* is not a propaganda novel or *roman à thèse*. It is significant that, unlike our other authors, Mahfuz situates the events of October–November 1956 in Cairo rather than the Suez zone. It is also interesting to discover in his novel some disgruntled characters who deep in their hearts sided with the foreign powers, even with Israel, in the hope that their incursion would bring down Nasser and his regime. Nevertheless, Mahfuz is at one with the other Egyptian writers in portraying the Suez war as a moment of awakening (short-lived though it was) for his protagonist.

NOTES

1. Cf. M.M. Badawi, *Modern Arabic Literature and the West* (London, 1985), pp.1–25 (chapter entitled 'Commitment in Contemporary Arabic Literature', first published in *The Journal of World History*, 1972); see also: S. Ballas, *La littérature Arabe et le conflit au proche-orient 1948–1973* (Paris, 1980), p.8.
2. Salah Abd al-Sabur's play *Al-Nas fi Biladi*, second edition (Cairo, n.d.), p.143.
3. E.g. Naguib Surur's play *Ah Ya Lel Ya Qamar* (Cairo 1968).
4. In Yusuf Idris' volume of plays *Nahwa Masrah Arabi* (Beirut, 1974), pp.98–170.
5. Abd al-Hamid al-Sahhar, *Al-Suhul al-Bid* (Cairo, 1965), pp.347 and *passim*.
6. Ibid., p.243 (Sheikh Hasan referring to the Battle of Badr).
7. Latifa al-Zayyat, *Al-Bab al-Maftuh* (Cairo, 1960).
8. Naguib Mahfuz, *Al-Summan wa al-Kharif* (Cairo, 1962). The quotations in this article are based (with some alterations) on the English translation of this novel by Professor Roger Allen (Naguib Mahfouz, *Autumn Quail*, Cairo; 1985). On this novel see also: S. Somekh, *The Changing Rhythm: A Study of Najib Mahfuz's Novels* (Leiden, 1973), esp. Ch.6.
9. *Al-Summan wa al-Kharif*, p.155; Allen's trans., p.114.
10. Al-Summan, p.154; Allen's trans., p.113.
11. Al-Summan, pp.144–5; Allen's trans., pp.107–8.

13

The Sinai Campaign as a 'War of No Alternative': Ben-Gurion's View of the Israel–Egyptian Conflict

Selwyn Ilan Troen

All wars have both public and secret aspects and there is usually at least some debate over their justification. Controversy has persisted over the Suez–Sinai conflict since it was a war initiated by a surprise attack that was a product of 'collusion'. Certainly British and French leaders have been subjected to continuing criticism over both the wisdom and justification of their actions and the failure to carry them out to successful conclusion. Ben-Gurion was undoubtedly the central figure responsible for shaping Israeli policy, and any analysis of Israel's role in the conflict must focus on his motivations, decisions and behaviour.[1]

On the third anniversary of the Sinai Campaign in 1959, Prime Minister and Minister of Defence David Ben-Gurion began his address on the war at a conference of army officers by declaring that 'many years will pass, perhaps several tens of years, until all its history is written. I will not be among those who will write the whole story, even though it is known to me, more or less, or perhaps because it is known to me.'[2] With the elapse of the thirty years required for disclosure of public papers, he can finally speak for himself through his diary and explain why he decided for war and how he carried out his designs.[3]

Since Ben-Gurion was the most powerful figure in Israeli society during its formative years and had great influence on the decisions that brought about the Sinai as well as the Suez campaigns, his testimony is important for understanding Israeli behaviour during this period as well as the nature of the British–French–Israeli collaboration. As a conscientious reporter who often noted in detail what others told him and what he learned, he maintained in his private diary a singular running account of important information that crossed his desk as well as his mind. These privately-recorded notes are invaluable since in both these operations crucial decisions were taken by only a few leaders none of whom provided us with similar documentation. This was particularly true in the case of the Israeli role in the Suez Crisis where there was an identity between the Israeli position and that of Ben-Gurion.[4]

Ben-Gurion's public and private records indicate that he never doubted the total justification for leading Israel into conflict with Egypt. His diary reveals that he expected war and systematically prepared his country for it. During the year before the war[5] Ben-Gurion repeatedly articulated his country's two major grievances against Egypt. The first was the long-standing complaint that by closing the Suez Canal and blockading the Straits of Tiran, Egypt interfered with Israeli shipping. However, aside from protests to the United Nations and appeals to international law, Israel never retaliated militarily. A second grievance was Egypt's more recent policy of sending fidaiyyun across Israel's borders. Ben-Gurion did not react to these incidents with a call for all-out war but favoured a policy of armed reprisals. Thus, although there was frustration and a continuing search for an effective response to Egypt's provocations, there is no indication that Ben-Gurion intended to go to war over these grievances.

There is considerable evidence that it was the arms deal between Czechoslovakia and Egypt, which Nasser revealed in September 1955, that caused a fundamental change in his thinking about the nature and scope of the dangers from Egypt and convinced Ben-Gurion to go to war. He concluded that this agreement would directly threaten vital Israeli security interests through the introduction of large quantities of modern weapons and the projection into the region of Soviet power, a force he deemed dangerous and hostile to Israel. It was especially these new circumstances that would require taking the field against the Egyptians. Ben-Gurion defined his task as ensuring that the coming conflict would be conducted under conditions that would be most favourable to Israel.[6]

The record of how he set about accomplishing this task is preserved in his diary. In the course of preparing for war, he systematically presented Israel's grievances before the court of world opinion and brought before his countrymen the justifications for taking up arms. Simultaneously, behind the scenes, he recorded in his diary the frantic search for the arms with which to defend Israel against the new Egyptian arms. Since through his public statements

181

he was attempting to win the approval of public opinion at home and abroad, in these he emphasized legal arguments concerning the freedom of the seas and the protection of citizens and property from terrorist attack. However, in his diary he recorded the practical steps he was taking to enable Israel to mount a pre-emptive strike. Thus, the record from the diary shows that while he publicly expressed alarm over Egypt's actions, he was carefully laying the political and military foundations for a preventive war.

Nevertheless, the war that Israel ultimately fought was not the one he anticipated. He assumed that Israel would fight alone and never imagined a conflict against Egypt with Great Britain and France as Israel's allies. The joining of Israel's campaign in Sinai with the British and French invasion of Egypt was an unanticipated consequence of Nasser's success in effecting the nationalization of the Suez Canal during the summer of 1956. For Ben-Gurion, then, this unexpected alliance influenced the timing and the character of the conflict with Egypt, but did not determine its occurrence.

POLITICAL PREPARATIONS

During the course of 1955, Ben-Gurion secured the internal political reorganization of the Government as a necessary precondition for countering the Egyptian challenge. From the beginning of the year, tensions over policy had been exacerbated by debates over reprisals to terrorist attacks. In early April, 1955 Ben-Gurion had found himself in the unaccustomed position of unsuccessfully arguing over defence policy in a Government headed by someone else. Lacking faith that his chosen successor, Moshe Sharett, would deal effectively with the threat created by the Czech arms deal, Ben-Gurion engineered his own return to power at the expense of Sharett's political demise. For this reason it is appropriate that he begins his official history of the Sinai Campaign with his address to the Knesset on 2 November, 1955. On that occasion he presented his new Government as the incoming Prime Minister, thanked Sharett for his service as Prime Minister in the previous Government, and, leaving Sharett to head the Foreign Ministry, Ben-Gurion retained for himself the additional post of Defence Minister. With these steps Ben-Gurion had again taken firm control over the reins of power.[7]

Ben-Gurion's return to the pre-eminent position in the Government caused considerable consternation among those who had believed that 'the old man', as he was then generally called, had appropriately relinquished responsibilities to younger colleagues.

182

In 1953, at age 67, Ben-Gurion had proclaimed his intention to retire and settle in the desert kibbutz at Sede Boqer. However, in February 1955 he returned to the Government as Minister of Defence before assuming complete control later that year. Significantly, problems with Egypt were major factors in his decision to do so. He returned to the Defence Ministry because he believed that his personal involvement was required for resolving an ill-advised and ill-fated security scandal involving Israeli agents in Cairo, an incident later known as the Lavon Affair, and because of policy disputes regarding the use of force against Egyptian-sponsored fidaiyyun.[8]

In a review of the war period which he confided to his diary on 14 December, 1956 Ben-Gurion explained that Sharett had to be shunted aside in view of the challenges and responsibilities facing the Israeli leadership during the year before the war.

> The correct setting of priorities among the many needs that abound and contradict one another is the beginning of political wisdom, at least in Israel. Our major needs are: security, economic independence, absorption of immigration. The abstract ideal is the fulfillment of these needs completely at all times, but this in practice is impossible since it is for us to know what has priority. Until the Suez Campaign, – after Egypt armed itself with the goal of destroying us – security stood as our major concern. Moshe [Sharett] did not understand that our foreign policy must serve our security needs. The change in the Foreign Ministry facilitated the obtaining of arms, because we were freed from the official, departmentalized approach that was so deeply ingrained in Moshe. Our arming ourselves and unorthodox connections with France made the Sinai Campaign possible. In this campaign we destroyed Nasser's military power and prevented the rest of the Arab nations from conniving against us.[9]

MILITARY PREPARATIONS

Ben-Gurion also linked Sharett's final expulsion from the Government to his own efforts to acquire arms. He had been concerned about a war for a long time. There was never in fact a real peace. Israel had to contend with problems of rights of passage in the Suez Canal and the Red Sea; the incursions of fidaiyyun; the concentrations of enemy troops in such sensitive places as Nitzana and Gaza as well as the usual frontier problems of two hostile nations. This situation might have continued except for the introduction of Czech arms in late 1955. Ben-Gurion's analysis in both public pronouncements and the diary was that the Czech deal had radically upset regional stability. It continually weakened Israel's position relative to Egypt's and it introduced the unsettling influence of Soviet power and ambitions. Hence, for Ben-Gurion, from the autumn of 1955 the question was not *would* there be a war with Egypt, but *when*. He considered the most pressing problem was how to redress the growing unfavourable balance in weaponry.

Ben-Gurion connected in his diary Sharett's resignation as Foreign Minister in June 1956 with Israel's contracting with France for the receipt of an unprecedented quantity of French aircraft – 72 Mystères – many tanks and other armed vehicles as well as large amounts of ammunition and spare parts. Ben-Gurion viewed Sharett, who had often urged military restraint and favoured negotiation, as a hindrance to vigorous retaliatory measures and preparations for a preemptive strike. In Ben-Gurion's evaluation, Sharett had become an impediment in the conduct of the security policy required by Israel. It was therefore also by design that in the crucial period just before and during the Sinai Campaign, Sharett was not only out of the Government but out of the way in the Far East on a mission Ben-Gurion had sponsored.[10]

Since significant shipments began arriving in Egypt in November 1955 and the best estimate within Israeli intelligence was that 8 months were required to absorb the weapons early projections had set the likely outbreak of war for the summer of 1956. In mid-January 1956, Ben-Gurion claimed in closed forums: 'I assume that they will attack at the beginning of the summer … . The logic of the situation is that they are liable to attack when they feel that they are likely to win.'[11]

There were many foreshadowings of conflict. There were aerial battles, border incidents, and men were mobilized. Although the dominant feeling among the Israeli military leadership was that Israel would win, the price was escalating in direct relationship to the absorption of new weapons within the Egyptian arsenal. Hence, the feeling was also growing that something must be done to minimize the costs and maximize Israel's advantages. It was in this context that Ben-Gurion was willing to consider a preventive war.

This step was but an extension of his approval of reprisals. In a debate at a meeting of the Knesset's Security and Foreign Affairs Committee in September 1956, he argued that punishment saves lives since it deters potential assassins: 'Retaliation does not stop the attacks entirely – but it does put many off – as every punishment does. Who knows how many lives have been saved thanks to these 'retaliatory' acts?' Similarly, if one was certain that one was about to be attacked, then one could initiate punishment in order to spare lives in future assaults. At the same meeting, he restated his conviction that 'There is no knowing where the Suez crisis may lead. There is no doubt that Nasser intends to attack Israel at the first opportunity ...'[12] The expectation of an Egyptian attack was also expressed in his diary shortly after nationalization of the Canal: 'if Nasser wins in the affair over the canal, and this is very possible, because the English will apparently do nothing against him, and without force Nasser will not submit. The increase in Nasser's prestige must bring about his desire to destroy Israel, not through a direct attack, but at first with a 'peace offensive' and an attempt to reduce territories, especially in the Negev, and when we refuse – he will attack us.'[13] It is not surprising, then, that at the same time as reprisal plans are drawn so, too, are plans for a defensive or a preventive war.[14]

Expectations of Egypt's hostile intentions had long influenced Ben-Gurion and his military advisers on how to establish Israel's military objectives and the means for attaining them. During the autumn of 1955, for example, a special unit was set up to attack Sharm el-Sheikh in the event of war in order to secure passage in the Straits of Tiran. There were far-ranging discussions of how to modulate the system of reprisals with one school – led by Chief of Staff Moshe Dayan – counselling for drawing the Egyptians into a war by escalating counter-attacks before they had a chance to absorb all their weapons. There were at the same time extensive civil defence preparations. There was a frantic search for money for funding arms purchases, including defence loans to which a large proportion of the population subscribed. Finally, there was an intensive effort to find a source of arms to counterbalance the weapons supplied by the Soviet bloc.[15]

Ben-Gurion devoted much attention to obtaining arms. He painstakingly noted in his diary the variety and amount of weapons Israel acquired, their costs, and the struggle to find adequate funds to pay for them. He was clearly very much involved in all aspects of this effort. The diary also reveals that he personally witnessed and recorded in great detail the arrival of nearly every ship and plane. The excitement of these nocturnal, secret landings on the coast of Israel, in Haifa harbour or at an airfield permeate his writings. Israel would soon be able to take the initiative in protecting its interests. If the war did not break out in the beginning of the summer of 1956 as initially expected, then it would come later, and so much the greater would be the Egyptians' surprise at the force of Israeli arms.

ALLIANCE WITH FRANCE AND GREAT BRITAIN

Until shortly after the nationalization of the Suez Canal Company, there had been no indication that any conflict in the region would involve outside forces. On 3 August, Ben-Gurion learned from Shimon Peres, then Director-General of the Defence Ministry, that the French were interested in strengthening Israel as quickly as possible. Peres reported that the French considered Nasser's expropriation of the canal as a calamity no less significant than a defeat in Algeria. Peres had also learned that the French and the British had agreed to take military action against Egypt. While he reported that the British were adamant about excluding Israel from a joint attack against Egypt so as to avoid bringing other Arab states to the defence of Nasser, there had been hints that the French would welcome some form of Israeli cooperation. In fact, during August, Ben-Gurion agreed to limited assistance to the French, primarily in the area of supplying intelligence including aerial photographs – a fitting response considering that the French were helping to provide Israel with an up-to-date air force.[16]

Through the end of September 1956, or but one month before the war, there is still no mention of an alliance or even any reference to coordinated military action. Ben-Gurion still saw the coming conflict as one in which Israel would fight alone, though he was interested in being helpful to those who similarly identified Nasser as an enemy. That he did not predict an alliance is apparent from his constant speculation all during August and through the end of September about possible actions France and Great Britain might take. For example, on 10 September, he wrote: '... it is still hard to accept that two governments of European powers would make laughing stocks of themselves by threatening to dispatch armies, navies and air-forces – and would then submit to the Egyptian dictator.' Again, two days later: ' I still find it hard to believe that Eden's government will act forcibly against the Egyptian tyrant. At least it is clear that up to now it does not want Israeli aid.' On 13 September, in his record of the conversation with the Italian ambassador, he writes: 'We do not rely on Eden. Eden did not take care of our rights even when he controlled the canal and there was a favourable decision of the Security Council.'

Nevertheless, what had been a relatively simple and direct conflict between Israel and Egypt had given way to a far more complex situation in which the imponderables increased in geometric proportion to the number of actors. On 25 September, he went with Dayan to meet Peres who had returned from Paris with new information. It was at this moment of tension, uncertainties and pressures that Ben-Gurion had to respond to a major change in the situation. Even before the meeting, Ben-Gurion notes in his diary: 'What he [Peres] may have to say could be fateful.' From Peres Ben-Gurion learned that the French, who claimed that they had lost patience with the British, were interested in launching a coordinated attack with the Israelis. The date proposed for attack was a mere three weeks away – as early as 15 October. It is germane to note here that Ben-Gurion expected that Israel would not fully integrate the new tanks in its armoured corps for many more months. Joint action with the French would necessarily mean putting the original timetable aside. A time for decision was at hand.

Prior to this, there had been many voices calling for Israeli action. Opposition party leaders Menachem Begin and Jacob Meridor urged an immediate attack on Egypt. Others argued for intervention in Jordan while the Egyptians and everyone else were so occupied with the crisis over Suez. On the other hand, the Baghdad Pact nations warned that Israel must not take advantage of the new circumstances. In the midst of these divided and contradictory counsels, Ben-Gurion decided to pursue the French invitation because, in spite of the dangers, he was motivated by the desire to have an ally for the first time in his country's history. As he wrote in the diary: 'My own opinion was that this was our first chance of getting an ally (and, by the way, an ally who has assisted us ever since the War of Independence right to this very day), and it is only due to her aid that we are not standing helpless today.'[17]

NEGOTIATIONS FOR AN ALLIANCE

From the end of September until the signing of the Protocol of Sèvres on 24 October, there was a month of extraordinary activity to conclude the terms of agreement, or the 'scenario', between Israel, France and Great Britain. The discussions were complex and the consultations of a small group of political and military officials necessitated much travel, primarily between Tel-Aviv, Paris and

London, with important conversations being held in New York at the United Nations. The matter was complicated further by the fact that until the tripartite meeting at Sèvres, Israel and Great Britain communicated and negotiated through the French rather than directly with one another. Ben-Gurion informed a very small circle of advisers of what was transpiring and communicated only limited knowledge to several members of the Government. He carefully controlled information as well as decisions.[18]

During this crucial period, he recorded in his diary analyses of the interests, strengths and weaknesses of the various parties to the unfolding drama:

(1) *Egypt* He never wavered in believing that they meant to attack Israel and he saw in Nasser a particularly dangerous leader with aspirations and tendencies Ben-Gurion associated with Hitler. Moreover, he expected that the longer the crisis over the Canal continued, the greater the possibility of Egyptian success in maintaining control. He was also convinced that an Egyptian victory on this issue would increase pressure against Israel in the future. It was thus in Israel's interests to cooperate with France and Britain. Although he shared his allies' wish to change the regime in Egypt, he was very sceptical that this could be accomplished by inducing the Egyptian people to overthrow Nasser. Indeed, he challenged both French and British leaders on this issue, predicting that even if Nasser were defeated at the Canal, he would withdraw, possibly to southern Egypt, and engage in guerrilla warfare. We now know that, in fact, this assessment of Nasser's intentions was accurate. Nevertheless, Ben-Gurion was willing to cooperate in any enterprise that would diminish Egyptian power and that might, despite his assessment, rid Israel of the threat posed by Nasser.[19]

(2) *Great Britain* Ben-Gurion understood Britain's interest in toppling Nasser. He also viewed as natural and desirable that Great Britain should continue as an important power in the Middle East. He shared Great Britain's concern about the apparent deterioration of King Hussein's regime and he was also concerned that Nasser's sympathizers threatened Hussein's control as well as British influence in Jordan. Unlike his French allies, he shared the British appreciation of the importance of American agreement to military action, even if only tacitly given.

There were serious disagreements as well: (a) Britain had been pressing throughout the second half of 1956 for Iraqi intervention in an apparently disintegrating Jordan. Israel, however, objected to the presence of a hostile and powerful enemy on her Eastern flank. Ways would therefore have to be found for ensuring that conflict with Egypt would not spread to a two-front war, with Britain and Israel fighting against a common enemy on the Egyptian front and against each other on the Jordanian; (b) although Britain became interested in an Israeli attack against Egypt, she did not want to be associated with Israel, even indirectly, for fear of losing Arab goodwill. Ben-Gurion objected to doing the dirty work, taking risks and possible blame while Britain reaped the benefits.[20]

Related to this issue, was the profound mistrust with which Ben-Gurion regarded the British leadership, even though he admired the English people. More than once during this period, as on many other occasions, he extolled the courage and character of the English based on what he had witnessed during the blitz on London during the Second World War. That memory was now evoked by the vision of Egyptian pilots flying over Tel-Aviv in Russian bombers. One striking example of this mistrust is found in the diary on 17 October, the same day he receives Guy Mollet's invitation to come to Paris. Commenting on yet another British scenario in which Israel was assigned the role of initiating the war without any apparent connection to European partners or guarantees of support from them, he wrote: 'It appears to me to be a British plot! They get us involved with Nasser, and meanwhile bring about the conquest of Jordan by Iraq.'[21] Decades of conflict between Britain and Zionism had resulted in a legacy of deep suspicion. Nevertheless, Ben-Gurion recognized the potential significance of Great Britain as an ally and was unwilling to join the French unless the British were an active part of the plan.

(3) *France* Ben-Gurion was fully aware that an important factor in the French interest in supplying Israel was the desire to undermine Egyptian support of the rebellion of France's colonies in North Africa. He sympathized with their desire to overthrow Nasser and their anxiety over potential humiliation if France were defeated over a crucial issue like control over the Canal. He understood that failure on Suez would not only damage strategic and commercial interests, but encourage further rebellion in Algeria. Finally, Ben-Gurion perceived France as a friendly power which, ever since the War of Independence, had cooperated on a variety of issues of mutual concern.[22]

It was natural, in this situation, that the French should play a major role. They were the crucial intermediary, anxious that both

Britain and Israel join them in the endeavour they all wished to advance. Of all the parties the French were the most flexible and offered the most alternatives. They were less sensitive to American opinion and less hesitant about using their own power and benefiting from Israel's. Both by supplying Israel with arms and repeatedly pressing their British allies to take action, they played a catalytic role in the coming of Suez.

What emerges, then, is that the interests of France, Britain and Israel were not evenly balanced. Ben-Gurion saw Israel as engaged in a long-term battle for survival with a dangerous and ambitious neighbour. A year had already passed since he first perceived the likelihood of conflict with Egypt and began preparing for it. Yet, that war need not be fought immediately. For the British and French, however, the issue of war with Egypt was one of *now* or *never*. For Israel, it was one of *now* or *later*.

Ben-Gurion well understood that the pressures were uneven. Because he was aware of the pressures that acted on Israel's potential partners and because of a fundamentally positive assessment of her strength, he could exercise considerable leverage in establishing the terms under which Israel would join in the alliance. There were scenarios that he could and did reject since, in his judgment, Israel could afford to forgo the cooperation in battle of two major world powers. For this reason, his evaluation and decisions were crucial to the shaping of the possibilities and the parameters of cooperation.

Ben-Gurion's calculations included assessments of the super-powers, which he predicted would play a crucial role in the outcome of any conflict. He valued American friendship as vital to the well-being of the State of Israel and to the successful conclusion of a war. He believed that Israel and her supporters could successfully press the United States since the forthcoming Presidential election would encourage candidates to be sensitive to Israel's position. He placed confidence in the continuance of the historic alliance between Britain and the United States even as he recognized that a serious rift in Anglo-American relations could endanger the effort against Nasser. In Ben-Gurion's mind, the United States was the key to significant change in the region.[23]

He had negative views on two other outside actors. He was critical of the United Nations which neglected its responsibilities when Israel's interests were concerned but supported the claims of her neighbours. He was also convinced that Dag Hammarskjöld, the

U.N. Secretary-General, was personally antagonistic and biased. He viewed the Soviet Union and its leadership in even darker terms, convinced it would not hesitate to deploy its power against the Jewish State. The letters that Soviet Premier Bulganin sent after the war began were, in Ben-Gurion's judgment, worthy of Hitler. This made it all the more necessary to maintain the friendship and cooperation of the United States and of whatever other allies might be found.[24]

THE PROTOCOL OF SÈVRES[25]

When Ben-Gurion left for the villa in Sèvres, where the responsibilities of the three allies in the Suez–Sinai campaigns were worked out as well as the timetable for action, he was doubtful that an agreement could be reached. Nevertheless, he sketched out his own scenarios. The most far-reaching and far-fetched was predicated on American support for a British–French–Israeli action that would achieve fundamental changes in the Middle East. In the outcome of this script, a Middle East without Nasser would contain a concert of pro-Western nations. The non-Christian portions of Lebanon would form a separate, independent state and all of Jordan would disappear as Iraq, Syria and Israel would amicably reassign the region's borders. The route to oil would be preserved and the sources of rebellion from the Persian Gulf to Northern Africa would be squashed. He labelled this vision with the appropriate code-name, 'Fantastic'. This was appropriate, for the idea was far removed from reality. Although Ben-Gurion recognized that an essential element in the success of any such plan was American support, he failed to understand how committed Eisenhower and Dulles had become to decolonization. They would not permit the United States to participate in a reenactment of imperialistic strategies in reapportioning the Middle East while at the same time being supportive of dismantling the British and French empires elsewhere. It was, in part, for this very reason that Eisenhower would cut the ground from under the British and French effort against Nasser over the far more modest goal of asserting their traditional and arguably legitimate rights over responsibilities for the Suez Canal.

An eminently more practical plan, which he came reasonably close to achieving, included terms he sketched out a month before the negotiations at Sèvres, just after hearing from Peres that Israel would be invited to participate in the action against Egypt. On 25

September, he listed in his diary three principles of negotiation with the French and the British. These were expressed in terms of negatives:

(1) Israel would 'not' initiate the war. He withstood considerable pressure in holding out for a plan of a *joint* operation, and insisted on a signed document to that effect even though he voluntarily kept its existence secret during his lifetime. Although he ultimately agreed that Israel would initiate hostilities, he interpreted this, in light of the signed Protocol, as a tactical illusion, not the deception demanded by the British. The document was his insurance that Israel would have protection from Egyptian planes and would not have to bear the onus of world opinion if her allies backed out after the first Israeli shots were fired.

(2) Israel would 'not' participate unless the British were involved and promised to keep the Jordanians quiet and the Iraqis out of that country and far from Israel's borders. Israel received the pledges she required and quiet on the eastern border with Jordan was maintained.

(3) It was the third 'no' that was not achieved. Ben-Gurion pledged that Israel would not become involved if the Americans opposed the action. Here he deferred to his allies who could not deliver the American support he correctly foresaw as crucial. The disappointment was tempered by the fact that American displeasure was also directed towards the allies and that it was far less costly to Israel than to them.

Through the negotiations at Sèvres, Ben-Gurion obtained arms, the writing-off of many French loans for weapons purchases, the coveted aerial umbrella for her cities, valuable assistance in destroying the military threat of her most dangerous enemy, understanding of her need for freedom of passage through the Straits of Tiran, and a deepening cooperation with the French. Ben-Gurion was able to exact as much as he did because he exploited Israel's strengths with skill, particularly the need of two world powers to have Israel fire the first shot. This may seem far-fetched today. It also did then. Dayan captured the mood of the Israeli delegation very well on the return flight from Sèvres on the 25th of October. He sketched a cartoon showing a well-attired and elegant male with a top hat next to an attractive woman. They were standing before a small figure in shorts wearing the typical, rounded Israeli cloth hat. The gentleman was labelled 'England', the lady – 'France'

Caricature drawing by Dayan on the plane returning from Sèvres

and the little fellow – 'Israel.' Behind Israel was a map of Egypt. The drama and the humour of the cartoon are expressed in both the gentleman and the lady stretching out an arm before them as they both say to the little fellow: 'After you!'[26]

*   *   *

193

This reading of Ben-Gurion's diary suggests that the alliance with Britain and France and the connecting of Israel's campaign in Sinai with her allies' campaign against Egypt were hardly the inevitable culmination of a long chain of events. Rather, they were unanticipated developments in a year-long effort to prepare for what Ben-Gurion believed was the coming conflict between Israel and Nasser's Egypt. Ben-Gurion himself reflected directly on the Suez–Sinai campaign during a review conducted by the army not long after the war and duly recorded his observations in the diary. He noted that the alliance with outside powers was a one-time episode in Israel's history. Israel had fought alone in the past and he expected that was how future wars would be conducted. The alliance had only brought a temporary advantage in a long-term struggle in which the Sinai campaign was an unavoidable episode. Since Israel could expect to act alone in the future, she would continue to need the latest technologies. This, he argued, would be especially true of the air force which would become an even more important factor in future conflicts. Finally, he accurately foresaw that Israel could also be subject to a surprise attack and that she might have to fight on two fronts. In sum, he assumed that the Sinai campaign was not the last war and that there would never be one like it again.[27]

His understanding of the Sinai campaign as a unique event was part of a deeply-held philosophical position about the nature of wars. In this conflict a window of opportunity had been opened for Israel as a consequence of Nasser's challenge to Great Britain and France with the nationalization of the Suez Canal. The peculiar chain of events set in motion in the summer of 1956 would not recur. Leaders would always have to be alert for the unexpected and the novel. In keeping with what he held to be a fundamental principle in the analysis of wars, he wrote in his diary well before and without reference to the Sinai campaign: 'I very much value the study of military history, even though it is not a science, since from one military event one does not learn about another.'[28]

NOTES

1. For an important recent discussion of the issue see Michael Walzer, *Just and Unjust Wars* (New York; 1977), pp.80–5. Note that he has chosen the Six-Day War of 1967 rather than the Suez Campaign as his example of the 'justified' pre-emptive strike.
2. Ben-Gurion Archives, *Speeches*, 11 Nov. 1959.
3. His official history of these events was published as David Ben-Gurion, *The Sinai Campaign* (Tel Aviv; 1959) [Hebrew]. See, too, David Ben-Gurion, *Israel: A Personal History* (Tel Aviv; 1972), pp.444–536. Moshe Dayan has written the most complete account of any of the Israeli participants in *Story of My Life* (London; 1976), chs. 13–15. Mordechai Bar-On, who was also a participant as a member of Dayan's staff, has written the most complete analysis in a four-volume study, *Tagar v'Tigra* [Hebrew]. It is being prepared for publication by the Ben-Gurion Research Center. See, too, Shimon Peres, *David's Sling* (London; 1970). The best consistent work by an Israeli historian who had access to most of the relevant documentation, including the diary, is by Michael Bar-Zohar. See, for example, his *Ben-Gurion; A Biography* (New York; 1986), chs.13–14. See, too, Michael Brecher, *Decisions in Israel's Foreign Policy* (London; 1974), ch.6.
4. Important collateral accounts are to be found in the memoirs of allies directly involved in forging the alliance and the negotiations at Sèvres. See Abel Thomas; *Comment Israel fut sauvé*; Christian Pineau, *1956 Suez* (Paris; Robert Laffont, 1976); Anthony Eden, *Full Circle; The Memoirs of Anthony Eden* (Boston; 1960); see, too, Robert Rhodes James, *Anthony Eden* (London; 1986), chs.11–13.
5. Ben-Gurion, *The Sinai Campaign*, pp.21–4, 95–103.
6. Ben-Gurion, *The Sinai Campaign*, pp.76–7, 192–210.
7. Ben-Gurion, *The Sinai Campaign*, pp.7–8, 24–5.
8. Bar-Zohar, *Ben-Gurion*, pp.217 ff.
9. *Ben-Gurion's Diary*, 14 Dec. 1956. An edited translation is found in Part IV of this book. The Hebrew originals are at the Ben-Gurion Archives in Sede Boqer.
10. *Ben-Gurion's Diary*, 29 Dec. 1956 and Ben-Gurion, *Israel; A Personal History*, p.492; Moshe Sharett, *Yoman Ishi* (Tel Aviv; 1978) [Hebrew], pp.1411–78.
11. Quoted in Bar-On, *Tagar v'Tigra*.
12. *Ben-Gurion's Diary*, 28 Sept. 1956.
13. *Ben-Gurion's Diary*, 10 Aug. 1956.
14. *Ben-Gurion's Diary*, 3 and 9 Sept. 1956.
15. Bar-On, Volume I; *Ben-Gurion's Diary*, 29 Dec. 1956.
16. *Ben-Gurion's Diary*, 15, 19, and 24 Aug. 1956.
17. *Ben-Gurion's Diary*, 25 Sept. 1956.
18. *Ben-Gurion's Diary*, 27 and 28 July, 30 Aug., 19 Oct., 1956.
19. *Ben-Gurion's Diary*, 22 Oct. 1956; see Bughdadi's memoirs in Part IV.
20. *Ben-Gurion's Diary*, 17 and 22–24 Oct. 1956.
21. *Ben-Gurion's Diary*, 17 Oct. 1956.
22. *Ben-Gurion's Diary*, 25 Sept. and 23 Oct. 1956.
23. *Ben-Gurion's Diary*, 13 Aug., 22 Oct., and 10 Nov. 1956. See Nadav Safran, *Israel; The Embattled Ally* (Cambridge; 1981), chs.19, 27.
24. *Ben-Gurion's Diary*, 3 Sept., 7, 8 and 10 Nov. 1956.
25. *Ben-Gurion's Diary*, 22–26 Oct. 1956.
26. Cartoon is appended to concluding volume of Bar-On, *Tagar v'Tigra*.
27. *Ben-Gurion's Diary*, 27 Dec. 1956.
28. *Ben-Gurion's Diary*, 15 Jan. 1955, in a conversation with the historian, Israel Beer.

14

The Influence of Political Considerations on Operational Planning in the Sinai Campaign

Mordechai Bar-On

Moshe Dayan, in an interview with the newspaper *Ma'ariv* after the publication of his first book, *Diary of the Sinai Campaign*, observed: 'From its inception, the Sinai Campaign was in a political vice; a very crowded oyster bed imposing severe limitations.'[1] This article will describe that Procrustean bed and changes made by headquarters during both the planning and execution of the Sinai Campaign, as well as their political significance.

Most Israeli accounts of the campaign were published before Israel publicly acknowledged its secret contacts with France and Great Britain prior to the operation, as well as the agreements signed at a secret meeting attended by Ben-Gurion, the French Premier, and the British Foreign Secretary, in the prestigious Paris suburb of Sèvres less than a week before IDF paratroops landed in the Mitla Pass. As a result, even the best accounts do not accurately explain the reasons behind various major moves, while the worst offer irrelevant analyses.[2] In an uncontrolled flight of fancy, authors have described the opening phase of the operation, i.e., the paratroop landing in the Mitla Pass, the penetration of the rest of the brigade via the Kuntilla–Themed–Nakhl axis, and the advance introduction of the 7th Armoured Brigade via Quseima to the rear of the Egyptian deployment in the Abu Ageilla and Um Kattef ranges, as brilliant operative insight based on the IDF's traditional indirect approach.[3]

These moves, in fact, had more to do with political constraints than with military theory or even the operation's own imperatives. Thus a disparity developed between the constraints, unknown to various command levels, and the traditional IDF aggressiveness guiding field commanders. This gap seriously disrupted execution of the High Command's orders, as dictated by these political constraints.

Since Operation Horev at the end of 1948, in which Palmach forces penetrated deep into the Sinai Peninsula, the IDF General Staff had been preparing for the possibility of another battle in Sinai. IDF doctrine then held that a war had to be shifted into the enemy heartland as soon as possible.[4] This doctrine was especially important in the Egyptian theatre.

The IDF feared that Egypt would use the Gaza Strip as a springboard for launching attacks against Jewish population centres, and that an Egyptian offensive toward Beersheva and the Hebron Mountain area would cut off the Negev. The IDF General Staff therefore based its planning in this sector on an early breakthrough into the expanses of Sinai, making a major effort to circumvent the dense Egyptian deployment at the peninsula's northeastern end, especially in the Abu Ageilla–el-Arish–Rafah triangle. The archives of the IDF Operations Department were full of periodically updated and modified files detailing the IDF's plans in Sinai in the event of an outbreak of war with Egypt.

In the early 1950s such contingency plans were routinely drawn up as a measure of general precaution. But during 1955, these plans became real and more urgent: tension surged on the Egyptian border following Israel's retaliation on Egyptian army camps north of Gaza (28 Feb. 1955),[5] the massive arms deal Egypt signed with Czechoslovakia which became widely known that September and Egypt's official announcement of the enforcement of the blockade of the Straits of Tiran to Israeli shipping.

In autumn 1955, Israel and the IDF General Staff were rife with talk about the need for a pre-emptive war, and Ben-Gurion ordered that a special brigade be readied to capture the Sharm el-Sheikh area by means of parachute airlift and a landing action from the sea.[6] The Israeli government ultimately rejected this proposal, but the General Staff continued to plan. In the spring of 1956, it became necessary to revise the plans to reflect the incorporation of newly-acquired French arms, the establishment of additional combat units,[7] and the nationalization of the Suez Canal, which created the possibility of hostilities between Egypt and Great Britain and France.

In the spring and early summer, the General Staff increasingly discussed its operational posture in the imminent showdown with the Egyptian army. The dramatic increase in Israeli armour following Israel's large-scale arms deal with France led the High

197

Command to reorganize the Armoured Corps under Major General Haim Laskov and his deputy, Colonel Meir Zorea. Within the General Staff a pointed argument raged on its deployment. Apprehensive about the fighting ability of the Infantry Corps' reserve brigades, Moshe Dayan preferred to scatter the Armoured Corps in aid missions among the infantry, while the corps' commanders insisted on a concentrated deployment. The issue was finally brought to Ben-Gurion, who resolved it in favour of the armour commanders.[8]

Air Force deployment remained undisputed. Fearing a surprise attack on Israeli airfields before the planes could take off, and seeking to maximize air superiority immediately, the IDF strove – then as always – to launch any campaign with a full-force, concentrated pre-emptive air attack on enemy airbases, quickly eliminating most enemy aircraft while still on the ground, and freeing the Air Force for interception and ground-forces aid.[9] Paratroop deployment was also obvious. With highly-experienced soldiers, these units were able to penetrate deep into enemy territory by parachute drops and airlifts, as well as by ground operation. The paratroops would therefore be assigned to the most vital targets deep in the enemy heartland at or near zero-hour and could be recalled for another mission during the same campaign.

The underlying concepts and detailed operational plans became increasingly clear during the summer, but only in early October did they finally crystallize. On 2 October, 1956, the Chief of Staff, Lt. General Moshe Dayan, returned from Paris, where, as part of a secret delegation headed by Foreign Minister Golda Meir, he had held detailed talks with French statesmen and generals about a possible Israeli–French war effort against Egypt.[10]

The joint operation was politically premature, but it had become extremely likely that the IDF would soon have to attack the Egyptians in Sinai. The scenario remained hazy but talks pointed towards two separate but coordinated French and Israeli operations. The IDF would deal with all territory east of the Suez Canal, defeat the Egyptian army in Sinai, and seize the peninsula. This would enable the IDF to base its battle orders on the most pertinent operational considerations, without concerning itself with political constraints, excluding the setting of D-Day.

It was sharply sensed that the talk was serious this time, and that the files piling up in the Operations Department's archives would soon translate into the supreme effort of thousands of soldiers, a reality of blood and sweat, fire and dust. The feeling that seized the

General Staff when the Chief of Staff read them the alert order is described by Moshe Dayan in his memoirs:

> The report that we were to ready ourselves for battle was electrifying. Those present felt they had already gone into the campaign with their hearts and souls. Around the table sat the army's top leadership: area commanders and commanders of the armour Corps, the Air Force, and the Navy. Not only their youthful age but also their nature determined their response. In the preceding years, young commanders who themselves had gone through battle, as commanders of units from squad to brigade strength, were chosen to command the larger battle units. They correctly understood the implications of the alert order, and even so not only were they not deterred by it but were eager to respond.[11]
>
> Briefing the Supreme Command staff, Dayan stressed several concerns: The key point is speed. We have to wind up the campaign as quickly as possible ... We can build our operation on units independent of one another; their commands, which have to receive reports and issue orders, would be in the front lines, among the fighting units ... The paratroop units should land in the vicinity of the final objectives at the very beginning of the campaign, so as to block the paths of reinforcement from Egypt and to capture tactically important strongholds.[12]

In the batch of orders issued for 8 October, the Chief of the General Staff set priorities for the IDF's operations:

A. Parachute or landing at zero hour
B. Rapid advance, bypassing the enemy's deployments
C. Breakthrough.

What this order of priorities meant was that it was better to capture first those objectives that were deep in the enemy's territory, by airdrops and parachute landings of Israeli forces, than to reach them by frontal and gradual progress, capturing one position after another. Then, in greater detail:

> First we have to capture strongholds in the vicinity of the Suez Canal, which is our final objective in the West. This, of course, is possible only by a parachute landing. Then [we take] el-Arish, followed by Abu Ageilla and Sharm el-Sheikh. Only in the end [do we take] Gaza, on the Israeli border.[13]

Beyond the operational importance of the Chief of Staff's guidelines was their significance in terms of inspiration and leadership. This determined the 'spirit of the orders' and was congruent with the atmosphere Moshe Dayan sought to cultivate within the IDF upon his appointment as Chief of Staff in 1953. The commanders absorbed the message, and it became an ethos.

The General Staff, directed by Major General Meir Amit, translated the guidelines into detailed operational directives over the next few days and submitted them to the Chief of Staff for approval in an operational order bearing the name by which the campaign was to become known: 'Kadesh'.[14] The plan was based on an attack along two axes and one diversionary operation. On zero hour two paratroop battalions and a third battalion landing from the sea would attack el-Arish frontally. Simultaneously, a division commanded by Major General Haim Laskov, which would include the Golani Infantry Brigade and the new 27th Armoured Brigade, would attack the Rafah sector as the infantry shattered the array of Rafah positions and the armour would pass by from the south and quickly join the paratroops in the vicinity of el-Arish.

The breakthrough on the central axis, along the Nitsana–Ismailia road, was entrusted to a division commanded by Colonel Yehuda Wallach. This division included the conscript 7th Armoured Brigade and two reserve infantry brigades. It would attack the Quseima region, intending to execute a prompt, deep flanking operation from the south using the Armoured Brigade, and would ultimately storm the Abu Ageilla–Um Kattef strongholds simultaneously from east and west.

The 9th Mechanized Reserve Brigade was set aside for a diversionary operation. One of its battalions would occupy Ras el-Naqab and advance west via Themed and Nakhl toward the Suez Canal, while the rest of the brigade would exploit the conquest of Quseima to join the brigade through the Quseima–Nakhl or Bir Hasne–Mitla axis. All this had to occur on D-Day or no later than the following day. In the second stage, the 7th and 27th Armoured Brigades would approach the Suez Canal and finish clearing the peninsula's northern half, while the paratroop brigade would be relieved from the el-Arish area to undertake a second parachute and airlift operation meant to occupy the Sharm el-Sheikh area, roughly along the lines demarcated in Operation Omer which was planned during the autumn of 1955.[15] Dayan assumed the IDF could reach the el-Arish–Jebel Libni–Nakhl line on the second day of the battle, and the Canal within four to five days. The Chief of Staff insisted on small-scale parachute landings of one or two platoons near the Suez Canal as early as zero hour to set up ambushes and road-blocks, thus enabling the IDF to 'confuse the Egyptians, disrupt supply lines, and prevent the movement of reinforcements from the Canal area east into the Sinai interior'.[16]

The plan was audacious, but the General Staff believed that with speed and decisiveness it was feasible, possibly even reducing the casualty rate and preventing political complications. It limited French partnership to the supply of additional equipment, primarily transport planes to be used for the airborne missions and 4 x 4 and 6 x 6 vehicles that could quickly penetrate the interior of Sinai using dirt roads or even river beds. Nevertheless, it was apparent even then that if the British or the French participated in one way or another, it would be their responsibility to destroy the Egyptian air force and attack its bases west of the Canal. The operation, code-named 'Kadesh 1', reflected the assumption that the Israel Air Force would be assigned to 'assist the ground forces and protect Israel's airspace'.[17] The Navy's major duties involved landing at el-Arish and the Straits of Tiran; its combat fleet – which then consisted of two Z-class destroyers, one old frigate and several torpedo boats – would provide cover and defend Israel's shores against attack by the Egyptian fleet.

This operational order remained in effect less than three weeks. Meanwhile, the French turned out to be either unable or unwilling to fight the Egyptians without the British, who refused to fight a tripartite campaign involving overt Israeli partnership. To break the deadlock the French tried to persuade Israel to initiate independently a campaign against Egypt in the Sinai. Britain and France would intervene later to 'separate the warring parties' and seize the Suez Canal to guarantee safe shipping.

This article will not analyse all the ramifications of these negotiations or describe in detail the secret Sèvres conference that led to the Tripartite Agreement.[18] It will note only those steps necessary to elucidate the changes in the operational planning.

Israel had a primary interest in the realization of the Tripartite Agreement. Ben-Gurion and most of Israel's political and military leadership assumed that Israel would eventually have to face the Egyptian army and, perhaps, other Arab armies as well.[19] Before Ben-Gurion departed for Sèvres, Dayan told him:

> ... We have to weigh and examine the consequences of refusing and of acceding [to the British and French call to go to war].

201

If we refuse, we shall have lost a historic opportunity that will not recur, and shall have to continue contending with Nasser alone, without the French and English armies, and without the equipment assistance that the French are giving us within the framework of the joint campaign. Are we really confident that, politically, we can launch the campaign alone and capture Sharm el-Sheikh in order to ensure free shipping to Eilat?[20]

A joint operation with two major powers seemed like a golden opportunity. Ben-Gurion indignantly rejected the British demand that the partnership be kept circumspect so that Israel would look like an aggressor, with the two powers interceding between it and Egypt. Ben-Gurion's opposition was chiefly political and ethical. He feared American anger, Russian intervention, and world condemnation of Israel as an aggressor. Furthermore, he was highly suspicious of the British and asked for guarantees in case they backed out or waged a two-faced policy by exploiting the war on the Egyptian front to effect changes on the Jordanian front – such as facilitating an Iraqi military penetration of Jordan and, perhaps, even the West Bank.

Ben-Gurion also worried that while Great Britain and France completed the diplomatic steps preceding military intervention, Israel, fighting alone, would be exposed to the full Egyptian strike force. A year after the Czechoslovak–Egyptian arms deal became known, Israel overestimated the Egyptian army. Ben-Gurion feared that the Israeli Chief of Staff would suffer extensive casualties in Sinai from the hundreds of tanks supplied by the Soviet Union to Egypt the year before, and dreaded the possibility that Egypt's new, modern jet bombers would reach Tel-Aviv and other Israeli population centres, inflicting heavy civilian casualties on Israel at the campaign's outset. Memories of his stay in London during the German blitz of 1940 repeatedly surfaced during the Sèvres talks, underscoring his anxiety.[21] It was clear, however, that Britain would not enter the campaign unless Israel launched a broad offensive in the Sinai, threatening the Canal Zone early on and thereby allowing Great Britain and France to intervene on the pretext of safeguarding the Canal from war.

To reconcile these conflicting positions, several conditions were necessary:

a. To minimize the time lapse between the beginning of the battles and the beginning of the allies' bombing;
b. To 'threaten the Canal' without getting too deeply and inextric-

ably entangled with the Egyptians, while offering maximum protection to the troops in the initial phases of the war;

c. To maximize Israel's links with its allies, or at least with France, in order to create a stable and irreversible international commitment.

The Gordian knot was cut on the second day of the Sèvres talks.[22] Two weeks earlier, while poring over maps of Sinai, trying to show Operations Department where it was possible for the paratroops to set up disruptive ambushes deep in the peninsula, Moshe Dayan had noticed the topographical advantages of the Mitla Pass. The pass appeared to be narrow, with precipitous mountains permitting a bilateral defence. Now, however, Dayan was attracted not to its topography but to its location. The pass was only about 40 kilometres east of the Canal, but was removed from the major Egyptian deployments concentrated in eastern and northern Sinai.

Only after all sides had agreed to reduce the time gap between the start of the Israeli offensive and the first British–French bombings from 72 to 36 hours,[23] and after the French had undertaken to station three fighter squadrons on Israeli soil and position several French warships along the Israeli coast, did Dayan make the operational proposal to Ben-Gurion that made it possible to sign the Sèvres protocol and carry out the joint offensive:

> A battalion of paratroops will be dropped near the Mitla Pass at zero hour. Simultaneously, only limited operations will be undertaken, namely only those moves necessary to assure IDF ability to join up quickly with the paratroop battalion. These operations will include the capture of three openings along the border and rapid penetration of the rest of the Paratroop Brigade along the Kuntilla–Themed–Nakhl axis toward Mitla. This operation will enable the battalion at the drop site to retreat if the war does not develop as planned, or to be reinforced by the rest of the brigade as the campaign develops, while the main IDF force reaches the Canal zone and relieves the paratroops from their isolation.

The intent was to wage a cautious, restrained campaign during the first 36 hours, one that left all options open – a kind of 'hot and cold' operation. Israel had to take drastic action close enough to the Canal to ensure England's and France's joining the war; yet that action had to be minimal and permit withdrawal if necessary in case the allies did not join. This would be achieved by presenting the opening of the campaign as a kind of a broad retaliatory action, rather than a move for permanent conquest; like the usual Israeli retaliatory raids, it might end with a pre-planned withdrawal if necessary. This approach, however, required that in its initial phases the IDF refrain from any superfluous action that would increase hostilities beyond the level necessary to implement the diplomatic agreement. The full IDF breakthrough needed to achieve its own territorial goals would have to be postponed for two days.

Dayan did not disclose to the British and the French the details of his new plan. However, as a result of his proposals, Ben-Gurion promised in writing that, within the framework of the Sèvres Protocol, Israel would launch 'a real act of war and would create a real threat to the Suez Canal'.[24] The General Staff was certain of Israel's ability to defeat the Egyptian army in the Sinai single-handed, but at stake were the campaign's ramifications for Israel's political and international status on the one hand and the number of probable casualties on the other. These considerations impelled Israel to cooperate with the two European superpowers which presented their own demands and constraints. These constraints required some essential changes in the 'Kadesh 1' operational plans.

When Dayan returned from the Sèvres conference on Thursday, 25 October, 1956, a difficult problem loomed before him. Although war preparations had been continuing for almost three weeks and many in the IDF were familiar with Israel's close contacts with the French army, the General Staff knew little of the more recent developments that had brought Britain into the circle. The Sèvres agreements were meant to be Israel's most guarded secret, not so much because of the need to conceal the war preparations, but because of Ben-Gurion's personal moral commitment to Britain's leaders.

Israel did not consider the agreements as a conspiracy, since it felt it had nothing to hide morally. Indeed, Israel had an interest that the world should know that it had not gone to war alone. Ben-Gurion reasoned that French and British involvement would strengthen Israel in waging its campaign and in protecting its gains. But the British sought a real conspiracy, considering it essential to conceal the plot in order to protect their vital interests in Arab countries. Ben-Gurion was determined to keep his word to the British on this matter for years after the campaign, a fortiori beforehand. Dayan was loath to broaden the group of parties in on the secret, or even to release too many details to those on its fringes, but it was very difficult to explain the changes in planning without spelling out the Sèvres agreements and constraints.

That afternoon, Dayan convened a small number of senior officers on the General Staff, headed by Major General Meir Amit, and told them of the agreements without going into detail. He described the principles according to which it was necessary to redesign the plan of action:

a. There would be a complete differentiation between what the IDF had promised the allies and what it had to do to achieve Israel's goals.
b. Every possible action would be postponed until after the allies' military involvement had commenced. 'For the first 36 hours in which the IDF will be acting alone, it is essential to minimize clashes both on land and in the air and to prevent an escalation of the war.'
c. After the allies intervened, Israel would quickly seize all ground targets of interest, with the Straits of Tiran at the top of the list.
d. Secrecy would be the most important consideration apart from victory itself.

Everyone would be familiar only with the details essential to his own mission, and might not understand the overall scheme. In light of the political factors involved, orders would be given in apparent contradiction to previous planning, and sometimes even defying pure military logic. Nevertheless, all command levels were instructed to follow their orders faithfully and exactly. This referred in particular to the surprising but justified decision – by those fully familiar with the political circumstances – to launch the war by conceding to the enemy the air initiative and the total loss of the element of surprise.[25] Major General Meir Amit, who was responsible for the planning and relaying of orders, was most helpful in attempting to solve the Chief of Staff's problem. But, as we shall see below, the problem remained, since the field commanders did not understand some of the reasons behind the orders, creating certain operational malfunctions.

The political pressures resulted in five important deviations in principle from the original plan and the IDF's standard war doctrine.

a. *Air force deployment.* Contrary to doctrine and the strong aspiration of the pilots and commanders, the air force was not permitted to employ its full operational capability. In the first stage, it was to avoid any unnecessary confrontation, contenting itself with defending both the forces penetrating Sinai and Israel's skies as passively as possible. Even in the second stage the air force could not carry out any missions west of the Suez Canal or intervene in attacking Egyptian airfields, for these missions were assigned to the British and French air forces. The Israel Air Force would have to be satisfied with any air battles that happened to break out over the Sinai, and principally with preventive missions and ground support.

b. *Paratrooper deployment.* Originally, the IDF's elite brigade was to conduct two major missions central to the entire campaign: capturing el-Arish and Sharm el-Sheikh. The new scenario subordinated the IDF's best brigade to meet essential *political* needs and barred it entirely from active participation in fulfilling major IDF military objectives. Parachuting at the Mitla Pass and assaulting the Kuntilla–Nakhl axis was militarily of secondary or even tertiary significance, since this was originally intended as a diversionary tactic only. Now it had become the political key to the entire operation. The IDF's best shock troops were no longer assigned to the main fighting against the Egyptian bastions in the Sinai.

c. *Deployment of the Armoured Corps.* Instead of exploiting the advantage of surprise and early initiative and breaking through with the armoured corps by means of sweeps into the heart of the enemy's fortifications close to zero hour, as mandated by the doctrine formulated by the corps several months earlier, the armoured corps now had to wait 36 hours until the allies intervened, and even then it was left with breakthrough missions that were more frontal than flanking and circumventing.

d. *Capturing Sharm el-Sheikh.* The campaign's major objective was now assigned to a mechanized reserve brigade. Rather than a vertical or naval landing, it would be conducted by a land approach through one long obstacle course.

e. *French aid.* Even though the General Staff did not consider it operationally necessary, Ben-Gurion and Dayan, acting under political considerations, required the integration of some French forces into the IDF's order for war. The addition of two dozen French transport planes for paratroop needs, and the parachuting in of supplies, were important. However, the IAF considered the stationing of three French fighter squadrons in Israel to defend the country's skies virtually humiliating. Even reliance on French warships to defend Israel's coasts and naval bombardment of Rafah positions seemed superfluous. But Ben-Gurion preferred to create a situation in which the treaty between France and Israel would have operative significance in the field.

The guideline that the Chief of Staff was forced to give the IDF due to the political constraints contradicted the spirit that Moshe Dayan had tried to create for the IDF since his appointment as COGS in December 1953. For three years Dayan had frequently spoken of 'horses bursting ahead', of galloping forward, of speed and aggressiveness – and his teachings had penetrated deeply into the consciousness of commanders of every rank. Now he was trying to instruct the army to walk a tightrope, to lead an operation where diplomacy dictated caution, restraint, and operational minimalism.

The field command did not understand what was happening – why did the Chief of Staff suddenly change his mind and rein in his sprinting horses? In spite of his strict demand for maximum discipline, an impulse of sorts was created, spreading quickly from the bottom up and disrupting all his cautious plans and the senior command's tightrope-walking.

AIR FORCE ACTIVITIES

In the realm of airborne activity, control was easier. Over the past few weeks, the senior echelons of the Israeli air force had already accommodated the possibility that the main work of silencing the Egyptian air force would be handled by the French or the British. Moreover, the air force by its nature was always activated through the command centre at GHQ and the order not to cross the Suez Canal westward could be clearly defined: 'For us, the Suez Canal was like the Yalu River in Korea; it is forbidden to cross it! It was forbidden to pass through! We were treating Sinai as if it were ours, but we dare not pass beyond!' Thus Ezer Weizman, then a wing commander in southern Israel, quotes the orders of Air Force GOC Dan Tolkowski.[26]

Nevertheless, these orders left the pilots bitterly frustrated. 'The order not to cross the Canal clipped our wings,' Weizman recalls in his memoirs.

We feared for the paratroops' fate, since the Egyptian air force was at the height of its power. We spoke bluntly to Dan [Tolkowski]: 'Give us the OK! Let us attack the Egyptian planes in their bases, in Fayid, Cabrit, Abu Suweir, and Cairo

West! We'll get there, destroy them, and return. We can do it!'[27]

The air force pilots were compensated in part at dawn the day after the parachute drop, when Egyptian planes tried to attack the paratroops in Mitla. Several dogfights ensued, and pilots could soon perform extensive ground support actions in the Sinai. However, they were not able to put their full power to use.

In this field nothing went wrong; the pilots meticulously followed the Chief of Staff's orders. It is fitting to add that by restraining the air force in the Sinai Campaign, Israel acquired an advantage of the first order in the Six-Day War. It is doubtful that Israel could have delivered the crushing blow that liquidated the Arab air forces in the early hours of the 1967 war had it performed a similar exercise 11 years earlier. At the time, however, no one could have imagined this advantage or placated the angry pilots.[28]

THE MITLA BATTLES

Many commentators have tried to explain the paratoop operations on the Kuntilla–Mitla axis as a bold stroke designed to disrupt the Egyptians once hostilities broke out, and an indirect, brilliant operational procedure that accelerated the Egyptian army's collapse in Sinai. Even official IDF publications, such as the 1986 booklet by Aviezer Golan, state: 'By basing itself on the Parker Monument, the IDF in effect bisected Sinai, split its south from its north, limited Egyptian army mobility there, and blocked one of the three avenues along which the Egyptian command could rush reinforcements to its attacked units.'[29]

This appraisal is not backed by fact. Moshe Dayan did not ask the paratroops to split, block, or do anything else connected in any way with subduing the enemy in Sinai. All he sought was an operation that would be viewed by the British as 'a real act of war and a genuine threat to the Canal', while leaving him the option of rescuing the paratroops as swiftly as possible if anything went wrong.

What is important for our discussion is that the paratroop commander himself, Lt. Colonel Ariel Sharon, presumably thought like Aviezer Golan under the circumstances. He could hardly have imagined that the elite brigade under his command was not assigned to one of the major operative missions in the campaign.

Moshe Dayan, who knew the paratroops' strong desire to storm and race ahead, conveyed an explicit order to their commander forbidding any advance beyond the positions seized by the battalion commander, Lt. Colonel Rafael Eytan (Raful), who was parachuted in on the first night. Dayan sought to prevent unnecessary casualties in an unimportant sector, after the paratroops had already completed their mission by the very act of parachuting. 'I again ordered them not to advance to the west,' Dayan wrote in his diary. 'At this stage we have no interest in giving the Egyptians further provocation to broaden their military activity, and we must strive as much as possible to get through the next 24 hours without additional battles ...'[30]

Originally the parachute drop was planned to land at the western opening of the pass. Aerial photographs taken the day before the parachuting revealed new tents at this locale, and the drop site was reset for the eastern opening, near the Parker Monument.[31]

When the brigade commander reached the Parker Monument, however, he realized that his unit was spread over difficult terrain. His natural inclination and the original plan on the one hand, and his utter ignorance of the political background on the other, led him to push his forces into the pass on Wednesday morning, two days after the campaign's opening. Disobeying explicit orders, he entangled himself in the Mitla Pass. Major Davidi, the deputy commander of the brigade, justly claims that

> the Mitla battle was brilliant. I don't remember a similar case in which a relatively small unit entered so perfect a trap, and managed to overcome its ambushers in a bitter battle that continued for hours while inflicting enemy losses ten times greater than its own.[32]

Nevertheless, the historian must conclude that it was a bloody but utterly unnecessary battle, inflicting heavy losses on the IDF while contributing nothing to the campaign in Sinai.[33]

At the end of the Suez Campaign, the General Staff dispatched the paratroop brigade to develop a parallel effort along the Gulf of Suez towards Sharm el-Sheikh. Mordechai Gur's battalion parachuted into the little town of el-Tur, while Rafael Eytan's came down by motor vehicle from Mitla, past Ras el-Sudar and onwards to the southern end of the peninsula. This manoeuvre was designed to ensure the capture of Sharm el-Sheikh if the 9th Brigade ran into difficulties, but the paratroopers arrived too late and in the end were not needed to bring the campaign to an end.

The interesting aspect of the paratroop deployment in Operation Kadesh relates neither to the Mitla battle nor to the role the paratroops played on the shore of the Gulf of Suez, but rather to the way the Chief of Staff was ready to forgo entirely the participation of the IDF's major elite brigade in deciding the campaign in Sinai. Moshe Dayan had to sacrifice one of his best cards to ensure the realization of the campaign as planned. It may even be said that he traded in his 'card' for the advantage Israel acquired in the political and military involvement of the two superpowers who were to become Israel's partners in the campaign. The results indicate that the gamble was calculated and successful.

THE DEPLOYMENT OF THE ARMOURED CORPS

The IDF had at its disposal in the Sinai Campaign two armoured brigades: the experienced standing-army 7th Brigade under Colonel Uri Ben-Ari, and the reserve 27th Brigade, under Colonel Haim Bar-Lev, a brigade that had been recently organized after the arrival of the new French equipment procured by the IDF throughout the late spring and summer. A third brigade, commanded by the late Colonel Shmuel Galinka, the 37th Brigade, was just being organized and when brought into the campaign it was no stronger than one armoured battalion.[34]

The doctrine formulated by the IDF held that it was necessary to use armour in large units and in fast, deep penetrations as soon as possible after the start of the campaign. In view of the political pressures the activation of Haim Laskov's division, which included the 27th Brigade, was delayed until two days after D-Day. The 7th Brigade was left in a waiting position at Be'erotayim, near the demilitarized zone at Nitsana. The 4th Infantry (reserve) Brigade was to capture at D-Day the Egyptian positions at Quseima in order to ensure an early joining with the paratroops at the Mitla Pass. The 7th Armoured Brigade was to exploit the breach in the Quseima sector, only after the General Staff had given the order for continued wide-scale activity. It was assigned to outflank Um Kattef and Abu Ageilla from the south and the west. In any event, the Chief of Staff intended to leave the 7th Brigade on guard for at least the first 24 hours, using it only if the paratroops became bogged down in battles with enemy armour, and send it in only after the allies' involvement permitted the IDF to act under 'clear skies' and with other operational advantages.

The 4th Brigade's attack on Quseima was unexpectedly delayed for a few hours as a result of difficulties on the approaches. Only at 0400 hours did it begin. At dawn the Egyptian soldiers still held a number of strong points west of the town. At this stage the OC Southern Command, General Assaf Simhoni, who had positioned his command post in the Be'erotayim region, was worried that the reserve infantry brigade would be unable to complete its mission and, in blatant violation of the Chief of Staff's orders, he commanded the 7th Brigade to enter the Sinai and finish conquering the Quseima region.

In the late morning, General Dayan arrived at Simhoni's command post and found to his dismay that even though the capture of Quseima had been completed by the 4th Brigade's patrol, the 7th Brigade's tanks were already advancing way past the conquered site, making direct contact with enemy units in the outer ranges of Um Kattef. The entire armoured brigade was already spreading out fast into the expanses of the Sinai.

This was an outstanding case of insubordination by a commander at the front who well knew his orders, even if he did not understand them entirely. 'Yesterday I clashed harshly with the southern regional commander,' writes Moshe Dayan in his memoirs:

He deployed the Armoured Corps' 7th Brigade before the appointed time, despite explicit commands that the Armoured Corps would not take action before October 31. He, the regional commander, was unwilling to rely on the fact that 'someone' [i.e., the British–French forces] would enter the action, and thus he saw no justification for delaying our assaults for 48 hours. He regarded the Chief of Staff's orders on this issue as a political and military blunder for which we would pay dearly.[35]

Moshe Dayan, angry and indignant, continued west and met with the armoured Brigade commander Uri Ben Ari near Ras Abu Matmir. 'The brigade was already spread over about 40 km within Sinai, while according to the plan it should have been 40 km within Israel,' writes Dayan in his book:

If the advances of the armoured brigade into Sinai indeed prematurely caused intensified Egyptian action (mainly by air), we were already unable to prevent it. Therefore, it was best at least to derive the maximum operational benefit from the armoured brigade's entry into the campaign.[36]

The Chief of Staff therefore commanded the armour to advance rapidly and break out westward along the central axis, Jebel Libni–Ismailia. Now there was no longer any reason to delay the other actions in this section, and the 10th Reserve Infantry Brigade also received the command to advance its attack on Um Kattef from the east by 24 hours, and, in preparation for this, to conquer during the night the Egyptian outposts in Uja al-Masri and Tarat-Um-Basis.

Even before noon of that same day the armoured forces succeeded in penetrating the narrow Daika Pass and took up positions along the central axis west of the Abu Ageilla salient; another battalion soon deployed for its attack on this salient from west to east, while other forces of the brigade continued to gallop westward towards Jebel Libni and Bir Hasne.

The premature armoured penetration at the Quseima section put paid to all the cautionary measures and restraining orders of the General Staff. Now there was no longer much point to them; but the Chief of Staff's fears had been proved groundless. True, the Egyptian air force entered the fray at dawn, but for some reason did this only half-heartedly and the IDF formations deployed in the desert suffered little from aerial attacks.

Both the Mitla battle, which led to unnecessary casualties, and the armoured penetration on the central front, which in retrospect bore significant fruit and caused no damage, stemmed from a measure of lax discipline among the senior command of the IDF. But even more, they stemmed from the clear contradiction between the cautious diplomatic plan for the campaign and the ethos that had taken over the IDF, to its benefit: an ethos of running ahead, storming the enemy, and continuous movement to attain tactical goals with daring and rapidity.

More than any other person, Moshe Dayan, who infused this new spirit in the IDF, was aware of this positive aspect of the hitches that occurred. In an interview with Dov Goldstein, conducted nine years after the Sinai Campaign, he explained why he did not take disciplinary action against the paratroop commander and the OC Southern Command:

> My chief criticism was directed at those soldiers who did not make a supreme effort to carry the burden of the battle – and not at the opposite situation, that of commanders and soldiers who did more than their assigned mission. I'm not saying that this is a good thing. Sometimes it can cause disaster, but such outbursts, which contain massive displays of courage – are a great asset to the IDF. We need to preserve this active and energetic spirit.[37]

Or, as he put it in his diary: 'It is better to struggle with rushing horses

– where the problem is how to restrain them – than to tug and pull at oxen who refuse to budge ...'[38]

THE CONQUEST OF SHARM EL-SHEIKH

This mission was undoubtedly the principal objective of the entire campaign. The Israeli Government and the General Staff assumed that, at the end of the campaign, Israel would be able to retain at least this essential ground accomplishment. The original plan, therefore, assigned this mission to the paratroops, to guarantee with utmost confidence in advance the achievement of this objective.[39]

Originally, the 9th Mechanized Reserve Brigade, commanded by Colonel Avraham Yaffe, was to penetrate the Sinai on the Kuntilla–Nakhl–Suez axis, considered of secondary value since its defence from the Egyptian side was scant. Although among the reserve brigades the 9th Brigade was known as one of the best, its skill was not comparable to that of the regular army brigades, not to mention the paratroop brigade. However, the Chief of Staff did not foresee very stiff opposition at the Mitla axis. From the beginning, it was meant as a diversion.

Since political constraints had removed the paratroop brigade from the conquest of Sharm el-Sheikh, the mission was assigned to the 9th Brigade, which was supposed to reach its target in a difficult and exhausting trek, over the trackless wastes and desultory roads along the coast of the Gulf of Eilat. Thus the 9th Brigade could not be sent into action until it had been guaranteed that the Egyptian air force would no longer be able to hinder its progress or inflict upon it unnecessary casualties along the open terrain of the desert. Problems along the way, as well as some difficulties in conquering the two-battalion Egyptian position at Sharm el-Sheikh, led to a significant delay in the completion of the entire campaign. Political pressures at the United Nations and by the United States and the U.S.S.R. increased in proportion as completion of the conquest was delayed. At a certain stage Abba Eban, the Israeli ambassador to the UN, was even forced to announce Israel's acceptance of a cease-fire, while the coveted goal was still not in hand.

The laggardliness of the French and British forces and the astonishing delay in sending their ground forces into action in Port Said permitted the IDF to continue its offensive. In order to hasten the completion of the conquest, Dayan finally threw into the battle one of the paratroop battalions that had been freed of its mission at Mitla. In the end there was no hitch, and the 9th Brigade managed

213

to complete the conquest of its target a short while before the paratroopers reached the western edge of the fortified position at Sharm el-Sheikh.

The bitter fortune of the British and French forces, whose prey was stolen from them before they had finished their action at the Canal, can serve as a good illustration of what could have happened as a result of the changes in the operative planning of the Israeli campaign as far as the conquest of Sharm el-Sheikh is concerned.

Political circumstances four months after the end of the campaign eventually forced the IDF to withdraw from the Straits of Tiran, but there is no doubt that had Israel been compelled to call off the battle before it had conquered its main goal, the entire significance of the war would have been utterly changed.

FRENCH AID

The most significant assistance provided to Israel by France on the eve of the Sinai Campaign and during the conflict found expression in the supply of ammunition and various weaponry. From the beginning of July there arrived from France increasingly voluminous shipments of tanks, self-propelled cannons, armoured half-tracks, transport vehicles with front-wheel drive, Mystère 4A planes, large quantities of replacement parts and ammunition, etc. Describing this episode goes beyond the purpose of our discussion. Here we will concentrate only on the French army's direct involvement in the Sinai campaign as a consequence of the Sèvres agreements. The only direct aid that proved essential and brought the IDF great utility was the provision of Dakota and Norad transport planes for parachuting, air supply, medical evacuation, and transporting commanders and troops throughout the campaign.

Either because Ben-Gurion feared Egyptian air raids on Tel-Aviv and other cities or because he sought to involve the French in the campaign in a way that would bar them from withdrawing or dislocating, the French air force was requested to position in Israeli air fields two fighter squadrons and enough additional air crew to man the Mystères that the IDF had received but for which pilots had not yet been trained.

The aerial umbrella remained unused. Only one Egyptian plane, flying blind, penetrated Israeli airspace and dropped two bombs, causing no real damage. To appease the idle French pilots, the Israeli air force saw fit during the campaign's later stages to involve them in ground support missions in the Sinai, but overall these precautions proved entirely unnecessary, although they caused no damage and strengthened the friendly connections between the IDF and French army officers.[40]

The deployment of the French Navy was unnecessary and even damaging. In accordance with the political plan, it was agreed that during the first 48 hours three French destroyers would be stationed near the coasts of Haifa and Tel-Aviv to fortify coastal and even anti-aircraft defence. One of these destroyers happened to participate in subduing the Egyptian destroyer *Ibrahim al-Awwal*, but it was unnecessary.

Additionally, it was agreed that a French cruiser would aid the Division's attack on the Rafah fortifications through softening-up barrages from its heavy guns, an operation in which the IDF had no experience. Images from the Second World War created the impression that the heavy naval bombardment could plough through the enemy's fortifications and would lessen his resistance. Whether because the shelling was imprecisely aimed or because by nature this device had limits, this action was of no use and only destroyed the surprise element. The sound from the bombardment alerted the Egyptian forces before Golani soldiers reached the perimeter of Egyptian positions.[41]

In my capacity as Head of the Chief of Staff's Bureau, I summarized the importance of direct operational aid provided by the French army to the IDF campaign in the Sinai, immediately after the operation ended, as follows:

> [it] was primarily political, since it established the ironclad fact of the political agreement between Israel and France. The actions of the French pilots and planes in conjunction with the Israeli air force, the execution of an attack on Rafah in coordination with the French navy, the valuable transport assistance, and, above all, the cooperation of French staff officers alongside the Israeli General staff – all accorded the French–Israeli partnership the clear character of a military treaty in action.[42]

NOTES

1. Dov Goldstein, interview with Moshe Dayan. *Ma'ariv*, 8 Oct. 1965, p.5.
2. The best factual description of military processes remains Lt. Colonel Ben-Zion Tehan, 'Sinai Campaign', *Ma'arachot*, no.113, May 1958 [Hebrew]. Moshe

Dayan's book, *Sinai Campaign Diary*, was also published in 1965, before it was permitted to publicize the 'collusion' with the French and the British. Therefore, despite a few hints as to the real considerations shaping events, this book lacks clarity and consistency.

3. See Tuvia Ben Moshe, 'Liddell Hart and the IDF; a Reappraisal', *Mednina, Mimshal ve Yahasim Beinl'umiim*, no.15 [Hebrew]; Meir Pa'il, 'The War of Independence, Operation 'Kadesh', the Six Days War – a Comparative Study', *Ma'arachot*, no.192, June 1968 [Hebrew].

4. See Yigal Allon, *A Curtain of Sand*, p.69 [Hebrew]. A comprehensive description of the IDF doctrine is found in Dan Horowitz, *The Israeli Approach to National Security: Constant and Variable in Israeli Strategic Thought*, and in Edward Luttwak and Dan Horowitz, *The Israeli Army*.

5. An authoritative report of this battle is found in *Hetz Shakhor*, published by the IDF History Branch, GHQ.

6. For Operation 'Omer' see Moshe Dayan, *Avnei Derekh*, ch.10.

7. The formation constructed for Operation 'Omer' became a permanent para-brigade. A new armoured brigade (no.27) was established and a third armoured brigade (no.37) was in the process of construction.

8. *Official Diary of the Bureau of the COGS*, 9, 10 and 13 Sept. 1956. IDF Archives [Hebrew].

9. Ezer Weizman, *Yours are the Heavens, Yours is the Earth*, p.100 [Hebrew].

10. Mordechai Bar-On, 'The St. Germain Mission', *Ma'ariv*, 29 Oct. 1971 [Hebrew]; also see Dayan, *Avnei Derekh*, pp.231–40.

11. Ibid., p.242. Also in *Official Diary*, op. cit. 8 Oct. 1956.

12. Ibid., pp.243–44.

13. Ibid., pp.245–46, and *Official Diary*, 8 Oct. 1956.

14. Earlier operation plans for attack in the Sinai carried the code name 'Safiah'.

15. Operation Command 'Kadesh 1' order, files of the Office of the Chief of Staff, IDF Archive.

16. Mordechai Bar-On, *Etgar ve Tigrah* (Hebrew draft), p.479.

17. Dayan, *Avnei Derekh*, p.252.

18. The Sèvres conference is described with notable detail in many books. Of primary value and those which have had access to original documentation: Michael Bar Zohar, *Ben-Gurion*, vol.3, pp.232–61; Moshe Dayan, *Avnei Derekh*, ch. 17; Yosef Evron, *Beyom Sagrir*, pp.119–42 [Hebrew]; Mordechai Bar-On, *Etgar ve Tigrah*; Christian Pineau, *1956 – Suez*, pp.149–85; Selwyn Lloyd, *Suez – 1956, A Personal Account*, pp.167–94; Abel Thomas, *Comment Israel fut Sauvé*, pp.105–200.

19. Concerning the motives behind the decision to embark on the campaign, see Mordechai Bar-On, 'The Sinai Campaign 1956 – Objectives and Expectations', *Zemanin*, no.23, autumn 1986 [Hebrew].

20. Moshe Dayan, *Avnei Derekh*, p.252.

21. *Official Diary*, 21 Oct. 1956. The costly results of the Qalqilia operation only a few days earlier also loomed large in Ben-Gurion's thoughts.

22. *Official Diary*, 22 Oct. 1956.

23. Ultimately the bombings were carried out 48 hours after the paratroopers landed in Mitla.

24. Bar-On, *Etgar ve Tigrah*, p.716; *Official Diary*, 23 Oct. 1956.

25. Paraphrased from *Official Diary*, 25 Oct. 1956.

26. Ezer Weizman, *Lecha Shamaim, Lecha Aretz*, p.155 [Hebrew].

27. Ibid.

28. Relations between the Israeli Air Force pilots and the French pilots stationed in Israel were so close then that when one French squadron was authorized to attack the airfield in Luxor from Israeli bases, the French invited the participation of several top Israeli pilots.

29. Aviezer Golan, *The Sinai Campaign*, an Official Publication of the IDF Chief Education Officer, p.23 [Hebrew]; similar assertions are in Uri Milstein, *The*

216

Paratrooper Wars, p.81.
30. Dayan, *The Sinai Campaign Diary*, p.72.
31. It was later discovered that those tents belonged to a public works group which was unarmed.
32. Quoted by Milstein, op. cit., p.81.
33. For Moshe Dayan's criticism of the paratroop activity at Mitla, see *Avnei Derekh*, p.282. See, too, J. Erez and I. Kfir, *Talks with Moshe Dayan*, p.42. Dayan is quoted, 'This was only a diversionary operation. There was no need to be in the western side of the Pass.' For the early reactions of the Egyptians to the Israeli drop at the Mitla Pass see Mohamed Heikal, *Cutting the Lion's Tail*, p.174.
34. Colonel Glinka was killed in this operation.
35. Dayan, *Avnei Derekh*, p.277.
36. Dayan, *The Sinai Campaign Diaries*, pp.81–2.
37. Dov Goldstein, *Ma'ariv*, 8 Oct. 1965, p.5.
38. Moshe Dayan, *The Sinai Campaign Diaries*, p.85.
39. For a full analysis of the campaign objectives see Mordechai Bar-On, 'The Sinai Campaign 1956 – Objectives and Expectations'.
40. Bar-On, *Etgar ve Tigra*, p.760 and p.767 and the final report on 'Operation Kadesh' by General Dan Tolkowsky.
41. The Brombergers' claim that the IDF called for help from the French cruiser after its forces became stuck is incorrect. Merry and Serge Bromberger, *Les Secrets de l'Expédition d'Egypte*, p.127.
42. Bar-On, *Etgar ve Tigra*, op cit., p.760.

217

15

Changes in Israel's Concept of
Security after Kadesh

Elhannan Orren

The aftermath of Operation Kadesh, as well as of the Anglo-French Operation Musketeer, necessarily called for a reassessment of the Israeli conception of security (*bitachon*).* Before a detailed discussion of what changed and what did not, it should be noted that the term 'conception' is commonly used in a somewhat vague sense. It is intended to convey a certain community of thinking, or a consensus, regarding cardinal issues, which supposedly affects planning and is expressed in practical deductions. In the case of Israel, however, one may question the degree of commitment of statesmen and soldiers, before and after Kadesh, to a presumed set of hard and fast concepts, clearly defined and outlined in detail.

Although from time to time, from the end of the War of Independence, Ben-Gurion expressed his thinking on 'basic issues of security' both in public and in inner councils, other Israeli statesmen and governments tended to avoid clear-cut definitions of their long-term outlook. The General Staff, because it must proceed from clear decisions on missions, objectives, and priorities in order to obtain the annual budgets, produced policy drafts and forecasts for government approval. But such a process of routine annual submission of proposals and their approval necessarily falls short of a schematic formulation of 'conceptions'.

Furthermore, the word 'conception' implies a logical process, resulting from methodically coordinated high-level planning, based on 'appreciations' (or 'estimates' in U. S. military parlance) and elaborated into directives, schedules and training 'doctrines' (another term which is used loosely). Also, by speaking of 'con-

* The use of the term 'security' is of significance, because it is seen to be more comprehensive, in the Israeli context, than the more common term defence (*haganah*), which is frequently substituted in translations, e.g. Minister of Defence.

cepts' one may convey the false impression that warfare is an activity controllable solely by logic and rational considerations. Yet warfare is permeated with attitudes, emotions and ideals, and the case of Zionism in the Israeli context is no exception. For example, during the weeks of suspense before the outbreak of the Six Day War the Israeli public heard premonitions of a 'final solution', while in the ranks of the leadership there was talk of the 'trauma' of the aftermath of 1956. One should not underestimate the importance of such moral and emotional aspects in military affairs at all levels, from the public at large to the political leaders and policy makers. For these reasons, then, a discussion of the conception of security, or the rational approach of a government and a military staff to a conflict which erupts into a violent crisis, must also take account of the prevailing mood, or what some historians call 'the climate of opinion'.

In the enquiry into 'conceptions', one can easily be misled by what was said in public at the time or subsequently, but what was said matters less than what was done under the circumstances prevailing at the time. Indeed, in a study of military thought, one might be well advised to proceed on the notion that 'the proof of the pudding is in the eating', or – to use a U.S. Army expression – that 'battle is the pay-off'.

Conceptions on policy express lessons of experience and the outlook (or even the forecast) on trends of change in years to come. More than a decade passed from Kadesh to the next outbreak of war, indeed a long period for changes to occur in the volatile Middle East. This paper confines itself to regional affairs, although due consideration is given to the shifting Great Power constellation and its regional impact. Among the major developments were the following:

1958 – In February Nasser of Egypt and Quwatly of Syria founded the 'United Arab Republic' (Ben-Gurion commented at the time that 'Egypt conquered Syria'); the merger lasted until 1961.

   – In July Qassem brought off his coup in Iraq; the shock waves disrupted Lebanon so much that Eisenhower dispatched marines to the shores of Beirut.

1960 – The Soviets started building the High Dam at Aswan which was considered essential to the future of Egypt.

1962 – By then Egypt had recovered from the blows of 1956 to the extent that Nasser ventured to intervene in the Yemen, but his expedition got bogged down for years.

219

1963 – In Syria the Ba'th took power.
– In Israel Ben-Gurion retired to Sede Boqer with Eshkol replacing him as Prime Minister and Minister of Defence.
1964 – There was an escalation of the Arab–Israeli tensions, as Israel's National Water Carrier neared completion:
– In January an inter-Arab Cairo summit decided on the diversion of Jordan sources.
– In May the Water Carrier was duly inaugurated.
– One Arab countermove was made by Syria, which adopted and activated the PLO; this organization declared its commitment to the destruction of the Water Carrier. As Y. Harkabi points out, it is the tragedy of the conflict that Arab leaders could see the inspired and complex irrigation scheme for the Negev only as an affront and a challenge.[1]

This is the background to our consideration of the problems which Israel faced after 'Kadesh'. Ben-Gurion held the portfolios both of Prime Minister and of Defence; when Eshkol succeeded him in 1963, he followed this example.[2] Students of Israel's security are aware of the underlying continuity of Arab belligerence and the threat to Israel's existence. In an outline of Arab–Israeli Wars, for example, the historian Netanel Lorch carried the story back to 1920 and entitled it 'One Long War'. Such continuity notwithstanding, changes do occur, and it is obvious that 1967 ushered in a new era. Therefore, current perspectives may obscure problems of earlier times.

Before we consider what changed after Kadesh, it would be useful to recall what has *not* changed. Since 1949, Israel has had to live with a dual security problem. In terms coined by A. Yariv, there exists the problem of 'fundamental' or 'basic' security – how to cope with a full-scale inter-Arab military onslaught to be launched at a time of their choosing.[3] Here this will be referred to as the 'major' problem. The second problem is the ongoing one of border-zone and internal security, posed by infiltrators, marauders and fidaiyyun guerrillas, a continuous preoccupation at variable intensity, mainly during between-war periods. This will be referred to as the 'minor' problem.

Each of these aspects, although linked, has a different impact on affairs, on attitudes and on policy-making. Ben-Gurion's outlook on the 'major' issues of security was marked by deep concerns. In 1949 he expressed the fear that an Arab leader cast in the mould of Ataturk might rise and incite the Arabs to 'take out' Israel.[4] He was deeply disturbed by what he saw on the map – the encirclement, the odds in numbers and materiel. Could Israel's lead in morale and quality balance or tip the scales and deter the enemy? The constant threat and the very narrow margin of safety led to nagging pangs of insecurity, even if these were subdued, suppressed, or even denied in public expressions.

What then did Kadesh change?

In terms of minor security problems, Kadesh brought in its wake a period of relative tranquillity. Until Kadesh Israel lived with the spiral of escalating strikes and reprisal raids, culminating at the Qalqilia Raid just about a fortnight before the campaign.[5] The period of calm after Kadesh brought welcome relief especially to army reservists who had undergone frequent call-ups and alerts in those uneasy times which preceded Kadesh. Such relief, however, was not to extend to major security problems.

After all, in the aftermath of the Kadesh campaign, the IDF had to evacuate the Sinai, and go back on the 'Green Line' demarcated according to the armistices of 1949. This meant that the centres of population were still exposed to shelling; airfields could be paralysed by long-range artillery; and there was almost no time for a so-called 'early air warning'.

Thus, in contrast to the respite in the 'minor' or ongoing security situation, the more fundamental 'major' threats persisted and intensified with the passing of time. These emanated mainly from Egypt and Syria. As Egypt rallied round Nasser, his radiating appeal inspired the Arabs to rally to his banner of 'one aim' and later they accepted his demands to form 'one line', in order to 'set back the clock' (to 1947). In the north, Syrian plots to divert the sources of the Jordan stemmed from the same urge as the Egyptian blockade that was broken by Kadesh – to prevent or impede Israel's development and the integration of waves of new immigrants who continued to arrive at the rate of tens of thousands per year. Moreover, Syria and Egypt extended the scope of their belligerence by involving the Palestinian refugees in violence. Their policy stood in contrast to that of Jordan, which endeavoured to absorb the West Bankers into its civic and political system. Well before 1967, Syria adopted Arafat's PLO, while Egypt sponsored Shuqayri's Palestinian Liberation Army; it should be noted that PLO terror was directed at Israel within the Green Line well before the occupation which followed the Six Day War and the Arab refusal to negotiate a peace.

When the IDF pulled out of Sinai and the Gaza Strip in early 1957,

Israel continued – or rather returned – to regard the 'Green Line' as permanent. This outlook was apparent in government policy, in party polemics, and where it counted most – in practice. This point may not be fully understood, since circumstances changed so radically in 1967. Therefore, it calls for some illustration.

First, the National Water Carrier was planned and constructed in full acceptance of the constraints resulting from the division of the centre of Eretz Israel along the Green Line, a partition which before Independence was considered to be incompatible with a country-wide irrigation scheme. For example, 20 years earlier the 'moderate' Chaim Weizmann had argued, in favour of the Biltmore Plan of 1942 (which called for a 'Jewish Commonwealth' in the whole of (western) Palestine), that the Negev irrigation scheme proposed by the American engineer Walter Clay Lowdermilk ruled out a partition of Palestine.[6] Thus the post-Kadesh decision to build the National Water Carrier indicates the significance of that pragmatic policy. Second, Israel obviously regarded the 1949 borders as long and vulnerable. But rather than undertake extensive fortifications, it continued with its settlement policy which was strategically directed to bolster 'regional defence.' The Nachal Command* was especially prominent in setting up 'foothold settlements' at sensitive spots near the border (e.g. Almagor, near the estuary of the Jordan into Lake Tiberias).

The consideration of security issues fell within the understanding that the central theme and vital interest of Israel was constructive development, coupled with absorption and integration of immigrants. It will suffice to mention some prominent examples of the nation-building effort in the post-Kadesh decade. As a direct outcome of Kadesh, Eilat rapidly became a port and a pump-head for Iranian oil, which was pumped north via a pipeline laid along the length of the Negev to a terminal at Ashkelon. A second deep water port in the Mediterranean, to serve the south, which had been under construction at the new city of Ashdod since 1955, was opened in 1966. The Dead Sea Works went into full-scale production, and shipped most of their products via Eilat and Ashdod. The

---

* 'Nachal' – a Hebrew acronym for 'Pioneering Fighting Youth'. The Command trains settler groups from the youth movements. Their tour of service combines military training and service with on-the-site life and training in settlements. Most groups, on completion of their tour of duty, augment existing communal settlements; some are chosen to set up new ones, including the type of 'foothold settlement' ('He'achzut') – a settlement on a site significant for border defence, which is developed gradually, until it can be converted to civilian status.

production of electrical current was tripled to meet consumption. The activation of the above-mentioned Water Carrier of course also deserves mention in this context. As for immigration, Ben-Gurion had hoped to bring in two million, half of them from the USSR.[7] Reality fell far short of this goal. Nevertheless, in the decade after Kadesh the Jewish population of Israel grew from 1,700,000 in 1956 to 2,300,000 in 1967. By then, the minorities, mainly Muslim Arabs, numbered 300,000.

The improvement of Israel's armaments in quality and quantity was, of course, a basic requisite within the context of development. In this vital concern Israel was largely dependent on the Western powers. A significant development in external defence contracts and relations occurred with the switch from an almost exclusive reliance on France for the supply of strategic weapons, to a growing dependence on the United States, causing some internal friction within the Israeli defence establishment. In the 1960s the green light was given by President Kennedy, and the process was stepped up under President Johnson, who responded to the appeal of Eshkol. Soviet advances in the Middle East probably influenced the U.S. to open up to Israeli defence needs.[8]

Turning from the overall policy of development to concepts of security, one axiom can be seen to dominate policy: there would never be another Kadesh; Israel must be prepared to face all the Arab armies, and on her own.[9] Soon after the campaign, in December 1956, a command conference discussed the lessons of Kadesh. Ben-Gurion, who attended and summed up, concentrated on the theme that the 'next war' would be different. He pointed out that in the future Israel might not again reap the benefits of the initiative; she might be the attacked, and by more than one army; the country might not gain external support; the war might be prolonged, and Israel would suffer more casualties. The main difference might be that the enemy air forces would not be paralysed from the outset; the enemy would hit at Israel's rear and lower morale; and when the IDF rallied to take the offensive to the lands of the enemy, the army would not move into an empty desert, but would be faced by a hostile populace.[10]

After the War of Independence the IDF had to strike a fine balance between alert preparedness at all times and preparation for an eventual war. When General Yigael Yadin served as Chief of Staff (1949–52), he used to point out the distinction between 'being' prepared (*konenuth*) and 'getting' prepared (*hithkonenuth*). Before Kadesh, Israel had been preoccupied with 'minor' security,

223

with frequent alerts and call-ups of reserves. After the campaign, rather than *konenuth* – having to be prepared and on the alert most of the time – the IDF could concentrate on 'major' security , namely to reorganize, equip and train in preparation for an expected 'next round'.

Aware of Egypt's military recovery due to Soviet military assistance, Israel soon found herself involved in a renewed arms race, and even some 'rocket-rattling' occurred. The immediate aim was to maintain deterrence. To this end, in the political sphere Ben-Gurion initiated attempts to reach out beyond the Arab confrontation states and cement ties with their non-Arab neighbours. He tried to form two linked triangular groupings with states on the periphery of the Middle East: a northern one with Turkey and the Shah's Iran, and an eastern one with Haile Selassie's Ethiopia and Iran. Very useful relations were developed.[11] In addition, Israel was helped by France to develop a nuclear potential.

The GHQ planners had to provide for a variety of strategic eventualities, which called for flexibility in contingency plans and a willingness to adapt to unforeseen circumstances. In their evaluations Egypt was regarded as the greatest threat; a crossing of the Suez Canal into demilitarized Sinai was seen as a *casus belli*. Jordan and Iraq were seen as a combined threat; the entry of an Iraqi contingent even into the East Bank, was also seen as a *casus belli*. Syria was perceived as posing the least threat.

Political constraints became an item of major concern in the consideration of operational policy, since these could affect a first strike option. In the context of war policy, terms such as 'preventive war' are used rather freely, but in Israel such a 'pre-emptive' (or spoiling) war was in fact ruled out, because after Kadesh Israel was very wary of being branded an aggressor. Instead, much consideration was given to a pre-emptive counter-attack in the event of an obviously impending Arab attack. Attention was centred on the sensitive issue of political prerequisites for such a strategy in the prevailing power constellation.[12] The conclusion of the military planners was that given government approval, the IDF would preempt an attack on one front in order to carry the battle to enemy territory, and then swiftly switch its main effort, making the most of Israel's central position, or 'interior lines'.

In addition, Israel had already learnt in 1948, and once again with Kadesh, that the IDF would have to race against the clock of a Superpower-imposed cease-fire. Dayan spoke of a 'political sandglass' or even a 'sword of Damocles'. It was difficult to reconcile the speed required for a pre-emptive strike and for time-saving 'accelerated combat' tactics with the precepts of the 'indirect approach' as formulated by Liddell Hart, the military thinker who was held in esteem in Israel, because he advised preliminary time-consuming moves of deception, diversion and distraction.

While the IDF focused on 'major' security issues, 'minor' security problems demanded attention particularly since 1965, as Israel responded in kind to Syrian harassment and to the raids of the Fatah fidai organization that were activated under Syrian sponsorship. Ongoing incidents on this front appeared to be so significant that even the International Institute for Strategic Studies in London came to the mistaken conclusion that Syrian–Israeli tension was the direct cause of the eruption of the Six Day War.[13] To Israeli observers the Syrian-adopted activities of Fatah were a resurgence of the hitherto dormant Palestinian issue, which they tended to view in a rather narrow and practical context. The IDF saw terror as a problem of 'minor' security, not as a 'major' problem of strategy, and even less of politics. To the extent that it affected 'major' security, it fell within the larger threat from the relevant 'host state' in which the terrorists were based.[14] Moreover, military planners considered the Palestinians a negligible military threat in the event of war and, indeed, they were proved correct during the swift West Bank Campaign in 1967. Politically, the Palestinians were seen in contingency plans as an issue for a 'military government' engaged in the problems of occupation.

Such attention to 'minor' security problems notwithstanding, the foremost policy issue after Kadesh was how to build up the IDF for full-scale war in order to cope with an all-Arab threat on several fronts. Within a decade IDF strength more than trebled, and American good will towards Israel's defence needs enabled it to achieve this rate of growth. It should be noted that the rise in defence imports persisted, because of the 'major' security threat, even when an economic recession set in.[15]

That the emphasis in the IDF was on the offensive, and on quality, rather than quantities of men and arms, is illustrated by the specific changes in the various services and branches of the IDF after Kadesh:

The Air Force completed its conversion and became fully jet-powered. Numbers of combat aircraft were more than tripled and the Mirage 3 became prominent. Maintenance schedule-timings were trimmed to achieve a rate of turn-around that enabled air crews to fly a number of sorties which seemed incredible. (When the Israeli squadrons attacked Nasser's airfields in successive waves on 5 June, 1967, Nasser probably did believe that the U.S. Sixth Fleet was involved.)

The Navy now became a 'two-sea' force, with a flotilla in the Gulf of Eilat.

The ground forces underwent development on the following lines:

• Armour became the main arm, with ex-Palmachniks converting to the Armoured Corps, and some becoming prominent tank commanders.[16] The numbers of tanks more than trebled, with British and French makes in the lead. At the same time IDF Ordnance 'beefed up' and reconditioned the ageing Shermans.
• The artillery was converted from drawn to self-propelled, to keep up with armour.
• Infantry brigades were mechanized and grouped with armoured brigades in divisions of a flexible 'corps-type' composition.
• Airborne troops were reinforced and equipped to become also copter-borne.
• Tactical training in all the corps of the ground forces was directed to cope with defence layouts constructed according to Soviet doctrine, as applied by teams of advisers and instructors in the Egyptian and Syrian armies.
• The 'Regional Defence', based on the extended layout of settlements, was bolstered for its vital function – to provide a defensive shield along the long borders, in order to enable field forces to concentrate in order to punch with a 'mailed fist'.
• The logistic system was reformed and computerized, with the aim of pushing fuel, ammunition and supplies forward, thereby relieving formations of the need to draw from dumps in the rear.

Additional changes were made to increase inter-service and nationwide preparedness. The infrastructure was developed to improve communications in order to take full advantage of Israel's compact 'interior lines'. In view of the threat to the rear, Civil Defence was reorganized with improved equipment. A special staff department was established with the task of putting the economy on an emergency footing in the event of full mobilization. To improve mobilization capability, call-up processes were constantly tried out and improved on, with the result that there was a significant reduction in the time required. (The pay-off came in the Yom Kippur War, despite the hasty and improvised call-up.)

To sum up, after Kadesh Israel prepared and geared itself for a war on several or even all fronts, and planned to take the strategic initiative on one front, strike decisively and switch swiftly to another. How did these concepts and plans stand up to the impact of mid-May 1967, when Nasser's army suddenly marched into the Sinai? In 1966, commemorating a decade after Kadesh, Chief of Staff Rabin wrote of the 'vindicated lessons' of 1956.[17] In May 1967 some of those lessons were invalidated: first, by the very fact that Nasser made this move; and second, when his forces, having crossed the Canal, sat tight in the Sinai. The Egyptians 'double-crossed' Israel – once when they did cross the Canal and again when they did not attack forthwith. This grave and unforeseen threat ushered in three weeks of a suspenseful waiting and soul-searching, when Israel called up the reserves and engaged in full-scale military preparations, while the government made last-minute efforts to prevent a clash or, if war was inevitable, at least to secure some political support from the USA. At last a 'national coalition' government was formed, with Dayan brought in to serve as Minister of Defence, and this emergency government decided to act. When it did, Syria was expected to join Nasser; instead it stood back while Jordan's Hussein – also unexpectedly – rushed in. However, by the onset of June Israel's post-Kadesh concepts had been flexibly readjusted to the political constraints and the loss of strategic initiative, enabling the IDF to deal with the closing ring of Arab armies by seizing the operational initiative in the air and on the ground.

In conclusion, the post-Kadesh experience – to which one can add the lessons of the 1973 Yom Kippur War – suggests that terms like 'deterrence' or 'early warning' tend in time to be regarded as axioms or are taken for granted, as if they were absolute guarantees. They should be regarded in relative and flexible terms as declared intentions, rather than attained ends. For instance, the effect of deterrence, not unlike physical health, should be judged by its duration – and Kadesh provided a respite of 11 years.

Another reflection is that whatever the conceptions to which a government and a GHQ are committed, they should still be viewed with 'open minds,' allowing a flexibility of approach. After all, statesmen and soldiers should expect the unexpected.

In 1967, Hussein followed Nasser's lead into war. Ten years – and two wars – later, Sadat took his momentous leap to peace. More than a decade later one may conclude with the reflection that Israel, having come such a long way in conflict and confrontations, has still to realize the third aim of the policy formulated by Ben-Gurion in 1947. On the eve of the impending War of Independence, and at its end, he listed three aims of long-term policy in the following sequence: first – security; second – independence; and third, in the fullness of time – Israeli–Arab peace.[18]

NOTES

1. Author's notes from a lecture on the asymmetries of the Arab–Israeli conflict, Tel Aviv University, 1975.
2. Eshkol held both posts until the formation of the 'national coalition' government on the eve of the Six Day War, when Moshe Dayan was brought in and replaced Eshkol as Minister of Defence. Moshe Sharett, Prime Minister from 1953 to 1955, separated the posts.
3. Gen. Aharon Yariv, '30 Years of Security' [Heb.], in *Sekirah Hodshit* (IDF Monthly), March–April 1979, pp.6–13.
4. D. Ben-Gurion, *The War of Independence; Ben-Gurion's Diary* [Heb.], Eds. G. Rivlin and Dr. E. Orren, Tel Aviv, 1982 (below – BG, *War Diary*), pp.863, 964.
5. Gen. M. Dayan, *Diary of the Sinai Campaign 1956*, ch.3 – Qalqiliah.
6. P. Goodman (ed.), *Chaim Weizmann – A Tribute on his Seventieth Birthday*, London, 1944, p.316 (speech on 30 Jan., 1944).
7. On the fourth anniversary of 'Kadesh', Ben-Gurion spoke of the necessary addition of 2 million immigrants, and expressed his hope that half of them would come from the USSR (D. Ben-Gurion, *Yichud Ve'ie'ud* [Heb., Singularity and Destiny], Tel Aviv, 1971, pp.321–2.
8. I. Rabin, *Pinkas Sherut* (Heb., Memoirs; literally: [Army] Service Record), Tel Aviv, 1979 (below – Rabin), pp.105–6, 113–14. See also Gen. T. Tsur, in *Tsahal be'Cheilo* [Heb.], IDF Encycl., vol.1 – *Army and Security, 1948–67* (below – IDF Enc), p.165. On U.S. arms supply see Nadav Safran, *From War to War; The Arab–Israeli Confrontation*, 1948–67, New York, 1969 (below – Safran), pp.131–79.
9. It seemed to many Israelis at the time that Gary Cooper, in the classic movie 'High Noon', aptly expressed the mood.
10. The relevant extract from Ben-Gurion's Diary, 27 Dec. 1956 – see Part IV.
11. Rabin, p.102.
12. Y. Allon discussed the problem in his book, *A Curtain of Sand* [Heb.], Tel Aviv, 1968, pp.67–77.
13. Michael Howard and Robert Hunter, *Israel and the Arab World: The Crisis of 1967*, Adelphi Papers, International Institute for Strategic Studies, London, Oct. 1967, pp.10–11, 13–15.
14. 'Host state' is the term in common use. However, to describe the interrelations between Arab states and the variously sponsored terrorist groups, a more apt term would be 'foster state'.
15. The figures of Israel's annual outlays come from IDF Enc, tables on p.144, 152, 186, and are correlated to the 1979 cost index. Safran provides a wealth of comparative data (see ch.III). He presents defence expenditure as percentages of the respective GNPs. However, it should be noted that the superpowers not only supplied arms, but also contributed massively to the economy of the parties.
16. Palmach (Heb. acronym, Assault Companies) were the regular element of the Haganah (Heb., defence), the Zionist underground army-to-be, before independence, and during the 1947–9 war rapidly expanded to form three infantry brigades, which became the outstanding battle formations of IDF. Many combat-

proven commanders of the Palmach were selected to convert to armour, and distinguished themselves. Some prominent ex-Palmach armour generals were Bar-Lev, Elazar and Adan.
17. I. Rabin in *Ma'arachot* ([Heb.], IDF Military Review), No. 178–9, p.13.
18. E.g., see BG, *War Diary*, pp.345, 999.

This paper is based mainly on Hebrew sources. Some additional studies in English are recommended:

Ben-Horin, Yoav and Barry Posen, *Israel's Strategic Doctrine* (Rand Corp; Santa Monica, 1981).
Cordesman, Anthony, *The Arab–Israeli Military Balance and the Art of Operations* (American Enterprise Institute for Public Policy Research: Occasional Papers; Washington, Oct. 1986), esp. pp.9–12.
Luttwak, Edward and Dan Horowitz, *The Israeli Army* (London, 1975), esp, chs. 5–6.
Schiff, Zeev, *A History of the Israeli Army* (New York, 1985), pp.86ff.

16

Operation Kadesh: A Legal Perspective

Yehuda Z. Blum

The Kadesh Campaign (29 October – 5 November 1956) poses some very interesting and intriguing legal problems, for it brings together some of the fundamental problems of contemporary international law, as they relate to the use of force in international relations. How should a State respond to ongoing provocations, acts of terrorism, initiated across its boundaries in a neighbouring country, with the encouragement, blessing, logistic support etc. of that neighbour? How should a State respond to an ongoing naval blockade of international waterways recognized as such, affecting not only vessels flying its own flag but also vessels of other States bound for its ports? How should a State respond to ongoing threats to its very existence, coupled with an intensified rearming of its neighbour with the avowed and declared purpose of liquidating it? These are but some of the problems that come to the mind of an international lawyer in connection with the Kadesh campaign.

It would seem appropriate to discuss all these questions within the broader framework of the legality of the use of force rather than from the perspective of the *just war* concept, since the latter (*bellum iustum* of the Medieval Christian philosophers) is basically a theological, as distinct from a legal, notion.[1] Thus it is bound to be a subjective concept depending upon the theological outlook of those who resort to it. To be sure, it is not only Christianity that was preoccupied with this concept of a just war.[2] A parallel concept is also found in Islam. *Jihad* is basically a just war, conducted against infidels, for the greater glory of Islam,[3] just as the *bellum iustum* of the Middle Ages in Europe was essentially a war conducted by Christians against infidels.

In Judaism there does not appear to exist a similar distinction between just and unjust wars. The distinction drawn by Maimonides between *Milchemet Mitzva* and *Milchemet Reshut*,[4] apparently does not parallel the distinction between *bellum iustum* and *bellum non-*

justum. Milchemet Mitzva, an obligatory war (although the concept is difficult to translate accurately), is a war waged for the conquest of the Land of Israel or a war of self-defence, whereas *Milchemet Reshut,* roughly corresponding to the concept of optional war, comprises all other wars conducted by the Kings of Israel, with the consent of the Great Sanhedrin. However, the concept has not been developed in Judaism mainly, it seems, due to the fact that with the destruction of the Second Temple in the year 70 C. E. and the resulting disappearance of Jewish statehood, this branch of Jewish Law was sorely neglected for nineteen centuries and has not been duly revived since.

The role of the concept of *bellum iustum* was greatly diminished as a result of the schism that occurred within Christianity with the advent of Protestantism. It underwent a process of secularization and in fact was practically discarded until the end of the nineteenth century.[5] This was done for a very good reason, for with the emergence of the national State based on the principle of sovereignty all wars became equally just and consequently legal. As a result, the old distinction between just and unjust wars was rendered useless and irrelevant. In fact, the virtually unlimited right of a State to wage war came to be considered as one of the fundamental attributes of statehood. International lawyers of that period right up to the outbreak of the First World War, when listing the attributes of an independent State, regularly mention, alongside the capacity to establish diplomatic relations and to conclude international agreements, also the right to wage war without any limitation.

It is only with the end of the First World War and with the establishment of the League of Nations that international law started to limit the right of States to wage war, mainly through various procedural devices. Without going into the rather elaborate provisions of the League of Nations Covenant, which are now mainly of historical significance, suffice it to state here that war as such was not prohibited under the Covenant.[6] Even the Kellogg–Briand Pact of 1928, often referred to as the treaty outlawing war, does not really outlaw war entirely. It confines itself to condemning war as an instrument of *national* policy and pledges the parties to the pact (virtually all the States of the world had joined the pact by 1939) to settle all their international disputes by peaceful means.[7]

Again, there is no complete and total renunciation of the resort to war in international relations. What is more, and this is perhaps even more disturbing: all these documents and instruments of the inter-war period refer only to war as such, and thus leave open the question of the legality of the use of force that does not amount to war or is not defined as such. They thereby open up a very dangerous loophole from which the potential aggressors and other violators of international law can always benefit.

This in fact is exactly what happened on numerous occasions between the two World Wars. Japan never waged war against China. Japan did not want to characterize its military actions as war for fear of being condemned by the League of Nations. China was not interested in declaring war on Japan for fear of being embargoed by foreign powers, primarily the United States, during those years. So it suited both sides to treat the war that was going on between them as if it did not exist. And there are also other instances of that period that highlight the inadequate stage reached by international law in curbing the recourse to war and force in international relations.

The founders of the United Nations thought they had learned the lessons of the past. The U. N. Charter thus no longer prohibits recourse to war as such, but more specifically speaks of the prohibition of the use of force in any form. What is more: it is not only the use of force that is prohibited; even the *threat* of force is unlawful under the Charter.[8] The difficulty with all this, of course, is that there is no institution in place to supervise and enforce adherence to this prohibition and to impose on States the duty to settle by peaceful means their international disputes.

The Charter, to be sure, does in principle impose this duty on States. Under Article 2(3), Member States pledge to settle their disputes by peaceful means.[9] However, the jurisdiction of the International Court of Justice is of an optional nature and is predicated on the parties' consent to such jurisdiction.[10] Thus, a situation has arisen in which a State is legally prevented from using force to enforce its rights, while at the same time being unable to compel its opponent to submit to the jurisdiction of the International Court of Justice.

There is an important exception to the general prohibition of the use of force, namely, 'the inherent right of self-defence' preserved under Article 51 of the U.N. Charter. Under the Charter regime, States have not given up their natural right to protect themselves against attacks from the outside. However, under Article 51, this right of self-defence is generally believed to be confined to a response to an *armed attack*. According to Article 51, 'Nothing in the present Charter shall impair the inherent right of individual or

232

collective self-defence if an armed attack occurs ...' Not every act of aggression is necessarily an *armed attack*. How, for instance, should we categorize terrorist activities sponsored by a neighbouring country? Do such terrorist activities invariably amount to armed attacks, within the meaning of Article 51? And if not – does international law expect the target State of such activities to act as a sitting duck and to endure them without any response on its part? Most authors and scholars in the field would answer these questions by pointing out that *individual* acts of terrorism do not normally qualify as *armed attacks* to justify counter-attacks in self-defence. However, the question then arises as to whether one should view each terrorist outrage in isolation, or whether one should not rather take a broader view and consider the *accumulation* of terrorist activities in their entirety as amounting to an armed attack.[11]

In this connection it should be mentioned that in 1955 and 1956 a long series of terrorist outrages occurred in Israel which could be traced to Egypt, directly or indirectly. If one takes the broader view of the legitimacy of State response to terrorist outrages, one may validly treat all these terrorist activities as amounting to one concentrated attack, rather than consider them as isolated incidents. In referring to terrorist activities of this kind, German international lawyers have been speaking of the application of a *Nadelstichtaktik* – tactics of the needle prick. The implication of this concept is that while each of such needle pricks, when viewed in isolation, probably would not justify an armed counter-attack in self-defence on the part of the target State, they nevertheless do justify such response when viewed as a whole.[12]

Moreover, in evaluating the legitimacy or otherwise of Operation Kadesh, one also has to bear in mind the naval blockade imposed upon Israel by Egypt at the time. As is well known, ever since the establishment of Israel in 1948, Israeli or Israel-bound vessels were prevented by Egypt from passing through the Suez Canal, in violation of the 1888 Constantinople Convention.[13] Simultaneously, Egypt also blocked passage for Israeli and Israel-bound vessels through the Straits of Tiran.

Admittedly, these two questions are not identical. The legal regime of straits[14] is different from that of the legal regime of the Suez Canal. However, what these two blockades had in common was that in both instances Egypt violated its obligations under the international law of the sea which imposed on it the duty to grant free and unimpeded passage to the vessels of all States through these international waterways.

On a narrow reading of Article 51, Egypt's conduct was probably not in the nature of an *armed attack*, but this does not necessarily mean that Israel had to put up forever with the situation thus created. Some of Egypt's acts unquestionably qualified as acts of aggression under the definition of aggression adopted by the U.N. General Assembly in 1974.[15] Admittedly, the Kadesh campaign preceded the adoption of that definition by 18 years. But it was generally accepted even prior to the adoption of the 1974 definition that a naval blockade amounted to an act of aggression and that it could be justified only in time of war. Israel, it will be recalled, had since 1949 a general armistice agreement with Egypt under which acts of hostility, including the sending of armed bands into the territory of the other State, were also forbidden.[16]

Finally, one must, of course, face the most difficult question of all: what does international law expect a State to do when it is in possession of conclusive evidence that its neighbour is bent on its destruction and is taking all the necessary steps to bring about the realization of that objective? To phrase this question differently: is self-defence confined only to the actual occurrence of an armed attack, or is it permissible also at an earlier stage when the impending armed attack becomes a virtual certainty? Under traditional international law, a broad answer was given to this question, namely, that the right of self-defence exists not only in those situations where an armed attack has already occurred, but already at the moment when the danger of such an attack has become instant and overwhelming.[17] Numerous scholarly authorities have taken the view that it is in the light of this traditional concept of self-defence in international law that the Charter provision contained in Article 51 has to be interpreted.[18]

These are all crucial questions; the Kadesh campaign has brought them all together. But Kadesh was not the only instance in Israel's history in which questions of this kind arose. Some 25 years later, in 1981, Israel was faced with a similar issue at the time of the destruction of the Iraqi nuclear reactor. That event is worth mentioning here because it too highlights the inadequacy of the traditional concepts and interpretations of the United Nations Charter when viewed against the background of the 1970s and the 1980s.[19]

Traditional international law was premised on the assumption that a State, once attacked, would always have the time and the ability to hit back and to repel the attacker. In other words, it would always have what we now call a *second-strike capability*. This was always a questionable assumption when applied to a small State like Israel, the total breadth of which was, in 1956, at its narrowest point (the so-called *narrow waistline*) only nine miles, that is the distance from the Mediterranean Sea to the slopes of the Samarian hills. It is certainly an utterly unrealistic assumption in this era of intercontinental ballistic missiles and of nuclear capability. Under these novel circumstances any undue patience on the part of the potential victim of aggression could easily become a prelude to national suicide. Such a course of action on the part of the potential victim surely cannot be reconciled with his right of self-defence.

One is therefore led to the inescapable conclusion that some of the traditional concepts of international law have become inadequate under the circumstances that have evolved since 1945. In fact, the United Nations Charter itself may already have been obsolete when it came into effect on 24 October 1945. The Charter had been drafted between April and June 1945, and was signed in San Francisco on 24 June 1945. Some six weeks later the first atomic bomb was dropped on Hiroshima and a new era was ushered in. Consequently, by October 1945 many people (including leading statesmen and legal scholars) asked themselves if, and to what extent, the Charter still met the requirements of the new nuclear age. This question remains with us some four decades later.

This, in fact, brings us to the much broader question of the relationship between reality and law in general. The law, as a rule, always lags behind reality; it is bound to lag behind it because it is shaped by the realities of everyday life. Moreover, the law, by its very nature, cannot be expected to adjust itself instantaneously to the changing scene of life, national or international. Such instant adjustment, even if it were somehow possible, would be irresponsible conduct on the part of legislators.

Having said this, and having entered these few words of caution, one should add that when the law lags too far behind reality, then eventually the loser is bound to be the law. This in fact is precisely what has been happening to international law, insofar as it relates to the use of force since the Second World War. Operation Kadesh was only one of the examples in which the inadequacy of contemporary international law relating to the use of force became painfully evident. If one surveys the international scene of recent years – whether in Afghanistan, Grenada, Libya or the Persian Gulf, to mention but a few examples – one realizes how great the discrepancy between international law and reality has become.

NOTES

1. According to Clive Parry, the earliest writers on international law 'adopted from Roman law a distinction between just and unjust war which had been developed and extended by the Christian theologians, and notably by St. Thomas Aquinas. ... The medieval theologians ... looked at the question of the justice or otherwise of the cause of a party purely subjectively. The activities of rebels were thus *bellum iniustum*, whereas the countermeasures of a legitimate prince were *bellum iustum*. Such a classification ... was incapable of objective application to determine, for instance, which of two plausible dynastic claims was the better, for each might have some justice about it.' C. Parry, in M. Sorensen (editor), *Manual of Public International Law*, 1968, p.27.

2. See J.L. Kunz, 'Bellum Justum and Bellum Legale', in 45 *American Journal of International Law* (1951), 528 ff.

3. See entry on 'International Law, Islamic', in R. Bernhardt (editor), *Encyclopedia of Public International Law* (Heidelberg), Installment 6 (1983), pp.227 ff.

4. Maimonides, *Ha'yad Hahazakah*, Hilkhot M'lakhim, Chapter 5, Sections 1 and 2.

5. See M. Shaw, *International Law* (2nd edition), 1986, pp.540 ff.

6. See Articles 12–16 of the Covenant. For a detailed legal analysis of these provisions, see W. Schücking and H. Wehberg, *Die Satzung des Völkerbundes*, 1921, pp.289–393.

7. For the text of the Pact (the official name of which is 'General Treaty for Renunciation of War as an Instrument of National Policy of August 27, 1928') see *League of Nations Treaty Series*, vol.94 (1929), p.59 ff.

8. Under Article 2(4) of the Charter, 'all Members [of the United Nations] shall refrain in their international relations from the threat or use of force against the territorial integrity or political independence of any state, or in any other manner inconsistent with the Purposes of the United Nations.'

9. Article 2(3) provides that 'all Members shall settle their international disputes by peaceful means and in such a manner that international peace and security, and justice, are not endangered.'

10. See Article 36(1) of the Statute of the International Court of Justice. For a more detailed analysis see S. Rosenne, *The World Court*, 3rd rev. ed. 1973, pp. 72–4.

11. See D.W. Bowett, 'Reprisals Involving Recourse to Armed Force', 68 *American Journal of International Law* (1974), 1, at 5–7.

12. See P. Wittig, 'Der Aggressionsbegriff im internationalen Sprachgebrauch', in W. Schaumann (editor), *Völkerrechtliches Gewaltverbot und Friedenssicherung*, 1971, pp.33–75, at p.55.

13. The text of the Convention may be found in the Supplement to 3 *American Journal of International Law* (1909), 123.

14. See Articles 34–45 of the Law of the Sea Convention of 1982. For a general discussion of the legal regime of straits, see T. Koh, *Straits in International Navigation*, 1982.

15. See Annex to Resolution 3314 (XXIX) of 14 Dec. 1974.

16. Under Article II(2) of the Egypt–Israel General Armistice Agreement of 24 Feb. 1949 'no element of the land, sea or air military or para-military forces of either party, including non-regular forces, shall commit any warlike or hostile act against the military or para-military forces of the other party, or against civilians in territory under the control of that party.' It is noteworthy, though, that the agreement in question does not contain a provision similar to that found in Article III(3) of the General Armistice Agreements concluded between Israel and Lebanon, Syria and Jordan, respectively, under which 'no warlike act or act of hostility shall be conducted from territory controlled by one of the Parties to this Agreement against the other Party.' However, according to Rosenne, oral undertakings to this effect

were also exchanged with Egypt. See S. Rosenne, *Israel's Armistice Agreements with Arab States*, 1951, p.46.

17. These are the criteria laid down by U.S. Secretary of State Daniel Webster in 1837 in the well-known *Caroline* case, reported in Moore's *Digest of International Law*, vol.II, 1906, p.409.

18. See e.g. D.W. Bowett, *Self-Defence in International Law*, 1958, pp.185–6; J. Stone, *Aggression and World Order*, 1958, pp.95–6; D.P. O'Connell, *International Law*, 2nd ed., 1970, vol I, pp.316–18.

19. On the legal aspects of the destruction by Israel of the Iraqi nuclear reactor, see A. D'Amato, 'Israel's Strike upon the Iraqi Nuclear Reactor', 77 *American Journal of International Law* (1983), 584 ff.; J. Birnberg, 'The Sun Sets on Tamuz I: The Israeli Raid on Iraq's Nuclear Reactor', 13 *California Western Journal of International Law* (1983), 86ff.

17

The Sinai Campaign and the Limits of Power*

I. Yitzhak Rabin
II. Shlomo Avineri

I. Yitzhak Rabin

If I had to sum up the Suez operation I would say that the winners were Egypt and Israel. The losers were Britain and France.

The British and the French discovered that through military action they could not achieve their political goals. This was not because of an inability effectively to use the forces at their command. It was because of their inability to withstand the political pressure of the United States and the Soviet Union, who compelled them to withdraw from the Canal and Egypt. This operation symbolized more than anything else the end of the primary role of Britain and France in the Middle East. A new era was inaugurated in which the two Superpowers filled the vacuum with their competing interests.

Nasser won politically although he lost militarily. He could not withstand Israel nor could he stop the British and the French so long as they wished to continue the military action. Nevertheless he successfully prevented Britain and France, who until then had been considered world powers, from regaining control over the Canal or from deposing him and changing Egypt's internal political structure. He also brought about the withdrawal from Egyptian territory of all British, French and Israeli forces. As a consequence of these achievements he gained great prestige throughout the Arab world.

---

* The following selections are from addresses on 'The Limits of Power' by the Minister of Defence Yitzhak Rabin and Professor Shlomo Avineri at the International Symposium on the thirtieth anniversary of the Suez–Sinai Campaigns held at Ben-Gurion University of the Negev in October 1986.

Israel won militarily as well as politically since it was willing to settle for limited goals. Although Nasser remained in power and Israel did not gain any territory, fidaiyyun raids were stopped, the number of Egyptian forces in Sinai were limited thereby freeing Israel from the danger of imminent attack, and the Straits of Tiran were opened to Israeli shipping. In the eleven years of peace that followed Israel was able to focus on other issues such as the development of the economy, education and improving social services. This was because Ben-Gurion was willing to forgo the unattainable and settle for what could be practically and realistically achieved.

What are the lessons that can be drawn for Israel's defence problems from the Sinai Campaign as well as from the other Arab–Israeli wars? In my presentation, I am not representing the official position of the Ministry of Defence or of the Government. I am speaking for myself.

All of Israel's wars, from the War of Independence and including the war in Lebanon, can be divided into two categories. The War of Independence, the Six Day War, the Yom Kippur War and the War of Attrition could be considered Wars of No Choice. The other wars, the Sinai Campaign and the war in Lebanon, were different in their structure and character. These were the only ones which we initiated or where we were party to their initiation. They were intended as wars for achieving far-reaching political goals. This distinction does not imply that these were not just wars. As in all the other conflicts, they were also just wars since the opposing parties had repeatedly stressed that they were at war with us and were unwilling to enter into peace negotiations. We were therefore justified in initiating war rather than allowing the other side to decide when and where to initiate a conflict with us.

Nevertheless, the question is not merely one of whether wars are just. The crucial issue is one of the wisdom and of the potential benefits of initiating a war. Israel's problem with the Arab countries and until 1978–79 with Egypt has been their unwillingness to become reconciled to the existence of Israel as an independent, viable and Jewish state. This has been their position no matter where the boundaries were located. The reality of the State of Israel was rejected in 1947, 1949, 1967, and 1973. With the exception of Egypt since 1979, when we signed a treaty of peace with her, we have been living under a state of war and have suffered from continual acts of terror. Thus, the primary question before the Israeli policy-maker and the military-planner throughout these years has been

239

whether it is possible to have a war that will bring an end to further wars. That is, is it possible, by utilizing all our resources and by undertaking comprehensive preparations, for us to achieve the kind of military strength that will enable us to engage in the war that will end all wars? Can one plan to use military strength to accomplish the ultimate purpose of using force to impose our political will on our enemies – those Arab countries that are in a state of war with us?

When I served as Chief of the General Staff of the IDF, I asked myself why Israel could not implement Clausewitz's axiom – that war is the extension of policy by other means and that through war one attempts to destroy the armed forces of the enemy in order to impose upon him your political will. This is what the Allies did during the Second World War by carrying out Clausewitz's maxim on a global scale. Having joined together against the Axis powers – Nazi Germany, Fascist Italy and Imperialist Japan – the Allied forces fought the war until they destroyed the armed forces and the will of the Axis nations so that they could impose their own political solution on these countries. They not only divided Germany between East and West but changed the entire structure of the German political system in the Western zones; they brought about a total political and social reform in Italy; and there can be no doubt that General MacArthur effected lasting reforms in Japan during an extended military occupation. Thus, profound changes were made on a global scale through the instrument of military power employed to its ultimate political purpose. The recent historical record clearly shows that Clausewitz's maxim can be implemented.

Can Clausewitz be realized in terms of the Arab–Israeli conflict? I have consistently believed over the past 30 years and still believe today that what was possible for the Allied forces in their war against the Axis powers is impossible for Israel, although not for military reasons. I believe that if Israel decided to undertake austerity measures in order to build the kind of military forces that we have the potential for organizing, we could reach all the capitals of the Arab countries. But what would happen after that? To what extent, by military strength alone, could Israel really impose what the Allies managed to do in Japan, Italy and Germany?

The reason for our inability to impose our political will through military means and why Clausewitz should not guide Israel's overall political and defence policy is very simple. Between Israel and the Arab countries there are at least two superpowers and they are deeply involved in whatever happens in the Arab–Israeli conflict. A precise and accurate analogy for the Arab–Israeli conflict can be defined in terms derived from London transport. The conflict is a 'double-decker' in which there are two levels: the local one and the superpower one. However, unlike the London buses, it is not divided into two clear-cut levels since there is much vertical interaction.

I do not believe that the superpowers would allow Israel to operate as a free agent or that they would stand aside if Israel attempted to achieve political goals by military means. In addition, I do not believe, as the war in Lebanon has demonstrated, that by capturing the capitals of Arab countries, we could really bring about new political systems that would be cooperative and peaceful with us. Peace cannot be imposed on our neighbours, nor can force of Israeli arms change their political systems or control them. These are significant and real limits to Israel's power. Any attempt by Israel to initiate war without taking these principles into consideration is doomed to failure.

The war in Lebanon provides ample illustration of this point. I am not referring to the need to destroy certain areas close to Israel. Whatever was required militarily in this regard was done. Going to war with the purpose of obtaining the 'Peace Treaty' that was signed between Lebanon and Israel on 17 May 1983 is another matter. The paper that was signed was patently inadequate and ineffective.

The use of military forces to achieve a political goal of this kind is clearly mistaken. This is borne out by the historical record in which we have a share. For the British and the French, the Suez War is an example of the inability to attain significant political change by relying on the application of force. Moreover, a review of the Sinai Campaign and the war in Lebanon – both of which were successful militarily for Israel – yields the same conclusion. In the Sinai Campaign, Ben-Gurion had the courage and wisdom to shift from the illusion of far-reaching political changes in Egypt and the region to far more limited goals. In so doing he was able to provide his country with 11 years of peace. On the other hand, we were mistaken in the war in Lebanon when we tried to extend our power beyond the relatively limited objectives of destroying the infrastructure of the terrorists in southern Lebanon. Military force alone could not achieve more than this. My conclusion is therefore simple and painful. Through military means – as we say in Hebrew: *z'bang v'gamarnu* ('just one shot and it's all over') – the attempt to bring about a war that will end all wars is a dangerous course of action and an illusion.

At the same time, I must state that Israel's military strength is vital to the country's existence. It is the only factor that can persuade an Arab leader to enter into a process that can produce peace. Without impressing on Arab leaders that force cannot be effectively employed against Israel, there is no chance for a political agreement with them. Only our military strength can convince Arab leadership to shift the focus of dealing with Israel from the battlefield to the negotiation table. Nothing else will be effective so long as they believe that through military means they can achieve total or even partial gains in the conflict with us.

As I reflect on the long-term implications of this perception of the limits to our military power in the face of the continuing threat from war and acts of terrorism, I have come to the conclusion that force of arms alone cannot bring about the desired termination of the Arab–Israeli conflict. We must understand that we must persist in developing our country with commitment, patience and endurance in the face of unresolved problems with our neighbours. There is no magical solution to this problem or any other complicated problem elsewhere in the world. Although I am not an orthodox Jew, I believe that there is much to learn from the Jewish tradition of 'Lo D'chikat Hakketz' – or 'not hastening the coming of the End [of Days].' I do not believe that we must achieve everything now, whether that may be obtaining all the Land of Israel or Peace Now, at any price. Rather, I believe in continually moving ahead, bearing in mind that we are engaged in the historic process of the Return to Zion which has to be measured in terms of time relative to the length of Jewish history.

II. Shlomo Avineri

When discussing the issue of the limits of power, two aspects can be discerned: the politico-strategic one and the ethical and moral one. My main analysis will be devoted to the politico-strategic but I would like to comment on the ethical aspect as well.

The ethical aspect of the limits of power is, at base, a fairly simple question: under what circumstances, and with what aims in mind, is a country justified in using power to settle political differences with other countries? This is the issue, the right to wage war – *ius ad bellum* – which harks back to the medieval scholastics and to Hugo Grotius. During the period when France attempted to maintain her power in Algeria, as well as during America's involvement in Vietnam, the moral – and not only the strategic – issue was at the core of the public debate: did France and did the United States have the moral right to wage war in Algeria or in Vietnam? I would imagine that this question exists in a muted form even in the Soviet Union with respect to its involvement in Afghanistan since it appears that some moral arguments may not be now completely overlooked even there.

In France, and to a larger extent in Britain, opposition to involvement in Egypt during the Suez–Sinai war did include a moral critique. In Israel in 1956 – for reasons that have to do with the general context of the Arab–Israeli conflict, Nasser's general aggressiveness and the acts of the *fidaiyyun* – this issue was almost non-existent. There is some expression of misgiving by Moshe Sharett, who was sent on a mission to the Far East in the period before and during the war. In his diary he notes that he feels that he has returned to a different and transformed country: 'My country has run away from me.' Even here, moral disclaimers are muted.

Politico-strategic considerations were, then, the dominant concerns of France, Britain and Israel in the Suez–Sinai war. It is my contention that when entering the war both the British and French leaders on one hand, and the Israelis on the other, were labouring under the memories of traumas of previous wars, and their cognitive maps were determined by these past experiences. In the case of the British and French leaders, it was the traumas of Munich and the Second World War; in the case of the Israeli leaders, it was the memory of the War of Independence. These prisms fixed the respective leaders' perception of the enemy, of his aims and character, as well as their justification of the war, their aims, and the ways and methods they adopted to reach these aims.

For leaders like Anthony Eden and Guy Mollet, the psychological map of the world was very much determined by their experience of appeasement, the delusions of Munich and their own standing up to Hitler – much against the initial conventional wisdom of their own generation. The parallel drawn in 1956 by British and French politicians between Nasser and Hitlerite tyranny was not just a public relations ploy. Anthony Eden deeply believed in this similarity; Mollet's political reputation was based on resistance to Hitler and Nazism and a critique of Munich. It could be argued that in confronting Nasser, Eden and Mollet were replaying a script which they recognized from past experience. If wars do sometimes have an aspect of a morality play Eden and Mollet had no problem in identifying the apparent moral issues of 1956 in terms of 1938. In fighting Nasser, they were fighting Hitler and Mussolini once again.

This analogy between Nasser and Hitler also provided justifica-

243

tion for the British and French war aims in Suez. Even as in the Second World War the goal was to destroy Hitler and reconstitute the German body politic, the aim in 1956 was to topple Nasser and reorder Egypt. While not as extreme as the dismemberment of Germany after the Second World War, the objective of imposing on Egypt a friendly government, propped up by Anglo-French military power, was similar to what actually happened to Italy and Japan under the Allies. The power of this analogy must be understood if one is to grasp the self-righteousness which undoubtedly motivated the British and French leadership. Such considerations took precedence even over the more apparent reasons of state for which the war was waged – such as Algeria and control over the Suez Canal.

How realistic was the aim of creating a new government in Egypt, in circumstances that were very different from those that existed in Europe in 1944–45, is a separate matter. Nevertheless, such aims demonstrate that not only do generals occasionally fight the previous war all over again, so do politicians. In this instance, British and French leaders, in reacting to the trauma of overcoming the 1930s reluctance to employ power against Hitler, had no qualms in using force against what they perceived was an evil tyranny reminiscent of Hitler. This was also to become their undoing. Although the particular manner of their political demise was different in the respective cases of Eden and Mollet, both committed fatal errors in attempting to emulate Churchill who rallied his people against the Nazi threat, and de Gaulle in 1940.

The reasons for their failure are obvious. The total mobilization, the demand for total surrender and the quest for total victory were a unique Second World War phenomenon, almost unknown in the annals of men. These conditions could not be duplicated in the context of the limited military campaign of 1956. Nor was Britain the kind of world power it had still been during the Second World War; and neither did Britain or France have the kind of freedom to manoeuvre which the Allies had in 1945. For these reasons, it is wrong to view 1956 as the last and failed example of nineteenth-century gun-boat diplomacy. British and French planners were not merely reenacting another chapter in European imperialism. They were reliving the defence of Western democracies even as they had done but a few years earlier. Their language is a clear and accurate reflection of this. That they were wrong in both the factual assessment of their capabilities and in correctly identifying the issues is beside the point.

From the failure of Suez one can learn two crucial lessons about the limits of power. The first, which the United States learned at horrendous cost during Vietnam, is that it is difficult to mobilize public opinion in a democracy for a limited war. Democracies have proved extremely effective in mobilizing public opinion and resources in wars which are perceived as crucial to their own survival. Such was the case of the Western democracies in the Second World War and Israel in its Wars of No Choice. However, Suez proved to the French and the British – as Vietnam was to prove to America and Lebanon to Israel – that what a democracy can achieve under conditions of siege and existential war may be unattainable in a partial war.

The second lesson was to demonstrate the limits of power of highly industrialized societies with regard to the Third World. In this respect, Suez was a novelty and a turning point for European powers. While there is no doubt that militarily, economically and politically, Britain and France in 1956 were stronger than Egypt, they still could not achieve victory and realize their war aims. This was due to a basic change in perceptions concerning the conduct of international affairs. This change was itself the outcome of the victories of Western democracies in the Second World War.

Western democracies fought in that war for ideological as well as strategic purposes. Dialectically, their victory resulted in limiting the use of their own power and their own superiority with respect to weaker nations, especially in the non-European world. The feelings of guilt associated with colonialism and the growth of Soviet power notwithstanding, the fact is that after the victory over Nazism and the ensuing decolonization, military power and economic superiority were no longer the ultimate arbiter in international affairs. In this respect, the nineteenth century came to an end in 1945. The Suez War was the first example of this lesson. No longer could a European power simply impose its will on a non-European power. Obviously there is a lot of moral hypocrisy in this new situation, and it sometimes allows some Third World countries and leaders to get away, literally, with murder. Iraq, for example, can use poison gas in its war with Iran; no European nation could now do this. These limits to the indiscriminate use of power are not applied equally, as is evidenced by the behaviour of the Soviet Union in Afghanistan. Nevertheless, limits on the use of power exist. In 1956, two European powers came up for the first time against the principles which they themselves had established in the United Nations Charter.

The dialectical paradox is that Eden and Mollet thought they were fighting the Second World War all over again. It was in their defeat that the principles for which Western democracies fought during that war ultimately triumphed. That it was such a flawed leader as Nasser who first reaped the benefit of such principles only suggests that history is much more ironic and cruel than most of its practitioners and observers usually care to admit.

If for Britain and France Suez offered an opportunity to replay the Second World War, for Israel Sinai was a replay of the 1948 War of Independence. In 1948, almost totally exposed and in mortal danger, Israel defended itself against extinction. This appeared to extend to the existential situation of 1956 as well. It is worthy of note that even in 1948 some leaders of the Yishuv had doubts, functional as well as moral, about the use of force, but they were overwhelmingly overruled by the unquestioned fact that had it not been for the sheer use of force, Israel would not have survived in 1948. World support and moral legitimacy would not have sufficed. Nasser's aggressiveness, his perceived support of the *fidaiyyun*, the real havoc which was caused in the daily life of ordinary citizens by murderers coming from across the armistice lines – all these tended to legitimize as justifiable self-defence Israel's involvement in the Suez–Sinai Campaign.

Initially, at least, Israel's aim in entering the Anglo-French alliance against Egypt was to bring down Nasser. Some subsequent Israeli accounts, including Ben-Gurion's own, suggest that Israel's war aims were more limited – putting an end to the *fidaiyyun* incursions, and guaranteeing freedom of navigation in the Gulf of Eilat. Israel, like France and Britain, intended to overthrow Nasser and bring about a transformation in the political structure of Egypt. Nevertheless, unlike her allies, Israel was able to wrest a limited political victory out of her military success. This was accomplished mainly because of Ben-Gurion's ability to change course in the midst of events and to recognize the limits of power. In my estimation, this was Ben-Gurion's finest hour, a supreme example of his ability to initiate policy changes rather than to get stuck – and fail – by adhering to what were the initial war aims.

Ben-Gurion's adaptation to new circumstances can be illustrated best by examining closely his now famous speech to the Knesset immediately after the termination of hostilities and his actions in the following two days during which he changed his policies. In this speech Ben-Gurion declared the Armistice Agreement with Egypt null and void – 'never to be revived again'. The implication was

246

clear: there would be border changes along the frontier with Egypt, especially with regard to Sharm el-Sheikh. To legitimize these territorial claims in the public mind, Ben-Gurion renamed Sharm el-Sheikh 'The Gulf of Solomon' ('Mifratz Shlomo' in Hebrew) – a neologism that was to survive 1956 well into the post-1967 era. In his Knesset speech he quoted, in the original Greek, an obscure passage from a little-known Byzantine historian, Procopius, who mentioned 'a Jewish realm' on an island in the Red Sea which Ben-Gurion identified with Tiran although it more likely refers to Gezirat al-Faraoun, a few miles south of Eilat. The point was clear: by force of arms Israel would change the political configuration of its southern border.

Within less than 48 hours, after Bulganin's letter and the clear indication from Eisenhower that Israel would be on its own against a Soviet threat, Ben-Gurion changed course completely. His response to Bulganin, which Ben-Gurion himself read over Israel radio, while aggressive in tone and language, clearly stated that Israel had no territorial claims on Egypt, and went to war only in order to secure its border against incursion and to guarantee freedom of navigation in the Gulf of Eilat. Historically, this amounted to falsifying an obvious record; politically, it was one of Ben-Gurion's most perceptive and momentous decisions. For a leader to climb down from such a lofty earlier statement, to 'eat' his own words, and to maintain at the same time his own credibility and carry his government, his party and his country with him is a feat of masterful leadership. At the same time, while retreating from his Grand Design about re-ordering the map of the Middle East, Ben-Gurion was able in four months of tough bargaining to guarantee for Israel the more limited aims of a quiet border with Egypt and free navigation to Eilat. This gave Israel the most peaceful decade of its history. Lesser leaders would not be able to perform such a feat of political acrobatics. Unable to swallow their own pride, they might have also brought down calamities and catastrophes on the heads of their people.

It is sometimes claimed that Nasser turned a military defeat into a political victory. The war's political casualties included Anthony Eden, Guy Mollet and eventually the French Fourth Republic. Ben-Gurion, too, could have become a casualty, though the impressive military performance of Israel in the war, compared to the messy Anglo-French effort, obviously gave Ben-Gurion better cards in the diplomatic game that ensued. Nevertheless, had it not been for his recognition of the limits of power, and his understanding that unlike in 1948–49 the borders of Israel would not automatically follow the extension of its armies, Ben-Gurion, and Israel, could have easily been defeated diplomatically as were France and England. Ben-Gurion even managed to derive from the Sinai Campaign an enhanced status for Israel among the nations and to improve its security situation despite the total withdrawal from all of Sinai and even the reversion of Gaza back to direct Egyptian rule in March 1957 contrary to agreements worked out through the Americans and the United Nations.

It is precisely Ben-Gurion's ability to achieve these limited aims after the breakdown of his Grand Design which is the lesson for Israel. The State of Israel is indubitably the strongest military power in the Middle East. Its power, however, does not enable it to dictate terms to its enemies. It does not stand in relation to the Arab countries, even if they are defeated in battle, as the Allies stood with regard to Germany, Italy and Japan after the Second World War. That was the lesson from 1956, so aptly described by Yitzhak Rabin.

For all the participants – France, Britain and Israel – there is also another lesson, and this is the relativization of Clausewitz. In democratic societies, where one needs to mobilize public opinion and reach a consensus about war, war is not merely the continuation of diplomacy by other means. This was learned in 1956, just as it was later learned by the United States in Vietnam and again by Israel in Lebanon in 1982.

Part III
THE SUPERPOWERS

18

The Impact of Suez on United States Middle East Policy, 1957–1958

Robert D. Schulzinger

The Suez Crisis of October 1956–March 1957 profoundly altered Washington's Middle-Eastern policy. The episode and its memory made the United States for the first time strive to become the major outside power in the Middle East, replacing Britain and France. After having joined with the Soviet Union at the United Nations to stop the British, French and Israeli attack on Egypt, the Eisenhower administration worried about Moscow. Suez convinced American diplomats that the Soviet Union was a major rival in the region. From January 1957, when President Dwight D. Eisenhower announced a new 'doctrine' for assisting non-communist states in the region, until July 1958, when 14,000 United States marines landed in Beirut, the Eisenhower administration applied what it believed were the three principal lessons of Suez:

(1) the United States had greater influence in the Middle East than any other outside power;
(2) communism was the major problem of the Arab Middle East;
(3) Gamal Abd al-Nasser of Egypt was an agent of the Soviet Union.

The results failed to confirm these propositions.

After Suez, American policy-makers chose to ignore the Arab–Israeli dispute. They did so on purpose, hoping to divert the attention of Israelis and conservative Arabs from what divided them to a common enemy. These attempts reflected American diplomats' frustrations with the limits of their new influence in the Middle East. An angry Eisenhower administration successfully turned back the Israeli–British–French attack on Egypt, but it had difficulty creating stability. By focusing on a communist threat,

251

Washington hoped to remodel the Middle East into a stable, pro-American area.

In fact, Washington did not shift the attention of the States in the region, nor, of course, did the Middle East become any more stable or pro-American than it had been before. The aftermath of Suez left Washington with a dilemma that no subsequent United States administration has solved, namely, the United States appeared omnipotent but its power seldom produced the desired results.

This paper traces the impact of the memory of the Suez crisis on the creation of a new Middle East policy. It describes how Suez affected the origins of and debate over the 'Eisenhower Doctrine' in early 1957. It concludes with an analysis of the implementation of the Eisenhower Doctrine, culminating with the action in Lebanon. Throughout these eighteen months American diplomats remembered the events of the Suez crisis, first explicitly and later implicitly. In either case, the Eisenhower administration found that it was easier to stop Britain, France and Israel than it was to make new friends in the Middle East.

On 5 January, 1957 President Eisenhower addressed a joint session of Congress on American policy in the Middle East. He reported that events in the region had

> abruptly reached a new and critical stage ... Just recently there have been hostilities involving Western European nations that once exercised much influence in the area. Also the relatively large attack by Israel in October has intensified the basic differences between that nation and its Arab neighbors. All this instability has been heightened and, at times, manipulated by International Communism.

The Middle East, he asserted, 'has always been coveted by Russia'. He therefore requested that Congress provide $200 million in military aid to the countries of the region in each of the next two years to counter 'International Communism'. He also asked lawmakers to authorize the President to 'employ the armed forces of the United States as he deems necessary to secure and protect the territorial integrity and independence of any such nation or group of nations requesting such aid against overt armed aggression from any nation controlled by international communism'.[1]

Congress did not leap to endorse this Eisenhower Doctrine. Instead, both House and Senate held two months of hearings before passing a modified version of the resolution in March. Scepticism reflected concern over Congress's war-making power, uncertainty that 'international communism' was the real problem in the Middle East, and doubts that $200 million was enough money.

Secretary of State John Foster Dulles argued the administration's position in Congress. He informed Senators that the doctrine originated in the belief that

> there is a highly dangerous situation in the Middle East, and that there is today a vacuum of power as a result of the recent British–French action, so that if we do not find some way in which to put our support back of the free nations of the area to reassure them and give them strength, then that critical area will almost certainly be taken over by Soviet communism.[2]

In other words, the Secretary worried about the results of recent American pressure on Britain, France and Israel. Having successfully stopped their invasion of Egypt, America had weakened the Europeans and enhanced the United States. At the same time, American diplomats regretted having joined the Soviets at the United Nations in demanding a cease-fire. At the end of 1956 it appeared that Egyptian President Nasser credited Moscow more than Washington with stopping the war. Eisenhower told Dulles, 'we regard Nasser as an evil influence ... While we share in general the British and French opinion of Nasser, we insisted that they chose a bad time and incident on which to launch corrective measures.'[3] In order to limit Soviet efforts to capitalize further on its UN efforts, the United States wanted to alert other Arab states to the dangers of Nasserism.

Eisenhower and Dulles had developed a negative view of Nasser in 1955 and 1956, and they did not change their minds about the Egyptian leader even though they helped save his regime from the Anglo-French–Israeli assault. Briefly, American policy-makers disliked Nasser for his independence from their influence and his willingness to deal with the Soviets and the Eastern bloc. His acceptance of Soviet aid for the Aswan Dam and of Czech weapons for his armed forces, and his recognition of the Peoples' Republic of China, all offended Dulles. Nasser's promise to unify the Arab world also puzzled and troubled Americans. In Washington's view, Arabs united behind Nasser would pay little attention to the interests or wishes of the United States.[4] In that sense, Eisenhower's and Dulles's opinion of Nasser differed little from that of the British and French leaders who had planned the Suez war. Washington's outrage over Suez derived more from anger at being ignored by allies, continued support for the collective security provisions of the

United Nations system, and a belief that gunboat diplomacy was outmoded, than from support for Egypt. In the aftermath of Suez, therefore, the United States developed the Eisenhower Doctrine to project the United States as the saviour of conservative Arabs from Nasserism. The method was designed to be more acceptable in the Middle East, even if the aim was indistinguishable from the goal of Britain and France in 1956.

Law-makers questioned many of the assumptions underlying the Eisenhower Doctrine. Senators wondered about the extent of authority granted to the President. Hubert Humphrey (Democrat, Minnesota) called the Eisenhower Doctrine a 'predated declaration of war'. Richard Russell (Democrat, Georgia) asked, 'Why is it necessary to make this commitment here in such broad terms of permanent military and economic aid to these countries? It leaves us open now to be blackmailed by every little dictator and leader there.'[5] Senator Wayne Morse (Democrat, Oregon) offered that the Doctrine 'presented a great constitutional question as to the operations of a system of congressional checks'. J. William Fulbright (Democrat, Arkansas) summarized a great deal of congressional scepticism when he observed, 'I cannot see the emergency ... because not very long ago the Secretary himself assured this committee that things were in very good condition in the Middle East.'[6]

On the other hand, Senators from the President's own Republican party noted what Alexander Wiley (Republican, Wisconsin) called 'the significance of the changed world in which we live. Wisconsin is nearer to attack now than New York City.' For such reasons, Wiley explained, 'I shall be willing to give the President the stand-by power [for] which I think he is going to ask.' Leverett Saltonsall (Republican, Massachusetts) also supported Dulles' reasoning that 'things move very fast today, jet planes and everything that goes with an attack, and the purpose of this resolution is to show, not that this country will act as a great nation, but that Congress will support the Executive in taking action under the terms of this general resolution, if trouble comes'.[7]

After two months of such debate a modified version of the Eisenhower Doctrine was adopted by Joint Resolution. Congress omitted an assertion that 'the peace of the world and the security of the United States are endangered as long as international communism and the nations it controls seek by threat of military action, use of economic pressure, internal subversion, or other means to attempt to bring under their domination peoples now free and independent'.[8] More significantly, Congress, jealous of its war-making prerogative, did not authorize the President to send troops in the event of a Middle East crisis. Instead, the resolution asserted that the United States was 'prepared to use armed forces to assist any nation...requesting assistance against armed aggression'.[9] One legislative historian concluded that Congress anticipated that 'the President ... would use this emergency power when necessary and report to Congress when appropriate'. Arthur Schlesinger Jr. notes that the effect of changes in the resolution 'was to convince [President Eisenhower] less of the need for serious consultation with Congress than of his inherent authority to employ armed forces at presidential will'.[10]

Even as Congress debated, the States of the Middle East expressed widely different opinions of the Eisenhower Doctrine. In January, Lebanon hailed the declaration and three members of the Baghdad Pact (Turkey, Iran, Iraq) supported the general approach. Yet Egypt and Syria denounced the United States for mistakenly substituting an imaginary danger – international communism – for the real ones – 'Western imperialism and Zionism'.[11] Saudi Arabia and Jordan also proclaimed that they would not permit foreign spheres of influence in their region. King Saud soon reversed himself, however, after a late January visit to Washington, and spoke in favour of Eisenhower's anti-communism at a February meeting in Cairo. By March, therefore, the Eisenhower Doctrine had hardened divisions in the Muslim world between the 'Northern tier' of mostly non-Arab states in the Baghdad Pact, which supported the U.S., and those closer to Egypt, opposed to it. Lebanon, confronting Syria and Israel, welcomed any outside support.

Reaction in Israel was lukewarm. Israelis were preoccupied in early 1957 with American demands that they quit the Sinai and Gaza in return for United Nations guarantees. Yet some officials saw benefits in endorsing the American plan. Ambassador Abba Eban convinced the Cabinet to support the Doctrine if it included Israel. Privately he mocked it as the 'Doctrine of the Immaculate Assumption', namely that the Arab states would substitute anti-communism (or anti-Nasserism) for hostility to Israel. Nonetheless, if Israel were included, Washington might come to value the Jewish state more highly.[12]

Once Congress had enacted the Joint Resolution, James P. Richards, a South Carolina Democrat who had once chaired the House Committee on Foreign Affairs, went to the Middle East to offer assistance. From March to May he visited fifteen countries

(Afghanistan, Ethiopia, Iran, Iraq, Lebanon, Libya, Pakistan, Saudi Arabia, Turkey, Greece, Yemen, Sudan, Israel, Tunisia, and Morocco). He did not stop in Egypt or Syria, now aligned with the Soviet Union, or Jordan, whose government had several pro-Nasser ministers. He produced agreements for military and economic assistance with nine countries (Iran, Turkey, Pakistan, Iraq, Afghanistan, Lebanon, Libya, Saudi Arabia, and Ethiopia) totalling about $119 million.[13]

While Richards travelled, the first of three crises testing the Eisenhower Doctrine broke out in Jordan. Over the next year the United States intervened in intra-Arab politics in Jordan (April 1957), Syria (August–October 1957), and Lebanon (May–July 1958). As one recent analyst has characterized the three episodes:

> In the crisis atmosphere of the post-Suez era, Eisenhower and Dulles were no longer wooing the whole Arab world to gain allies in the conflict with the Soviet Union. Now they were intervening in intra-Arab affairs to assure that those individuals and forces inclined to reject Soviet influence either rose to power or remained in authority. The effort to co-opt Arab governments into the program for containing the Soviet Union had been replaced by a doctrine which projected the international hunt for communists into Arab politics.[14]

In the Jordanian case, the United States invoked the Eisenhower Doctrine to help suppress a pro-Nasserist Prime Minister, Sulayman al-Nabulsi. In April 1957 King Hussein became alarmed that a Palestinian element in the Government and civil service was plotting with Egypt and the Soviet Union to overthrow the monarchy and establish a Nasserist republic. Prime Minister Nabulsi had denounced the Eisenhower Doctrine in January and in April promised to open diplomatic relations with Moscow and accept Soviet aid.

Perceiving a threat to his throne from the Palestinians, the King sought army support to oust Nabulsi. He asked for and received succour from Washington when the President invoked the Eisenhower Doctrine in April 1957. Within a week the United States dispatched an aircraft carrier to the eastern Mediterranean and reinforced its troops in Turkey. A new Royalist government took over in Amman and the United States immediately provided a $10 million emergency grant. An additional $20 million followed in the next two months.

It is hard to say that the Eisenhower Doctrine determined the outcome in the Jordanian crisis. The President's report to Congress in July 1957 noted that 'no action' had been required in the Jordanian crisis. The President did claim that invocation of the Doctrine and the ensuing military moves had deterred a communist attack against Jordan. What attack? From whom? Eisenhower did not specify and the deterrent power of the Eisenhower Doctrine remained unproven in mid-1957. One student of the Jordanian crisis asserts that 'the administration failed to consider ... that the successful intervention on Hussein's behalf also entailed important costs and that it did not remove the fundamental instabilities in Jordan and in the region'. John C. Campbell, writing soon after the events, noted that the intervention placed the United States in the eyes of Arabs in a position 'hardly distinguishable from that which the British had just been forced to relinquish'.[15]

That autumn another 'equally indecisive' application of the Eisenhower Doctrine took place in Syria.[16] In August the Government of Syria reported uncovering an American conspiracy to overthrow the Government of Prime Minister Asali. Patrick Seale, a British journalist who studied the Syrian charges in 1966, concluded that 'it is hard to dismiss them as fabrication. Convinced that Syria was 'going communist', the United States had been exploring ways of reversing the trend. Its officials had had clandestine contacts with members of the Syrian armed forces with a view to organizing the overthrow of the government'.[17] A few months before, Syria had concluded a massive arms agreement with the Soviet Union, and it appeared to Washington as if the communist penetration of Damascus was complete. Eisenhower recalls that 'the entire action was shrouded in mystery but the suspicion was strong that the Communists had taken hold of the government'.[18] Syria replied with the expulsion of three officials at the U.S. Embassy, and the Chief of Staff of the Syrian Army, reportedly friendly to the United States, resigned. Syria's neighbours, notably Lebanon, Jordan, Turkey and Iraq, feared that the new weapons would be used by the pro-Nasserist regime against them. They therefore wanted United States support against a possible Syrian attack.

Lebanon took the lead in asking the United States for help against pro-Soviet Damascus. It requested prompt action, to prevent Syria from becoming a fully fledged satellite of the Soviet Union. Washington was willing to defend Lebanon, but wanted to wait for further evidence that Damascus was moving against its neighbour. Before an actual attack took place, the United States followed the earlier pattern by flying planes from Europe to Turkey and moving the Sixth Fleet into the eastern Mediterranean. The State Department also dispatched Deputy Undersecretary of State Loy Henderson to the region.

Henderson was cautious about joint military action with the states of the region. While reflecting the fears of Syria's conservative neighbours that Damascus planned to subvert their Governments, he believed that intra-Arab rivalries undermined joint military action against Syria. In mid-September only the non-Arab Turks, bordering the Soviet Union, and Lebanon, the traditional adversary of Syria, still favoured military action.

At this point Secretary of State Dulles announced that under the terms of the Eisenhower Doctrine the United States was hastening deliveries of economic and military assistance to the countries neighbouring Syria.[19] He affirmed that the United States could use troops if three conditions were met: (1) that the President determined that a country was controlled by international communism, (2) that aggression took place and (3) that the victim of aggression requested United States aid. The Secretary said that the United States had not yet determined that Syria was dominated by international communism, 'and I might say at the present time that I don't think it likely that those three things will occur'.[20]

Now the crisis threatened to escalate into a confrontation between the superpowers. Soviet Foreign Minister Andrei Gromyko charged that Turkey and the United States plotted to attack Syria. Nikita Khrushchev warned Turkey that 'if the rifle fires, the rockets will start firing'. Dulles stormed back: 'Certainly if there is an attack on Turkey by the Soviet Union, it would not mean a purely defensive operation by the United States, with the Soviet Union a privileged sanctuary from which to attack Turkey.'[21]

After the superpowers had growled, the crisis subsided. No coup took place against Syria, no Soviet attack occurred against Turkey, and no American military movement ensued. Most observers regarded the affair as a setback for the United States and a success for the Soviets. Nasserists were encouraged that Soviet pressure had forced the United States to suspend plans for a coup against the Syrian government. A student of deterrence concluded that 'more than the earlier Jordan affair, the Syrian crisis revealed that Arab nationalism and neutralism placed important constraints on the behavior of even those pro-Western Arab governments that benefited from certain aspects of Washington's new Middle East policy'.[22]

One year after the Suez crisis, Washington had not achieved what it had expected from the Eisenhower Doctrine. The Soviet Union was as important as it had been in October–November 1956. The Arabs remained bitterly divided regarding the United States but united in opposition to Israel. Nasser's supporters appeared emboldened, and in February 1958 the Government of Syria entered a political union with Egypt. The new United Arab Republic disturbed the United States. Eisenhower confessed confusion: 'It was unclear whether this union was prompted by Communist influence or whether the Communists were merely going along with Nasser's ambitions eventually to unify the Arab world.'[23] The latter probably was the case, as Nasser, who became President of the new republic, abolished all political parties including the communist. The Soviet Union recognized the UAR on the day it was created, hoping to maintain the same influence in Syria it enjoyed in Egypt.

While the UAR was not the communist satellite feared by some, it threatened to upset the system Washington wanted in the Middle East. A month after the new republic came into existence, Nasser commenced a violent press and radio attack against King Saud whom the Egyptians accused of intriguing with the United States. Saud was forced to yield control over Government operations, including foreign affairs, to his brother Prince Faysal, who officials in Washington believed was sympathetic to Nasser. Eisenhower lamented the fall of a 'man we had hoped might eventually rival Nasser as an Arab leader'.[24]

Accordingly, by the spring of 1958, Washington feared that it had not effectively used the influence it appeared to have gained during the Suez crisis. When a civil war broke out in Lebanon in May 1958, American leaders decided to view it as part of a larger picture. United States interests appeared threatened by internal Lebanese disorder, Nasserist sentiment throughout the Arab world, and a lurking Soviet presence. Having refrained from using troops in Jordan and Syria, the Eisenhower administration felt compelled to do more in Lebanon. American policy-makers used force to demonstrate that the promises of the Eisenhower Doctrine were real. One analysis of the planning for the Lebanon intervention concludes:

> Washington felt itself under pressure to take more drastic action in Lebanon than it would otherwise have contemplated in order to reaffirm its interests throughout the Middle East. The eventual intervention in Lebanon on July 15, 1958, can be

259

explained partially as a last resort by which U.S. leaders hoped to reverse, or at least arrest, this anti-Western trend.[25]

The Lebanon crisis contained two distinct phases. The first erupted in May and subsided in about one month. The second took place suddenly in mid-July and led to the dispatch of 14,000 American troops who remained until October.

The first phase began when President Camille Chamoun, a Christian, became concerned that the Muslim and possibly Druse portion of the population wanted him out. A civil war flared on 8 May, 1958 when a critic of Chamoun was assassinated. Rebels reportedly received support from Syria, and radio broadcasts from the UAR urged the President's overthrow. Chamoun had been one of the earliest and most enthusiastic backers of the anti-Nasserist promises of the Eisenhower Doctrine, and on 13 May he asked Eisenhower if the U.S. would provide military support. Eisenhower recalled that 'behind everything was our deep-seated conviction that the Communists were principally responsible for the trouble'.[26] He demurred, however, at promising troops to extend Chamoun's term of office. Instead, he once more ordered the fleet to the eastern Mediterranean and increased the number of marines in the region. He also sent tear gas and small arms to the Lebanese government to maintain order.

Later in May the United States began military talks on Cyprus with Great Britain to develop contingency plans should Syria attack Lebanon. The two decided that the United States would send troops to Lebanon and Britain would send them to Jordan in the event of Syria's army attacking Lebanon. In the meantime, Lebanon brought the issue before the United Nations, where the United States supported Chamoun's complaint of 'massive intervention' by the UAR. In June a UN observer team failed to confirm this interpretation, and Secretary General Dag Hammarskjöld reported that the Syrian infiltration had not been as sizeable as Lebanon asserted.

As June wore on the situation stabilized in Lebanon. President Chamoun opened conversations with the rebels and agreed not to seek another term as President. He also promised to find a candidate suitable to both Christians and Muslims. Washington watched carefully, and Secretary of State Dulles asserted on 1 July that it reserved the right under the UN charter to send troops to protect Chamoun's government from 'an armed revolution which is fomented from abroad'.[27] Nevertheless, Dulles expected that the civil war would soon end quietly.

It might have done had not the aftermath of a revolution in Iraq brought the United States directly into Beirut. On 14 July Iraqi General Abd al-Karim Qassem took over the Government, murdering the pro-Western royal family and prime minister. Eisenhower was bewildered at the fall of 'the country we were counting on as a bulwark of stability and progress in the region'. He saw Nasser's hand, as he explained that day to Vice-President Richard Nixon: 'We have come to the crossroads. Since 1945 we have been trying to maintain the opportunity to reach vitally needed petroleum supplies peaceably without hindrance on the part of anyone.' The President thought that the revolution in Iraq resulted directly from 'the struggle of Nasser to get control of these supplies – to get the income and the power to destroy the Western world'.[28] President Chamoun was equally frantic in Beirut. Early on the morning of the 14th he summoned the British, French and American ambassadors. He told each that unless they sent troops within the next 48 hours 'he would be a dead man and Lebanon would be an Egyptian satellite'.[29]

Eisenhower and his advisers concluded that the United States had to do something and be seen doing something in response to the collapse of the Baghdad government. At a meeting with Dulles officials concluded that the effects of the United States doing nothing would be:

1. Nasser would take over the whole area;
2. The United States would lose influence not only in the Arab states, but in the area generally, and our bases throughout the area would be in jeopardy;
3. The dependability of United States commitments for assistance in the event of need would be brought into question throughout the world.[30]

Eisenhower met with a bipartisan group of law-makers on the afternoon of 14 July to inform them of plans to send marines to Beirut. House Speaker Sam Rayburn (Democrat, Texas) feared U.S. involvement in a civil war and Senator William Fulbright (Democrat, Arkansas) doubted the communist origins of the crisis. Eisenhower replied that the UN observers had not seen very much and 'some of our own observers definitely doubted the competency of the team'. He insisted that 'authority for such an operation lay so clearly with the Executive'. Congressional concerns about the war-making prerogative carried little weight.[31]

The President also telephoned his friend, British Prime Minister

261

Harold Macmillan, to inform him of the intention to land in Beirut. Macmillan joked, 'You are doing a Suez on me.'[32] The Prime Minister wanted to act jointly, but Eisenhower resisted any appearance of Western collusion, such as had occurred in the Suez invasion. Instead, Eisenhower asked Britain to prepare to land paratroopers in Jordan with American logistical support. 'In a farcical twist', writes Steven Spiegel, 'the British and Israelis now found themselves cooperating with the Americans in another Mideast intervention.' The British requested overflight rights over Israel to Jordan. Israel's Prime Minister David Ben-Gurion telephoned Dulles in the middle of the night to make sure of United States approval.[33]

On 15 July, the first of 14,000 U.S. marines landed on the beaches of Beirut to the astonishment of the peaceful sunbathers. A few shots were fired, but for the most part there was a festival atmosphere in Beirut, not the chaos expected in Washington. Over the next few weeks the civil war cooled and the United Nations addressed the Lebanese problem. Accompanying the marines was Deputy Undersecretary of State Robert Murphy, a longtime troubleshooter for Eisenhower. Murphy opened conversations with the rebels and concluded that President Chamoun could not maintain his power. On 31 July, the Lebanese parliament confirmed a compromise candidate, General Fouad Shehab, as President. On 21 August the UN General Assembly passed a resolution sponsored by the Arab states in which they pledged non-interference in one another's internal affairs and insisted that no one else intervene either. In late August the United States and Britain announced their intention to withdraw their troops, and all were gone by November.

The Soviet Union did not intervene in the crisis, something Washington regarded as a victory. Nasser also appeared intimidated into keeping his support for the Lebanese revolutionaries at a minimum. Murphy reported that Eisenhower believed dispatching the marines changed attitudes in the Middle East about American will. The President told Murphy that

> the sentiment had developed in the Middle East, especially in Egypt, that Americans were capable only of words, that we were afraid of Soviet reaction if we attempted military action. Eisenhower believed that if the United States did nothing now, there would be heavy and irreparable losses in Lebanon and in the area generally. He wanted to demonstrate in a timely and practical way that the United States was capable of supporting its friends.[34]

The Lebanon intervention has been described as a 'catharsis' for America's Middle East policy.[35] Having demonstrated that it was willing to use force in the region, the Eisenhower administration now felt comfortable in paying less attention to Nasser, Arab nationalism, and the Middle East in general. In their own minds the Eisenhower policy-makers no longer feared immediate dangers from Nasser and the Soviet Union. The Middle East became a subsidiary issue for American policy-makers until the 1967 Arab–Israeli war.

The American understanding of the Suez crisis did not develop into a coherent or successful policy. The United States based its post-Suez activities on the premise that the era of British and French domination in the Middle East had ended. True enough: the United States and the Soviet Union, for reasons of their own, had succeeded in October and November 1956 in finally ridding the region of two long-term rivals. In late 1956 and early 1957 America believed that the Soviet Union stood poised to fill that vacuum, either directly or through the proxy of Nasserism. Therein lay part of the problem in creating a new policy. American policy-makers never decided how much of an international communist Nasser was. What began as an effort to block the Soviet Union changed into an American challenge to Nasser. Americans also considered the Arab–Israeli dispute a gnawing annoyance, diverting Arab attention from more serious problems.

The Eisenhower Doctrine originated in an effort to change the subject from relations between Israel and its neighbours, to relations between conservative Arabs and others – the Soviet Union, Nasser, domestic radicals, etc. Israel reluctantly approved of the Eisenhower Doctrine, hoping that the United States would stop putting pressure on it. The Eisenhower Doctrine was more problematic for the Arab states. It did not smooth divisions within the Arab world and may have exacerbated them. The Doctrine also did not block Soviet gains in the region. By 1957, the Baghdad Pact, designed as the bulwark of the Northern tier against Soviet encroachments, had fallen. The United States intervened in Lebanon and Britain in Jordan and no Soviet base emerged there. But the Lebanese action came more out of concern that the United States should not appear as a blusterer than out of a belief that the Soviet Union was plotting with Nasser against Lebanon. Once the United States had left Lebanon in the autumn of 1958, the Eisenhower Doctrine fell into obscurity and the United States ceased to stress the principle of the defence of friendly states in the Middle East.

What precisely were the mistaken American lessons drawn from Suez?

(1) American policy-makers exaggerated the power of the United States after stopping Britain, France and Israel. It was easier to stop that invasion than to dominate the region.

(2) Americans also exaggerated the power of the Soviet Union. Joining the Soviets at the United Nations in October 1956 shocked the American people. To this dismay was added American revulsion at Soviet behaviour in the Hungarian revolution. Secretary of State Dulles and President Eisenhower decided by the end of 1956 that the Soviets would determine events in the Middle East unless the United States moved quickly and forcefully. In fact, however, the Soviets had even less opportunity to dominate the region than had Washington.

(3) Nasser was a problem, but America did not go much beyond that unhelpful formulation. If he was a major threat, then had the United States acted properly in saving him in 1956? Was he a communist? American policy-makers could not answer these questions even during the following two years.

One recent analysis of the Eisenhower administration's Middle Eastern policy concludes: 'the tactics devised, though unsuccessful, were not lacking in ingenuity. Indeed ... this administration ... can be criticized for over-activity in the Middle East'.[36] The United States had sought to construct a policy based upon close ties to the conservative Arab states. That ignored Israel and offended radicals. It was a one-dimensional policy, but even its concentration on the conservative Arabs produced enormous complexity that exceeded the American capacity to manage. The events of 1957 and 1958 did not fulfil the promise of American influence which resulted from the Suez crisis, and the United States was less visible in the Middle East for at least a decade.

THE IMPACT OF SUEZ ON U.S. MIDDLE EAST POLICY

NOTES

1. United States Department of State, *United States Policy in the Middle East*, September 1956–June 1957: Documents (Washington, 1957), pp.15, 16, 20, 24.
2. U.S. Senate, *Committee on Foreign Relations, Executive Sessions of the Senate Committee on Foreign Relations*, Vol. IX, 85th Cong. 1st sess., 1957 (Made Public 1979), p.3.
3. Steven L. Spiegel, *The Other Arab–Israeli Conflict: Making America's Mideast Policy from Truman to Reagan* (Chicago, 1985), p.83.
4. Recent views of the Eisenhower administration's view of Nasserism appear in Stephen Ambrose, *Eisenhower*, Vol.2 (New York, 1984), pp.347–75; Spiegel, op. cit., pp.66–82. Useful traditional studies are Townsend Hoopes, *The Devil and John Foster Dulles* (Boston, 1973), 318–44; Herman Finer, *Dulles over Suez: The Theory and Practice of His Diplomacy* (Chicago, 1964), pp.10–113.
5. U.S. Senate, *Committee on Foreign Relations*, op. cit., pp.20, 22.
6. Ibid., p.26.
7. Ibid., pp.27, 25.
8. Ibid., p.758.
9. Ibid., p.iii.
10. Arthur M. Schlesinger, Jr., *The Imperial Presidency* (Boston, 1973), p.162.
11. John A. DeNovo, 'The Eisenhower Doctrine', in Alexander DeConde, ed., *The Encyclopedia of American Foreign Policy* (New York, 1978), p.296.
12. Spiegel, op. cit., p.65.
13. DeNovo, op. cit., pp.296–7.
14. Spiegel, op, cit., p.86.
15. Stephen J. Genco, 'The Eisenhower Doctrine: Deterrence in the Middle East, 1957–8', in Alexander George and Richard Smoke, *Deterrence in American Foreign Policy: Theory and Practice* (New York, 1974), p.332. John Campbell, *Defense of the Middle East* (New York, 1959), pp.130–1.
16. DeNovo, op. cit., p.297.
17. Patrick Seale, *The Struggle for Syria: A Study in Postwar Arab Politics, 1945–58* (Oxford, 1965), p.294.
18. Dwight D. Eisenhower, *Waging Peace, 1956–61* (New York, 1965), p.131.
19. Genco, op. cit., p.334.
20. Department of State, *Bulletin*, 37 (30 Sept. 1957), p.532.
21. Genco, op. cit., pp.336–7.
22. Ibid., p.337.
23. Eisenhower, op. cit., p.262.
24. Ibid., pp.263–4.
25. Genco, op. cit., p.339.
26. Eisenhower, op. cit., p.266.
27. Department of State, *Bulletin*, 39 (21 July, 1958), p.105.
28. Eisenhower, op. cit., p.269; Ambrose, op. cit., p.470.
29. Genco, op. cit., p.348.
30. Spiegel, op. cit., p.88.
31. Eisenhower, op. cit., p.272.
32. Ambrose, op. cit., p.471.
33. Spiegel, op. cit., p.32.
34. Genco, op. cit., p.353.
35. Spiegel, op. cit., p.89.
36. Ibid., p.92.

19

The United States and the Suez Crisis: The Uses and Limits of Diplomacy

Alfred Atherton

I am sure all of us at some point have indulged in the pastime of asking, 'Where were you when?' Where were you when the Japanese bombed Pearl Harbour? Where were you when President Kennedy was assassinated?

I start by where I was when the Suez War began – not just to play the 'where were you when' game, but because it says something about where the United States Government was on that occasion. I was a junior Second Secretary at the American embassy in Damascus. The State Department had approved our Ambassador's recommendation that the United States should open a Consulate General in Aleppo and that I should be its first principal officer. On 29 October, 1956 I was in Aleppo with two missions from my Government. The first was to look for suitable property for the Consulate General – business as usual on that mission. The second mission was to contact the small American community in north Syria, consisting largely of educators and missionaries, and to tell them that in view of the intensifying crisis in the area, their Government advised them to leave Syria. The official American community in Damascus had already been evacuated to the safety, stability and comfort – bizarre as it may seem today – of Beirut.

With both missions accomplished, I started the drive back to Damascus and made the usual rest stop in Homs. There, while having a cup of coffee at my favourite local restaurant, reports began to come over the radio that Israeli troops had moved into Sinai. I had one consolation for having been caught that much by surprise and not being told very much by my Government about why I was alerting Americans to leave Syria. The President of the United States, who was on an electoral campaign trip at the time, reportedly did not hear the news until nine hours later.

266

The United States Government had of course been aware of the rising tensions and the risks of war in the area. Washington was not caught totally unaware. It was not possible at the late stages of the preparations for the Suez operation to conceal military movements. Our intelligence people were not totally uninformed of what was going on, although so far as I know they had not succeeded in putting all the pieces together. Despite the fact that some officials within the Government did correctly foresee what was coming, there was, right up to the last minute, confusion created by Israeli disinformation about whether Israeli military preparations were directed against Jordan or against Egypt. Washington's efforts to elicit the intentions of the Governments of Israel, Great Britain and France had been met, to put it mildly, with less than full candour. As the Suez crisis gathered force, the American Government sought to influence the course of events, without fully understanding the nature of the events it was seeking to influence. The essence of my thesis is that the power of a state to influence events in the affairs of nations is often limited not by its potential, which may be great, but by a flawed understanding of the situation it seeks to influence and by a consequent failure to bring its potential power to bear effectively at the right time, at the right point, and without ambiguity as to its purposes and intentions. As a corollary, I would say that the effective exercise of power must be based not only on a clear understanding of the situation one seeks to influence, but also on a clear-headed assessment of the relationship between the means a state is prepared to employ and the ends achievable. States prepared to go to war to protect their interests as they perceive them will generally have an advantage over those which seek to avoid war.

It is my contention that, in the years preceding the Suez crisis, the Eisenhower Administration did not fully understand the nature or the intensity of the imperatives driving either the Government of Israel or the Government of Egypt under its new leader, Gamal Abd al-Nasser. It failed to understand how American efforts to promote an alliance of regional states, including the Government of Iraq, against what it perceived as a Soviet threat to the region, and its willingness to provide arms to states which would join the alliance, coupled with its unwillingness to provide arms to Israel, contributed in that period to Israel's sense of insecurity. The Eisenhower Administration also failed to understand how, by doing nothing to enforce the resolutions of the United Nations concerning Israel's right of passage through the Suez Canal, it contributed to Israel's sense of isolation and pressures within Israel to act alone. The

267

United States Government disapproved and made known its disapproval of Israel's policy of military reprisal and joined in condemnation of the several Israeli raids during this period, from Qibya to Gaza to Khan Yunis. But, in Israeli eyes, the United States at the same time offered Israel no alternative.

Turning to America's perception of the Arab position, the Eisenhower Administration also failed to understand the forces that compelled Nasser to align himself with the non-aligned nations, and to seek arms from the Soviet bloc when the Western powers, guardians of the 1950 Tripartite Declaration, refused his requests for arms. It failed to understand the depth of Arab nationalist resentment and rejection of Israel, and the Arab sense of humiliation at their military and political weakness. It was slow to appreciate how, as Nasser sought to assume leadership of the Arab nationalist movement, these forces would move him from his initial seemingly pragmatic, or at least not highly emotional, approach to the Palestine problem to a position of challenging Israel – for example, by tightening the blockade of the Straits of Tiran in September 1955.

My purpose here is not to try to answer the question which has been posed over the years of whether Nasser's policies were the cause or the result of Ben-Gurion's tough strategy of using military measures to force the Arabs to understand that Israel was here to stay. My focus is on how the United States Government interpreted and reacted to this situation. With its eyes fixed on the Cold War, the American Administration failed to appreciate the strength and irreconcilability of the forces gathering strength in the Middle East.

While seeking to woo Egypt as part of this global anti-communist strategy, the Administration also had to cope with pressures on the American domestic front to provide arms to Israel. At the same time Washington was grappling with the problem of how to maintain its close ties with its NATO allies, Britain and France, while encouraging the liquidation of the remnants of colonialism in the world, represented *inter alia* by these two allies. There was no desire to take over what was left of the British Empire or the French colonial position. American leadership at that time had come to believe that the age of colonialism had passed and that it was important to get on the side of the wave of the future – the freeing of nations under colonial rule. This was in the legacy and tradition of America and was certainly the American people's understanding of the policy of their Government.

The fact was that, while the United States was going in the direction of trying to develop relations with Egypt, the British saw

Nasser as a growing threat to their position in the Canal zone and the Gulf and further east. While Algeria was perhaps not the only or the predominant reason why France was concerned about Nasser's policies, I think it is generally accepted that France did see Nasser as a threat to its position in Algeria and that this was a factor in the French decision to go into what became known as the Suez Operation.

The ineffectiveness of United States efforts to influence the course of events during this time reflected the limits of American power in the pre-war period. Warnings to Israel to exercise restraint in its reprisal policies, and to Nasser not to accept Soviet arms, had gone unheeded. Finally reacting to a series of setbacks to its policy of seeking to win Nasser, which up to that time had been a centrepiece of American Middle East strategy – setbacks consisting of the arms deal with the Soviets, the failure of the secret mission of President Eisenhower's emissary, Robert Anderson, to promote understanding between Ben-Gurion and Nasser, and Egyptian recognition of Communist China – and also bowing to strong anti-Nasser and pro-Israel sentiment in the American Congress, the United States Government on 19 July, 1956, withdrew its offer to help finance the Aswan High Dam, an offer it had made only the previous December. There is irony in the fact that this effort to exercise American power through economic pressure on Egypt precipitated the chain of events which culminated in the war Washington sought to avoid – a chain of events that began with Nasser's nationalization of the Suez Canal Company one week later, which Nasser attributed to the withdrawal of the Aswan Dam offer. I know there is a school of thought which holds that Nasser was going to find a way to do this in any case. Even if that is true, the fact is that withdrawal of the Aswan Dam offer did provide him a pretext.

Efforts by the United States to prevent the Suez war, including warnings to the British and French that they would be alone if they resorted to military force, were ignored and probably disbelieved. In fairness, it has to be pointed out here that Mr. Dulles sent mixed signals about what his attitude was towards Nasser, and that probably did not help the British and French to understand the depth of President Eisenhower's feelings about not being associated in any way with military action against Egypt.

Once hostilities broke out, American policies and actions did indeed have an impact on the course of events. By this time, Washington had come to adopt the objective of weakening and isolating Nasser. It had lost its enthusiasm about Nasser; the honeymoon in effect was over. It opposed military action, not to *save* Nasser, but because it was convinced that such action would unify the Arab world *behind* Nasser, and also because it would offer an opening to the Soviet Union. By siding against Britain, France and Israel in the United Nations, and by such actions as withholding emergency oil supplies from Europe after the Canal had been blocked and withholding funds to stabilize the British pound, the United States undoubtedly contributed to the collapse of the Anglo-French military effort, which was already under severe pressures at home, at least in Britain. At the same time, the United States did summarily reject a Soviet offer of joint action and warned against Soviet intervention, thereby seeking to make clear the difference between American and Soviet intentions. On 6 November the British and French announced their intention to withdraw, and their forces were out of Egypt by the end of December.

Dealing with the Israeli presence in Suez proved more complex. The Israeli Government, unlike the British and French, had solid support on the home front and had won a decisive military victory. It was not until March that a combination of American pressures and promises and also, probably, Israel's concern about the long-term importance of its relations with the United States brought about Israeli withdrawal from Sinai.

Belatedly, the United States had succeeded in bringing effective influence to bear to help resolve the immediate Suez crisis. With the British and French positions in the Middle East in shambles, with the need to provide a counter-weight to the Soviet Union, and with commitments both to the new United Nations peace-keeping force and to Israel in return for its withdrawal, the United States emerged from that crisis as the principal Western presence in the Middle East and has remained so ever since.

That the United States, in the immediate wake of the crisis, was nevertheless unable to turn this outcome to its longer-run advantage again demonstrated how a flawed understanding of the situation America faced imposed limits on the effective use of American power. The key point to understand United States policy is that Washington sought to pick up after the crisis where it had left off before the war began, without regard for the reality that the Suez war had altered power relationships and perceptions in the Middle East. The war had also if anything hardened attitudes on both sides of the Arab–Israeli conflict. The dilemma for the United States remained what it had been before the war, only more so – it could not reconcile its commitment to Israel on the one hand, and its desire on the other to increase its influence in the Arab world, which refused to accept Israel, and to keep the Arabs out of the Soviet camp. Yet in the wake of the war the United States — its perceptions no doubt reinforced by the Soviet suppression of the Hungarian revolt — pursued policies which made that already difficult dilemma even more difficult.

At a time when the Arab world had just seen one of its own attacked by Israel, Britain and France, the United States declared that the enemy was the Soviet Union and announced what became known as the Eisenhower Doctrine. In the name of that doctrine, it invited all States in the area to join in an alliance against international communism and in effect against the Soviet Union, which in Arab eyes had championed their cause in the recent crisis. The invitation was on the whole positively received in Israel although there were some differences of opinion arising, I believe, from the fact that Israel was interested in ascertaining whether an alliance would be created which Israel could join. The invitation was rejected in most of the Arab countries and greeted at best with reserve in the rest.

The popularity the United States enjoyed in the Arab world in the immediate aftermath of the war, because of the position it took against the tripartite invasion, quickly evaporated in the fulminations against the Eisenhower Doctrine, which was popularly portrayed in much of the region as an effort to ensnare the Arabs in a neo-colonialist embrace. The limits of American power were again revealed. Clearly this was not solely America's fault, but the anti-American reaction that set in very shortly in much of the area was greatly exacerbated by the failure of the United States to assess correctly the forces at work in the region and to take them into account in formulating its own policies.

American policies in the 1967 and 1973 crises make an interesting epilogue to the experience of 1956. Again on those two latter occasions, the United States was caught unprepared by a sudden outbreak of hostilities, and again its last minute efforts to prevent their outbreak were unavailing. In the course of those wars, the United States was again able by its actions and policies to be a factor in determining how the crises were resolved. Compare, however, the American approach in the period after Suez with that following the 1967 and 1973 wars. A better understanding of the political realities and of the perceptions of the parties to the conflict enabled the United States to project its influence, both through the United

271

Nations and directly with the parties, into the post-1967 and post-1973 diplomatic efforts in ways it was unable to do in the aftermath of the Suez crisis.

There is a further point that needs to be made about the limits and uses of American power and diplomacy. The very knowledge that the United States was there and engaged in the Middle East itself exercised influence on Soviet policy, in the sense that it was something the Soviets had to take into account and something that, in real moments of crisis, constrained them. It is also true that to some extent this worked both ways and that the United States was also very conscious of Soviet interest and potential power in the region. It is revealing that in 1967 and 1973, in the very early moments of hostilities, one of the first things the United States and the Soviet Union did was to open the hotline between them. Both clearly wanted to avoid the situation leading to a confrontation at the superpower level.

Finally, I do not want to exaggerate the successes of American diplomacy in the period after 1967, and of course the context was very different from 1956. Israel in June 1967 was seen as having responded to a threat rather than as having taken unprovoked military action. Also, unlike 1956, there was no United Nations resolution calling for immediate Israeli withdrawal. In fact, Resolution 242 recognized that Israel should remain in occupied territories until the Arabs recognized and made peace with Israel. Although American efforts in this period produced no major breakthroughs toward peace, the United States role – even though it had no diplomatic relations with most Arab states – was more relevant than it had been in the period immediately following the 1956 Suez crisis. Much of American diplomacy after 1967 – and it was a very active diplomacy – was not entirely to Israel's liking. I am thinking in particular of the Rogers Plan of 1969. There was one important success worthy of note, the Rogers initiative in the summer of 1970, which produced a ceasefire between Israel and two Arab parties, Egypt and Jordan, that lasted until the 1973 war.

The period after the 1973 war is probably the best example of the projection of American influence into post-war Middle East diplomacy. It is true that Henry Kissinger kept a close eye on the Soviets during this period and did his best to exclude them from the Middle East diplomatic scene. But he also did not see the situation entirely in U.S.–Soviet terms. He came to grips with the issues between the parties themselves and produced a series of agreements that eventually bore fruit at Camp David and in the Egyptian–Israeli peace treaty.

American influence in the Middle East on the issue of paramount concern – the process of continuing to work for comprehensive peace in the region – in my view began to diminish again when we forgot the lessons of earlier periods and began in 1981 to talk about giving priority to establishing a strategic consensus in the area – a phrase that evoked some of the failed concepts of the Eisenhower–Dulles period. There are many reasons why the peace process has slowed since 1981. I believe there is enough blame to go around among all those with an interest in this problem. An important factor, however, is that the United States has not always in recent years remembered what its priorities should be.

20

The Soviet Union and the Suez Crisis

Galia Golan

Soviet–Egyptian relations began virtually only after Stalin's death. There is some controversy over changes which Stalin sought or planned to make in foreign (and domestic) policy in the last year or so of his life. Nonetheless, pending a thorough reassessment and change in foreign policy, Stalin had little room for a relationship of any duration with a country like Egypt. His was a strictly bi-polar, two-camp view of the world (expounded by Zhadnov in 1947) which advocated revolutionary militancy and loyal alignment. Given this attitude, Stalin failed to see the shades and nuances developing in the Third World, and thus was fated to dismiss the revolution-making Free Officers in Egypt as lackeys of imperialism. Similarly, neither before nor after the Egyptian revolution did Stalin initiate a shift towards the Arabs or a 'pro-Arab' stand in the context of the Arab–Israel dispute, despite the fact that his policy towards Israel had been increasingly unfriendly since the end of 1948. Only after Stalin's demise, the rethinking surrounding the succession and the rise first of Malenkov and then Khrushchev, did Soviet policy undergo significant change. This change, which basically opened the way for relations with a 'Third' non-aligned world, was generated by concern over the risks inherent in the nuclear era. Finding Stalin's militancy too risky and believing in the inevitability of escalation of war, including local war, to nuclear confrontation, the new leaders sought reduction of international tensions and peaceful coexistence through deterrence. Khrushchev took this competition overseas, well beyond the outer edges of the Soviet bloc, and he defined deterrence as nuclear power even to the point of nuclear 'sabre-rattling'. Yet he saw this, apparently, as brinkmanship, i.e., the employment of the threat of nuclear strike as a deterrent, without in fact getting involved in a war, which Khrushchev believed could not remain limited or conventional.

Much in Khrushchev's personality and views was flamboyant and contradictory. But within the above perception of Soviet policy there was a certain consistency. There was a competition for the new, neutral nations. No longer the militant but dangerous revolutionary approach, the new tactics called for cooperation with bourgeois nationalists, who were appreciated for their anti-imperialist orientation, even if this fell short of Marxism or alignment. Indeed, non-alignment could be particularly useful inasmuch as the West, not Moscow, was the party seeking alignment in the form of treaties and bases. Anti-imperialism and non-alignment were both definable in the 1950s in anti-Western terms. The more sophisticated, less risky peaceful-coexistence policy of Khrushchev therefore, might well provide openings which the militant, two-camp, continental orientation of Stalin overlooked.

It was the post-Stalin reappraisal of the Third World which led to Soviet relations with the Arab states, and a shift towards the Arabs, specifically Egypt, in the Arab–Israeli conflict. These were evidenced by the use of the Soviet veto in the Security Council in 1954 against Israel, in one case against the right of Israel to passage through the Suez Canal on which the Soviets had merely abstained a few years earlier in 1951. It was also evidenced by a Soviet–Syrian arms deal in 1954 and the $250 million Czechoslovak–Egyptian arms deal of 1955.[1] The relationship opened with Egypt was made possible by the general policy reassessment in Moscow; it was occasioned by a number of specific factors, such as the mutuality of Soviet and Egyptian interests vis-à-vis Western attempts to forge the Baghdad Pact (building on Egypt's arch-rival, Iraq), as well as a general lack of American responsiveness to Egypt's economic and military demands, and Egypt's efforts to free itself of Britain.

THE SUEZ CRISIS

The 1956 Suez Crisis was the first test of the Soviets' newly found interest and commitment to the area. Indeed it could be said that because this *was* the first crisis situation in a relationship that had only just begun, little can be learned from it or that it constituted something of an exception from today's vantage point. Thus it may be argued that the Soviet commitment was not yet, in fact, particularly great; Soviet involvement in and influence over Egypt was not quite fully developed; Soviet familiarity with the Arabs was not great and, therefore, Moscow was not particularly responsive. To some degree these things are true. Soviet interests in the region at the time were primarily political, part of the competition with the

275

West. This was an area which Moscow appreciated as being more important to the West than to the Soviet Union, even if it were geographically close to the Soviet Union. Only later did Soviet interests expand, as newer interests were added to the political and the traditional interest in the region to the south of Soviet borders. Only in the 1960s did Moscow develop a definite military interest in, and need for the area. As a result, its involvement and commitment became much greater in the late 1960s. It can be maintained, however, that the basic outline of Soviet behaviour in the Suez Crisis became, in fact, a *pattern* for Soviet behaviour in the Arab–Israeli conflict and subsequent crises. There were variations and additions, to be sure. These were in part the result of a certain learning process and in part because of changing capabilities. Nonetheless, certain basic points remained consistent in subsequent years.

THE PATTERN: OBJECTIVES

Two major considerations guided Soviet actions in this crisis, and in subsequent wars. The first was the objective of exploiting the opportunity, however it was created, to improve Moscow's own position in the region with its Arab clients; the second was to avoid direct confrontation with the United States. These two objectives, while not necessarily mutually exclusive, could nonetheless prove contradictory or at times difficult to juggle. With regard to the second objective, it must be remembered that this was a period of definite American strategic nuclear superiority, as well as regional superiority, with the sixth fleet in the Mediterranean. It was also a time of Khrushchevian belief in the inevitability of escalation of local wars to nuclear confrontation, and, probably of an exaggerated Soviet belief in the power of Washington over its allies, particularly Israel. This last estimation could lead Moscow to consider the United States more loyal to its allies than it claimed to be; at the very least it contributed to some uncertainty over the American factor.

At the same time, the crisis offered a great opportunity to improve Moscow's position in the region, to evict the British altogether and to discredit the West, including if possible the United States. Indeed, the Soviet propaganda line varied between one which portrayed the United States as directly involved as Britain and France, or the line that the United States wanted to replace Britain and France as the central power in the Middle East and, therefore, welcomed a conflict which discredited the two. It may be

276

noted that this effort to indict the Americans was indicative of a basic difference in the attitudes of the Soviet Union and Egypt prior to the war, and which persisted, causing some tension between the two countries. The Soviet Union viewed (and continues to view) the Arab–Israeli conflict in East–West terms, particularly the role of the United States, while Egypt understandably viewed it in Arab–Israeli terms.[2]

THE PATTERN: BEHAVIOUR

Moscow was slow to respond to the Egyptians' nationalization announcement and, also, to the outbreak of hostilities in October. In the pre-war period of negotiations regarding the Canal, the Soviets championed Egyptian rights and action, making propaganda profit of the anti-colonial nature of the action. Moscow may have calculated, as the Egyptians claim, that Egypt would have the Canal running and the crisis would subside before the use of force could be prepared.[3] On this estimate, the Soviets presumably sought to prolong the negotiation period, while dispatching assistance to Cairo in the form of navigation pilots (and grain for Egyptian currency, once Britain froze Egyptian accounts). The Soviets may also have been concerned, however, that France and Britain would strike some compromise deal with Egypt. For this reason, amongst others, the Soviets sought to be a party to any negotiations taking place. Moscow also had an interest in the assertion of freedom of navigation, preferring an international forum even as it asserted Egyptian sovereignty and rights over the Canal. Moscow did send letters of concern and warning to the British and the French, referring to the dangers of escalation, as well as to Soviet interests in the region.[4] But these communications were by no means in the form of a threat or commitment; they were not even particularly strongly worded. Nor was there apparently any Soviet–Egyptian coordination of actions at this time. Cairo may have been encouraged by the informal comment regarding the possibility of Soviet volunteers made by Khrushchev at a Rumanian reception in Moscow in August.[5] This remark was published by the Egyptian press, but not by that of the Soviet Union. In fact, according to Heikal, Nasser actually cancelled a trip to Moscow planned for August, because of the crisis.[6] Far from seeking co-ordination, Heikal claims that Nasser purposely avoided such consultation for fear of Soviet over-cautiousness and restraint.[7] While it seems unlikely that the Soviets would have urged Cairo to

277

back down, Moscow did become increasingly cautious as the crisis augmented, rather than receded, and the actual use of force by Britain and France became a more immediate possibility.

With the outbreak of the fighting the Soviets took several steps – none of which indicated an intention of becoming involved. The 45 Ilushin 28s provided to Egypt, with their Soviet instructors, were transferred to Luxor in Upper Egypt, for further removal to Syria.[8] Thus the Soviets obviously sought to avoid the destruction or capture of these aircraft, as well as their possible involvement in the conflict. In so doing, however, Moscow was in effect removing Egypt's striker-bomber offensive air capability. Following British and French air attacks on Egypt, the Soviets transferred some 380 Soviet and Czechoslovak advisers out of Egypt to the Sudan, for eventual evacuation from the region. This move followed orders issued earlier to the advisers to refrain from any involvement in the fighting.[9] This was particularly significant inasmuch as these advisers included the instructor-crews for some 200 Soviet tanks (which the British had apparently believed they would have to fight).

On 31 October, the day after the British–French ultimatum, the Soviet Union proposed that the crisis be referred to the Security Council, and on the next day, it urged India and Indonesia to activate the Bandung Conference nations.[10] Thus, neither politically nor militarily were the Soviets prepared to take a direct role. Moreover, when asked directly for assistance, on 1 November, by Syrian President Quwatli visiting in Moscow, the Soviet leadership was almost contemptuous in its reply. Marshal Zhukov is reported to have pulled out a map and demanded to know how Moscow could in fact intervene.[11] The Soviets' offer at this point reportedly was limited to political support, particularly through the UN. A similar message was conveyed to the Egyptian ambassador in Moscow on 2 November, i.e., that the Soviets would not provide military assistance but would mobilize world opinion.[12] (Nasser later claimed that Moscow did offer to supply tanks and technicians, but that the offer was rejected because Egypt did not require such aid.)[13] In light of the evacuation of the Soviet tank crews already in Egypt, it is unlikely that such an offer was actually made or that it was meant – or taken – seriously.

The direct, and strong, Soviet move came only on the night of 5 November: the ultimatum. This ultimatum came in the form of five letters, including one to Britain and France (a threat of rocket attack), one to Israel (the possibility of placing the existence of the

State of Israel in question), one to the Security Council (a twelve-hour deadline for cessation of hostilities) and one to the United States (a proposal for a joint force including the American sixth fleet).[14]

THE PATTERN COMPARED

The picture *prior* to the night of 5 November was one of lack of involvement and caution, both in messages to the Arabs and in responses to such measures as the closure of the eastern Mediterranean and the northern Red Sea, and the American SAC alert (Soviet forces had been on alert since the beginning of the Polish and Hungarian crises in mid-October). Political measures were indirect even to the point of supporting the American resolution at the UN. Certain basic moves in the period prior to 5 November were repeated in the 1967 war and even, to some degree, in the 1973 war. In both the later cases, Soviet aims were the same: improvement of the Soviet position (which in 1967 held hopes for Soviet naval expansion, but in 1973 was actually in decline) and the avoidance of confrontation with the United States. In 1967 and 1973 Soviet personnel and equipment were moved out, although in 1973 it was only an evacuation of civilians, combined, however, with the movement of the Soviet fleet westward (as in 1967), away from the area of conflict.[15] In 1967 and 1973, as in 1956, there were Soviet warnings to the Egyptians that they might expect no more than political assistance or that they were not to expect Soviet intervention. In 1967 as in 1956, no Soviet assistance was dispatched during the conflict – in 1967 the Soviets reportedly claimed there was no place to land such aid, just as in 1956 they reportedly claimed logistic problems. Nor were there any military moves. In 1973 there was aid, even massive aid delivered during the hostilities, although Sadat complained that it was insufficient, merely fulfilment of prewar orders, and, more important, supplied only in return for hard currency cash payments, which were provided by Algeria. Indeed, this resupply during hostilities was probably prompted, at least in part, by the lessons of 1956 and particularly 1967, for the Soviets had been severely criticized by Arab circles for refusing such aid in the earlier conflicts.[16] In 1973, there were Soviet military moves in the form of augmentation of their fleet, although this was located off the coast of Crete, and designed to neutralize the American fleet rather than provide for intervention.

279

There are similarities with regard to the threats of 5 November as well.[17] In all three cases, 1956, 1967 and 1973, Soviet moves, as presented by Moscow, were credited with bringing the conflict to a halt (stopping the 'aggressors' against the Arab states). In 1956 the questions were: why did the Soviets wait until the night of 5 November, and was there any substance to their threats? Indeed one could ask these questions with regard to all three wars. In 1956, it is generally explained, the Soviets waited because of their involvement in Hungary.

It is true that they were occupied with the Hungarian revolution, especially and acutely from the time of their first military intervention in Hungary on the night of 23–24 October until the second intervention on 4 November. It may be, however, that they waited to act in the Middle East for another reason – one which was typical of the subsequent Arab–Israeli wars as well. Moscow most likely awaited the American response to the Middle East crisis, acting only when relatively certain there would be no risk of confrontation with the United States. They also awaited the passage of the critical point in the field, when there would be little likelihood of any necessity to carry out their threatened actions. That is, they waited in all three cases until the crisis had reached its diplomatic peak, resolution was in sight, and the United States was likely to support the end of the conflict by restraining its allies or clients.

Thus, the timing of the threats was dependent upon the Soviets' own risk-taking propensity, rather than the Arabs' needs or plight. The threats added a further political objective, aimed at audiences in the Third World, for example, beyond the actual combatants, promising propaganda-political benefits with no need actually to implement the threats. It is true that the threats always came to save the Egyptians from further, more devastating defeat, but never to prevent them from reaching the point of defeat. In the Suez crisis a more effective time for the Soviet threat, from the Arab point of view, would have been immediately after the British–French ultimatum of 30 October, but at this time there was no certainty on the Soviets' part that the U.S. would *not* support its allies' action. The crisis was at its peak and the risk was high. Indeed the delay in Soviet action indicated the priority of the second Soviet objective in the war, avoidance of confrontation with the United States, over the first objective which was an improvement of the Soviet position in the Arab world. By the evening of 5 November the peak of the crisis had passed: the Egyptian air force was destroyed or crippled, a cease-fire had already been achieved with Israel and that fighting had ceased, the British were clearly ready to stop, a short-lived cease-fire had already been attempted in Port Said, and, most important, the United States was involved in trying to stop the British and the French.

Another interesting aspect, pointed out by Francis Fukuyama, was the wording of the threats in 1956. The language was conditional: the term 'could', not 'would', was used in relation to threatened actions. And joint action was sought with the United States, against America's allies and clients. This was a proposal which the Soviets knew could not be accepted. Chester Bohlen, U.S. Ambassador to Moscow at the time, later wrote that he could not believe that the Soviets actually expected him to deliver such a proposal when it was handed to him.[18] This part of the threat was also politically dictated, designed to embarrass the United States, at least in the eyes of the Third World, and even portray it as colluding with the British and French.

In June 1967 and October 1973 the Soviet threats also came (1) after the major fighting and the peak of the crisis; (2) after the United States was committed, and trying, to restrain its client (the Americans had agreed to a cease-fire); and therefore (3) after the necessity of implementing the threat. In these cases too the threats were couched in conditional terms, lacking in precision, and in 1973 as in 1956 joint action in order to embarrass the United States was proposed. In 1956 and 1967 there were no military moves to back up the threat; in 1973 such moves were highly ambiguous and subject to much controversy amongst analysts. In fact most such moves in 1973 preceded rather than accompanied the threat (e.g., the passage of nuclear material through the Dardanelles on 14 or 15 October and the airborne alerts from the beginning of the war).

The 1973 threat was taken much more seriously than the previous ones, probably because Soviet military capabilities had greatly expanded in the interim. One might question the Soviets' ability, even in 1973, quickly to introduce large numbers of forces into battle against Israel.[19] But in 1956 and 1967 it was certain that no such capability existed. Thus, not only did the Soviets wait until there was no necessity to implement their threats; they actually had no ability, or intention, to implement the threat. In 1956, when Moscow threatened Britain and France with rockets, it actually had only a fraction of the American missile capability. What little the Soviets did have, according to John Erikson, were first generation rockets which were modified V-2s with the limited range of 400 to 450 miles.[20] Erikson has concluded that they could have used these only

281

in a sporadic, uncoordinated way and then only from points in Eastern Europe – at a time when Eastern Europe was in turmoil. With regard to intervention – not actually threatened (the Soviets spoke publicly of volunteers only on 10 November) – this too was unlikely. There were no Soviet airborne divisions until the late 1960s and no large transport planes to bring large numbers even of volunteers. There were long-range bombers capable of hitting the British, for example at their Cyprus staging position, but there were no signs of any preparation or intention to deploy them. And the Soviets had virtually no marines at the time (or, for that matter, since then). Thus the standard explanation that Moscow was tied up in Hungary does not fully explain the delay in the Soviet threat. The delay until after the second intervention in Hungary conceivably might have accorded the Soviet threats greater credibility. But it is unlikely that involvement in Hungary actually prevented an earlier threat, since this kind of empty, purely symbolic threat could have been made at any time. There was no more or less ability to back it up during or after the Hungarian crisis. What was different was the U.S. factor.

In 1967 there was still no airborne capability, nor a significant marine corps. Most of the same problems for intervention existed then as in 1956. In 1973 the airborne capability did exist, including the large Antonov aircraft necessary for transporting these forces, but what remained consistent, despite improvements in the Soviet military position, was the concern over taking on such an intervention. This concern was based on (1) the continued American superiority in the strategic sphere (at best parity was only being neared) and the risk of direct confrontation; (2) the superiority, despite the augmentation of the Soviet fleet, of American forces in the region; and (3) the cost of engaging in battle against the Israeli airforce and its armoured corps (which may well have been more than a match for the Soviet airborne infantry). There were differences, of course, in the three crises, but in spite of changes in Soviet capabilities, increased Soviet commitment, and even military moves in 1973, the pattern apparent in 1956, of limited, delayed action and caution remained characteristic of Soviet policy in all three cases.

THE EFFECTS OF 1956 ON THE SOVIET POSITION IN THE MIDDLE EAST

One interpretation of the outcome of the crisis, an interpretation nurtured by Moscow, is that the Soviet Union was the major beneficiary of the 1956 crisis. Britain and France were discredited and their influence virtually ended in the region. The United States was to some degree linked to its allies, or at best a poor ally; the Soviet Union however, saved the day, brought about an end to the hostilities and emerged as the champion of the Third World in general, the Arabs in particular. In fact, however, several elements of dissonance entered, or became apparent, in Soviet–Arab relations as a result of Soviet behaviour.

First, the Egyptians resented the Soviet attempt to take credit for the political defeat of the West. The Egyptian attitude was evident in their media emphasis and careful insistence upon the exclusive Arab role in the crisis.[21] The Egyptian press did not even give the Soviet threats editorial coverage nor did it express any gratitude. And Nasser actually credited other outside factors (including the efforts of President Eisenhower) equally with those of the Soviet Union.[22] Second, the Egyptians resented the Soviet delay and inaction during the crisis. Nasser made several statements which clearly referred to this, saying for example, that the Soviets waited nine days to make up their mind.[23] Sadat has said that his own disillusionment with Moscow began at this time (and he credited the Americans with the major role in ending the crisis).[24] Heikal reports the same, claiming on one occasion that this was the beginning of the deterioration which was to come to a head in the 1958–60 crisis in Soviet–Egyptian relations.[25]

Third, the Arabs became aware of Soviet priorities, noting that concern over war with the United States, and the placement of Soviet interests over those of their clients, were linked to if not dictated by American strategic superiority. It was clear to the Arabs that all else was secondary to this concern, the Soviets willing to do little more than engage in symbolic, propagandistic actions, while exploiting the crisis to their own political benefit. Conversely, it may be that the Soviets, for their part, saw the poor performance of the Arab armies even with the recently supplied Soviet arms. This could have fortified those within the Kremlin who argued for the provision of newer and better equipment and training for the Arab armies, but by the same degree, it may have fortified those who opposed the

283

involvement altogether – creating if not continuing a difference of opinion on the issue. Neither group, if indeed there were groups, can have concluded, however, that an Arab–Israeli war in the near future would be a positive option. Such a conclusion would have had to be based on the Soviets' unwillingness directly to intervene, highlighting what was probably the major lesson to both sides: the importance of the United States, the centrality of the response of and risks emanating from American military strength and the possibility of superpower confrontation.

Indeed, although the crisis may have augmented Soviet prestige in the eyes of some in the region, another result of the crisis was the Eisenhower Doctrine, i.e., a stronger American commitment to the area. While this was a negative phenomenon for the Soviet Union, Moscow's reaction was not necessarily the one the Egyptians might have chosen. It was a Soviet proposal, in February 1957, for a Soviet–American cooperative approach to the region, including an arms embargo and a peaceful solution to the Arab–Israeli conflict.[26] These were just the two points which were to become serious bones of contention in the subsequent Soviet–Egyptian relationship. On the first point, the Soviets were, and remained, reluctant to deliver just anything and everything in the way of arms and equipment requested. In a Soviet retrospective of the Suez crisis it was even stated that one of the lessons of the crisis was that a State did not need military superiority and that hardware was not the most important factor in the conflict.[27] On the second point, there was, and remained, Soviet reluctance to support the war option, i.e., there was a preference for political means over military, because of the concern over Soviet–U.S. confrontation.

CONCLUSIONS

It is not my contention that the pattern and resulting behaviour of Moscow in 1956 became a hard and fast rule governing all subsequent and future Soviet behaviour in the Arab–Israeli context. On two occasions the Soviets actually assumed commitments for the air defence of two Arab states and went so far as to dispatch close to 20,000 military advisers including pilots. Yet the wars to date have followed the same general pattern, even though greater involvement was undertaken outside the region, in cases where a limited American commitment minimized the risks. This, then, is the primary factor to emerge: the American commitment, in the final analysis, is the determining factor restraining

284

Soviet behaviour, even with increased Soviet military capabilities. Changes in the future are always possible. A number of scenarios may be cited which might result in a different approach. Moreover, there was one more feature of the Suez crisis which had bearing on future Soviet behaviour. If the basic pattern set by Suez and repeated later was caution, or the priority of superpower concerns, it was also demonstrated that the Soviet Union assigned its interests in the Middle East, and the value of the region to both East and West, sufficient importance to demand recognition of Moscow's role. This demand was illustrated and given force by the Soviets' willingness to issue a threat, even without great risk-taking or willingness to implement. One could attribute this, in 1956, simply to Khrushchev's penchant for sabre-rattling and brinkmanship. The repetition of the threat pattern, however, in subsequent, post-Khrushchev conflicts, coupled with the fact that such threats have not been issued in many other Middle Eastern crises outside the Arab–Israeli context, suggest the greater importance attached to this conflict by the Soviet Union. It is not of sufficient importance to warrant high risk-taking but enough to warrant more than minimal action.

This then was another pattern set: a policy of threats, of arming and of a challenge to the West in what could be called competitive behaviour coupled with or followed by cooperative proposals, for joint political action, such as the February 1957 proposal. Somewhat similar may have been the dispatch to Egypt of the 20,000 advisers in 1970, followed by the transmission to the United States of Moscow's most moderate negotiating position to date.[28] In 1967 the Soviet threat was followed by the Glassboro meeting and the joint effort which produced Security Council resolution 242. In 1973 there was the almost simultaneous cooperative Soviet–American effort for a cease-fire and conference proposal (resolution 338) and the threat of 24 October, followed again by cooperation. The Suez crisis of 1956 marked the Soviets' role and demand for a role as co-superpower participant in the region, with all its limitations and specific priorities of a complex nature. These should not be exaggerated, but they are also not to be underestimated.

NOTES

1. See Yaacov Ro'i, *From Encroachment to Involvement: A Documentary Study of Soviet Policy in the Middle East, 1945–1973* (New York, 1974), pp.143–4 for details.
2. See, for example, the Soviet statement of April 1956, the first major pronouncement on the Arab–Israeli conflict in Khrushchev's time (*ibid.*, pp. 163–5). This statement saw the conflict purely as the result of the Western imperialists' actions, concentrated on the United States and the West in general, while it included Israel amongst those states whose independence was supported and to be consolidated.
3. Mohamed Heikal, *The Cairo Documents* (Boston, 1972), p.90.
4. Anthony Eden, *The Suez Crisis of 1956* (Boston, 1969), p.122; Hugh Thomas, *The Suez Affair* (London, 1967), p.81.
5. Peter Calvocoressi, *Suez: Ten Years After* (London, 1967), p.21.
6. Mohamed Heikal, *The Sphinx and the Commissar* (London, 1978), p.71.
7. Heikal, *Cairo Documents*, p.90.
8. J.M. MacIntosh, *Strategy and Tactics of Soviet Foreign Policy* (London, 1962), p.186; Calvocoressi, op, cit., p.49 (John Erikson).
9. *Ibid.* (both).
10. *Soviet News*, 1 Nov. 1956.
11. Heikal, *Cairo Documents*, p.111 and *Sphinx*, p.71; Stephen Kaplan, *Soviet Naval Diplomacy* (Brookings Institution, 1981), p.154.
12. Heikal, *Sphinx*, p.71.
13. Kenneth Love, *Suez: The Twice-Fought Wars* (New York, 1969), p.609.
14. See Ro'i, op. cit., pp.186–91 for documents.
15. For Soviet behaviour in 1973, see Galia Golan, *Yom Kippur and After: The Soviet Union and the Middle East Crisis* (Cambridge, 1977); for 1967, see A. Horelkick, 'Soviet Policy in the Middle East', in S. Alexander and P. Hammond, *Political Dynamics in the Middle East* (New York, 1972), pp.581–91.
16. Tunis radio, 12 April 1974.
17. For an analysis of Soviet nuclear threats see Francis Fukuyama, 'Nuclear Shadowboxing: Soviet Intervention Threats in the Middle East', *Orbis*, Fall, 1981, pp.579–605 and Galia Golan, 'Soviet Decision-Making in the Yom Kippur War' in Wm. Potter and J. Valenta, *Soviet Decision-Making for National Security* (London, 1983), pp.192–96.
18. Chester Bohlen, *Witness to History* (New York, 1973), p.432.
19. See Kaplan, op.cit.
20. Calvocoressi, op.cit., p.22 (Erikson). The Soviets had tested a 1000-mile range IRBM, but these were barely produced prior to 1957, according to Erikson.
21. Shahrough Akhavi, 'The Egyptian Image of the Soviet Union, 1954–1968' (Ph.D. thesis, Columbia University, University Microfilms, 1970), pp.103–5.
22. Oles Smolansky, *The Soviet Union and the Arab East Under Khrushchev* (Leninsburg, 1974), p.51; Love, op.cit., pp.611–12; Nasser interview, 7 April 1957.
23. *Ibid.*
24. Anwar Sadat, *In Search of Identity: An Autobiography* (New York, 1977), p.146.
25. Heikal, *Sphinx*, pp.73–4.
26. *Soviet News*, 13 Feb. 1957.
27. L. Medvedko, 'Uroki Suesta', *Aziia i Afrika Segodnia*, No. 11, 1981, p. 14.
28. Transmitted in July 1970 according to L.L. Whetten, *The Canal War* (Cambridge, MA, 1974), pp.115 and published in *Pravda*, 15 Oct. 1970 by Primakov.

Part IV

PARTICIPANTS RECORD THE EVENTS

21

Ben-Gurion's Diary:
The Suez–Sinai Campaign

Edited and introduced by Selwyn Ilan Troen

The following excerpts from the diaries of David Ben-Gurion comprise selections from the period of the Suez–Sinai Campaign. They begin on 30 July, 1956, shortly after Nasser's nationalization of the Suez Canal, with a report of the clandestine receipt of French arms; detail the contacts and negotiations between France and Great Britain that led to the campaign against Nasser; and continue through the post-war period, concluding with Ben-Gurion's evaluation of the Sinai campaign at the end of December.

This segment from the diary of 1956 represents approximately 20 per cent of the total notations for this six-month period. Items relating to party politics, and other non-Suez-related matters that engaged Prime Minister and Minister of Defence Ben-Gurion have been omitted; so, too, have some details that relate to the relationship with the United Nations, particularly over border problems that were considerable at a time when there were frequent fidaiyyun attacks and Israeli reprisals. A few entries will have to await yet one more generation before being released to the public by the Israel National Archives. Nevertheless, the materials presented here stand on their own as a prime resource for reconstructing the events leading up to the war.

The Suez diaries are part of a massive record Ben-Gurion kept from 1900 until nearly the day he died in 1973. Since they were notebooks intended to assist him in his work rather than private or intimate notations, there is almost nothing of a personal nature on himself, his family or his private life. He used the diaries to record his activities including meetings, letters, and conversations, to note what transpired, and to offer commentary, reflection and analysis. During the 1920s and 1930s he even shared them with his colleagues as a means of communication. In order to facilitate their use, he indexed them himself so that he could refer to them for needed information. From time to time he also wrote summaries and short histories of topics that were of interest to him.

The following selections from the diary of 1956 record Ben-Gurion's analysis of the very complex and dynamic political circumstances surrounding 'Suez' as well as his assessment of the motivations and calculations of the other major actors in the drama. Of particular value is his account of the meetings at Sèvres, France between October 22nd and 24th where the French, British, and Israelis negotiated the conditions and mutual responsibilities for their joint attack on Nasser's Egypt. Since there was no official stenographic record, Ben-Gurion's detailed entries are probably the most complete account of the decision-making process which for thirty years has been enveloped in secrecy.

During his own lifetime, Ben-Gurion forbade the use of this diary for publication and kept secret the conversations at Sèvres as well as the details of negotiations for arms with the French and many of the other activities noted here. Although several histories of Suez and biographies of Ben-Gurion have benefited from access to the diary after his death, they all necessarily lack the authority and consistent point of view of the author himself.

The critical researcher is aware of the lacunae in records of this kind. Ben-Gurion does not tell us all we would wish to know. For example, for the days of Israeli involvement in the war there are no notations whatsoever since Ben-Gurion became ill with the outbreak of the conflict. Apparently, he exerted himself to an extraordinary degree in the events leading to the actual fighting and this took its toll. Only at the end of the war does he resume writing in the diary. On the other hand, the diary includes an extraordinarily generous entry during the secret flight from Israel to France. The weather was bad and in the additional hours the plane circled over the landing field Ben-Gurion had a chance to pen a revealing projection of what the Middle East could become should the war against Nasser succeed. Such are the inevitable imbalances of a document of this sort.* Nevertheless, it should be noted that despite his expectation that his diaries would be read by posterity, or perhaps because he was conscious that he was creating a historical document, Ben-Gurion never erased or changed an entry. In all the diaries, the record of any particular day remains a reflection of what

---

* For a more systematic, legalistic justification and interpretation of the war see the collection of speeches Ben-Gurion published as *The Sinai Campaign* [Hebrew], 1959.

engaged Ben-Gurion at the moment. Thus the following selections provide revealing insights into how a central figure in the crisis over Suez endeavoured to comprehend the dramatic unfolding of events and a unique account of why and how Ben-Gurion led Israel into the Suez and Sinai Campaigns.

FROM BEN-GURION'S DIARY

Monday, 30 July 1956

At 2 p.m. I went down to Tel-Aviv to meet with the editors of our newspapers[1] to inform them of a vital secret with the aim that they should keep the secret and prevent any possible leak. – This is about our deal for tanks, airplanes and artillery which will be delivered to us during the next two months.

[Later that night ...]

[Pierre-Eugène] Gilbert[2] came a second time to greet the ship [bearing French arms]. Golda [Meir][3] came with him.

At 10:00 p.m. the ship docked and opened its doors. In twenty minutes the 30 tanks rolled out. Then the unloading of the crates with the spare parts and accessories continued.

Thursday, August 2

At noon, Nehemia [Argov][4] and [Yehoshafat] Harkabi[5] came to see me. Our [French] allies request information concerning the possibilities of the Port of Haifa. I asked that all the requested information be delivered to them. On our part we are requesting the use of Djibouti[6] – in the event that we break through to Eilat or that we have to sabotage Egyptian ships in the Gulf [of Suez].

Friday, August 3

At six, Moshe [Dayan],[7] Shimon [Peres],[8] Nehemia [Argov] and Moraleh [Mordechai Bar-On][9] arrived. The contract for 18 Vautour [airplanes] has been signed. The [French] air-force was asked whether they could give them up and replied in the negative, but the Minister of Defense [Maurice Bourgès-Maunoury][10] gave an affirmative order. This was done with the knowledge of the P[rime] M[inister] [Guy Mollet][11] and [Foreign Minister] [Christian] Pineau.[12] They have also agreed to the postponement for one year of the payment of 20 million dollars, but Shimon claims that he will be lacking funds ... [details of $116 million military procurement budget follows] ...

291

According to Shimon [Peres], the French have taken Nasser's decision [to nationalize the canal] more seriously than is reflected in the [French] press. They view a defeat over Suez like a defeat in Algeria.

On the first of this month Abel Thomas, Director-General of the Defense Ministry,[13] reported to Shimon that:

(1) The English and the French had decided in principle on a joint military action to conquer the Canal; (2) The estimated time of the operation would be in 3 weeks; (3) The English made the condition that Israel would not take part in this action, and would not even be informed of it at this stage (in order to prevent all the Arabs from uniting around Nasser).

In the conversation with the Director-General [Thomas] the question of our participation in planning and advice 'was raised' and if necessary – more than that. The Director-General asked whether we would be prepared to send a military man to France concerning this matter.

[Eliahu] Elath[14] cabled (on the 1st of this month), that Randolph [Churchill][15] had confided in him that Britain has a plan to take over the Canal should Nasser obstruct free passage of ships. A plan for the evacuation of 30,000 British subjects in Egypt has been worked out. The issue confronting [Anthony] Eden[16] is how to get the U.S. involved so that should action be taken, it will not be done with only the authority of France and England. Selwyn Lloyd[17] opposes Eden and demands that military action be taken even without the U.S.

At 8.30 p.m. I went down to the Kishon port [in Haifa] with M[oshe]. D[ayan]., Shimon [Peres] and Nehemia [Argov]. The third ship arrived at 10.00 ... Three ships are involved in this transfer and when they all return to Algeria they will go to Toulon and reload, each in its 'turn' – each one three times. On the 11th of this month they will leave Toulon again and the second shipment will arrive here on the 18th. The first ship will bring Super-Shermans, each boat [carrying] approximately 13–14 tanks, so that in only 3 ships forty 'Supers' will reach us.

The third shipment will again bring AMX [tanks]. On the 18th, the first 18 Mystères are also due to arrive. 3 Vautours are due in October–November.

Saturday, August 4

Several facts and figures concerning the 'Canal'. It was completed in 1869 ... [*There follows an outline history of the Suez Canal from 1869*

292

to the overthrow of King Farouq in 1952]. ... On July 26 of this year, Nasser seized the Canal. In 1954 the British occupation of the Canal came to an end. A month ago the last British soldier departed from the last British base on the Canal. The U.S. and England had hoped that Nasser would join the Western bloc. In December 1955, the U.S. and Britain had promised aid in the construction of the Aswan Dam that was to cost 1.3 billion dollars. They had promised Nasser a grant of 70 million and a loan of 200 million. Nasser, realizing the West's weakness, spread the information that the Soviets would assist him with the construction of the dam. Finally, in Washington and in London, they began to understand Nasser's true intention. In July, the U.S. and England notified Nasser that under the 'existing conditions' they would not participate in the construction of the dam for they were hesitant as to the ability of Egypt to carry out this plan. Two days later the Soviet Foreign Minister [Dimitri Shepilov][18] announced that Russia did not intend to assist Egypt in building the dam. On July 26, Nasser declared the nationalization of the Canal. Two days prior to that he sharply attacked the U.S. at the inauguration of a new refinery, claiming the U.S. was spreading lies concerning the economic state of Egypt: 'I look at you Americans and say: May you choke yourselves to death in your anger.' On Friday, July 27, Nasser declared a state of war in Egypt and on July 30 threatened that any 'intervention' may cause the closing of the Canal. ...

... [B.G. has read that] the Canal is not vital to the West, neither economically nor strategically. The importance of the Canal has risen due to the oil-fields in the Middle East, but oil pipe-lines from these fields to the Mediterranean make the Canal dispensable and it is also possible to travel by way of the Cape of Good Hope (in South Africa).

In the late afternoon I returned to Jerusalem.

Teddy [Kollek][19] came immediately. ... [He] believes that there is a possibility to lay down a pipe from Eilat to one of our ports on the Mediterranean ... [I concluded that] an estimated budget for such a pipe-line must be prepared.

Sunday, August 5

Abel [Thomas] informed [us] in the name of the chief of military intelligence in Paris, that they have known of Nasser's intention of nationalizing the Canal since February, as promised to the East[ern bloc] in the arms deal. It appears that France and Britain have decided to get rid of Nasser. The French fear that Nasser's retreat will unfortunately prevent them from exploiting this opportunity.

The implementation was fixed for after the naval conference.[20] The [United States] Sixth Fleet apparently had promised logistical assistance. They will not let us participate in order not to turn the event into an Arab–Jewish war.

For some reason I find it hard to believe that Eden will carry out his plot.

Monday, August 6

Elath informs that at a meeting of the members of the Baghdad Pact Britain declared that under no circumstances would it let Israel take advantage of the Canal complications.

Tuesday, August 7

In the morning meeting of the Security and Foreign Relations Committee in the Knesset Building. I opened [the discussion] with two remarks: about the events surrounding the 'Canal' and about our 'Deal' (somewhat camouflaged). From [Jacob] Meridor's[21] words it was clear he was greatly distressed to receive arms [from the French]. For he asked what was the value of some planes as opposed to the convenient 'constellation' [of circumstances] for a war against Nasser. [Menachem] Begin[22] explained that there is no problem of an opportune moment. Any time is opportune for a fight with Egypt. In my reply I indicated that with this position they [Meridor and Begin] constitute a danger to the existence of Israel but to our joy the people are not so foolish as to entrust them with the power to direct our policy.

Friday, August 10

Shaul [Avigur][23] believes that now with the Egyptians tied up is the opportune time to start work on the Jordan [River water project] once we receive the main equipment.

I do not regard the Jordan project as one of our major concerns – but the danger from Nasser. Should Nasser be victorious over Suez – which is very probable, for the English apparently will do nothing against him, and without force Nasser will not surrender – Nasser's growing prestige must strengthen his desire to annihilate Israel, not by direct attack but by starting with a 'peace offensive' and attempting to cut into our territory, especially in the Negev, and when we refuse – he'll attack us.

Monday, August 13

M[oshe]. D[ayan]. and Shimon Peres came. Yesterday they dined with Gilbert. He is pessimistic regarding the internationalization of the Canal. In his opinion, his government will be bitter following the failure of the [London] conference[24] – they will want to take action and will to turn to Israel –. But I do not believe that even with the assistance of France alone something can be done. U.S. agreement is needed. In G[ilbert].'s opinion the Sinai Peninsula must be conquered and then the Canal will become international. That was [Admiral Louis] Mountbatten's[25] opinion when he was here.

Wednesday, August 15

... Yuval [Ne'eman][26] was told [by the French] that they are willing to put at our disposal 2 Vautours for photographing the Canal. The pilots and the technicians must be our men. This is acceptable to me.

Sunday, August 19

During the cabinet meeting this morning I told the colleagues about the arms consignments. ... I suggested that three go to the beach tomorrow to meet the boat (the fifth), and another six go on Wednesday to meet the planes. I suggested casting lots to determine who would go where. They demanded that I decide who would go. ... I dined with the President. At the end of the meal I told him about the arms shipments. He expressed his wish to be present at the arrival of one of the boats. I have my doubts whether this is desirable.

Wednesday, August 22

I am not inclined to carry out the [military] operation on our own – at the present time. We have no interest and advantage in the operation and without [our] being in 'respectable company' it is certain that it is not desirable. There's no knowing how the London Conference will end and what will be done following it – if anything at all is done. A solitary 'operation' on our part may well turn out to be calamitous ...

Friday, August 24

In the afternoon there was an [army General] Staff meeting in my home ... I agreed to French planes using our airfields and [proposed] that any assistance they may need be extended to them.

Gilbert turned to [Robert] Lacoste[27] with a radical proposition:

that Israel conquer the Sinai Peninsula thereby *de facto* turning the Canal into an international waterway.

Saturday, September 1

– Yosef Nachmias[28] cables from Paris that there is no respite in the preparations against Nasser, neither on the French side nor the British. Despite publications in the press the Americans have consented to an operation should Nasser not accept the Dulles plan[29] in its entirety. The commander of the operation will be the British General [Sir Hugh] Stockwell[30] and his deputy the French Admiral [Pierre] Barjot.[31]

Our Deputy Chief of Staff [Meir Amit][32] was invited (by the French) to come to consultations about the operation. The main goal of France is to depose Nasser and this coincides with British interests.

Our Deputy Chief of Staff was invited to a meeting with Admiral Barjot on September 7. The French and the British forces are equal in the air and on the sea. On land the British forces are twice as large.

Wednesday, September 3

I told him [Gen. E.L.M. Burns of the United Nations][33] that I doubted whether there was any use at all to the U.N. observers and that I do not know whether there's any point in turning to them with complaints [about terrorist attacks]. The condemnations are of no consequence to our neighbours and the murdered are murdered. In any case we are not willing to accept double standards. The first two articles of the U.N. Charter are not being kept and the U.N. does not protest or prevent the injustice. The Security Council's decision regarding free rights of passage for our ships is not kept and no one raises his voice – until England is hurt – and then it does not turn to the U.N. but prepares to take action on its own.

... The experience of eight years has proven to us that agreements are worthless when neighbours want to uproot Israel. Without a radical change there's no value at all to the agreements. England is now evacuating all British women and children from Jordan – and Jordan is supposedly its ally. Does it not know what tomorrow may bring? We shall not evacuate from Israel any woman or child. – If according to its Charter, the U.N. cannot bind the Arabs to live in peace with us – let it not bother us with useless observers – even if they have goodwill.

I can imagine [Dag] Hammarksjöld's[34] wrath when he receives the report of this conversation.

At 9 p.m. Moshe Dayan came to me ... [I stated that] There are now forces in the world who would like to see our victory over Egypt. And we must take care of how to overcome the quantitative and qualitative superiority of the Egyptian arms. In the first stage this is possible by taking a defensive stand against an Egyptian armoured attack. Should we have to face three fronts – Egypt, Syria and Jordan – it appears that we would have to immediately attack Jordan and take Jerusalem and Hebron. In Syria we'll only endeavour to halt the enemy and on the Egyptian front we shall first try to bleed the attacker from a defensive position and later we'll strike and attack. But generally I expressed my agreement with what Moshe [Dayan] had said that we must take the offensive, mislead, confuse, surprise and destroy the enemy and this is possible despite the fact that the foe has the advantage in manpower and arms.

I asked Moshe [Dayan] what the strength of our forces would be if war should break out ...

Sunday, September 9

... We [Haim Laskov[35] and I] talked for about two hours. I told him that I did not agree with his war plan. In my opinion it is dangerous to concentrate all the armoured forces against the Egyptian armoured forces in the war. Jordan must be hit first and forced out of the game. In the beginning the Egyptians must be made to bleed from defensive positions and attacked later, but not necessarily in a concentrated effort. Different sensitive spots such as airports, the Canal, large cities must be assaulted and the spirit of the enemy broken. On the Syrian front we must [only] stop [them] for we are not interested in taking [their] land. Jordan is the main enemy from a point of view of land, Egypt – for power. We'll break both of them, one after the other ...

Monday, September 10

In the morning I left for Jerusalem, ... Moshe [Dayan] asked whether we should take action in the Red Sea Straits [where the Egyptians blocked passage of Israeli shipping]. I told him that we must see how things develop between France and England and Nasser. Even though from the start I did not believe that Eden would do something serious – it is still hard to accept that two governments of European powers would make laughing stocks of themselves by threatening to dispatch armies, navies and air-forces – and would then submit to the Egyptian dictator.

Wednesday, September 12

This morning the radio announced Eisenhower's declaration that the United States recognizes the right of England and France to use force – should all other peace efforts to settle the Canal affair prove to be of no avail, but he promised that so long as he was President, America would not go to war without a resolution passed by the Congress.

I still find it hard to believe that Eden's government will act forcefully against the Egyptian tyrant. At least it is clear that up to now it does not want Israeli aid.

Thursday, September 13

– At four the Italian Ambassador, Count [Benedetto] Capomazza[37] came to see me. We started the conversation by discussing the Canal. He has still not received any information from his government regarding Eden's statement in Parliament yesterday. All in all Italy's position is close to that of the U.S. They are interested in free passage in the Canal as the fourth power to use the waterway. France is the fifth. They [the Italians] do not want force [to be used]. They have a community of 45 thousand Italians in Egypt, but they do look favourably upon an Anglo-French action ... Finally, he asked me about our attitude to Suez and the war. I told him that we were interested in free passage – ours, too. That we do not trust Eden. For Eden had not respected our rights even when he controlled the Canal and there was a Security Council resolution. Here, the Ambassador had apparently reached the purpose of his visit: He explained to me that it was important that we should not interfere in the war – if it should come to war – in order not to give Nasser a pretext to rally all the Arab nations round him. Concerning the Canal he believes the other Arabs are not with him but a conflict with us would unite all the Arabs. Therefore, these days we must exercise self-restraint even if we are right, and not furnish Nasser with an excuse.

Sunday, September 23

[In this period of intensified border incidents, including atrocities by fidaiyyun terrorists who have infiltrated into Israel, Ben-Gurion devotes much attention to formulating an appropriate policy that will not interfere with plans for a possible large-scale campaign.]

Following clarifications with the [Army] General Staff members and Moshe [Dayan], I realized that an action in Mar-Elias[38] is liable to cause many deaths and after further consideration I reached the conclusion that there's no point in hitting a number of [Jordan] Legionnaires this time, and ordered Moshe [Dayan] not to do anything. But I shall request Golda to warn [General] Burns [of the United Nations] that if Jordan does not stop its capricious acts we shall reserve our right to act. I asked Moshe to plan some serious operations.

Tuesday, September 25

At 7:15 I left Sede Boqer by plane for Ramla. There I met M[oshe]. D[ayan]. and Shimon Peres who had just returned from Paris. What he recounted may turn out to be fateful. At a meeting with the Minister of Defence, Bourgès-Maunoury told him that after the London Conference, the [French] Government decided that it could not accept this plan [of the Suez Canal Users' Association][39] and that it is prepared to 'act' against Nasser – with the knowledge of the English and with their approval. They would like to cooperate with Israel – and this is also in conjunction with the English. Their only condition being not [to attack] Jordan. They would like a delegation of three, including at least one minister to come next Saturday to discuss matters with Guy Mollet, Pineau and Bourgès-Maunoury on the basis of mutual cooperation.

From Ramla I left for Jerusalem with Moshe [Dayan] and Shimon [Peres] ... After the meeting [of the Cabinet] I invited colleagues in the Government [for a talk] ... and I told them what had been decided by the French Government. Several colleagues expressed apprehension: (1) Russia will send 'volunteers' from Albania or China, (2) England will betray us, (3) all the Arab nations will join in war against us.

My own opinion is that this is our first chance of getting an ally (and, by the way, an ally who has assisted us ever since the War of Independence right to this very day), and it is only due to his assistance that we are not standing helpless today. – Suspicions still exist – but they will also exist when we have to stand alone and Nasser tries to liquidate us. But we shall only enter this partnership on certain conditions: (1) That France knows in advance of the limitations of our air and armoured forces. (The armoured forces will only be totally ready on January 1st and only on March 1st, 1957 – the air force [will be ready].) (2) If indeed England also backs France and the affair is carried out with the knowledge of the U.S. (3) That we shall obtain the coast of the Straits of Tiran thereby enabling us to exercise free passage in the Red Sea and the Indian

Ocean so that Eilat will truly become a port and the 'hinterland' of the Negev will be developed.

This summary was accepted by one and all present – who had committed themselves to secrecy. ... We agreed that a final decision would be reached after the members [of the mission] return from Paris – and of course their trip would be kept confidential.

The French demand that the [military] 'operation' will begin on October 15!

Thursday, September 27

This morning we held a consultation – Golda [Meir], [Peretz] Naftali,[40] Pinhas Sapir,[41] Moshe D[ayan]., Shimon Peres and myself – regarding the French proposal. ... I made three negative assumptions: (1) We shall not be the ones to open [hostilities]. (2) We shall not participate unless there is British agreement and their agreement must also include our defence against a Jordanian and Iraqi attack. (We on our part will promise not to attack either Jordan or Syria.) (3) That no action will be taken contrary to U.S. opinion and without it being informed. Our final decision will be made here following their return [from France] ...

Upon the conclusion of the Eden–Selwyn Lloyd talks in Paris[42] with the French Government a communiqué was issued saying that both governments hold the same views as to the steps that must be taken in the present crisis. Have they really reached an agreement on an 'operation' and did they also discuss the plan of our participation? ...

Next Sunday things will become clearer following the departure of our delegation.

– Tonight, the last ship bringing French arms is due to arrive. On it are the last 20 Super-Shermans, accessories and ammunition.

– Following my disclosure of this 'military secret', several weeks ago, the newspaper editors, who were true to their word, were taken today to watch the unloading of this precious 'merchandise'.

Friday, September 28

– At twelve I called in the Security and Foreign Affairs Committee [of the Knesset] ... I explained that the security situation was becoming more serious due to the following reasons: (1) Border clashes – there's no knowing to what they may lead. (2) Jordan has called upon Iraq for help and we shall not sit around with our hands in our laps while Babylon [i.e. Iraq] inherits Ammon [i.e. Jordan].

(3) There's no knowing where the Suez crisis may lead. There is no doubt that Nasser intends to attack Israel at the first opportunity ...

The debate, in general, was good ... [In the discussion on the appropriate response to fidaiyyun attacks, Ben-Gurion argued] that punishments for murderers that are acceptable in other countries do not stop the killings, but if no killer were punished then the reins would be let loose and many people would be murdered. Punishment does deter − even if it does not deter everyone. The killers from across the border − their government does not punish (it mobilizes them), the U.N. cannot or does not want to punish − so we have to do it. Retaliation does not stop the attacks entirely − but it does put many off − as every punishment does. Who knows how many lives have been saved thanks to these 'retaliatory' acts?

Sunday, September 30

− Amiel Najar[43] received a telegram from France saying that it was agreed between France and England to destroy Nasser, and that this will also be done with the assistance of America after the elections, even if Stevenson is elected.

Tuesday, October 9

− [Amiel] Najar recounted his talk with [Jean] Fernard Laurent,[44] Gilbert's deputy. France is worried by Iraq's entry [into Jordan]. They fear that the English want to conquer Jordan, [and] Syria with the help of the Iraqis. They do not trust the British partnership. They [the French] expressed their astonishment that we would let the Iraqis enter ...

Fernard Laurent confided to Najar that what the British have in mind is to notify Israel 24 hours in advance should it finally be decided that Iraq enter Jordan, and to tell us that if we react with force − they will act according to the Tripartite [i. e. U.S./British/ French] Declaration of 1950.[45]

Thursday, October 11

Fati [Yehoshafat Harkabi] notifies from N.Y. that he has met Pineau. The situation in the Security Council is terrible. The Egyptian is not moving [towards negotiation]. Selwyn [Lloyd] is weaker than Eden, and yet Pineau is of the opinion that the preparations must continue ...

Monday, October 15

We were notified from Paris, the day before yesterday, that the partners' willingness to carry out [the operation] has not been shaken despite the majority [against action in the U.N.]. The day before yesterday, Mollet sent [General Maurice] Challe[46] and a member of his cabinet, to Eden, [suggesting] that France, England and Israel will attack Egypt, or at least that he would agree that France, aided by Israel, would attack Egypt from bases on Cyprus. A third proposal is that they at least guarantee that other Arab countries will not attack Israel – should France and Israel attack Egypt not from Cyprus. Until now (11 a.m.) we have had no news as to Eden's reply. Fati [Yehoshafat Harkabi] cabled us from N.Y. on 12 October, [19]56 that Challe had informed Pineau that the French were ready, and that Pineau ordered the acceleration of preparations without procrastination and to speed up the dispatches of equipment which will take time. Challe has returned to France. Pineau discussed with Selwyn Lloyd the possibility of Iraqi intervention should there be any complications and Lloyd assured him that nothing would happen. Pineau told Fati that he had not let the British into the picture with the actual joint plan of Israel and France, but he estimates that they suspect something. It will be difficult to hide the preparations for war. Pineau does not see the possibility of a combined British–French operation except at a later stage ... Pineau thinks of returning home tomorrow. He has despaired of the Security Council.

At this time, three French boats are leaving carrying arms on 'loan' – 100 Super Shermans ...

Wednesday, October 17

Today, the political debate in the Knesset ended with my reply. It was followed by something that, I believe, has never occurred in the Knesset before. All the parties, except for 'Maki' [Communists] and 'Herut' [Revisionists] accepted the Government position as I had defined it in my opening speech, the day before last.

Today it was made clear that last night's notice about the decision of Eden and Guy Mollet to send a convoy down the Suez and to include an Israeli ship, was not true. In the evening we received information that in consultation between Eden and Lloyd and the French Government in Paris, the first alternative (cooperation between France and England) had been abandoned, as well as the

302

second [alternative] (French–Israeli cooperation with England's knowledge). And the English propose that we should start [the campaign] on our own, they will protest, and when we reach the Canal – they will come in as if to separate and then they'll destroy Nasser ... They pledge not to assist Iraq and Syria should these two attack us (they did not mention Jordan) ... I called in Golda [Meir], [Levi] Eshkol (who until now did not know of all the events),[47] and Moshe [Dayan]. Shimon Peres brought along the text of the telegram from Paris which concludes with Guy Mollet's suggestion that I come to Paris to examine the options and if it becomes necessary a member of the British Cabinet will [also] be invited. ...

I sent a reply that the British proposal was not acceptable. If Mollet, knowing that, still thinks that it is worthwhile that I should come – then I'll be willing to come after Sunday [October 21] (for I do not wish to be absent from the [Sunday] Cabinet meeting).

... Moshe [Dayan] is in favor of reaching an agreement with the English regarding the whole of the Middle East, destroying Nasser and partitioning Jordan between us and Iraq. The enormous difficulty – even if we thought that England would consent (and it is hard to even think about it) is what to do with all the Arab population ...

According to Rome 8000 Iraqis are about to go in [to Jordan].

I believe it is an English plot to get us entangled with Nasser and in the meantime to bring about Jordan's takeover by Iraq.

Thursday, October 18

I came to Tel Aviv in the morning. Here I found a second cable from Paris, which had been sent (yesterday) four hours after the cable which Shimon [Peres] had brought last night to Jerusalem.

Yosef [Nachmias] was invited by [Colonel Louis] Mangin[48] to a meeting with Pineau and there Pineau enumerated the five possibilities which had been discussed with the English: (1) An ultimatum to the Egyptians. (2) An English operation in Egypt. (3) A French–Israeli action with France operating from Cyprus. (4) A French–Israeli action from Israel. (5) An Israeli action with French and English guarantees. The first three were put aside. The fourth was rejected because if France were to go to war without England it would bring about Eden's fall. Therefore the only feasible way (?) is the fifth.

Eden has made two declarations: (1) Should there be fighting close to the Canal, France and England would call the sides to halt and retreat. If they agree then no [further] action will follow. Should they refuse – one side, or both – then France and England will intervene in order to ensure free passage through the Canal. (2) In case of war between Egypt and Israel – England will not come to Egypt's aid. Other considerations will apply to Jordan with whom they have a pact. – According to Pineau, Selwyn Lloyd's mind was not easy with either of these declarations but Eden's opinion was decisive.

How can England prevent intervention by Iraq and Syria? England will remind them that Egypt had also declined aid to Jordan when she was in distress ...

What position will the U.S. take? Pineau's opinion is that they will be angry, but if the operation takes place before November 6, no actions will follow the anger.

What about Russia? Pineau thinks they will not intervene. Pineau elaborated on his disappointment with Selwyn Lloyd. He expressed his joy at the prospects of meeting B.G. and participating in the discussions with him.

– This morning, [Meir] Amit returned from Paris. He departed at midnight. Double negotiations have taken place this week – military and political with no coordination [between them]. The planning headquarters were not aware of all the details of the political negotiations and therefore caused a bit of a mix-up. Amit's first meeting had been with Admiral Barjot and General Gazin[49] who had been entrusted with the planning. They said that after we start the action – they will also enter with full force. Meir told them that this contradicts his directives. In the meantime, General [André] Martin[50] (Air-Force who had been here) joined the talks. He tried to explain that there was some confusion: Headquarters had received orders to plan according to the British proposal. Martin promised to clear things up. (That was on Monday, 15th of the month.)

Amit suggested a meeting with Challe. On Tuesday morning (day before yesterday), Amit met with Challe and [André] Martin. Yosef [Nachmias] and Abel [Thomas] were also present. Challe showed the written directives they had received: Aim: – to assist Israel in attacking the Egyptian army (Amit stated that our purpose was not to receive aid but to act through mutual assistance). The plan: French forces will join the action on D-Day + 3. Second alternative: Joint action of the A[ir] F[orce], and coordination of the action of the infantry. Amit noted that in Israel the matter was discussed differently and read out the terms as they were defined back home [in Israel]. Martin admitted that that was the way things had been summed up, except for the cooperation of the infantry. It had not been agreed upon that they would act at one and the same time because France could not put its ground forces into action immediately. Amit proposed that first an air raid would take place and then a combined land operation ...

The directives Amit had were: (a) Everything depends on the [Israeli] Government's decision. (b) D-Day for the land forces must be the same. (c) Action by the Air-Force must precede ground operations. (d) Our reaching just as far as the Canal is only in regard to Stage I of the operation. There's no restraint from continuing – should the need arise. (e) The French must themselves take all or part of the Canal ...

Nehemia [Argov] woke me up at 1 a.m. and brought me the French reply. Guy Mollet had been given my message and yet he's still anxious for the meeting. They will send a plane here on Monday, with Mangin. I ordered to reply that I accept the invitation. I shall be able to come after next Sunday and will let them know who will be accompanying [me].

Friday, October 19

At eleven, Gilbert, who has just returned from France, came to see me ... I outlined to him my plan for the Middle East and he agrees with it. In his opinion his government will endeavour to influence Britain to accept my plan, for without England the plan cannot be. In general the plan is: oust Nasser, partition Jordan – [with the] eastern [part] to Iraq – so that it will make peace with Israel thereby enabling the refugees to settle there with the aid of American money. The borders of Lebanon will be reduced and it will become a Christian state. I am not quite clear in regard to what will be done with Syria. Gilbert thinks that [Adib al] Shishakli[51] is the man [to take into consideration] since America trusts him.

Monday, October 22

On the Airplane[52]

When I got to [the] Hatzor [airfield], I learned from Moshe [Dayan], who had been talking with Mangin throughout the day, that he [Mangin] had asked whether the second alternative was still in existence – the English proposal [that B. G. had rejected out of hand]. If so – what's the purpose of this trip? I fear that this may only harm our relations with France.

Throughout the night Challe formulated a slightly different plan – that we open [the campaign] at night against the Egyptians and three hours later, they (the French and the English) will start bombing the airports. They have 500 planes on Cyprus, 120 of which are bombers. They'll depose Nasser and form a new government.

I fear that in this there's a great deal of *wishful thinking* [original in English]. How do they know that Nasser will fall – even if they do take Cairo and defeat his army? He'll organize guerrilla [warfare]. Why should England agree? And why – and this is the greatest question of all – should our people agree? What will America have to say? And Russia?

Moshe [Dayan], speaking for [General] Challe informs that [General Paul] Ely[53] has gone to meet [Admiral Arthur] Radford,[54] [who acts] as if he agrees and has access to Eisenhower no less than does Dulles. However Eisenhower talks differently every day and stresses especially the issue of peace.

My comprehensive plan – even if it is rather dubious, because before everything else it requires England's good-will and trust-worthiness, it cannot be carried out in a rush. The U.S. must be won over to the idea – but in theory it does solve the question of the Middle East and fulfills England's needs, France's and Israel's – and also Iraq's and Lebanon's [through] Nasser's downfall (if it is at all possible ...); apportioning Eastern Jordan to Iraq on two conditions: (1) peace with Israel, (2) settling the refugees on their [Jordanian] territory; cutting into Lebanese territory in order to establish a Christian state, annexing part [to] Syria (Shishakli's) and part – as far as the Litani [River] – to us. This gives the French two states in the M[iddle]. E[ast]. which are allies (and maybe three – Syria), strengthens England's status in the oil area, frees France of the trouble of Nasser and enables a peace arrangement in Algeria and North Africa. But this will take time. I have discussed this plan with [Abba] Eban[55] and he suggested that Eisenhower invite me to Washington (he may even say during the elections that he'll go to the Middle East, as he said four years ago that he'd go to Korea). And he'll also invite some Arab king ...

We should have reached our destination this morning at eight, but due to a fog over Paris we waited some hours in Marseilles ...

At the Villa – 'Somewhere' in France. [At Sèvres]

– We circled over Paris for more than two hours without being able to land because the skies were so cloudy. They already wanted to return to the airport at Argent and go from there by train – a distance of 9 hours, but in the end we landed at a military airfield and at three [p.m.] I was brought to a French villa in the vicinity of Versailles, which belongs to the family of the young man who had killed Darlan in the Second World War.[56] Here we were offered a French lunch which I could not enjoy for I had eaten sandwiches on the plane. During the meal, the three: Guy Mollet, Pineau and Bourgès-Maunoury waited till we finished eating and then [we] started the meeting which lasted for three or four hours.

I explained my reasons for rejecting the 'fifth' proposal – that we start the war against Egypt and 48 hours later, after an ultimatum to both sides, the English and the French would take the Canal. There are ethical, political and military reasons. Why should we all of a sudden become the aggressors – and have our friends in the world denounce us? (Pineau tried to explain that with their veto they will prevent a condemnation in the Security Council.) The U.S. would disapprove and there's no knowing what Russia would do. And most important – Egypt would bomb the airports in Tel-Aviv and in Haifa. Instead, I proposed a plan for a comprehensive settlement in the Middle East – not immediately, but following comprehensive clarifications with the U.S. and England. I called the plan 'fantastic' but one which can be executed on condition that the English prove to be of good will and good faith, something which I rather doubt. And the plan, as I had [previously] told the ambassadors at the meeting – [provides for] partitioning Jordan between us and Iraq, cutting the borders of Lebanon so that it will become a Christian state and limiting Syria – I said that I didn't know how and who could stabilize Syria, though the Americans trust Shishakli and our border will be the Litani.

Before everything else, of course – [there is the] overthrow and destruction of Nasser. For while Nasser is in control this [plan] will not be possible. The condition for turning eastern Jordan over to Iraq is peace with Israel and settling the refugees. This would give France two faithful allies in the Middle East, and possibly three (Syria), will guarantee British interests in the oil region and would keep peace in the Middle East.

Guy Mollet [said] that my plan is not fantastic and he is willing to accept it. But time is pressing concerning Nasser and the Canal because they [the French] have mobilized forces and cannot hold them for long. I said that we'd consent to an action soon – if after we start on zero night – at dawn, following an ultimatum to Egypt, they would bomb the Egyptian airfields. Guy Mollet explained that Eden insists on an operation but Selwyn Lloyd is looking for a compromise with Nasser (through [Mahmud] Fawzi).[57]

I remarked that in England a P[rime]. M[inister]. can replace a minister if he so wishes. And Pineau remarked that Eden is [also] bothered by Labour's opposition. Mollet said that he had talked with [Hugh] Gaitskell[58] for two hours and he [Gaitskell] had almost agreed with him, but Labour's general opposition to Eden and fear of Bevan tipped the scale against Eden's line. While we were talking – it was at six or seven in the evening, it was announced that the Number Two of the British cabinet had arrived in Paris for several discussions. There were guesses whether it was [Robert, Marquess of] Salisbury,[59] [R.A.] Butler,[60] or [Selwyn] Lloyd. It turned out to be Lloyd. To my astonishment, I was invited to the tripartite conversation – that took place in another room.

I explained to Lloyd my reasons for opposing the [delay of] two days [before the British join the attack]. And he said that the new plan – to attack the airfields the next morning – is totally new. England would be condemned for having taken such an action. I asked him: Why should we take upon ourselves an act for which we would be condemned? He said that Nasser was our enemy and he denied us our rights. I said that he had been doing it for years and no one had protested. Lloyd recognized my fear of the bombing of Tel-Aviv and Haifa and the airfields. But he remained opposed to the action. A suggestion arose that the next morning the French would take action and on the second day England would join in. Pineau is inclined towards this proposal but said that he had no bombers. I said: England 'will loan' bombers and pilots, and there was a precedent for such a loan when Roosevelt lent England 50 destroyers. Lloyd derided the destroyers as not having been worth anything. I answered that it had been of great political and moral value.

Lloyd and Pineau – Guy Mollet was not present at this discussion – pressed regarding the question of time, and it was agreed that the operation would take place – if at all – next Monday, the 29th of this month. We [the Israelis] would start the operation at seven p.m. near the border with mechanized forces near the Canal. The two cabinets [British and French] would immediately convene, would decide to present an ultimatum, would notify each other of their decision, and in the early morning would begin to bomb the Egyptian airfields.

The talk adjourned at 10 p.m. for dinner and later continued till twelve. When Lloyd persisted in his objection to [British involvement in] the operation after 12 hours, Pineau announced that they'd be willing to act on their own and that the English would join in the next morning. That is 48 hours later as had been discussed. But it turned out that in order to carry out a serious action they would have to operate from bases on Cyprus. Challe was of the opinion that the Mystères would be sufficient to bring down the Egyptian bombers if they should try to hit Israel. But I said that I did not think that this insured us against danger and I insisted that they must attack the Egyptian airfields.

It was concluded that Lloyd return that night. Tomorrow morning he'll convene the cabinet and immediately after the meeting he'll send an envoy to France to inform of their decision. During the conversation that continued with Pineau following Lloyd's departure, Pineau announced that he does not rely on Lloyd and that tomorrow night he will fly to London to talk with Lloyd, for he sees two difficulties: (a) Conflict among the English – [i.e.] Labour's objection. (b) Lack of French bombers. I suggested that they take a 'loan' of 50 bombers with their pilots from the English and paint the planes the French colors. The conversation concerning this matter did not end with a definite conclusion. Challe – who's an air force man – thinks that my hesitations are exaggerated and that they [the French] can defend us with the Mystères.

We'll see what will happen tomorrow. I fear that Pineau's trip will be in vain. Because Lloyd will ensure that the decision he desires is carried as opposed to French opinion and ours.

Tuesday, October 23

In France

From home, of course, there's no news. In Jordan the pro-Egyptians have not received a majority [in the election], as it appeared they would yesterday morning. The forces are almost equal and it will be difficult to form a government. This afternoon they will vote here in the French Parliament, the issue being a vote of confidence in the government. – Our friends feel certain that they will receive the vote, and at twelve-thirty, local time, we'll have lunch and continue the talks. Maybe by then we'll know what the British have decided.

It later turned out that the pro-Egyptians do have a majority in Jordan and Ibrahim Hashim[61] handed in his resignation. It is now clear that the Iraqis will not enter – for in the meantime others have 'entered'. Should the [Jordanian] Parliament – in the event its opening is permitted – cancel the Anglo-Jordanian pact, as it will undoubtedly do – we shall not be too sorry about it. It is better to stand against Jordan alone than to face both Jordan and England. In the meantime it was learned [here] that the French have caught five of the rebel leaders in Algeria.[62] The fools travelled in a plane whose pilots were French and they [just] entered the trap. A general strike broke out in Tunis in [support of the] demand to release the captives and in Morocco, too, there are riots.

    – Prior to lunch, before the cabinet members Bourgès-Maunoury and Pineau could arrive ... we had a talk with [Abel] Thomas, the Director-General of the Defence Ministry. He's very pessimistic and thinks that it's now or never. If action against Nasser is not taken immediately there'll be no power – especially moral power – for France to do it at any other time, and this may be true of the English as well. At present, the whole nation – except for the Communists – stands fast behind the government. Although the question of [a vote of] confidence is before the parliament, they have no doubt they'll win. No one wants to topple the government now – they have just mobilized the reserves, they've sent troops to Cyprus. If they have to return from Cyprus empty-handed there will be bitter disappointment in France – and [the feeling of] helplessness will grow. Nasser's prestige will rise and they'll have no hope of terminating the conflict in Algeria. Possibly the conflict in Morocco and Tunis will grow and [Habib] Bourgiba[63] is already wavering. Black children in Equatorial Africa already bear flags with Nasser's picture. And England will be expelled from Jordan and Iraq. At the moment spirits are high among the French and they are willing to make every effort and support the government.

    Should they stand about doing nothing – despair will grow and there'll be no strength to start over again. Now England is going along with them. In the new elections, Labour may well win. At the moment, America is involved with elections and will do nothing; after the elections – and it is believed that Eisenhower will be elected – America will make some arrangement with the Soviet Union. They will divide spheres of influence, neglect the Middle East which will fall to the Russians and their [the French] situation in North Africa will be desperate. They cannot retreat from Algeria – and somehow they must tie it – and not by the flimsiest connection, to France. This will become possible only after Nasser's downfall.

    It is clear that this is not only Thomas' view but the opinion of the whole government, and indeed, this afternoon I heard the same things from Bourgès-Maunoury.

    – To the meal, which was delayed a while according to French custom, Bourgès-Maunoury came, followed by Pineau. Challe explained his new plan of how to bridge over the first day after our clash with the Egyptians on Sunday night: – We [Israelis] stage an air-attack on Beer-Sheva and this will enable England to enter the action immediately. Pineau said that he would have agreed but that the English would not accept it. I announced in my own name – as a Jew – that I could not participate in deceiving the whole world. Though we have many grievances against the world regarding the past and the slaughter in Europe, yet we have not despaired, and we have persisted and established a state and defeated our enemies for we believed in the righteousness of our cause. And when we fight – we shall fight out of this belief, but I do not see how we can mislead the world and stage such a thing.

[General Maurice] Challe and his airforce colleague ([General André] Martin) then proposed some other plans to defend Israel from Egyptian aerial attacks on the third day and Moshe [Dayan] sat down with them to discuss the matter. Pineau took leave of us as he was off to London and I had a conversation with Bourgès-Maunoury who explained to me France's current position, her difficulties and her prospects.

At the dinner table, Pineau recounted that in the morning they had met with President Coty – he [Coty], the P[rime]. M[inister Mollet]. and Bourgès-Maunoury. They informed him of the talks with us and with Lloyd and explained to him that the difficulty lay in the fact that the Israelis had faith in the French but did not trust the English. I told him that that was exactly so.

– Due to Pineau's trip and the P.M.'s concerns in their 'Knesset' [i.e. Parliament] – they are troubled by the question of the [Algerian] leaders they have captured – our departure has been postponed till tomorrow, and only after Pineau's return from London will the discussions take place at 3 in the afternoon.

The whole group is in town and Nehemia [Argov] has also joined them. In the evening only Artur [Ben-Natan][64] stayed with me. For a long time we searched for the Voice of Israel and I couldn't find it. At a late hour Artur discovered a small radio and managed to pick up the Overseas Voice of Israel. At 10.30 we heard the news from home in French: Two fidaiyyun who had come from Lebanon were caught in Nazareth. They were sent by the Egyptian military attaché or his envoy.

Wednesday, October 24

Nehemia did not return from Paris till the morning and until now (10.00 Israeli time), I still have no news of what's going on in the world, for Artur has also disappeared.

Meanwhile, I have considered the situation and if measures to protect us from aerial attacks are taken on the first day or two, until the French and the English bomb the Egyptian airfields – it seems to me that the operation must be carried out. This is the only chance that two not-so-small powers will try to destroy Nasser, and we shall not stand alone while he grows stronger and conquers all the Arab countries.

The action which is demanded of us is like a 'raid', though on this occasion with larger forces. If we succeed then we will have achieved free navigation in the Straits of the Red Sea, Sharm el-Sheikh and the Isle of Tiran – historic Yotvat – and *maybe* the whole situation in the Middle East will change according to my plan. But there's no certainty that Jordan and Syria, and possibly Iraq, will try to attack us, and who knows if Russian 'volunteers' will not come. In any case, we shall have to ensure our freedom of action with Jordan – should it attack us.

– I requested Moshe [Dayan] and Shimon [Peres] to come here immediately (it is 11:00 Israeli time). I have made a list of questions which we must clarify amongst ourselves and questions to be raised between us and our friends –

(1) D-Day – for us, for the French, for the English.
(2) Will the Egyptian airfields be bombed, when, by whom?
(3) What amount of French and English forces will immediately enter the campaign and where, – on both sides of the Canal[?]
(4) Will they go on to conquer Cairo and will they form a new Egyptian government.
(5) How long will they remain at the Canal?
(6) Can England ensure the neutrality of Jordan and Iraq? And if they or one of them should attack will we have the freedom to take action?
(7) What will be the fate of the British force in Aqaba and Amman?
(8) Can we conquer and hold onto the Red Sea Coast and the Isle of Tiran?

Questions for ourselves:

(1) What is the force that we shall send across the border (Rafah or Sinai) and to the Canal?
(2) How will we protect our force on the Canal and how shall we bring it back?
(3) How do we secure our Eastern border – facing Jordan and Syria?
(4) How many must we mobilize immediately?

(5) What is the strength of the French assistance in the air on the day following our incursion?
(6) In what form shall we present the decision to the government?

Thursday, October 25

On the plane:

Yesterday – may well have been – a great day. After Pineau broke Selwyn Lloyd's opposition, ... they [the British Cabinet] voted in favor of the 'campaign'. ... At lunch – which began at three – only Bourgès-Maunoury participated and Pineau joined in later – Two Englishmen came – [Donald] Logan,[65] who turned out to be Lloyd's second private secretary (he has 4) and not Eden's envoy, and [Patrick] Dean,[66] the Director-General under Minister of Defence [Anthony] Head.[67]

Before that, I had a discussion with Guy Mollet. I told him about the discovery of a great deal of oil in South-Western Sinai, and that it is worthwhile to detach this peninsula from Egypt for it does not belong to her, but the English had stolen it from the Turks when they thought that they had Egypt in their pocket. I proposed laying down an oil pipeline from Sinai to the refineries in Haifa, and Mollet expressed interest in this suggestion. By the way, he apologized to me for a charge of antisemitism that had apparently reached me. I told him that I had heard that he had been a Prof[essor] but I had not heard that he was antisemitic. He complained about the Jewish members in the Party. That they are extreme and I explained to him about the inferiority complex from which Jews in the Diaspora suffer, which forces them to be more French than the French [themselves].

We had a conversation between us and the French and there was a discussion between the French and the English. Finally – a triangular discussion took place. The English proposed as a pretext to our attack – sending an Israeli ship through the Canal. I expressed doubt whether the lack of time would enable us to carry that out, since we have only a total of 4 days left following our return home and we have sufficient pretext in the [Egyptian] violation of the U. N. Charter, the [failure to honor the] cease-fire agreement to the Security Council decision concerning free passage [in the Straits of Tiran] and the [establishment of the] fidaiyyun organization.

The time for the start of the operation was set – for 7 p.m. on Monday, 29th of this month. Immediately on the next morning the two states [Great Britain and France] will 'call' upon the two sides

[Israel and Egypt]: to cease fire and to retreat 10 miles from the Canal. Egypt will also be required to permit French and English forces to hold the Canal until an arrangement is reached. Israel will not be obliged to halt any activity until Egypt accepts the three conditions and has fulfilled them.

The critical day for us will be Tuesday [October 30]. The French will give us two squadrons (one of Mystères and one of F-84s), apart from the 'volunteers' for our Mystères. They will also send two warships to Haifa and Jaffa with very powerful anti-aircraft guns.

I asked what would happen should Syria or Jordan attack us? The English answered that they had no interest in Syria. But they would not assist Jordan if it should attack. I promised that we would do nothing against Jordan if it would remain quiet.

On the evening of Wednesday [October 31], at an hour which is agreed upon by the commanders – the French and the British will start to bomb the Egyptian airfields. I told them that for us the Suez [Canal] was not so important; our Suez was the Straits of Eilat and we wanted to take the coast of Eilat to the islands in the south including the islands themselves. They asked who owned the islands. I told them that until a few years ago they were no man's land, for they are desolate with no water, though until the sixth century [A.D.] an independent Jewish state had existed there. This was conquered by the Emperor Justinian. Egypt claimed the islands just a few years ago and we must take hold of them in order to guarantee free passage in the Red Sea.

After clarifying all the points, I proposed that we draw up a protocol of these conclusions which would be signed by the three sides and approved by the three governments. This was accepted and six – two from each side – promptly sat down to formulate the conclusions: on our part Yosef Nachmias and Moshe [Dayan] participated. The minutes were edited in French – we signed them – each one [signed] three copies, and it was agreed that tomorrow, i.e. today, the British Government would announce whether it approved it or not. As soon as we receive in Israel the British confirmation through the French Government – we will announce our confirmation. In addition, every government will send out two letters – to each of the partners – concerning the confirmation. Those who signed were Dean (Director of the British Ministry of Defence), Pineau and myself.

Already last night, Moshe [Dayan] sent directives to Headquarters to mobilize the armored forces. On the plane he drew up the order of the campaign. We left our house at Sèvres at about ten and at eleven we took off from a military airfield in the same airplane in which we had come (De Gaulle's plane).

If when we reach home in approximately two hours we find the British Government's approval, we shall then be facing great days in our history. But I have grave doubts whether the approval from London will come.

– At twelve we landed at Hatzor and at a quarter past one I reached Jerusalem. In the morning papers I saw that Guy Mollet has made up with [Nikita] Krushchev or vice-versa, and that in Hungary the people's revolt has been crushed with military force. Moscow is still very much in command.

Meanwhile, a united headquarters has been established for Jordan and Syria. That means that Egypt now commands the two countries. The situation is becoming more complex.

Friday, October 26

The news which was expected from Paris and which arrived yesterday was not clear: the formula we received in reply from the English indicates an agreement to the plan of operations, but does not state agreement to the 'Sèvres' protocol. ... I sent a telegram to Yosef [Nachmias] requesting clarifications from him whether both Britain and France have ratified the Sèvres protocol. This morning came Yosef's reply saying: Pineau officially informs you that both France and England have ratified the Sèvres agreements. Therefore I am noting that the agreements are approved by the Government of Israel and I am notifying the British Government of this.

Waiting for Artur [Ben Natan] to come today at lunch (I am writing at 4 p.m.) in a French plane with the documents from France and Britain ... Artur brought three documents.

(1) A letter from Guy Mollet in which he writes –

'Mon Cher P.M. – Je vous confirme l'accord du gouvernement français sur le résultat des conversations de Sèvres et les termes du protocole final auquel elles ont donné lieu. J'ai d'autre part, reçu de Sir Anthony Eden une lettre par laquelle celui ci me confirme l'aigrement [sic] du gouvernement britannique. Pour votre information personnelle, je vous communique une photo copie de la dite lettre. Croyez, mon cher P.M., à l'assurance de mes sentiments les plus cordiaux.

(–) Guy Mollet.'

(2) A letter from Bourgès-Maunoury that the French Government is committed to put on Israeli territory for the purpose of air

defence, for the period from October 29 to October 31, a squadron of Mystères 4 and a squadron of Chasseurs bombers. Apart from that two battleships will come for the same duration to Israeli ports. (3) In Eden's letter to Mollet it was said:

'Her M[ajesty's]. G[overnment]. have been informed of the cours[e] of the conversations held at Sèvres on October 22–24. They confirm that in the situation there envisaged they will take the action described. This is in accordance with the declaration enclosed with my communication of October 21. Yours, etc.

(–) Anthony Eden.'

This letter is typical of the British Foreign Office for it can be interpreted in various ways, while the French state clearly to what they have committed themselves, as was discussed with them without adding or subtracting.

There's a message from Pineau (though I do not know on what it is based) that 'the Government of England [sic] and the Government of France have both confirmed the terms of Sèvres.' Therefore I am hereby noting that the terms are also confirmed by the Government of Israel and making notification of this to the English Government.

– Eden's declaration which is mentioned in his letter was given to us on Pineau's return from London on October 23rd. According to what Shimon [Peres] has written based on memory, it is as follows: (a) England agrees that the operation will start as a military raid and not as a full scale war. Eden requests that the raid will take place as near the Suez [Canal] as possible and that it will be as 'noisy' as possible. The English support the passage of an Israeli ship through the Suez and should the Egyptians stop it, it will be possible to declare Egypt an aggressor according to Security Council resolutions. (b) The English agree to the following time-table and actions: The Israeli raid will start on Monday at 7 p.m. The next morning at 7 a.m. England and France will present Egypt with the ultimatum as it has been agreed upon. Should Egypt not accept – the joint air force (of England and France) will begin bombing Egypt's airfields during the night between Tuesday and Wednesday at approximately 4 a.m. (There are about five hundred planes on Cyprus, 140 of them are bombers.) (c) In the request to Egypt there will be three conditions: (1) To withdraw their forces 10 miles from both sides of the Canal within 12 hours. (2) To halt all acts of aggression immediately. (3) To consent to the entry of French–English forces in order to ensure peace on the Canal. They will turn to Israel with two demands: (1) That our forces retreat 10 miles east of the area of the Canal. (2) The termination of acts of hostility. They will inform Israel of the third demand which was presented to the Egyptians.

Saturday, October 27

– At ten all our members of the Cabinet gathered and I informed them of the Sèvres agreements. Following some clarifications – without objection to the plan itself – the meeting was favorably adjourned ...

Sunday, October 28

Even though all the members of the Government already knew the complete story and each of them had already expressed his view – I again recounted the matter, and the debate continued as if they had just heard it for the first time. ...

From the meeting I went to [see] the President and after dinner I gave him a report of the decision and the plan.

No entries in the Diary from October 26 through November 6.

Wednesday, November 7

An act of the Devil – I fell sick and was bedridden following the Government approval of my plan, a day before actions in Sinai began. I had an attack of high fever and weakness and even yesterday, Prof. S[hlomo]. Zondak[68] forbade me to go up to Jerusalem to the Knesset. But I could no longer take his advice, since the Knesset had been put off from Monday till today. At eleven o'clock this morning I gave my report of the military actions of the biggest campaign in the history of our people – the campaign to conquer the Sinai Peninsula (including the Gaza Strip). (I could not give an account of the political background of the military operation.)

In bed in Tel-Aviv, I was in constant touch with military headquarters on the one hand, and with the Ministry for Foreign Affairs, on the other. I wasn't sure whether Eden would keep his part of the arrangement. And though he was twelve hours late – in turning [with the ultimatum] to Egypt as well as in the start of the bombings, I was anxious with fright that Tel-Aviv and the other airports might be bombed – the partners did keep most of their commitments. On two occasions Eisenhower poured out his anger at us – twice before the start of the operation (during mobilization) and twice following our commencing the operation. But by the time we managed to explain to him the reasons for our actions he was informed that the

English and the French were also taking action, and in his broadcast to the nation that night – October 31 – he was more moderate towards us.[69]

In the beginning the entire affair seemed like a dream, then a fable and in the end like a night of wonders.

The dispatch with which [Nikolai] Bulganin[70] honored me – if his name hadn't been signed on it I could have thought it had been written by Hitler. There's not much difference between these hangmen. It worries me because Soviet arms are flowing into Syria and we must presume that the arms are accompanied by 'volunteers'.

Thursday, November 8

... Eban, all terrified, called. His cables also sow fear and horror. [Herbert] Hoover [Jr.][71] has warned [Reuven] Shiloah[72] that they [the Americans] will sever all ties with us, will stop all assistance and possibly expel us from the U. N. Apparently the fear of Russia has fallen on them. According to the information, large quantities of arms with 'volunteers' are flowing into Syria.

[Walter] Eytan:[73] The whole world, except for France, is uniting against us because of our staying in Sinai. But even France will not be able to support us to the end. Such a situation existed in November 1948 when we were required to pull back our forces. ... – (Eytan continues). We must generate foreign interests in our remaining in Sinai. There is a strategic aspect to this: if it is desired that the Canal will be international then it is desirable that we remain in Sinai (the English will say – that they will stay, thereby achieving this aim). There are [also] economic interests: Italy and Belgium have already turned to us to protect their oil rights. We could ensure them a more efficient exploitation [of the oil] (both of them are only 'flies' in comparison with the world powers). If Egypt remains – it will be able to nationalize the oil. We would protect them from nationalization. There are mines in Sinai (copper, manganese, etc.) that have not yet been exploited. If we don't get them for ourselves but give concessions to foreign companies that have not yet been utilized – we'll be creating interests (why should not a multi-national force ensure that? Because it is not a sovereign force, but a police force). There is a possibility of settling refugees in Sinai.

– Today was a horrifying day: listening [to] news from Rome, Paris and Washington one item kept chasing another concerning information of a flow of Soviet planes and volunteers to Syria, the promise to bomb Israel – airfields, cities, etc., whether the Syrians and Jordanians will go to war against us ... There may be a great deal of exaggeration in these news items. But Bulganin's dispatch to me – a letter which could have been written by Hitler – and the frenzy of the Russian tanks in Hungary are evidence of what these Nazi Communists are liable to do.

Saturday, November 10

I have formulated an outline of principles for our diplomatic information [services] in the United States, in England, in the Scandinavian countries ...

(1) The Egyptian army cannot be permitted to return to the Sinai desert, thereby the Canal will become an international waterway at least *de facto* (if not *de jure*).

(2) The multi-national force must remain both east and west of the area of the Canal but only in the area of the Canal. Thereby free passage will be ensured to every nation without depending on the Egyptians or the Soviets who stand behind them.

(3) Egypt must be required to negotiate a permanent peace directly with Israel. The cease-fire agreement has been irreparably destroyed. From the beginning it was not meant to be an extended rule but a transition until the establishment of a permanent peace.

(4) The Straits of Eilat and the western coast of the straits are vital for Israel. Only Israel's hold on them will ensure Israeli free passage and the freedom of international navigation in the Red Sea, and will guarantee free access to the ports of Eilat and Aqaba to maritime trade of all nations, as well as the transfer of oil to the Mediterranean without the need of the Suez Canal which Egypt can block from time to time as it has done now.

(5) The danger of the Soviets taking control in the whole of the Middle East with the aid of the Egyptian dictator and the Syrian president Shukri al-Qawatli[74] who has just returned from Moscow as a Soviet instrument.

Should this Soviet takeover not be stopped shortly (and the most efficient means to do this is to remove Nasser and Qawatli from power) the whole continent of Africa will fall into Soviet hands in the near future.

(6) The true nature of Nasser's rule: a Fascist military dictatorship which crushes and impoverishes the Egyptian people in order to establish an inflated military force on which their rule can lean; exploiting religious, Moslem, and racist Arab instincts against every other people in order to carry out aspirations of expansion and

domination over the whole of the Arab world. [This is] as Nasser himself describes his aspirations in his book, *The Philosophy of the Revolution*, which is a kind of *Mein Kampf* of the Egyptian tyrant. Though the military junta which rules Egypt is not rigid in its communist doctrine – it does in fact serve as an instrument in the hands of the Soviets in order to penetrate into the African continent and the Middle East. Nasser's temporary pretence of being friendly towards the West is but an act of deceit.

(7) The stand taken by the Arab and Moslem countries (except for Turkey) in the [U.N. General] Assembly on the issue of the cruel suppression of the Hungarian people by the Soviet army – is a proof of the strong cooperation which exists between these two powers. This partnership is a danger to all the free world.

Nasser and Qawatli are the two personages in the Arab world who are handing over the Arab nations to the Soviets. And if these two are not confronted by an efficient and determined opposition on the part of the free world – they will impose their authority over the entire Arab and Moslem nations.

(8) There exists in the Arab world – inside Egypt as well as in Syria – many forces and persons who oppose the rule and the aspirations of Nasser and Qawatli, but they need the active assistance of the free world in order to be rid of these two malignant people.

... Having read the dispatch [from Pres. Eisenhower] I poured out my heart to [U.S. Ambassador to Israel, Edward] Lawson[75] about Hoover's threats in his talk with Shiloah. I asked him whether they had made threats like these when Nasser violated the U. N. Charter or the Security Council resolutions. And did America understand that she was strengthening the position of the Soviet Union in the Middle East by assisting Nasser and did it understand that Nasser and Qawatli will hand over the entire Middle East to the Soviets, and after the Middle East the whole of the African continent. Do they understand that the bombing of Budapest by the Soviets only raises the prestige of the Soviets in the eyes of the Arabs for they scorn the U. N. resolutions, which nobody keeps – unless they are directed against Israel and that the two most dangerous men in the free world are Nasser and Qawatli and instead of assisting in deposing them – the U. S. A. elevates them[?]. I made a particular point of the danger of Egypt's return to Sinai, which had never belonged to Egypt and that their return will endanger our very existence.

Wednesday, November 14

Yesterday, Reuven [Shiloah] cabled about the long talk with [General Walter] Bedell Smith[76] according to the guidelines I had set for the Foreign Ministry on Saturday. [see above for Nov. 10] He found B[edell]. S[mith]. to be 'sick and depressed'. [He was] angry with the English who had not dared to land and advance. According to B[edell]. S[mith]. they should have conquered the entire Canal in five days at the most. Then there would have been no Nasser, no Soviet threat and the world would have sighed with relief. Those are my exact same words.

Shiloah informs that he [Bedell Smith] accepts the P.M.'s (i.e. – mine) assessment in full and as far as he can he will try to impart it to others. He is also in favor of a meeting between the P.M. and the President, but felt it to be his duty to warn Reuven for he doubts whether it will be possible to overcome the existing attitudes in the Administration. He is sorry that Dulles is sick, for despite all his mistakes he understood the Soviet danger better than all the others …

– In the early evening [Ya'acov] Herzog[77] and [Walter] Eytan came to see me. Ya'acov tried to summarize the situation as it is reflected in the telegrams from our envoys in the neighboring countries and particularly in the U.S.

The stand taken by Britain and France is that we do not have to evacuate Sinai. France has publicly announced that we do not have to leave the Gaza Strip. Their army will not leave the Canal until international supervision is guaranteed. Israel must be assured of free navigation through the Canal. Britain has announced that the British force will not move from the Canal until international supervision is guaranteed. As for Israel – in their opinion the I[srael] D[efense] F[orces] do not have to withdraw from Sinai until an Israeli–Egyptian settlement is reached.

The Italian Foreign Ministry is of the opinion that we will not leave the Gaza Strip until Egypt undertakes not to concentrate military forces in Sinai, and the U.N. will guarantee the security of Israel, and that an immediate solution be found for the refugees in Gaza and that Nasser will commit himself to a peace treaty or a non-aggression pact and will stop the fidaiyyun activities.

– Hammarskjöld – our No. 1 enemy after Russia – has finally decided to go to Hungary and [this] will give us a respite for a couple of days.

There's a favourable shift in the U.S. Speaking before members of the Congress, the President has spoken of Nasser as 'the most wicked man in the world'.

Thursday, November 15

Shimon [Peres] informs me that the French now want to turn to the English requesting them to carry out my Plan for the Middle East (the partition of Jordan, etc.). I advised against it at this time. Any comprehensive plan for the Middle East would not be appropriate now for a precondition to any arrangement would be the termination of Nasser's rule. Due to Eden's procrastination and hesitation, Nasser was not wiped out. Therefore the urgent need at present is:

(1) To assure that British and French military forces will remain on the Canal.
(2) To reaffirm and strengthen the American–French–English union.
(3) To insist vigorously against any Russian intervention in the Middle East and to undermine Nasser's and Qawatli's regimes.

Without achieving these three goals – no changes and arrangements can be made in the Middle East.
– At eleven p.m. [Ya'acov] Herzog brought me Bulganin's second dispatch which had left Moscow today. It is no better than the first dispatch in its truth, honesty or humanity. Dispatches which I presume to be slightly more polite have also been sent by him to France and England.[78]

Friday, November 16

– At three-thirty Golda [Meir] called from N.Y. [asking] whether to present Bulganin's dispatch to the Security Council? ... When I told her that I shall send my reply to Bulganin only on Sunday, she asked if it was worthwhile to answer at all. I told her that one must reply for the sake of world public opinion, and the falsehood in his letter must be denounced.
– According to [the British journal] the *New Statesman* of November 10th, 60,000 British and 30,000 French troops participated in the Anglo-French campaign, as well as 1,200 jet planes and two-thirds of the active British navy. If they had only appointed a commander of ours over this force – Nasser would have been destroyed in two days.

322

Saturday, November 17

[Abba] Eban and Golda [Meir] spoke with Pineau in N.Y. – concerning the need to renew the pact with the U.S. and about the danger of reviving Nasser. Pineau is in agreement. It was agreed to act separately but with coordination. Pineau agreed that the Egyptian forces must not be returned to Sinai and the islands. According to him he was taken by surprise when Hammerskjöld refused to accept Nasser's condition and insisted on the ideas which are acceptable to France. Lodge has hinted to Pineau that should Israel solve the greater part of the refugee problem it [Israel] will not find it difficult to gain international recognition for its position in Gaza. According to Pineau, the situation in Syria is more worrisome than in Egypt.

– This morning I edited a draft – answer to Bulganin.

– In the evening Fati [Yehoshafat Harkabi] came to see me, asking whether we should make public the list of our casualties in the Sinai War. They number about a hundred and sixty. There are several missing. I told him to publish [the list] for we are duty-bound to honor [them].

– We have the following prisoners of war: 180 Egyptian officers: 2 generals, colonels and others. The captains are the most talkative of them all. Altogether we have about five thousand prisoners.

This time the nation is united more than it has ever been. The first voices of woe which were heard following my broadcast to the nation are dying out. There's a growing realization among the people that we took a wise and necessary stand.

Saturday, November 24

Allen Dulles[79] is angry with Issar [Harel][80] for not telling him the truth. But he does understand us. Beddel Smith, [General Lucius] Clay[81] and the military realize the danger posed by Nasser, though over there they think that Qawatli poses a greater hazard.

Clay visited the Foreign Secretary and defined the Administration's policy thus:

(1) The U.S. Government feels itself morally committed to ensuring the existence and independence of the State of Israel. But a Soviet conquest of the Arab world would put an end to all Western interests and Israel. Therefore, the U.S. Government must beware of losing its influence and prestige in the Arab world that has not yet been enslaved to Nasser.

(2) The Administration views Nasser as a most negative factor and would like to see his downfall, but the way taken by France and England only achieves the opposite results. If the British had hastened to end their part of the operation the situation would have been different. But the British military failure was a most shocking event. On the 'other hand, Israel's military success has been most impressive and is worthy of military appreciation despite the differences of opinion concerning the wisdom of the initiative.

(3) It is obvious that there's no going back to the former unstable situation but a permanent arrangement must be accelerated.

(4) The main point is to prevent Soviet intrusion.

(5) The U.S. will renew its close ties with Britain, France and Israel. But it is important that while doing this it will not abandon the Moslem world into the hands of the Soviets.

(6) There's no harm in the fact that the Canal will be closed for a while. The Arabs, including Nasser, will suffer financial losses.

(7) He listened very attentively to our claims and suggestions concerning the situation and volunteered to be constantly in touch.

Sunday, November 25

– At five p.m. [the British Ambassador to Israel Sir John] Nicholls[82] came to see me. He took a piece of paper out of his pocket and while looking at it from time to time, said that he had been requested by the Prime Minister to say that Eden had full confidence in him and that whatever I wished to pass on to Eden I could tell him, for Eden did not know when he would have the chance to meet me. I told him that I had a plan as to how matters in the Middle East could be arranged and whose cornerstone was Nasser's elimination. When I spoke with him several weeks ago I had the basis for assuming that [Nasser's] destruction would take place but what happened – happened. The British operation in Egypt did not succeed, and Nasser exists. Nicholls observed to me that nothing has changed the position of the English Government as to the necessity of getting rid of him [Nasser] ... Then he continued to talk about those who are inquiring about the collusion, and it seemed to me that that was the purpose of his visit, or one of the aims of his coming ... Altogether he was very friendly, almost fawning. I suspect that this is due to the fear of the collusion being discovered.

Saturday, December 1

At eleven Issar [Harel] came to see me. ... [He informed me] that the Americans will not make up with the English until Eden goes [resigns] ... Issar presumes that there's an agreement between the Soviet Union and the U.S. that there will not be [another] world war although subversion, competition and the Cold War will continue. Each side was supposed to be responsible for its followers so that a war would not start. And now, without informing Eisenhower, Eden has started a war. (Why isn't there any anger at Mollet? Isn't he a major partner?)

– More telegrams have been received in the Foreign Ministry but they have not yet been decoded. Truman was spoken with and he claims that he [Nasser] should have been destroyed already a year ago. I have no doubt that he [Truman] would have done it.

Sunday, December 2

– At five [U.S. Ambassador Edward] Lawson came by my invitation. Following a short friendly conversation, I told him that we were moving away from the Canal in accordance with the [U.N.] Secretary General's demand and in order to keep our promise to the President. But [I asked] what about the relevant arrangements on which our promise had been conditioned? How will they keep the Sinai from becoming a base for a military invasion and a fidaiyyun center; how will fidaiyyun attacks be prevented – Cairo radio has announced large-scale fidaiyyun actions in Israel; how will our freedom of navigation in the Suez [Canal] be guaranteed if Nasser becomes the only one in control of the Canal; how will we maintain freedom of navigation and aviation in the Straits of Eilat if we are forced to withdraw? ... Lawson promised to convey these items to Washington immediately. I reminded him of the fine words the President had written me in his three despatches and [told him] I was sure his words were sincere – but where are the actions?

Tuesday, December 4

[Abba] Eban cables that the Americans are continuing to wonder why the British ceased firing suddenly instead of going on for another day and finishing the conquest of the Canal. (Why had the Americans pushed them?) The tension with the U.S. would not have grown if the English had persisted for just another day.

Tuesday, December 11

... In the afternoon I had a meeting with Shimon [Peres] (who has returned from Paris) and with Moshe [Dayan]. Shimon is satisfied with his talks with the Government members in Paris. In his opinion this Government will continue to exist for a few more months and there is no depression in France due to the 'operation' which was unsuccessful. There's no fear of a reaction against those who had carried it out nor against Israel. They have agreed to leave the arms they have loaned us. (Shimon believes their value is $15 million.)

Thursday, December 13

– At four-thirty [Richard] Crossman[83] came to see me.

I asked him what was the point of Eden's actions concerning the Canal? Why did he start and why did he not finish, though he could have done it in two or three days. He said that there were two factions within the Tories. 'The Suez Group' and the liberals. Eden had wanted to satisfy both sides and so spoke to each with what he thought they would like to hear. He didn't really know what to do. He sent the army but did not dare to take any action. All of a sudden he acted – then hesitated and gave an order to engage [in hostilities] without casualties. If Churchill had been in his place he would have first spoken with the Americans and he would have either convinced them or not. Eden, in fact, cheated everybody as well as himself. He will not return to power, in Crossman's opinion ...

He asked about the situation in Jordan. I said that in my opinion that state had no future, but for the time being it's better that England will not sever its ties for otherwise it [Jordan] would become a Soviet satellite like Syria. He admitted that England was now totally dependent on the will of the U.S. I said to him that I saw danger in that. The U.S. had become the leader of the non-Communist world. Eisenhower is a frank and honest man, with goodwill who strives for peace with all his heart, but he's no politician and is dependent on the advice of his counselors. There's no knowing who will take his place and it is not possible that the entire free world – and the fate of the world – should be dependent upon one man and the U.S. It is imperative to establish a United States of Europe ... The existence of two free forces in the world, independent of each other but friendly and allied, will ensure world peace.

Friday, December 14

– The correct setting of priorities among the many needs that abound and contradict one another is the beginning of political wisdom, at least in Israel. Our major needs are: security, economic independence, absorption of immigration. The abstract ideal is the fulfillment of these needs completely at all times, but this in practice is impossible since it is for us to know what has priority. Until the Suez Campaign, – after Egypt armed itself with the goal of destroying us – security stood as our major concern. Moshe [Sharett][84] did not understand that our foreign policy must serve our security needs. The change in the Foreign Ministry facilitated the obtaining of arms, because we were freed from the official, departmentalized approach that was so deeply-ingrained in Moshe. Our arming ourselves and our unorthodox connections with France made the Sinai Campaign possible. In this campaign we destroyed Nasser's military power and prevented the rest of the Arab nations from conniving against us. A respite from our enemies is not guaranteed to us for ever or even for a long time. But for now we have a relaxation although it is hard to define how long it will last. However there's no doubt that there will not be a war for the next two or three years. If we only strengthen our air force then we shall have discharged our duty to security.

Thursday, December 27

All day at [the army base] Tzrifin, a continuation of the clarifications about the Sinai Campaign. Moshe [Dayan] concluded and after him there were only 15 minutes left, for I was called to dinner in honour of Montell, Chairman of the Foreign Affairs and Defense Committee of the French Parliament ... I only managed to observe that the main lesson from the Sinai Campaign was that there was no way of learning from it regarding the next war, for the following reasons:

(1) Here we were the initiators and the advantage of having the initiative is well known. In the next war we may be the ones attacked and the first initiative will be in the hands of the enemy.
(2) This time we fought only against the Egyptian army. It is possible that in the next war there will be many attackers. The Egyptian soldier is, except perhaps for the Iraqi, the worst among the neighboring Arab armies.
(3) We shall have no external assistance – and there is no way to estimate [the value] of foreign aid in weapons, and those who took up arms (pilots) and in other ways ...
(4) The [next] war could go on for an extended time. This time we knew in advance quite precisely that we would complete the conquest of Sinai in five days. And as we planned – so we carried it out (only the conquest of Sharm el-Sheikh took another two days). There were special conditions which are not likely to return. The

next war could last longer and might entail a heavy burden on the army, the people and the economy.

(5) There will be many casualties. On this occasion we were aware that we would have few casualties due to the characteristics associated with the campaign. A portion of the casualties were hit by our own forces and we knew in advance that our casualties would be small. This will not be the case in the next war.

(6) The main difference − in the next war the enemy's air force will not be paralyzed. The air force itself will not be able to conduct the war but without it, the navy and the land forces will be powerless. There is no estimating the importance of the assistance we received this time from the French air force in paralyzing the Egyptian air force. It will not be this way next time.

(7) In the next war, the homefront is liable to be hit. The high morale which this nation (in the 'homefront') demonstrated during the days of the Sinai Campaign is without a doubt this nation's virtue. Tel Aviv and Haifa were not bombed and no enemy plane was seen over Israel's skies − not so in the next war. The attacks will have a bearing on the morale.

(8) Should the war − as we want and hope − take place on enemy territory, we shall not confront [the enemy] in an empty desert as on this occasion − but among a hostile population.

Therefore − [we must] strengthen the air force (despite budget cuts), improve the quality of the army morally and professionally, and unite the people. Now, too, it is an educational force − for those who are discharged from the army are more educated than when they entered. This is especially true of the immigrants. The army, and above all the commanders, must serve as a model for the nation − in friendship and in discipline.

Saturday, December 29

− Yesterday I checked with Peres the dates of the French deal.

The contract for the first 12 Mystères was signed on December 26, 1955 with General Bailly[85] ... without the consent of the Americans.

The 12 Mystères were received on April 11, 1956.

The second contract for an additional 12 Mystères was signed with Bourgès-Maunoury in mid-April 1956 ... − this time, too, without American consent. Later, the Americans agreed to release 12 [planes] from NATO.

Meeting about 'Geut' [code name for the arms deal with the French] took place on June 22, 1956 (four days after the change in

328

the Foreign Ministry – M[oshe] Sh[arett] resigned on June 18, 1956) – we agreed upon 72 Mystères, 120 AMX, 40 Super-Shermans, ammunition, rockets, radar, 105 mm mobile guns. The first Geut Mystères arrived on August 18, 1956. The first boat with tanks, ammunition and spare parts arrived on July 24, 1956. The Geut deal was made with the Government of Guy Mollet. I told the journalists about this deal on July 30, 1956.

NOTES

1. Newspaper editors: Beginning in the pre-State period, editors of the Jewish press were organized in a forum that provided for self-censorship and cooperation on matters affecting security. They met on a regular basis with political and military leaders for the purpose of receiving reports that were not for publication.
2. Pierre-Eugène Gilbert (1907–), French Ambassador to Israel 1953–56.
3. Golda Meir (1898–1978), Israeli Foreign Minister 1956–1965; Prime Minister, 1969–1973.
4. Nehemia Argov (1914–1957), Military Secretary to the Prime Minister.
5. Yehoshafat Harkabi (1921–), Major-General, Director of Military Intelligence.
6. Djibouti, an enclave on the the Gulf of Aden formally under French control, now an independent nation.
7. Moshe Dayan (1915–1981), Chief of the General Staff, 1953–1958; Minister of Defence, 1967 and Minister of Foreign Affairs, 1977–1979.
8. Shimon Peres (1923–), Director General of the Defence Ministry 1953–1959; Prime Minister 1984–1986.
9. Mordechai Bar-On (1928–), Head of the Office of the Chief of General Staff, 1956–1957; later Chief Educational Officer in the Israel Defence Forces.
10. Maurice Bourgès-Maunoury (1914–), Minister of National Defence, 1956–1957; Prime Minister, 1957.
11. Guy Mollet (1905–1975), Prime Minister of France, 1956–1957.
12. Christian Pineau (1904–), Minister of Foreign Affairs, 1956–1958.
13. Albert Thomas (1920–), Director General of the French Defence Ministry, 1956–1957.
14. Eliahu Elath (1903–), Ambassador to Great Britain, 1950–1959.
15. Randolph Churchill (1911–1968), son of Winston Churchill, politician and journalist.
16. Anthony Eden (1897–1974), Conservative Prime Minister 1955–1957.
17. Selwyn Lloyd (1904–1978), Secretary of State for Foreign Affairs, 1955–1960.
18. Dmitiri Shepilov(1905–), Soviet Minister of Foreign Affairs, 1956–1957.
19. Teddy Kollek (1911–), Director General of the Prime Minister's Office 1952–1956; Mayor of Jerusalem, 1965– .
20. On August 2, 1956 the United States, Great Britain and France called for a conference of the original signatories to the 1888 convention which guaranteed the right of free navigation through the Canal together with special interests in Suez to meet in London on August 16 to discuss the establishment of an international board of management for the operation of the canal.
21. Jacob Meridor (1913–), Herut M.K.; Member of the Knesset Committee on Foreign Affairs, Minister of Economic Coordination and Planning, 1982–1984.
22. Menahem Begin (1913–), Leader of the Herut opposition party; Prime Minister, 1977–1983.
23. Shaul Avigur (1899–1978), Chief Assistant to Minister of Defence, David Ben-Gurion; later served in special capacities on behalf of the Ministry of Defence.

PARTICIPANTS RECORD THE EVENTS

24. see fn. 20.
25. Admiral Louis Mountbatten (1900–1979), First Sea Lord 1955–1959.
26. Yuval Ne'eman ((1925–), Colonel and Director of Planning Section IDF; Minister of Science and Development, 1982–1984.
27. Robert Lacoste (1899–   ), French politician, Minister Resident in Algeria, 1956–1958.
28. Yosef Nachmias (1912–), Deputy Director-General of the Defence Ministry, 1953–1957.
29. John Foster Dulles (1888–1959), U.S. Secretary of State, 1952–1959.
30. General Hugh Stockwell (1903–1986), Commander of the British Ground Forces.
31. Vice-Admiral Pierre Barjot (1899–1960), French Assistant Commander of the Anglo-French operation.
32. Meir Amit (1921–), Deputy Chief of Staff, 1956–1957; Minister of Transport and Communications, 1977–1978.
33. Lt. General Eedson Louis Millard Burns (1897–1980), Canadian Chief of Staff of the UN Truce Supervision Organization in Palestine, 1954–1956; Commander UN Emergency Force Sinai–Suez, 1956–1957.
34. Dag Hammarskjöld (1905–1961), Swedish Secretary General of the UN, 1953–1961.
35. Haim Laskov (1919–1982), Commander of Armored Corps, 1956–1957.
36. Shelomo Kaddar (1913–   ), Israeli Minister in Prague, 1953–1957.
37. Benedetto Capomazza, Marquis Di Campolattaro, Italian Ambassador to Israel 1953–1958.
38. Mar Elias Monastery is situated on the southern outskirts of Jerusalem on the Jordanian–Israeli border.
39. After the failure of the London Conference, U.S. Secretary of State Dulles put forward the idea of a Suez Canal Users' Association (SCUA). The object was to create an association of those countries that used the Canal which would employ their own pilots and other personnel to assure proper passage. It was to have paid Egypt a share of the receipts collected from ships using the services of the SCUA.
40. Peretz Naphtali (1888–1961), Minister of State, 1955–1957, and Mapai MK.
41. Pinchas Sapir (1909–1975), Minister of Commerce and Industry, Mapai MK.
42. Eden and Lloyd had public meetings in Paris on September 23 and then secretly returned to meet Mollet and Pineau on September 27.
43. Amiel Najar (1912–1980), Director, Western European Division at the Ministry of Foreign Affairs.
44. Jean Fernand-Laurant (1917–), Counsellor at the French Embassy in Tel Aviv.
45. The United States, Great Britain and France issued the Tripartite Declaration in May 1950 in order to limit arms shipments to Israel and her neighbours, guarantee the armistice agreements and promote a regional defence scheme.
46. General Maurice Challe (1905–1979), French Deputy to the Chief of Staff for Air Force Affairs.
47. Levi Eshkol (1895–1969), Minister of Finance 1952–1963; Prime Minister 1963–1969.
48. Col. Louis Mangin (1912–), Political adviser to Minister of Defence, Bourgès-Maunoury.
49. General Maurice Gazin (1904–), Chief of Bureau to General Ely 1956–1958.
50. General André Martin (1911–), Second in command to General Challe, Chief of the French Air Staff.
51. Adib al' Shishakli (1909–1964), Former President of Syria 1949–1954; leader of the opposition in 1956.
52. General Charles de Gaulle loaned his own DC-4 for this mission.
53. General Paul Ely (1897–1975), French Chief of General Staff, 1956–1958.
54. Admiral Arthur William Radford (1896–1973), Chairman of the U.S. Joint Chiefs

330

of Staff.

55. Abba Eban (1915–), Israeli Ambassador and Chief Delegate to the UN, 1950–1959; Minister for Foreign Affairs, 1966–1974.
56. François Darlan (1881–1942), French Admiral assassinated for his collaboration with the Nazis.
57. Mahmud Fawzi (1900–), Egyptian Minister of Foreign Affairs, 1952–1958.
58. Hugh Gaitskell (1906–1963), Labour Opposition party leader.
59. 5th Marquess of Salisbury (1893–1972), Leader of the House of Lords, 1951–1957 and Lord President of the Council, 1952–1957.
60. Richard Austin Butler (1902–1982), Leader of the House of Commons 1955–1961.
61. Ibrahim Hashim (1878–1958), Prime Minister of Jordan 1956–7.
62. Algerian rebel leaders including Ben Bella and Ben Khider had been captured by the French on October 22 while in transit to Tunis from Cairo.
63. Habib Bourguiba (1903–), President of the Tunisian National Assembly, Prime Minister, Minister for Foreign Affairs, 1956–1957; later President of Tunisia.
64. Artur Ben-Natan (1921–), Representative of the Ministry of Defence in Europe; later Ambassador to France and West Germany.
65. Donald Logan (1917–), Assistant Private Secretary to the Secretary of State for Foreign Affairs, 1956–1958.
66. Patrick Dean (1909–), Deputy Under-Secretary of State, at the Foreign Office, 1956–1960.
67. Anthony Head (1906–), Secretary of State for War, 1951–1956; on October 18, 1956 became Minister of Defence (1956–1957).
68. Professor Shmuel Zondek (1894–1970), Head of Internal Diseases Department, Hadassah Hospital.
69. On November 5, British and French troops landed in Egypt; on November 6, Eisenhower was re-elected and turned his attention and anger to the Suez Crisis. He placed great pressure on the allies for a cease-fire even as he warned the Soviets about intervening.
70. Nikolai Bulganin (1895–1975), Soviet Prime Minister, 1955–1958.
71. Herbert Hoover, Jr. (1903–1969), son of the former President Herbert Hoover; Under-Secretary of State, 1954–1957.
72. Reuven Shiloah (1909–1959), Minister at the Israeli Embassy in Washington, 1954–1957.
73. Walter Eytan (1910–), Director General of the Israeli Foreign Ministry, 1948–1959.
74. Shukri al-Quwatli (1892–1967), President of Syria, 1943–1949, 1955–1958.
75. Edward Lawson (1895–1962), U.S. Ambassador to Israel, 1954–1962.
76. Walter Beddel Smith (1895–1961), Director of CIA, 1950–1953. Ben-Gurion met him while visiting Jewish DPs after World War II, had a warm memory of their association and expected him to be sympathetic and helpful to Israel.
77. Yaacov Herzog (1921–1972), Advisor to Ben-Gurion on U.S. affairs during the Suez Crisis; later Ambassador to Canada and Director General of the Prime Minister's Office, 1969–1972.
78. Bulganin's telegram of November 15 denied Israel's grievances and contained such threatening phrases as 'Israel's policy ... is dangerous to the cause of general peace and fatal for Israel ...'; 'The Soviet Government has cautioned the Israel Government about the dangerous consequences for Israel ...'
79. Allen Dulles (1893–1969), Director of the CIA, 1953–1961.
80. Issar Harel (1912–), Head of the Mossad (Israeli Intelligence), 1952–1963.
81. General Lucius Clay (1897–1980), Retired General, adviser to the Pentagon.
82. Sir John Nicholls (1909–1970), British Ambassador to Israel, 1954–1957.
83. Richard Crossman (1907–1974), Pro-Zionist author and Labour MP; Member of the 1946 Anglo-American Committee of Inquiry to Palestine.
84. Moshe Sharett (1894–1965), Prime Minister, 1953–1955; Foreign Minister 1948–

1956.
85. General Paul Bailly (1903–   ), Chief of Staff to the Commander in Chief of the French Air Force, 1955–1957.

22

Abd al-Latif al-Bughdadi's Memoirs*

Edited and introduced by Moshe Shemesh

INTRODUCTION

The Western practice of opening up national archives to the public does not exist in the Arab countries. There are only scant Arab primary sources at the disposal of researchers of the contemporary Middle East. They largely consist of memoirs, diaries or personal archives and official publications. Therefore, the publication of the personal memoirs of senior Arab politicians is an important occasion for scholars. Such is the case regarding most sources on the policy and involvement of Egypt in the Suez–Sinai crisis. Although Muhammad Hassanein Heikal's books are important primary sources they are stamped by the seal of a confidant and adviser to Nasser.

The diaries of Abd al-Latif al-Bughdadi, a high military officer and a member of the Egyptian Revolutionary Command Council (RCC), and of Engineer Sayyid Mar'i, an expert in agriculture and Minister for Agrarian Reform, are important contributions to the primary sources on Suez. Previously published only in Arabic, they present two approaches to understand different aspects of Nasser's regime and shed light on special angles of the Egyptian position in the Suez–Sinai crisis.

Abd al-Latif al-Bughdadi was born in 1917. He graduated from the Military College in 1938 and Flight College in 1939. As a wing-commander he took active part in the revolution of the Free Officers (23 July 1952). He was a member of the RCC from the day of its inception. In June 1953 he was appointed Minister of War. In September 1953 he was nominated chairman of the Revolutionary

---

* Abd al-Latif al-Bughdadi, *Mudhakkirat* (Memoirs) (al-Maktab al-Misri al-Hadith, Cairo, 1977), vol.I, ch.VII–VIII, pp.307–67. For biographies of participants, see Notes.

Court. In April, 1954 he was named Minister for Municipal and Agrarian Affairs. In July 1957 he was elected chairman of the first parliament to be established following the Revolution. After the union between Egypt and Syria in February 1958, he was appointed Vice-President of the Republic in charge of production. In October 1961, following the dissolution of the Union, he was nominated Vice-President for Production as well as Minister for Finance and Planning. In November 1962 he became a Member of the Presidential Council. In March 1964 he retired from public life. Bughdadi himself testified that he resigned his posts three times due to conflicts with Nasser. Twice he withdrew his resignation and returned under pressure from Nasser and his colleagues – in April 1954 and in August 1958. But the third time, in March 1964, he finally resigned in protest at 'the way the Presidential Council functioned and the fact that it was not fulfilling its duties as a collective leadership'.

Bughdadi states that his decision at the end of 1953 to write a diary stemmed from his evaluation that 'the development of the Revolution was threatened ... when signs of a conflict appeared, or more precisely a serious struggle between General Naguib and members of the RCC'. He adds: 'I decided to note down these events and dangers which threatened the Revolution so that the truth will not be lost when we die.' In order to strengthen this claim he points out that it had not been his intention to publish his diary during his lifetime. Nevertheless, he felt impelled to publish it due to the results of the October War 'which gave back the Egyptian soldier and the Arab soldier their honour and dispelled the humiliation of the June 1967 defeat'. Bughdadi admits that he does not give the full account but only a 'presentation of the events to which I myself was a witness or in which I participated'. He claims to give details of the events as he noted them down in his diary 'limited by my knowledge of the events at the time of writing without analysing them or interpreting them.'

There are several points to be made concerning Bughdadi's recounting of the Suez–Sinai crisis events:

(a) This is Bughdadi's personal record including his emotional and critical attitude towards Nasser. Despite this, it is an important primary source written by a person who took part in the discussions leading to the most important decisions which changed the face of the Middle East. He was a witness to the conduct of the Egyptian leadership throughout its most critical crisis since the Revolution in

334

July 1952. Yet the question remains – to what extent did he keep the original text of his writings? To this we have no answer. But it does appear that the diary was edited prior to its publication.

(b) Bughdadi's special relationship towards Nasser is evident. His attitude is far from being positive. Indeed, it is very critical. Although he does not directly present him negatively, he does so without enthusiasm. It must be noted that the diary was published during the height of the de-Nasserism period in Egypt. Bughdadi presents himself as having been very close to Nasser, someone who accompanied him throughout the war, who advised him and as one who acted as an intermediary between Nasser and Abd al-Hakim Amir, the Minister of War and Commander-in-Chief, and the High Command. He endeavours to be correct and straightforward towards Nasser while stressing Nasser's critical moments throughout the war. These he presents quite dramatically in a fashion far from complimentary to the leader. He points out Nasser's detachment from the army and 'his weakness and helplessness despite his being the leader of the revolution and president of the republic'. We may assume that his conflicts with Nasser and his retirement from the political scene are reflected in this approach. In contrast to Heikal he does not stress Nasser's part in the decision to retreat from Sinai. He does mention Egypt's political achievements following the war but finds it sufficient to note: 'The results of nationalizing the Canal and the tripartite aggression were political victory for Egypt and for Nasser in particular. He [Nasser] became the uncontested leader of the Arab nation and a hero of Arab nationalism.'

(c) Bughdadi paints a rather grim picture of the Egyptian leadership's reaction and behaviour towards the Anglo-French military initiative. His critical attitude is particularly aimed towards Amir and his functioning amongst the military high command. Well aware of this austere state of affairs, as well as of Nasser's condition (as he described it), and as if to convince the reader of the truth of his words he states twice: 'This is what I wrote down in my diary concerning that day. My diary expresses the difficult and cruel circumstances we had to go through in the course of that crisis.'

FROM THE *MEMOIRS* OF ABD AL-LATIF AL-BUGHDADI

Our goal, following the nationalization of the Canal [Company], was to gain time and to try to prevent, as far as possible, a clash in particular with England, and with France and the USA. Our evaluation was that time would be in our favour, so long as world public opinion was convinced of our right to nationalize the Canal. Our belief was that Britain, who more than any other country would use military force against us, would need time to organize the force required for such an operation. We had this time at our disposal in order to raise world public opinion in our favour. The possibility of Britain's cooperation with Israel in order to attack us never dawned upon us. For we thought that Britain would never take a step that would raise hostile reactions in the whole Arab world as well as harm her own interests – a certain result of such an act.

The Egyptian Military High Command, when estimating the military situation, had assumed that should Britain use military force, the bulk of it would reach Egypt from the direction of Alexandria and Rashid. Therefore, the defence plan was determined on the basis of this possibility. So much so that when Khalid Muhi al-Din[1] told Gamal Abd al-Nasser[2] of the reports that he had received from one of his friends in Paris, which said that France would cooperate with Israel in attacking us, Gamal did not take this information seriously. He and Abd al-Hakim [Amir][3] believed that the purpose of passing this information on to us was to pressure us into concentrating our defence forces in the direction of Israel, thereby abandoning Alexandria and Rashid which were on the expected route for the British troops to take, as we had already estimated, without sufficient defence forces to enable us to repel them.

To avoid any skirmish or clash with those same forces [of Israel], Gamal Abd al-Nasser ordered all Egyptian fidaiyyun units stationed in the Gaza Strip to be taken out and their sabotage activities in Israel to be halted. We also decided on a passive stand concerning the freezing of our accounts deposited in banks in Britain and France. We also stressed continuously that those who owned Canal stocks would be compensated for their stocks and would receive their value according to the value of the stocks at closing time of the London Stock Exchange on the day preceding the nationalization.

Mahmud Yunis[4] was also instructed to make every possible effort

336

not to prevent the passage of any ship which wanted to go through the Canal, even if it failed to pay its passage dues. We wished to evade clashes and wanted to let these ships through the Canal so that preventing them would not serve as a pretext against us or a justification in world public opinion to attack us.

[Monday, 29 October 1956]

On Monday, 29 October 1956, at approx. 22:30 Gamal Abd al-Nasser's adjutant, Major Mahmud al-Jayyar, called and informed me that the President requested that I come to him immediately at the Joint Military Headquarters in Misr al-Jadida [Heliopolis]. I quickly went over there. There I found Gamal Abd al-Nasser and Abd al-Hakim [Amir] from whom I learned that Israel had attacked our forces. According to the reports Israeli parachutists had been dropped in the Mitla Pass in the Sinai Desert that same night. Up to that moment the exact situation was not yet known. We began looking at several maps and while doing so Zakariya [Muhi al-Din][5] arrived. Kamal [al-Din Hussein][6] arrived later and then Hussein al-Shafi'i.[7] Following a review of the situation and an assessment of the Israeli intentions, it was decided to respond to this aggression with force, that is – war. After ascertaining that a force had [indeed] been dropped in the Mitla Pass, it became clear to us that the operation was much larger than just an Israeli military attack on one of our posts, as had been its habit until now.

It appeared necessary to make use of our air-force that very same night in order to bomb the enemy's forces which had been dropped in the Pass. Also early the next morning to concentrate our bombing of the enemy's airfields and its planes. Also [our airforce] was to do its best to gain air superiority in order to be free and flexible to take action against the enemy's land forces.

Muhammad Sidqi Mahmud,[8] the Air Force C-o-S, arrived. He had received orders according to which our airforce was to immediately bomb the forces which had parachuted in the Pass, as well as the enemy's airfields.

Faced with this order, it was discernible that he [Sidqi Mahmud] was uneasy and embarrassed. He said that several difficulties arose which prevented our bomber planes from carrying out these missions at once. His excuse was that there wasn't enough fuel for [the planes] at the airport of Cairo West, which was the airfield for the bombers. As the general regulations were to refuel the gasoline tanks of the planes at the end of their daily flights, I suggested to him, after he mentioned this obstacle, that the planes would execute the orders that same night [by using] the fuel which was already in their tanks. Simultaneously, means would be taken to supply the needed quantities of fuel for the base in the morning ...

[Tuesday, 30 October 1956]

On Tuesday, 30 October 1956, the second day of the war, I went at 9 a.m. to the Joint Command [building] where I found Kamal al-Din Hussein with Abd al-Hakim. I noticed that Abd al-Hakim was nervously conducting the campaign giving out orders to every large and small unit, and the commanders in the field were not enjoying any freedom of action. [They] only took action after turning to him. This is a serious flaw when conducting battles. He [Abd al-Hakim Amir] as the C. in C., in the course of war should only deal with important matters. I also noticed that he was sending many forces into the battlefield with no clear justification. Apparently he wished to gain a quick victory, for as time went by without hearing of the victory he so desired, he kept sending new forces into the fray.

That same evening the Government convened. During the meeting we were informed of the [details of the] Anglo-French ultimatum.

While the contents of the ultimatum were being discussed in the Government I noticed that Gamal Abd al-Nasser was not taking it seriously. He was of the opinion that its aim was to cause most of our forces not to move towards the battlefield in Sinai, thereby giving Israel a chance to gain a victory as a result of the weakness and the limited forces fighting them. Gamal believed in that despite the previous events, and the seriousness with which England and France had moved their forces to Malta and Cyprus and [in spite of] their stand towards the different peaceful solutions [to the crisis].

Following a debate in the Government regarding the situation, it was decided to reject the ultimatum.

[Wednesday, 31 October 1956]

The next morning, Wednesday, 31 October 1956, I left for Military Headquarters. Zakariya [Muhi al-Din], Kamal [al-Din Hussein] and Gamal Abd al-Nasser arrived and we began discussing the military situation in light of the information which was coming in from the battlefield. However, I noticed that Abd al-Hakim [Amir] was continuing to despatch forces to the front, more than were necessary according to my estimation. This was in order to gain a quick victory.

When we analysed the course of the war while looking at the

maps, we expressed our fear of the possibility that the English and the French would drop forces in the Canal zone in order to cut off our forces in Sinai. But Gamal looked upon this as an unlikely possibility and was not convinced of this view.

... At seven p.m. Gamal came in and immediately following his arrival there was an air attack over Cairo. We learned that British Air Force planes had carried out this attack. We also found out that in the air battles that had taken place over Sinai, the number of Mystère planes which participated far exceeded the number of such planes in the Israeli Air Force. The obvious explanation for this was that the French Air Force was also participating in these operations over Sinai. It became clear that the goal of England and France with Israel's cooperation was to push our army into Sinai. Then later, under the pretext of defending the Canal and ensuring free passage through it they would intervene and drop their forces in the Canal zone, thereby isolating our army which was in the Sinai desert east of the Canal. They would then move to destroy and annihilate it. On the basis of this evaluation we discussed the withdrawal of the whole army from Sinai, even from the Gaza Strip, Rafah, el-Arish and Sharm el-Sheikh. At 22:20 the decision was taken to totally withdraw all our forces from these areas. Abd al-Hakim started to give the orders for the retreat.

At about eleven p.m., a second air-attack was carried out over Cairo. We went down to the shelter in the Headquarters building. We were later informed that enemy paratroopers were being dropped in the area of the (horse) racing [arena] in Misr al-Jadida, which is near the Military Headquarters building and Gamal's home. Following this news the situation became tense and nervous. Abd al-Hakim said: 'Take shelter everybody and leave me with the army.' Salah Salim[9] insisted that we leave the Headquarters building at once and take shelter. He asked us to come to his house in order to discuss the situation calmly far away from any danger. Zakariya mentioned three flats that had been equipped for use in an emergency, should we in any circumstances have to go underground. [Bughdadi wrote 'underground' in English.]

This excitement was a result of a misleading estimate on the part of several officers from Headquarters who surmised that the purpose of dropping the soldiers was to break into the Headquarters building and to Gamal Abd al-Nasser's house in order to arrest him. They had forgotten that such a suicide mission would be doomed to shameful failure and no military command would think of such a thing.

What [really] happened is that several attacking planes threw a number of flares over the racing course in Misr al-Jadida in order to illuminate the military targets they intended to bomb. Several air-defence people who were in the area thought that soldiers were being dropped. They notified Headquarters. The news was quickly picked up for a fact which caused all the confusion and excitement.

However, after some time Gamal [Abd al-Nasser] gained control over himself. The situation at that moment was critical. The fate of our country, and possibly that of future generations, was dependent upon Gamal Abd al-Nasser's behaviour. Our honour and the honour of this generation were dependent upon him.

I felt that suddenly we were overcome by confusion and many of us were paralysed when it became clear that England and France had entered the war. Indeed, it was a very difficult situation, for the result of the campaign was predictable. It was unreasonable to assume that we could overcome both of them and their protégé Israel. The question which bothered each one of us at that moment was whether to continue with the war and bear the consequences of destruction and devastation, or to save our country from ruin by surrendering and going underground in order to maintain the struggle against this conquest which would be thrust upon us. Most [of us] were inclined to go underground in order to fight. Gamal was confused and did not express his opinion immediately nor did he reveal his inclination.

Our evaluation was that the British Air Force would concentrate its bombing of our airfields early the next morning in an attempt to destroy our planes to enable it [the RAF] to have [total] air control. Relying on this estimation [Nasser] demanded that precautions be taken to defend those airfields and the planes stationed there, as well as actions to strengthen the defence measures for them.

[Thursday, 1 November, 1956]

On Thursday, 1 November 1956 I woke up early to the sound of exploding bombs from the planes attacking the airfields of al-Maza and Misr al-Jadida. I went to Gamal's home. I found him in a much better mood than the previous day. I found him even lively. He had started to prepare the address he was to read to the nation over the radio. In it he explained the reasons which had compelled him to take the decision to withdraw our forces from Sinai. Later we walked to Military Headquarters at Kubri al-Quba. Gamal read the address from there. I went with Gamal to his home. [Gamal] requested Mahmud al-Jayyar[10] to contact the ministers and to convene them to a meeting at 7 p.m. We discussed the need to go on resisting even if we lose the battle. For in so doing we would be continuing the mission which we preached.

During the Government meeting Gamal spoke about the enemy's plan and aims and the reasons that had compelled us to withdraw our forces from Sinai. But the Government members kept silent.

At the end of the meeting we returned to his [Gamal's] house. We continued to discuss the situation. I told him my opinion concerning the war as it was being conducted by Abd al-Hakim and his bad mood following what had happened. I asked him to have a talk with him.

[Friday, 2 November 1956]

On Friday, 2 November, we woke up to the sound of explosions caused by an aerial attack and the thunder of anti-aircraft guns. When the attack was over, Gamal spoke on the telephone with Abd al-Hakim and asked him to come over to have breakfast with us. Abd al-Hakim arrived and Gamal requested him to visit the military units in the Canal zone in order to uplift his spirits as well as [thinking] that the soldiers' morale would rise if they were to see him amongst them. Abd al-Hakim agreed to conduct such a tour and said that he would do so in a few days' time. He claimed that if he were to go that very day he would find the forces in disarray due to their retreat. He [Nasser] asked about his [Amir's] opinion as to sending Kamal al-Din Hussein to Ismailia in order to take over the command of its defence. He [Amir] did not object. Gamal contacted Kamal by telephone and asked him to come. Following his arrival, Gamal asked him to accept the defence of the area of Ismailia and Kamal readily accepted. He left for his mission that same day.

I went with Abd al-Hakim [Amir] to Military Headquarters. I stayed in Abd al-Hakim's office till 15:30.

Then I decided that it was only right for me to see my children at the house of one of my relatives to which they had been taken in al-Duqa. But a couple of minutes after I got there Gamal called and asked me to come to his bureau in the P.M's Office. He told me that Abd al-Hakim was with him. I discerned from the sound of his voice that something was bothering him. When I got there only Gamal and Abd al-Hakim were in the office. I started to talk with them about the people's morale and their behaviour as I had observed them during the aerial attack while I was on my way from Headquarters to al-Duqa [and about] the scorn with which the people greeted these attacks and their high morale. Then Zakariya [Muhi al-Din] arrived. Salah Salim telephoned Gamal Abd al-Nasser and asked to meet with him. Gamal set the meeting with him an hour after the telephone call. Then Gamal got up and asked to be excused. He asked Abd al-Hakim to discuss with us the subject he [Amir] had previously raised with him.

Abd al-Hakim's opening remarks were: 'The continuation of the war will bring about the destruction of the country and the death of numerous citizens. As a result of this the people will hate the regime and those who uphold it. He [Abd al-Hakim Amir] prefers, in order to prevent such devastation to ask for a cease fire.' This was in short the content of his words.

As I had not expected to hear such things from him I was completely taken aback. I therefore reacted very emotionally and excitedly. I noted that although we were about to lose the campaign we must give in honourably. Our surrendering now would only give rise to the people's scorn for us. The hatred he [Amir] fears is far easier to bear than the scorn. All that we have lost until now have been only a few material things. Even if there were to be a number of human sacrifices these would be on behalf of the mission and the duty to which we were bound. The present situation demands that we go on with the war until the capital [Cairo] falls. Then we shall review our situation. I do not mean that we should behave like Hitler and never surrender until all the country is totally destroyed. But in my opinion we should continue the war so that we shall not lose the people's esteem nor the respect of other nations.

Gamal returned and heard some of my words. He sat down but did not utter a word. He frowned. I did not know how he had reacted to Abd al-Hakim's words when they had discussed this subject. Zakariya's opinion was that we must go on with the war if only for a while.

During the course of this debate Salah [Salim] arrived. He started by saying: 'We must prevent further calamities and destruction in this country.' He repeated what Abd al-Hakim had said previously. He proposed that Gamal address the nation and declare that for the benefit of the people and in order to prevent [further] disaster and destruction he [Nasser] was about to request a cease-fire and a surrender. Then he added: 'Let us rise and give ourselves up to Trevelyan, the English Ambassador.'

But I could not put up with these words of his and I answered him:

342

'My opinion, Salah, is that it is more honourable for me to commit suicide, before doing such a thing [surrender].'

Here Gamal interjected: 'Far better for us all to commit suicide here, before taking such a step.' He asked Zakariya to bring some vials with phosphate-cyanide so that there would be enough for us all should the need arise. He stressed: 'I am serious about what I've said.' Here Salah said that he was withdrawing his proposal.

The debate continued with our trying to explain that we were honour bound to continue the fighting until the capital fell and until we reached the limit where crossing it and continuing to fight would be madness. After that we could go underground in order to continue the resistance. Before going underground Gamal would empower somebody to negotiate with the aggressors to end the fighting, so that we should not abandon the country without leadership when we went underground. Salah expressed his consent to this approach. Abd al-Hakim said that this had been his intention and also agreed. After that the issue was never raised again.

During the meeting Lt. Colonel Salah Nasr[11] came in and told Gamal that Sulayman Hafiz[12] wanted to meet him, Gamal, that night concerning an important matter. Gamal said: 'I cannot meet him for I do not want anybody to see him meeting me.' He requested me to meet with him [Sulayman Hafiz] in his place. But Salah Nasr returned and informed us that Sulayman Hafiz wished Abd al-Hakim to be present at his meeting with me. We arranged to have the meeting in the house where my family was staying in al-Duqa, at 20:30.

I went with Abd al-Hakim to the house in al-Duqa accompanied by Major Ali Shafiq,[13] Abd al-Hakim's secretary. We later sent him to bring Sulayman Hafiz who arrived shortly.

We asked Sulayman what the matter was and he came straight to the point: 'I asked to meet with Gamal in order to raise before him the proposal I had previously set before Ahmad Husni,[14] Minister of Justice. Did he not tell you about it?'

We questioned him as to what proposal he had in mind?

He said: 'My suggestion is to present the attacking countries with the request to turn Egypt into a neutral country like Switzerland, as well as the Suez Canal. These countries will vouch for Egypt's neutrality. All this in order to evade the disasters of war, the destruction, devastation and conquest. This proposal would be submitted by somebody other than Gamal Abd al-Nasser. There was nobody more appropriate for this mission than Muhammad Naguib.'[15]

343

Abd al-Hakim replied that this proposal had already been presented by Gamal to the Menzies[16] Committee but had been rejected.

Sulayman said: 'But now the situation has changed.' He asked: 'What do you intend to do?' We answered: 'Continue with popular resistance.'

He said: 'Popular resistance requires organization and morale. It takes a long time to get organized and you haven't done a thing about it. Therefore you must trust the morale. This morale can only be achieved if at the head of the popular resistance there is a person as popular as Muhammad Naguib. Gamal Abd al-Nasser must return to the Sixth Infantry Battalion.'[17]

When we questioned him as to why Gamal should return to the Sixth Infantry Battalion he said: 'Because people say that Gamal Abd al-Nasser confuses his personal glory with the future of the country.'

I said to him: 'Who is Muhammad Naguib? People have forgotten him. It is Gamal's recent deeds which have caused Muhammad Naguib to be forgotten'.

He said: 'I am telling you the truth that [other] people will not reveal to you, Gamal is hated and unpopular.'

Abd al-Hakim asked him: 'If that is so how do you explain the results Gamal achieved in the national referendum? They prove just the opposite of what you claim.'

He replied: 'We all know how these matters are conducted, especially when the man in question stands at the helm of power in the country.'

I said: 'We all know that all those who had the right to vote were promised total freedom of choice.'

He said: 'That's true. But fear made them evade the problems that could bother each of them if they had not voted for Gamal.'

Abd al-Hakim answered him: 'You know Muhammad Naguib and I know him too. He will not succeed in such a mission.'

Sulayman Hafiz replied that that was true but he [Muhammad Naguib] would symbolize the popular struggle and perhaps Gamal Abd al-Nasser would serve as his deputy and in practice lead the struggle under Muhammad Naguib's banner.

Finally we made it clear to him that the struggle would go on but without Muhammad Naguib. That was the end of that subject. We discussed the past when he had cooperated with us at the beginning of the revolution. Then he realized we were in a hurry and asked to leave. We left the house with him.

... I went to my home in Misr al-Jadida. I preferred my home despite the fact that I knew it was totally exposed to direct hits from attacking planes as it was so near the al-Maza air-base, the airfield of Misr al-Jadida and the military area of al-Maza. These areas had been attacked by enemy planes. I did so in the hope that one of the pilots would make a mistake and my house would be hit by one of the bombs. I would thereby end my life and not be a witness to the impending disaster which I pictured to myself.

That is what I wrote down in my diary concerning that day. My diary expresses the difficult and cruel circumstances we had to go through in the course of that crisis.

[Saturday, 3 November 1956]

[Next morning] I telephoned Gamal Abd al-Nasser at the Revolutionary Council Headquarters [building] during one of the [air] raids. It was about 10 a.m. He asked me to come to him and added that he had looked for me the night before. When I reached him I found Major Salah Desuqi,[18] liaison officer of the Ministry of the Interior with him. I described the aerial attacks to him and the response of our artillery, and that one of the enemy planes had been shot down near the Misr al-Jadida air-base. I had passed by there to see the crashed parts on my way to him. In truth, I lied to him for what had fallen by this air-base were none other than the reserve fuel tanks of one of the planes. When Gamal heard these words he took my face between his two hands and kissed me.

He said that he did not know a thing of what the Army was doing and that the military forces had dispersed throughout the streets of Cairo leaving the Canal zone, despite the decision that they would retreat from Sinai in order to defend that area. He added that he was completely cut off from Military Headquarters and no information of battle orders, the movement of the forces or any defence plans reached him. He pointed out that after all he was the one who held primary responsibility in the state. [He added] that apparently it was Salah Salim who turned out to be in charge. For his [Salim's] proposals were being implemented and he was giving the orders. He also noted that he, Salah, was the one to persuade Abd al-Hakim to surrender and cease the fighting and that in fact Salah was ruling over him [Amir]. Gamal was excited as he said that. In fact he almost lost his self-control.

I asked him to calm down and to forget what had happened and to try to remedy what seemed to him to be a mistake. [I also told him] that he must think of what we should do in order to face the future. I offered to go and bring Abd al-Hakim to him so that we could discuss

345

all these matters with him and carry out all that could be consented upon. He agreed but remarked that Salah Salim was present at his [Amir's] office at Headquarters. He [Gamal] asked me not to bring him together with Abd al-Hakim. I left him and went to Abd al-Hakim. Salah Desuqi accompanied me and I went with him in his car. On our way there, Salah Desuqi suggested that we arrest Salah Salim, bring him to my house and have police officers guard him. But I turned down the idea. When we got to Abd al-Hakim's office I found Salah Salim and Hasan Ibrahim[19] there. After a while I informed Abd al-Hakim that Gamal wished to meet with him. He agreed and asked that we wait till he finished taking care of a number of matters. While we were waiting Gamal asked for Abd al-Hakim over the telephone and talked to him. At the end of their conversation Abd al-Hakim told Salah [Salim]: 'Go to Suez to be in charge of its defence.' I thereby concluded that Gamal wished to detach Salah from Abd al-Hakim.

Then I went with Abd al-Hakim to Gamal. We began discussing the situation. During the last part of the debate Zakariya and Hasan Ibrahim were also present. Gamal spoke at this meeting, frankly stressing to Abd al-Hakim that he [Nasser] was concerned about being out of contact with the military command and being in the dark as to what was going on despite his responsibilities. [He also said] that Salah [Salim] was in fact running the state . However, Abd al-Hakim answered him: 'You know that I have a personality and an opinion of my own and I shall not give in to Salah or anybody else.' Gamal was agitated as he spoke while Abd al-Hakim was self-controlled as he asked Gamal what he expected of him. He [Abd al-Hakim] added that he had no objection to Gamal taking upon himself the command of the army and that he was ready to act under his [Gamal's] command. However, Gamal replied: 'I am not asking to undertake the command but am asking to know what is going on and for our opinion to be sought. We have also had military experience and understand these matters.' Finally, after a heated argument it was concluded that Abd al-Hakim would send two officers from his staff who would act as liaison officers with Gamal's bureau. This would enable him [Gamal] to get a full and detailed picture.

That evening we met with the two liaison officers sent over by Abd al-Hakim and discussed with them the plan for the defence of Cairo. We learned that until that evening the plan had been to defend Rashid West, until the retreating forces reorganized. Gamal said to them: 'This means that now, we in Cairo are outside the protected area.' They answered: 'Yes.' While discussing the defence plan of the Canal zone we found it to be weak, for most of our military forces had already withdrawn to the Cairo region. He [Gamal] asked for the defence means of that area to be strengthened.

According to the two liaison officers it was difficult for enemy forces to land [inzal in Arabic] at Port Said or Suez. Should the enemy attempt such a landing it would take place in Western Alexandria. Therefore no great importance had been attached to strengthening the defence means of the Canal area. We pointed out the mistake in their estimation because the British–French ultimatum determined the area which they threatened to conquer. Politically, due to world public opinion, it was inconceivable that they would invade all Egypt in order to reach the Canal area – the subject of the dispute, because in that event their losses would be numerous. It would also lengthen the time of the operation. Anyhow, that was the assessment of the Egyptian Military Command.

At that time many [people] expressed strong criticism against Abd al-Hakim and the army. But we must be fair, for the burden was too heavy for Abd al-Hakim to bear alone, especially after England and France entered the war. The psychological factor had great influence over the behaviour of many people. Furthermore, many were paralysed when it turned out that the two countries had entered the war in addition to Israel.

When discussing the situation following the nationalization of the Canal Company, some of the colleagues had at that time expressed the view that, should things turn out as in fact they had, it would be like the flood. Those who at that time predicted the present situation were now the first to attack Abd al-Hakim, and compared him to General al-Muwawi, Head of the Military Operation during the Palestine War of 1948 – and his failure in that war.

[Sunday, 4 November 1956]

On Sunday, 4 November 1956 while we were still staying in the Revolutionary Council Building, having woken up, I went to Gamal's room in order to have breakfast with him. As I went into his room I asked him: 'How are you today?' He answered me that he had not slept all night. He admitted that he had wept and that he had apparently lost the state. I was moved by his condition. I sat down to breakfast with him while my mind was wandering. I did not know what to do to help him or myself in this difficult situation in which we were involved.

We watched the events closely till evening. At about 23:00 Gamal asked me, while I was sitting with Zakariya, to come up with him to the top floor of the Revolutionary Council Building on the pretext of getting some fresh air on the balcony overlooking the Nile. We left Zakariya and went up. Having stood there for a while, observing the waters of the Nile, darkness overcame all parts of the city and silence was everywhere. Gamal said: 'I have decided to leave for Port Said tonight to see how the army will react when they find out that their President has gone to Port Said to take part in the fighting himself. You must take care of political matters and propaganda.'

I answered him: 'I'll go with you. At least we shall die in the defence of our country.' But he asked me to rethink my decision. When he realized that I was insistent upon going with him he told me: 'We'll leave at midnight.'

[Monday, 5 November 1956]

A short while after midnight we left by car in the direction of Ismailia on our way to Port Said. Along this route we saw many destroyed military vehicles either turned over or abandoned. Some of them were burned out and some appeared to be whole. Apparently, at least some were damaged as a result of being hit by planes which continued to attack the forces moving along this road on their way to Cairo, following their retreat. Gamal asked me about each tank or vehicle as we passed by it: 'What happened to it?' I felt that he was in another world, lost in thought. I realized that he was very tired due to the situation. I tried to ease things for him. I thought it to be my duty when my country was going through such a time. I knew that Gamal was a symbol of the revolution and not only in Egypt, but in the entire region. All my hope was that this revolution would continue to exist and not die out. That was dependent on our behaviour during these days and particularly Gamal's own behaviour.

On our way to Ismailia Gamal said in a sad emotional tone, after he saw the wrecked vehicles and tanks by the sides of the road: 'These are the remnants of a destroyed army.' He was sorry about the sums that had been spent on armaments saying: '103 million Egyptian pounds down the drain.' He also added in English: 'I was defeated by my own army.' I replied: 'Don't give up.' And he answered me: 'You know I never despair.' But I felt that a broken man was in front of me, and upon him and how he behaved depended the future of my country. I felt sympathy towards him and even at that moment felt that my heart went out to him more than at

348

any other time in the past. I was ready to sacrifice myself for him the moment he would break down and the whole thing was over, and [even] now that he was weak and helpless.

This is what my diaries say and they are an expression of my feelings during a difficult situation and under cruel circumstances when emotions are very strong.

At about 03:30 we reached Ismailia. We turned to the building where the headquarters of Kamal al-Din Hussein was located. One of the guards directed us to an entrance that was not the main gate. We went up a wooden staircase to the first floor where Kamal was staying. I was watching Gamal and compared the way he looked at that moment and at other times when he was triumphant and felt powerful. I knew what was going on through his mind at such a situation: helplessness despite his being the leader of a revolution and President of a republic.

Kamal, who had [just] woken up when he heard of our arrival came towards us. I noticed that his morale was high in contrast to ours. Perhaps it was due to the fact that he was involved in preparing the defence of Ismailia, or to his lack of knowledge of what was going on in Cairo and the army. He was enthusiastic and confident as to his situation there. He knew of our plans to complete our journey to Port Said that same night, but advised us to stay in Ismailia till the following evening, for if we were to continue on our way we would be exposed to attacking enemy planes at dawn. We therefore decided that it would be preferable to stay in Ismailia and spend the whole of the next day with our military forces there and to continue on our way when it got dark. We went to bed at about 5 a.m. I stayed in one room with Gamal. A moment after we were left alone in the room Gamal turned to me: 'I am tired.'

We woke up at 08:00. Kamal came in and informed us that the enemy had dropped paratroopers in Port Said and that the first group had dropped over the al-Gamil airport, at the al-Raswa Bridge and in the vicinity of the cemetery. [Despite the fact that] this group had suffered heavy casualties the enemy returned and dropped another group and the fighting was continuing. He also informed us that Abd al-Hakim had contacted him to advise us to return to Cairo. Kamal supported this. Gamal did not object, for the situation had changed following these events, including the forces of enemy paratroopers being dropped in Port Said. ... Therefore, Gamal ordered his own car to be ready to return to Cairo. We descended to the operations room where the military situation in Port Said was explained to us over a map and we were given

349

information that had reached them concerning the battles there. Then we went out to one of the balconies of the Headquarters building and saw the townspeople as they were going back and forth as if life was going on naturally and the war was not taking place a couple of kilometres away. Each one of them had a rifle over his shoulder and even a street vendor sitting on the pavement had his rifle beside him. This scene encouraged us. We felt that the atmosphere in Ismailia was totally different from the atmosphere which had engulfed us at the Revolutionary Council Building in Cairo. Perhaps that was due to our isolation in the Revolutionary Council Building as we did not see anybody or hear anything except news about our military forces and their retreat from Sinai and what happened to them as they withdrew and the rate of their losses. But our observance of the people of Ismailia, who are the citizens closest to the Canal zone, assisted us to regain some of the morale which we had lost.

Having met several officers who were in Ismailia we made our way back to Cairo ...

At about noon we reached the Revolutionary Council Building. Zakariya began to give us the information he had at hand about the campaign going on in Port Said. We continued to follow this fighting throughout the day. When Lt. Colonel Salah al-Mughi, commander of the Egyptian forces in Port Said, called us, he stated that the British commander, in charge of the paratroopers who had been dropped near the pumping station had asked him [al-Mughi] to send somebody with whom he could negotiate the surrender of Port Said. Gamal gave the order that no man should go, and that he must demand that the commander of the enemy forces give in to him, together with his soldiers.

The communiqué of the allied command (the English and the French) that evening declared that the number of air attacks that their planes had carried out that day over Port Said alone had reached 473 sorties.

[Tuesday, 6 November 1956]

Tuesday, 6 November 1956 dawned and Port Said proudly continued its resistance. But from the early morning, the navy of the enemy had begun shelling al-Balah quarter very heavily, in preparation for the landing of its soldiers in that area. Their planes also bombed the city at the same time very heavily. But the people in Port Said and the armed forces stationed there, as well as the civilian police, heroically continued their resistance, despite the fact that they did not have the necessary means at their disposal. However, the forces which landed on the beaches of Port Said did not succeed in conquering the city. Fighting continued bravely till midnight. This was the battle for our honour and we should be proud.

The UN Secretary-General, Dag Hammarskjöld, that evening announced that Britain and France had agreed to a cease-fire in Egypt as of midnight of Tuesday, 6 November 1956 GMT, i.e. at 2 o'clock in the morning of Wednesday 7 November, Cairo time. [He also announced] that Britain and France had instructed their forces to carry it out.

[Wednesday, 7 November 1956]

However, the invading forces were put out by the fact that they had not managed to break into the city from any direction and had not succeeded in penetrating it. Therefore, on Wednesday, 7 November, despite the decision to cease fire, they began to besiege the town using their tanks in order to complete their blockade and in order to get out of their difficult military position. They opened fire on whoever tried to get close to them and broke into the populated quarter where they were met with strong popular resistance to their advance. They also began pillaging the customs warehouses which are situated there.

[Thursday, 8 November 1956]

On Thursday, 8 November 1956 in the morning, I went to Gamal's office in the Revolutionary Council Building. (Nasser began talking to Bughdadi concerning their personal relationship.)

Gamal's conversation with me was cut short because Zakariya came in. Following his arrival the conversation was conducted amongst the three of us regarding the mistakes the army had made during the war. We summed up that there was no escape from immediately transferring some of our military units to the Eastern Bank of the Canal in order to occupy positions in the Sinai Desert. These positions must be as far away as possible from the Eastern Bank, and all this prior to the arrival of the International Police Force which would clean out all Israeli forces from the Sinai Desert. We concluded that I would go with Zakariya to Abd al-Hakim to discuss these mistakes with him and [to talk] about the need to despatch several of our army units across the Canal to the Eastern Bank.

We met with Abd al-Hakim. He listened to us and to our remarks and reacted to them with a strange serenity. He controlled himself and did not even raise his voice.

351

[Saturday, 10 November 1956]

On Saturday, 10 November 1956 I was in the Revolutionary Council Building present at [a meeting] between Gamal Abd al-Nasser and Foreign Minister, Dr. Mahmud Fawzi[20] and Ali Sabri,[21] who was in charge of Gamal's office. When the meeting was over and Dr. Fawzi left, Gamal Abd al-Nasser used harsh words against the army. He explained to Ali Sabri his complaints about the army and about Abd al-Hakim and the spirit of surrender to which they had succumbed, the paralysis which had struck them following the entrance of the English and French into the war and the fact that the army did not heed his commands despite his contacting them repeatedly. He also mentioned Salah Salim's part. In other words he recalled the development of the various events during the last couple of days and the role each one played. I commented on his words and [said] that he is [like] Abd al-Hakim's elder brother. That the situation was difficult and that we must act to repair what had been spoiled and that he must be patient as that was one of his duties. Circumstances force each one of us to tolerate the other's behaviour. I suggested that he invite Abd al-Hakim to dinner or lunch and he would undoubtedly accept the invitation.

Following the conversation I felt the seriousness of the dispute and the tension between Gamal Abd al-Nasser and Abd al-Hakim. I decided to go and meet Abd al-Hakim in the afternoon to talk with him in an attempt to patch up the dispute.

I went to Abd al-Hakim's office at seven that evening. I met him and spent two hours with him. The conversation was about this dispute which existed between him and Gamal. I tried to bridge over their differences and overcome the misunderstanding. I noticed Abd al-Hakim's goodwill. He said that he was aware of the delicacy of the situation and that his manhood prevented him from behaving in any way that could harm the country. At the end of the meeting we hugged and kissed.

Following this conversation I went over to Gamal Abd al-Nasser in the Revolutionary Council [Building] and found Anwar al-Sadat[22] with him. He was speaking on the telephone, and I understood from the conversation that he was talking to Abd al-Hakim. He invited him to have dinner with us. I informed Gamal that I had met Abd al-Hakim and that he had shown goodwill. After a while Abd al-Hakim arrived and we had dinner together. The atmosphere was relaxed.

[Thursday, 15 November 1956]

Gamal Abd al-Nasser invited me to dinner on 15 November, and informed me that Abd al-Hakim would be joining us. When I went over I found him with Abd al-Hakim. The conversation amongst us turned to the events which had taken place in the last few days and the battles which our army had waged against the Israeli forces before taking the decision to withdraw. I told Abd al-Hakim what I had heard and gathered from the officers of the air force – that they had lost their faith in their commanders as a result of the mistakes which had been made. This in turn compelled him to take steps against those in command in order to rekindle the faith between the commanders and their subordinates. He was to hold an inquiry amongst those commanders whose negligence caused these errors and to relieve them for other duties. Gamal intervened in the conversation and giving Sidqi Mahmud, C-o-S airforce, as an example, suggested that he be transferred to the post of deputy War Minister for air affairs.

However, Abd al-Hakim answered saying: 'They have a justification for what has happened. If they were mistaken then you must look upon me as responsible and it is better that I too would resign.'

Gamal responded: 'You have a political position and we are discussing the principle.'

Gamal wished to stop discussing the issue in order to avoid a clash. He therefore continued the conversation with another topic.

[Sunday, 18 November 1956]

Three days having gone by since this conversation, I visited Gamal. He discussed with me Abd al-Hakim's words in which he had implied that he too was as responsible as the other military commanders, and that he preferred to resign his command of the army. Gamal noted that in his opinion Abd al-Hakim would take such a step but was only waiting for the right moment and for the atmosphere to calm down. He [also] noted that he knew Abd al-Hakim well and that he was obstinate. I recounted to him what Abd al-Hakim had said to me about the delicacy of the situation when I had called upon him to do away with any misunderstanding between the two of them.

I asked Gamal to take action in order to prevent Abd al-Hakim's resignation for that would raise various comments and would weaken the revolution.

353

Gamal answered: 'Time will solve everything. In my opinion we must leave Abd al-Hakim alone. He will think and will know whether he was right or wrong.'

[Tuesday, 1 January 1957]

On Tuesday, 1 January 1957 I returned from the town of Port Said, [having gone there] since I was in charge of its reconstruction. I visited Gamal who told me that Abd al-Hakim had sent him a letter with Zakariya in which he requested him [Nasser] to accept his [Abd al-Hakim's] resignation for he felt that his role was over. When I asked him on which day Abd al-Hakim had sent him this resignation he replied that it had been a week ago, last Monday. I said that the matter had to be dealt with for the [political] situation was still vague and the negotiations were still going on. This would have a bearing on our positions and also because Abd al-Hakim was well liked by the people and the army. I queried whether Gamal had contacted him in order to settle the matter. He answered in the negative saying: 'I am letting him think it over until he'll recognize the mistake he has made.' When I pointed out to him that Abd al-Hakim might interpret that as lack of interest in him, and that would complicate matters even more, he answered that he himself would talk with him and that the subject of the resignation must remain confidentially between us. I understood that he did not wish me to discuss the matter with Abd al-Hakim.

[Wednesday, 2 January 1957]

On Wednesday, 2 January 1957 in the evening, Gamal called me and said that the matter of Abd al-Hakim's resignation had been settled.

[Saturday, January 5 1957]

On Saturday, 5 January 1957 Gamal and Abd al-Hakim together visited the wounded [soldiers] in the al-Aguza Hospital in order to put an end to the rumours about their [strained] relationship.

[Sunday, 6 January 1957]

On Sunday, 6 January, Gamal telephoned me at Port Said. I learned from him that he had sent a letter to Salah Salim in which he made it clear to Salah Salim that since cooperation between them was impossible, he was relieved from his post as head of the newspaper.[23]

NOTES

1. *Khalid Muhi al-Din (1922–)*: member of the RCC; graduated from the Military College 1940; Major 1952; dismissed from the army and the RCC following his attempt to back General Naguib by leading a tank corp on 22 February 1954; went into exile; returned to Egypt in 1955; Editor of the daily *al-Masa* October 1956 to March 1959; Chief Editor of *al-Akhbar* 1964; Member of the Presidential Council of the World Peace Council; Secretary-General of the Egyptian National Peace Council 1967. He was depicted as the 'Red Major'.

2. *Gamal Abd al-Nasser (1918–70)*: member of the RCC from its inception and its chairman; graduated from the Military College 1938; posted to Sudan 1939; instructor at the military college 1941; as a major participated in the invading Egyptian force into Palestine 1948–49; Lt. Colonel 1951; one of the founders of the Free Officers who carried out the military coup d'état, July 1952; Deputy Secretary-General of the Revolutionary Council May 1953; Deputy Prime Minister and Minister of the Interior June 1953; Prime Minister February 1954; elected President in June 1956; President of the UAR February 1958–61; resigned following the June defeat in 1967 but withdrew his resignation; died in September 1970.

3. *Abd al-Hakim Amir (1919–67)*: member of the RCC; graduated from the Military College 1939; Major 1948; promoted to General and appointed C-in-C of the armed forces June 1953, and Minister of War, 1954; Field-Marshal, Vice-President, Minister of War, 1958; member of the Presidential Council 1962; First Vice-President and Deputy Supreme Commander of the Armed Forces 1964; after the defeat in June 1967 he committed suicide in prison.

4. *Mahmud Yunis (1912–)*: army engineer 1937; Military Operation Directorate 1943; Staff Officer's College 1944 and 1947; Director Technical Affairs Office, GHQ 1952; Chairman and Managing Director, General Petroleum Authority 1954; Managing Director and Deputy Chairman Egyptian Suez Canal Authority July 1956; Chairman of the Suez Canal Authority 1957; Deputy Minister for Transport and Communications 1965–67; Minister of Oil Transport 1967.

5. *Zakariya Muhi al-Din (1918–)*: member of the RCC; graduated from the Military College 1938; Major 1948; Lt. Colonel 1950; Minister of the Interior and Director of Intelligence and Internal Security Services 1953; Vice-President 1961; member of the Presidential Council 1962; Prime Minister 1965–66.

6. *Kamal al-Din Hussein (1921–)*: member of the RCC; graduated from the Military College 1939; Major 1948; Minister for Social Affairs 1954; Minister for Education 1956; member of the Presidential Council 1962–64, when he left public office.

7. *Hussein al-Shafi'i (1918–)*: member of the RCC, graduated from the Military College 1938; Lt. Col. 1950; Minister for War and Marine 1954; Minister for Social Affairs 1954; Minister of State for Planning Affairs 1957; Deputy Prime Minister for Social Affairs 1967; Deputy Prime Minister 1968–1970; later Vice-President under Sadat.

8. *Muhammad Sidqi Mahmud*: resigned as Air Force C-o-S on 11 June 1967; arrested for political reasons in September 1967.

9. *Salah Salim (1920–1962)*: member of the RCC; graduated from the Military College 1939; Major 1948; Minister for National Guidance and Minister of State for Sudan Affairs 1954–55; editor of the daily *al-Sh'ab* 1955–56; dismissed after the Suez War.

10. Nasser's adjutant.

11. *Salah Nasr (1920–)*: member of the Free Officers; graduated from the Military College 1939; Major 1950; Director of the C-in-C (Amir) Office for General Affairs 1953–56; later Director of General Intelligence Service.

12. *Sulayman Hafiz*, politician in Farouq's regime; chief Political Adviser to General Naguib after the July revolution; Deputy Prime Minister (Naguib) and Minister of the Interior September 1952 June 1953.

13. *Ali Safwat Shafiq (1925–)*: graduated from the Military College 1946; Captain 1950; officer in the C-in-C's Bureau for General Affairs 1953; later secretary to the C-in-C.

14. *Ahmad Husni*: Minister of Justice 1956; The Egyptian Region Executive Minister of Justice 1959–61; Minister of State of the United Government of the UAR 1961.

15. *Muhammad Naguib (1901–84)*: Graduated from Cairo University (Law) and Military College 1921; Colonel 1948; second in command of the Egyptian invading army in Palestine 1948–49; General 1950; Director General of Infantry 1951; Chairman of the RCC 1952; President and Prime Minister June 1953; resigned as Prime Minister April 1954; resigned as President October 1954 and placed under house arrest; released from house arrest in 1971 after Nasser's death.

16. *Robert Menzies (1894–1982)*: Australian statesman; Attorney-General 1934–39, leader of the United Australia Party from 1939; Prime Minister 1939–41, 1949–66.

17. Nasser served during the Arab–Israel War 1948–49 in the 6th Battalion which participated in the Egyptian invasion of Palestine. The battalion was the first to encounter Israeli forces in the South of Israel. He was beseiged in the al-Faluja pocket.

18. *Salah Desuqi*: police officer.

19. *Hasan Ibrahim (1917–)*: member of the RCC; graduated from the Military College 1938, and Flight College 1939; Squadron Commander 1952; State Minister of the Presidency 1954; Minister for National Production 1954–56; member of the Presidential Council 1962–64; Vice-President 1964–65.

20. *Mahmud Fawzi (1900–81)*: entered diplomatic service 1923; Vice-Consul New York and New Orleans 1926–29; Consul-General Liverpool 1937–40; Director, Department of Nationalities, Ministry of Foreign Affairs 1940–41; Consul-General, Jerusalem 1941–44; Egyptian delegate to the UN and Representative to the Security Council 1946; Ambassador to Britain 1952; Foreign Minister 1952–64; member of the Presidential Council 1962–64; Deputy Prime Minister for Foreign Affairs 1967–68; Prime Minister 1970–72; Vice-President 1972–74.

21. *Ali Sabri (1920–)*: member of the Executive Committee of the Free Officers; graduated from the Military College 1939 and Flight College 1940; Wing-Commander 1952; Free Officers Liaison with the US Embassy after the coup; Director of Nasser's Bureau for Political Affairs 1954–60; Minister for Presidential Affairs 1960; Prime Minister 1962–65; Vice-President 1965–67; Chairman of the Arab Socialist Union 1965–69; Vice-President May 1970–May 1971.

22. *Anwar al-Sadat (1918–1981)*: member of the RCC; graduated from the Military College 1938; Major 1950; Lt. Colonel 1951; announced the revolution over Radio Cairo July 1952; editor of the daily *al-Jumhuriya*; Minister of State and Secretary General of the Islamic Congress 1954; Secretary-General of the National Union 1958; Speaker of the National Assembly 1960; member of the Presidential Council 1962–64; Vice-President 1964–66; President September 1970–81.

23. The daily *al-Sha'b*.

23

Sayyid Mar'i's Political Papers*

Edited and introduced by Moshe Shemesh

INTRODUCTION

Engineer Sayyid Mar'i is one of the civilians who continued to fill official high positions after the Revolution. He reached the height of his career during the time of Sadat. Mar'i was born in 1913. He graduated from the College of Agriculture in 1937; was a member of the Egyptian parliament in 1944. Following the Revolution he became responsible for enacting the Agrarian Reform Bill. Most of the time between 1956 and 1971 he held the post of Minister and later Deputy Prime Minister for Agriculture and Agrarian Reform. In 1972–73 he was General-Secretary of the Arab Socialist Union (the ruling party). In 1975 he became Vice-President of the Republic and Speaker of the National Assembly. In 1978 he was named special assistant to President Sadat and then his advisor until Sadat's assassination. Mar'i has published many books on agriculture and food.

The civilian ministers under the revolutionary regime were mostly technocrats and experts in their field. Their position was secondary to that of the revolutionary officers. Decisions on significant topics such as defence and foreign affairs were taken by a small group of members of the RCC and, after 1956 (following the dispersal of the RCC), by ministers who had previously been members. The government debated and discussed subjects which were only technical or professional. As Mar'i himself points out the civilian ministers shared a 'silent solidarity'. These ministers, such as Mar'i, Ahmad Husni, the Minister of Justice and Aziz Sidqi, Minister for Industry, played no major role during the Suez–Sinai crisis. They were only observers.

* Sayyid Mar'i, *Awraq Siyasiyya* (Political Papers) (al-Maktab al-Misri al-Hadith, Cairo, 1978), vol.II, ch.XVI, pp.347–62.

Mar'i's *Political Papers* were published in three volumes in 1978. The first volume surveys the period up to the revolution of July, 1952. The second volume deals with the years 1952–67 and the third volume is about the period between 1968 and the October War, 1973.

In the preface to the *Papers* Mar'i notes: 'I made sure to write down the events as I actually experienced them, and as I witnessed them through every stage ... even if the events proved me to have been wrong in my estimation. I always noted down another opinion besides my own, in order to give the reader the freedom to choose between right and wrong.'

As to Mar'i's attitude to the Suez–Sinai crisis, it may be well to point out:

(a) His approach is more direct and critical than Bughdadi's. His view is that of an observer rather than that of a participant in the decision making. His account is inclined to be more objective than Bughdadi's. In fact, Mar'i did not accept the official Egyptian version that the Suez–Sinai campaign was a military victory.

(b) Mar'i is cautious in his esteem of Nasser regarding the nationalization of the Canal Company. He is rather sceptical concerning the repercussions of this move. Indeed, he was the only one who dared to challenge Nasser when he heard his decision, saying: 'This decision means war with Britain, France and all the West.' By these words he expressed the opinion of the rest of the civilian ministers in the government who shared his view.

(c) In general, his attitude to Nasser is more positive than that of Bughdadi. In fact he compliments Nasser and calls the nationalization of the Canal 'an historic step'. His views expressed the feelings of wide circles of Egyptian society following the nationalization. His enthusiasm for this action, which he expressed despite his criticism, was shared by many Egyptian people. Bughdadi could not have expressed such enthusiasm and emotion.

(d) Mar'i's attitude to the crisis and the war complements and balances Bughdadi's recounting. For Mar'i tells about the government debates and not just the discussions of the limited inner circle surrounding Nasser. Furthermore he added impressions, interpretations and analysis of Nasser's moves as well as details concerning the reaction of the people. One may also assume that side by side with his being proud of Nasser's actions he was fearful of the anticipated developments following the nationalization. Indeed, Mar'i proved to have been right in his misgivings.

FROM THE *POLITICAL PAPERS* OF SAYYID MAR'I

ON THE EVE OF THE NATIONALISATION
OF THE SUEZ CANAL

We left for Alexandria to be present at Gamal Abd al-Nasser's speech on the occasion of the anniversary of the King's departure. This is the speech that Nasser makes every year in Alexandria on the evening of 26 July.

Two hours before the time for which the speech had been planned I was summoned by the President's secretariat to an urgent meeting at his home at 'Luran' in Alexandria.

As I set out, it occurred to me that this was not a meeting of the Cabinet as such, but of a limited number of members of the Cabinet who had been individually invited to this sudden meeting by the President. In addition to him there were the Minister of War Abd al-Hakim Amir,[1] the Foreign Minister Dr. Mahmud Fawzi,[2] the Industry Minister Dr. Aziz Sidqi,[3] and myself.

The meeting began at once. Nasser's face looked serious. The occasion seemed to produce respect and fear and the participants looked as though they were frozen. My brain raced ahead, trying to predict the purpose of this meeting, but I completely failed to reach any conclusion. It was revealed when President Nasser began to speak and I found myself listening to the greatest surprise of my life.

The President began in a serious and direct manner by saying that he had invited us in order to inform us of a decision that he would announce in his speech that night. This decision was the nationalization of the Suez Canal.

This was not a decision; it was a bombshell – it was more than a bombshell.

The general political situation at that time revolved around the negotiations that were taking place with the International Bank and with America, Britain and France, regarding the finance for the High Dam construction project. This plan had become essential for Egypt's agriculture and economy. The costs were then estimated at E£460 m., of which E£136 m. in foreign currency was required over a period of 10 to 12 years. During the first stage the negotiations appeared to be progressing favourably since the USA had offered to provide $54 m. in aid and Britain had offered a further $16 m.

However, the negotiations started to go wrong when the International Bank began to impose its conditions for the granting of a loan to Egypt in the amount of $200m. (equivalent at that time to E£70 m.). It began to impose one condition after another ...

Thus 1956 opened with strained relations between Egypt and the USA and they reached a crisis point in July when John Foster Dulles[4] announced the cancellation of the loan which his country had granted as participation in the funding of the High Dam project. The significance of this was in fact the withdrawal of Britain and the International Bank from funding the project and the impact that this of necessity had on Egypt's political and economic reputation throughout the world.

This also meant that Nasser, followed by the whole of Egypt, had reached a dead end and there was no alternative but to escape from it. However, in all our predictions and suppositions, we did not even imagine the idea of nationalizing the Suez Canal, for which the operating contract was due to expire in 1968. The canal itself was the direct cause of all the aspirations of foreign elements towards us during the last 70 years.

And here was Gamal Abd al-Nasser telling us that within the next hour or hour and a half he was going to announce the decision to nationalize the Suez Canal.

I SAID: 'THIS DECISION MEANS WAR.'

This news reverberated around the room in which the meeting was taking place more powerfully than a bombshell. We were dumb-struck and filled with awe.

Gamal Abd al-Nasser turned to me and asked, 'Why don't you say something, Sayyid?'

It seems that my silence was more noticeable than that of the others and had attracted the attention of the President, who surprised me with this question whilst I was reflecting on the significance of the words Suez Canal in the political history of Egypt. The Canal had always been a symbol of imperialistic aspirations towards Egypt and thinking about it brought to mind perforce all the evil that was embodied in them. Thoughts of a closure had to take into account the fact that ultimately there would be no escape from direct confrontation with powers harbouring such aspirations.

At that moment God could not have helped me to provide a different answer than the one I gave: 'Mr. President, the decision you have made is the dream of every Egyptian. But this decision means that we shall become directly involved in a war with Britain, France and the whole of the West.'

President Nasser thought for a moment, his gaze shifting between Abd al-Hakim Amir and me. He then replied, 'I did not ask you to fight. If war breaks out it will be Abd al-Hakim Amir who will be fighting, not you.'

Silence then returned to the room in which the meeting was taking place. As for me, I do not remember anything about the meeting after Nasser's decisive reply to me. All I recall is that I went with Aziz Sidqi by car to where the speech was to be delivered in the al-Manshiya Square in Alexandria. We both remained absolutely silent during the journey.

Nasser began to speak.

There then came the moment when he announced his historic decision to the thousands of citizens in the square and to the outside world: 'In the name of the people ... the President of the Republic ... the Suez Canal Company is being nationalized. [It will become] an Egyptian public company and all its assets, royalties and liabilities will be transferred to the state ...'

The crowd gathered in the square would not let him finish. Thousands of people burst into cheers and began shouting patriotic slogans which made us, up on the stand, forget everything except that at this moment the independence of Egypt was being decided and that if the price of nationalizing the Canal was war, or even ten wars, this nation was prepared to sacrifice itself for it, just as it had paid for its construction with the lives of one hundred and twenty thousand of its sons.

We were suddenly overcome by a feeling of honour and self-sacrifice, the kind of feeling that affects every nation when destiny puts its patriotism, endurance and honour to a decisive test. The people's attitude suddenly changed from fear to honour, from hesitation to enthusiasm, from suspicion to solidarity and from doubt to pride.

The historic speech came to an end and we each went home so that our children could run after us with their hundreds of questions and their cheers. Each of the children began to feel an earthquake of pride and self-respect because his father was part of the great historic event that was taking place in Egypt and each one of them, their friends and their friends' friends, were prepared to offer up and sacrifice their cheap, humble lives faithfully to ward off any danger arising from the decision that Egypt had taken. It was as though Egypt was exacting an old revenge that had accumulated over the previous 70 years and the time had finally come to settle it.

I did not fall asleep that night until dawn, but I felt nothing of the

361

caution, fear or apprehension that had troubled me for a brief moment the previous day. But the worries began in the days that followed. These worries were not in the nature of fear, but due to the desire to ensure that we were preparing for every possibility, including the possibility of war.

Although there were few meetings of the government in the following three months, it was obvious from the meetings that took place that Nasser was completely drained by the political situation, the scale of which had begun to reach global proportions. It was also clear that the idea of war was not uppermost in his thoughts and that war itself did not enter his plans as a serious possibility.

It was clear that Nasser's assessments were made on the basis that the possibility of a solution to the crisis by peaceful means was far greater than through war; whether this assessment was based on political analysis or on information which reached him at the time, I do not know.

What I do know is that at the very moment when Nasser invited us to his house in Alexandria and when he was making his speech to the crowds, a group in Ismailia under the command of Engineer Mahmud Yunis[5] had effectively taken control of the management of the Suez Canal Company.

WORLD REACTIONS

It is clear that Nasser relied on two basic facts in his management of the political campaign following the nationalization:

(a) An effort to prove that the Egyptian administration of the Suez Canal was as capable as the foreign administration and even better.

(b) Flexibility in handling the political situation with the aim of softening the crisis in political terms and gaining as much time as possible so that the states using the Canal, and in particular Britain and France, would concentrate on political means to solve the crisis.

It was obvious that Nasser had made his decision and the matter was closed; no threats by the British Prime Minister Anthony Eden or the French Premier Guy Mollet would make him alter his decision.

Public opinion in Egypt was completely behind Nasser. Furthermore I remember a remark made previously by Sa'id Lutfi (Pasha), one of the senior political leaders of the pre-revolutionary period, who summed up Nasser's personality at the beginning of the revolu-

362

tion by saying, he is 'like a mill which grinds everything that comes in its way'.

I want to say that even Sa'id Lutfi, who had such a view of Nasser at the early stage [of the revolution], was proud of the historic decision to nationalize the Canal; this explains to what extent the return of the Suez Canal was a national aspiration (qawmiyya) which previous generations had seen as a dream difficult to fulfil.

Developments in the crisis regularly took first place on the government's agenda. Every meeting of the government began with opening remarks in which Nasser explained the latest developments and the most likely possibilities [for the future]. After that Dr. Mahmud Fawzi would speak and explain the international measures being taken by the UN and outside it.

The most striking report given by Nasser was at one of these sessions following his meeting with the then Prime Minister of Australia, Robert Menzies,[6] who had come to Egypt to negotiate in the name of a group of states using the Canal or the Canal Users' Association, as it was then called. Nasser pointed out to us that he had started the meeting with the intention of reaching a compromise with Menzies ... but the latter was arrogant and had provoked Nasser time after time until he had no alternative but to rise from his chair and expel Menzies from his office.

Despite this, Nasser's basic assessment was that the Suez Canal crisis would find a peaceful settlement. The maximum he anticipated was confrontation with Israel, since Israel regarded the nationalization of the Suez Canal by Egypt as an aggressive initiative against her and would therefore take action against this initiative. However Nasser expected that it [Israel's action] would happen only some time later. As for Britain and France, there was, of course, a possibility that they would act against Egypt, but in Nasser's opinion this was unlikely in military terms. If it were to happen, it would be indirect [in his opinion], through Israel and not at present. This was because Franco-British military action against Egypt, whether direct or through a pact with Israel, would be an act of political stupidity, amounting to the two countries' suicide in the whole Arab world.

Thus, the maximum that Nasser was expecting was military action by Israel against Egypt and if this were to happen, Egypt would of course react to it. He estimated, however, that the Canal crisis would be resolved by the UN or under its auspices, which would be the ideal solution from Egypt's point of view.

BRITAIN AND FRANCE DELIVER AN ULTIMATUM TO EGYPT

This position [of Nasser] was maintained until Israel launched her surprise military action against Egypt on 29 October 1956 and a few hours later Egypt received a joint ultimatum from Britain and France.

Gamal Abd al-Nasser summoned us to an emergency meeting of the government. Up to that moment Egypt had been successful in her political manoeuvring. She had rejected the requests of the committee headed by the Prime Minister of Australia, Robert Menzies, promoting the decision of the London Conference[7] regarding the internationalization of the Canal. The former management of the Canal Company began to incite the pilots to stay away or leave their jobs, with the result that within a month after the nationalization there were 59 pilots absent from work. After this, on 15 September, the foreign pilots and technicians resigned completely and only a quarter of the number of pilots remained in the Canal administration. However, the Egyptian management succeeded in working wonders and operated the Canal better than before ...

We had difficulty getting to where the government meeting was taking place because of the blackout that was in force due to the war with Israel that had already been going on for several hours in Sinai. We went into the meeting room and within a few moments President Nasser entered; as soon as he had sat down he took hold of a sheet of paper and then surprised us.

'A few hours ago Britain and France handed us a joint ultimatum, which was also delivered to Israel. Israel has of course accepted this ultimatum. They have conditions which they are asking us to accept. They have given us 12 hours to reply.' He then began to read: '... the ultimatum speaks of the two States' [Britain and France] firm decision that the land, sea and air forces of the two sides, Egypt and Israel, should withdraw to a distance of ten miles from the Suez Canal, in order to guarantee navigation in the Canal and that the Egyptian government should agree to the entry of forces from the two States (Britain and France) into positions controlling the Canal, as well as Port Said, Ismailia and Suez. This ultimatum has a time limit of 12 hours from the time it was delivered.'

Nasser looked up from the paper with an extremely serious expression on his face. He then went on to say, 'Before we begin the discussion I want to express a reservation, which is that we have to consider this ultimatum in the light of every possibility, including the possibility that it may be a threat.'

So up to this moment Nasser did not in any way estimate that this ultimatum was serious; this was in accordance with his existing political outlook, based as it was on the assumption of the political risks facing Britain and France and with which we had all agreed. Nasser opened the meeting but no-one spoke.

There was a frightening silence in the room which lasted for more than a minute until it was broken by Nasser himself, who turned to the Foreign Minister Dr. Fawzi and asked: 'What is your opinion, Dr. Fawzi?'

Dr. Fawzi replied: 'Mr. President, when the cannon speaks, the politician is silent. But the politician's silence does not mean that he has ceased to act, since his actions in time of war may be seen in the results of the military campaign.'

Once again there was silence.

After a short while the late Minister of Justice Ahmad Husni[8] said, 'Mr. President, I have a question. I wish to know what is expected from each of us at this time. Do we have to fight? Are we prepared to face them [Britain and France] if they become involved militarily? And I have a further question: if we fight, do we have sufficient arms or shall we throw bricks at them?'

At this point Nasser's face at once showed signs of unease in reaction to the remarks of the late Ahmad Husni, for which apparently he was completely unprepared, as were we. Nasser was silent for some time and then said: 'In my opinion we have no alternative but to take the following immediate steps.

'Firstly, we reject the Franco-British ultimatum formally and in practice; we shall not accept it whether it is genuine or merely a threat.

'Secondly, we must prepare militarily for every eventuality, and at once.

'Thirdly, as far as we the government are concerned, a number of ministers will have important assignments if there is Franco-British involvement in the Canal Zone. Dr. Mustafa Khalil,[9] for example, will be responsible for army signals and transport. Dr. Aziz Sidqi will be responsible for converting industry to serve the war effort. Engineer Sayyid Mar'i will be in charge of the supply system and organize the smooth evacuation of civilians from the Canal Zone to the rural areas. The Minister of Education and Culture[10] will make the schools available for the evacuation. The Health Minister[11] will declare a state of emergency in the hospitals, etc. etc. ...'

365

The meeting ended. Each of us went back to his home in the full blackout.

WE EMERGE FROM THE CRISIS

I returned home with an aching heart and in low spirits. The fact that I had expected war from the start and that this evaluation of mine had upset Gamal Abd al-Nasser, who had interpreted it as fear, did nothing to relieve my state of mind. In fact, I had hoped that my prediction would be mistaken. Furthermore when I expected war, my mind did not clearly grasp its dimensions or its significance. After all we were a nation that had been under English occupation for 74 years and this had only ended a few months ago. The English still have a military base on the Canal whilst our army has not yet been rebuilt. For these reasons we were surprised by a war at a level far higher than our direct capability. This was due to a plot against us, the success of which was not only conditional on our own capability, but also dependent on world opinion condemning this wild confrontation. The Franco-British ultimatum turned out to be in earnest, and the Israeli aggression was only part of a vast tripartite plot that had been planned months before.

When we started to follow the developments, the first of which was the landing of invading paratroops at the al-Gamil airfield in Port Said, each of us quickly began to carry out the tasks we had been assigned. I left home at seven in the morning and took my car to the districts, in particular the Daqhiliya district, which had been designated to absorb most of the civilians evacuated from the Canal districts, and in particular Port Said. During some of the following nights, I found myself crying at what was happening. At the end of the night I went over in my mind the sights I had seen during the day, the broken sentences I had heard, especially from those who, willingly or against their will, had left their homes in one of the Canal towns. The worst thing was that some of them were not at all interested in what was happening to their country, their homeland, but only in the pounds they were losing because of the shut-down of navigation or the departure of the English ... On the other hand I found that most people were overwhelmed by the feeling that nothing was more important than the great campaign which was Egypt's true war of independence. This independence was facing its decisive test.

It was certainly true that these ardent patriotic feelings were directing everything and that without them nothing would work

366

properly. There was no preparedness, no planning, no training nor anything else. The gravity of the crisis was increased by the fact that Egypt had to withdraw her army from Sinai after the scale of the Israeli–Franco-British conspiracy was revealed and by the need to organize shelter, supplies and equipment for all the civilians and military who were streaming to the towns in the eastern Delta and especially Daqhiliya.

This atmosphere lasted only for a few days. The USA, followed by the USSR, quickly acted to stop this extensive tripartite aggression against a small country, but it was clear that after the cease-fire the campaign turned into a clear-cut political campaign.

However, in those few days it emerged that we had been routed in the field, but this had been covered up by the Egyptian propaganda, which had invented imaginary battles and created heroic stories of popular resistance in Port Said. And yet the decisive factor in the whole affair was the political shrewdness with which the campaign was managed, which completely obscured the military débâcle.

I personally expected that there would be a political solution, especially in view of the respected moral position taken by the American President, Dwight Eisenhower, against the three aggressor states. But I did not anticipate such a decisive and wide-scale solution as came later.

In the light of the political developments of the crisis, which came day after day, one was forced to make inevitable comparisons. Although I and other citizens did not play a major role in this crisis, viewing it from inside, as it were, provided a yardstick for the fitness of the regime and there was sufficient material to compare it with what had happened in Egypt before the revolution.

First: regarding the actual decision to nationalize the Canal, the most striking aspect was the great courage involved in making it.

Second: as for the method by which the crisis was managed politically, there was an overriding feeling that it was a mixture of fear, dread and wonder.

Third: as the crisis developed and escalated, Gamal Abd al-Nasser placed his cards on the table one after another in order to avoid any military confrontation.

Fourth: the whole world was shocked by a decision that was one hundred per cent Egyptian. Egypt [before the nationalization] was the one that was shocked by what was happening in the world; it was she that was influenced by it rather than being the one to influence it. The world appointed a representative to meet Nasser, namely the Australian Prime Minister, Robert Menzies. This representative behaved with arrogance and insolence. When he displayed his arrogance in the presence of Nasser, he at once got up and asked him to leave his office.

When I remember all this, I also remember what runs parallel to it. For example, on 4 February 1942, when the British ambassador presented his famous ultimatum to the Egyptian king[12] ... every Egyptian politician was shocked and afraid ... I even remember the news about the same ambassador meeting a certain Egyptian politician. When it became known, the politician's reputation went up at once and the question, 'Will he return to the government?' became instead, 'When will he return to the government?'

When I remember all this and compare this event with another, I find myself full of wonder, but with mixed feelings. At the personal, emotional level I am filled with pride and honour; honour in how much has changed and in so short a time and pride that Egypt – after this great step [nationalization of the Suez Canal] – has an international importance that she never achieved in any previous period in her modern history. Egypt's political victory in the course of the crisis over the nationalization of the Suez Canal was by every standard an international victory, which made Egypt a leader of the Third World nations and a basic factor in every international calculation.

On a practical level all the hopes that had been impossible only a few years before ... became achievable for the first time ...

The dream of returning the Suez Canal to Egypt had been a dream for two or three generations and suddenly it came true by means of the courageous decision of a courageous leader. It reverberated throughout Egypt and the whole international arena.

The things that had been impossible became possible ...

NOTES

1. *Abd al-Hakim Amir (1919–67)*: member of the RCC; graduated from the Military College 1939; Major 1948; promoted to General and appointed C-in-C of the armed forces June 1953 and Minister of War 1954; Field-Marshal, Vice-President, Minister of War, 1958; member of the Presidential Council 1962; First Vice-President and Deputy Supreme Commander of the Armed Forces 1964; after the defeat in June 1967 he committed suicide in prison.
2. *Mahmud Fawzi (1900–81)*: entered diplomatic service 1923; Vice-Consul New York and New Orleans 1926–29; Consul-General Liverpool 1937–40; Director, Department of Nationalities, Ministry of Foreign Affairs 1940–41; Consul-General, Jerusalem 1941–44; Egyptian delegate to the UN and Representative to the Security Council 1946; Ambassador to Britain 1952; Foreign Minister 1952–64;

member of the Presidential Council 1962–64; Deputy Prime Minister for Foreign Affairs, 1967–68; Prime Minister 1970–72; Vice-President 1972–74.

3. *Aziz Sidqi (1920–)*: engineer, technical adviser after the July 1952 Revolution at the Prime Minister's Office; Director General of the Productivity Centre of the ILO 1955; Director-General of the Liberation Province Authority, Minister of Industry 1956; Central Minister of Industry after the union between Egypt and Syria 1958; Deputy Prime Minister for Industry and Mineral Wealth 1964; Adviser on Industrial Affairs to the President 1967; Minister for Industry 1968 and Military Production 1969–70; First Deputy Prime Minister 1971; Prime Minister 1971–73; Assistant to President Sadat 1973–75.

4. *John Foster Dulles (1888–1959)*: U.S. Secretary of State, 1952–59.

5. *Mahmud Yunis (1912–)*: army engineer 1937; Military Operation Directorate, 1943; Staff Officer's College 1944 & 1947; Director Technical Affairs Office, GHQ 1952; Chairman and Managing Director, General Petroleum Authority 1954; Managing Director and Deputy Chairman Egyptian Suez Canal Authority, July 1956; Chairman of the Suez Canal Authority 1957; Deputy Minister for Transport and Communications 1965–67; Minister of Oil Transport 1967.

6. *Robert Menzies (1894–1982)*: Australian statesman; Attorney-General, 1934–39; leader of the United Australia Party from 1939; Prime Minister, 1939–41 and 1949–66.

7. First London Conference on the Suez Canal was held on 16–23 August 1956. The Conference decided to appoint a five-member committee, headed by Robert Menzies.

8. *Ahmad Husni*: Minister of Justice 1956; the Egyptian Region Executive Minister of Justice, 1959–61; Minister of State in the United Government of the UAR 1961.

9. *Mustafa Khalil (1920–)*: civil engineer, Egyptian State Railways 1941, 1951–2; Minister for Communications and Transport 1956–64; Deputy Prime Minister for Communications and Transport 1964–5, for Industrial Wealth and Electricity 1965–66; Secretary-General of the Arab Socialist Union (established in 1962) 1977–78; Prime Minister 1978–81.

10. *Kamal al-Din Hussein (1921–)*: member of the RCC; graduated from the Military College 1939; Major 1948; Minister for Social Affairs 1954; Minister for Education 1956; member of the Presidential Council 1962–64 when he left public office.

11. *Nur al-Din Tarraf*: Doctor of Medicine; Minister of Health 1956; Chairman of the Executive Council of the Egyptian Region of the UAR 1958–60; Minister of Health 1961–62, member of the Presidential Council 1962–64; Deputy Prime Minister and Minister of Justice, Labour and Youth Affairs 1964–66.

12. On 4 February 1942, in the face of the growing military threat from the Axis forces and the pro-German foreign policy of the King and his Government, Britain compelled the King to replace the Cabinet with a Wafdist Government that was more acceptable to Britain by issuing an ultimatum and a show of military force. Then the King appointed Mustafa al-Nahhas, the leader of the Wafd, as Prime Minister.

APPENDIX

APPENDIX

The Egyptian Army Operation Order
1 September 1956
for the Defence of Egypt*

Edited and introduced by Moshe Shemesh

INTRODUCTION

The Operation Order 1 September 1956 for the Defence of Egypt, which was captured by the Israeli Defence Forces during the war, is published here for the first time. This document is important for understanding the Egyptian strategic, military and political evaluation of the situation for the critical period between the nationalization of the Suez Canal Company on 26 July 1956 and the outbreak of hostilities three months later. The Order is also essential for analysing the Egyptian perception of possible Anglo-French–Israeli courses of action.

The point of departure for this Order is the assessment that the Western Powers, particularly Britain and France, might initiate hostilities to take the Canal Zone, above all, and then possibly Cairo in order to topple the regime. At the same time, The Egyptian High Command assumed that Israel would not be likely to take part in any Western attack, although they thought that Israel would carry out local initiatives along the Egyptian border, particularly in the demilitarized Zone around Nitsana. In December 1956, Nasser explicitly expressed this evaluation by emphasizing that 'Our general assessment of the situation on which the deployment of our forces on the front was based is as follows: if Israel's aim was to perpetrate incidents or raids, then she would direct them either at the Gaza Strip or at our advance positions on the border.'** With the Sinai excluded as a possible major theatre of hostilities, Egypt's

---

* GHQ, Operations and Planning Branch, *Army Operation Order No. 50, 1956* (1 September 1956).
** *The Egyptian Gazette*, 6 Dec. 1956.

373

principal defensive regions were therefore defined as the Canal Zone, Alexandria and Cairo.

The High Command assumed that the Western Plan would be implemented in two main stages:

The first stage: Capture of the Canal Zone and possibly the area of Alexandria with air and naval forces and with both ground and airborne infantry playing a major part in the attack.

The second stage: Advance on Cairo with the aim of overthrowing the regime, together with the possibility of a landing in the Delta area.

Apparently the assessment of the High Command was that the balance of power, in general, and in every expected theatre of operation, in particular, would be favourable to the attackers. Therefore, the High Command mobilized all the regular and semi-regular forces for the campaign. Its aim was to gain time by conducting delaying battles to prevent, as far as possible, the enemy's advance. The assumption was that following the attack there would be political developments which would bring about a cessation of hostilities or a complete change in the balance of power. The element of delay is discernible in the general structure of the Order, although, each unit was expected to engage in obstinate defence.

It was obvious, in the light of the evaluation of the enemy's possible courses of action, that already in the first stage of the attack the High Command would aspire to prevent the seizure by the attackers of bridge-heads on Egyptian terrain.

For purposes of defence, the Order divided Egypt into six fronts (or commands): Sinai, the Gulf of Aqaba, the Canal and the Eastern Delta, Alexandria, Cairo and the Delta. The GHQ in Cairo retained the over-all command of all six fronts. The headquarters of each front consisted mainly of the then existing HQs of the areas (regions) after adjustment to the new assignments derived from this Order. All land forces, including the units of the Liberation Army (militia), were placed under orders of the commanders of the fronts. Each front commander received exhaustively defined assignments. However, the priorities concerning the vital defence areas were to be determined by the commanders of the fronts themselves. If they were not able to hold their positions and had to retreat, they were authorized to sabotage or blow up the various installations, but only after receiving the approval of the GHQ.

The Order only relates to four of the fronts. As to the other two (Sinai and the Gulf of Aqaba) the commanders were referred to orders which had previously been circulated.

Canal Front

The disposition of the forces shows that they anticipated that the Canal Zone would be the principal battle-ground, at least in the first stage. Therefore, most of the forces were allocated to it. The commander of the Eastern Front (responsible for the defence of Sinai) was given the command of the Canal Front. Thus, his authority encompassed the command of both the Canal and the Sinai fronts. The task of this front was the defence of the Canal Zone (including Bir Adib) and ensuring navigation through it.

The forces allocated to this front were: 2 infantry brigades (2nd division), 1 National Guard brigade, 1 armoured brigade and support forces. The forces were dispersed in such a way as to deal with the possibility that the main thrust of the enemy would be concentrated on the Canal Zone for the purpose of capturing it and advancing towards Cairo by utilizing the many transportation routes to the capital. It was determined that Ismailia and Suez, located at the head of the major routes to Cairo and Port Said, were vital areas in the Canal Zone.

The Alexandria Front

The task of this front was to defend the Alexandria area, within which the Egyptian naval base was located. Its importance was derived also from its location on the main road to Cairo. The Egyptian High Command thought this area might be used for the landing of a secondary military effort with the purpose of splitting the Egyptian forces and, if possible, carrying out an attack on Cairo. The forces allocated to this front were: 1 infantry brigade, 2 National Guard brigades and support units.

The Cairo Front

The assignments given to this front were the defence of the Cairo area and the maintenance of order in the capital. Its importance derived from its being the centre of government and the location of many airfields and army bases. The approaches to the city and its suburbs, especially the eastern approaches, were chosen as vital defensive areas, as was Bir Adib to the south-west of the Gulf of Suez. The Egyptian GHQ feared that its fall would open an easy route for an attack on Cairo.

The forces allocated to this front were: 1 armoured brigade (also serving as the HG reserve), 1 National Guard brigade, 2 reserve brigades, approximately 20 battalions made up from the staff and cadets of the military colleges, to be organized in time of emergency, and support units.

The Delta Front

The possibility of a landing in the Delta area did not seem very probable; therefore this front was not assigned specific tasks. Its assignments were detailed in the section of the Order entitled 'points to be given attention', namely to carry out sabotage to cut off communications lines and to secure the flanks of the other fronts.

Only small units were allocated to this front, whose main task was to take action against sappers and small units. It consisted of 1 National Guard brigade and semi-regular forces.

The location and mobility of the general reserves of GHQ were in accordance with the anticipated courses of action of the enemy. Being an 'assault force' their tasks were: first, to block the forces trying to break through on one of the Canal or Alexandria routes to Cairo by waging the principal battle outside Cairo, and second, to take part in the defence of the Cairo area and to secure domestic order within the capital as needed.

The Egyptian forces were combined on the basis of a regular army nucleus, including all the support and service elements, with the addition of reserves and semi-regular units. The battle framework on each front was the infantry brigade, except for the main Canal Front, where there was a divisional framework. The armoured brigade teams were not split up since they were to be committed to battle in their regular framework. The combination of forces on each front was balanced and permitted independent fighting without the need for support or service during the first phase of the combat.

*　　　*　　　*

General Head Quarters
Operations and Planning Branch
Date of publication: 1.9.56
Date of latest update: 27.9.56

ARMY OPERATION ORDER NO. 50, 1956

(No changes regarding verbal instructions already issued)*

General

1. It is expected that some Western states will carry out hostile actions against Egypt as a result of the nationalization of the Suez [Canal Company].*

Information

2. See Appendix A attached. [Appendix not attached]

Possibilities of Attack

3. Occupation of the Canal Zone by air and naval action.
4. Occupation of the Alexandria base by naval and air operations.
5. Attack on the Cairo region, following the occupation of the whole or part of the Canal Zone or the occupation or neutralization of Alexandria.
6. Naval landings and airborne drops in the Delta region.
7. One should not ignore what action may be taken by Israel in these circumstances.

Battle Fronts

8. The Republic (apart from Upper Egypt), due to present circumstances and for the purposes of military operations, is divided temporarily into the following fronts:

   a. Sinai Front
   b. Gulf of Aqaba Front
   c. Canal and Eastern Delta Front
   d. Alexandria Front
   e. Cairo Front
   f. Delta Front

---

* Parentheses – ( ) – enclose materials found in the original text. Square brackets –
[ ] – enclose explanatory additions by the editor.

9. The boundaries shown on the attached transparency are to be considered as temporary and for operations purposes only. [Transparency not attached]

10. The Sinai and Gulf of Aqaba Fronts will follow the orders already issued.

Canal and Eastern Delta Front

11. *Command*

    a. The Canal Zone and the Eastern Delta will be under the command of Lt. General Ali Ali Amir, commander of Eastern Command forces.

    b. In view of present circumstances the authority of Eastern Command will be extended to include the Canal Zone and the Eastern Delta.

12. Forces

2nd Infantry Division, including: 2nd infantry brigade, 3rd infantry brigade, 7th infantry brigade, support units of the above; 1st Armoured Brigade team and 2nd Armoured Battalion [reconnaissance battalion]; 21st Heavy Mortars Squadron; 19th Heavy Mortars Squadron, less 2 batteries; squadron from 19th Battalion [rockets]; National Guard Brigade; staff units.

13. *Tasks*

    a. Securing the Canal Zone from attack by air and sea.

    b. Securing the passage of traffic through the Canal.

    c. Strengthening the status of the nationalized [Suez] company if necessary.

14. *Points to be considered*

    a. The importance of the Suez region and the prevention at all costs of its occupation by the enemy.

    b. Steps to be taken to control the Bir Adib area, to immobilize any landings in this area and destroy all forces advancing from there to the north or the west.

    c. All hostile forces succeeding in landing at Port Said are to be prevented from moving towards, or reaching, Ismailia.

    d. The importance of intensified measures to destroy all hostile airborne forces landing or dropping in this area.

    e. Controlling Egyptian installations in the area and securing the Canal crossings, whilst drawing up necessary plans for the demolition of the important bridges in case of necessity.

f. Securing in a thoroughgoing manner the airfields at Abu Suweir, Fayid, Cabrit, and Casparit.

g. Preparation for the special blowing up and demolition operations, as set out in Army Operations Orders no. 41/56; any air drops by forces in the Canal Zone will necessitate the implementation of these orders.

h. Coordination with East Cairo forces and the armoured forces in the Cairo area as well as the Liberation Army, operating in the Delta and the Canal region.

The Alexandria Front

15. *Commander:* Lt. General Ahmad Salim, commanding officer, Northern Command.

16. *Forces*

18th Infantry Brigade; 2nd Infantry Battalion; 116th Battalion [guard battalion]; light company [armed jeeps]; battery from 18th Field Battalion [self-propelled S.U. 100 guns]; squadron of field artillery; squadron from 19th Battalion [rockets]; squadron from 5th Light AA Battalion; tank company from 3rd Battalion [Shermans]; engineer company; transport company; air control team, and 2 air support officer stations; 2 National Guard brigades; staff units.

17. *Tasks*

The defence of the Alexandria region against any hostile actions by sea or air.

18. *Points to be taken into account and considered*

a. Important and essential targets such as the port of Alexandria, coastal fortifications, airfields and combined operations rooms will be included in the defensive framework.

b. The importance of the elimination of all forces landing by sea during the initial stages of the landing, whether to the east or the west of Alexandria.

c. Implementation of the demolition plans, especially as regards roads related to shipping, whilst maintaining an open communication axis to the Delta (the al-Mahmudiya road).

d. Implementation of the special plans referred to in our letter no. 8155/2610 dated 1.8.56.

e. The necessary coordination will be maintained with forces of the Liberation Army which has the task of the defence of Alexandria. It is also necessary to maintain coordination with the Delta forces with regard to the securing of Alexandria forces from this direction or concerning all movements of forces of the Alexandria front through the Delta, if this should prove necessary.

f. These instructions cancel Army Operations Orders no. 42 of 1956, which were issued as no. 6280/2268 dated 1.8.56.

The Cairo Front

19. Western Cairo

a. *Commander:* Lt. General Mahmud Abd al-Aziz Mustafa, commanding officer, Western Cairo.

b. *Forces*
91st Infantry Brigade [reserve brigade]; 97th Infantry Brigade [reserve brigade]; battalion from 1st Brigade as support for armoured forces [armoured infantry battalion]; anti-tank company from 70th Battalion; 4th Armoured Division HQ staff; 9th Armoured Battalion [Centurion tanks]; 85th Medium Battalion [T-34/85 tanks]; 11th Armoured Battalion [Stalin tanks]; 5th Armoured Battalion [composite reconnaissance]; 10th Armoured Infantry Battalion; 13th AMX Company; support and staff units; battalion of 122mm. howitzers will be attached immediately following completion of training; 61st Medium Artillery Squadron [155mm]; 5th Light AA Battalion (less 1 squadron); 2 companies of engineers (to be exchanged with Eastern Cairo); 2 squads of military police; transport company; air control team and 2 air support officer stations; National Guard battalion; administrative units; 2 guard companies and company from 70th Infantry Battalion and 13th AMX Platoon, all this formerly posted to West Cairo airfield.

c. *Tasks*
Defence of the Western Cairo front against any land attacks or airborne drops.

d. *Points to be considered*

1. The importance of eliminating enemy armour before reaching agricultural areas.

2. The importance of the complete concealment of concentration areas of armour and guarding against the effects of enemy air superiority by application of the principle of surprise, destruction and night movements, in so far as conditions permit this.

3. Control the various approach roads from this direction.

4. Utilization of the natural obstacles in the agricultural areas to the west of the Nile for defence in depth.

5. Utilization of demolition and destruction, especially in the agricultural areas.

6. Application of the plans referred to in our letter no. 5518/2610 dated 1.8.56.

7. The defence of the west of Cairo airfield will be within the responsibility of this front.

8. Coordination with Liberation Army forces operating in the Delta as well as with forces of the Alexandria front.

20. *Central Cairo*

a. *Commander*: Lt. General Naguib Abd al-Hamid Ghanim, commander of Central Cairo.

b. *Forces*

16 battalions (formed into a special formation from training bases and schools and to be activated at the appropriate time); Republican Guard battalion; transport company (2 platoons or similar units) to be formed at the appropriate time; security and guard company, and a company from the Infantry School (to be posted at the appropriate time) [both formerly posted to the al-Maza airfield]; security and guard company for the Heliopolis airfield; 2 National Guard battalions, and 60th Staghound Company [armoured car] (less 3 platoons) [both] formerly posted to the defence of Cairo airfield; battalion from the Infantry School and under its command 2 Staghound platoons [formerly posted for anti-paratroop defence in the al-Maza and Heliopolis areas]; battalion from the Army Services Training Base [formerly posted for anti-paratroop defence in the Huckstep area]; battalion from the Infantry Advanced Training Base [formerly posted for anti-paratroop defence in the Wadi Hof area].

c. *Tasks*
1. Local defence of the city of Cairo.
2. Support for local security activities and assistance to the civilian authorities.

d. *Points to be considered*
1. The defence of al-Maza, Heliopolis and (international) Cairo airports will be included in the control zone of this front.
2. The special importance of defence against paratroop forces in the areas of Heliopolis, al-Maza, Huckstep and Wadi Hof, with coordination of the necessary communications between the local defence of the airfields and the other forces responsible for defence against paratroopers in these areas.
3. Concentration of the defence of the main approach roads to the heart of Cairo.
4. The importance of defence in built-up area combat and the training of forces in this type of warfare from now on.
5. Defence of the Nile crossings against sabotage.
6. Maintaining a local reserve force sufficient for internal security work.
7. The importance of coordination between forces of the Liberation Army operating in Cairo, and coordination with the defensive forces in Eastern and Western Cairo.

21. *Eastern Cairo*

a. *Commander*: Major General Ahmad al-Gharib Zayd, commander Eastern Cairo.

b. *Forces*
1. *under command*: battalion from the technical training base (to be used at the appropriate time); a company from 70th Infantry Battalion; border patrol car company (to be used at the appropriate time); 122nd Medium Artillery Battalion (when fully equipped); 2 engineer companies (each one with 2 platoons) in cooperation with Western Cairo; squad of military police; transport company (3 platoons or similar force); air control team and 2 air support officer stations (to be attached at the appropriate time); National Guard brigade, less 5 battalions [a National Guard brigade consists of 10 battalions]; administrative units; National Guard battalion and National Guard medium machine-gun platoon (both for Anshas airfield); National

Guard battalion and National Guard medium machine-gun platoon (both for Bilbeis airfield).

2. *under command at the appropriate time according to course of operations*: 97th Infantry Brigade [reserves]; 4th Infantry Brigade (10th and 12th Battalions and 290 Battalion [reserve battalion]); 1st Infantry Brigade (less 1 battalion) [armoured infantry brigade]; all other forces that circumstances will permit are to be concentrated in the Cairo area, apart from its current resources.

c. *Tasks*

The defence of Eastern Cairo from any hostile actions from that direction.

d. *Points to be considered*

1. Securing the various approaches to Cairo, whether from the direction of the Bilbeis Desert, Suez or Bir Adib.

2. Implementation of demolition and destruction in suitable places for this purpose, and especially on the approach roads to al-Ma'adi, Tara and Helwan.

3. Coordination with the armoured forces, the Central Cairo Command and the Eastern Command (the Canal) as well as with the Liberation Army forces operating in the Delta.

4. The Defence of Anshas and Bilbeis airports will be included in the area of authority of this front.

The Delta Front

22. *Commanders*: Col. Ahmad Hamdi Abid, Commander, Eastern Delta Sector; Lt. General Salah Hatata, Commander, Central Delta Sector; Maj. General Atif Nassar, Commander, Western Delta Sector; Col. Abd al-Mun'im Husni, Commander, Cairo Sector.

23. *Forces*

National Guard brigade; battalions of the Popular Resistance; Youth battalions; company of engineers (2 platoons).

24. *Points to be considered*

The importance of coordination with army forces operating in the various battlefronts – the Canal, Alexandria and Cairo – especially with regard to the defence of our forces' flanks to the East and West of Cairo, as well as to raids carried out by Liberation [Army] forces to cut and sabotage the enemy's communications whether on the Cairo–Alexandria road, the Ismailia road or the Suez road.

The General Reserve

25. *Forces*

    a. 1st Infantry Brigade – 1st Battalion, 3rd Battalion and 20th Battalion (armoured infantry); 4th Infantry Brigade* – 10th Battalion, 12th Battalion and 290th Battalion [reserve battalion]; armoured units; 40th Field Artillery Battalion [reserve battalion] – 118, 119 and 124 Squadrons; 120 Field Artillery Squadron (in process of formation); 94 Anti-Tank Squadron [17-pounders]; 5th Light AA Battalion (less 1 squadron); 17th Light AA battalion, less 1 squadron [which was in process of formation]; 6th Engineer Company; 3rd Infantry Workshop (less 1 section); 3rd Field Hospital; 32nd Armoured Transport Company, 6x6 armoured troop carriers (to serve with 1st Infantry Brigade immediately following its formation); 41st Transport Company; army services; troop transport platoon (for operation with 1st Infantry Brigade); 2 platoons military police (immediately following formation).

    b. 75th Paratroop Battalion; squadron of field artillery from the Gunnery Training Centre (following formation).

26. The forces in paragraph 25a are to be considered as assault troops and will carry out the following assignments:

    a. to operate in the Canal area or the Alexandria area and fight the main battle outside Cairo, according to developments.

    b. to participate in the defence of Eastern and Western Cairo.

These forces are to carry out all reconnaissance and make preliminary preparations in order to ensure the complete implementation of these assignments.

Secondary Plans

27. Armoured units in Cairo – in addition to their tasks in Western Cairo – will draw up secondary plans for action in Eastern Cairo with

---

* The 4th Infantry Brigade was actually stationed in Sinai and participated in the battles during Operation Kadesh.

the objective of destroying all hostile forces advancing on the city, whether from the Canal Zone or Bir Adib. This is to be done in coordination with the armoured units on the Canal and with Eastern Cairo Command and Eastern Command (Canal).

28. 97th Infantry Brigade [reserves] will draw up a plan for the defence of Eastern Cairo, after completing its plan for Western Cairo.

29. 1st infantry brigade will participate in the preparation of a defensive plan for Eastern Cairo, up to battalion level, to enable it to take part in the defence if circumstances so dictate. It will also study the situation in Western Cairo in order to carry out a counter-attack if necessary.

Liaison between the Liberation Army and other Land Forces

30. Elements of the Liberation Army operating on the military fronts will come under the command of the commanding officer of the front for operational purposes.

31. Army commanders will coordinate their actions with the commanders of Liberation Army units in the areas under their command.

32. Border and coastal [guard] forces operating within any of the army fronts will support that front.

33. Land elements of the naval forces taking part in the defence plan of the ports or land elements of the air force taking part in the defence plan of the airfields will come under the command of the commanding officer in charge of the land defence of the respective port or airfield.

Liaison between Commanders of the Fronts and the Anti-Aircraft Artillery for the Aerial Defence of the Republic.

34. All changes in the AA defence plan for the Suez Canal strip must be agreed by the officer commanding aerial defence in the sector and the officer commanding the AA defence in the sector. This agreement will be authorized by Eastern Command before implementation. AA Defence Command must notify about these changes immediately.

35. Commanding officers of Commands or Fronts may issue tactical orders to the AA forces operating within their commands or fronts according to the needs of the general tactical situation at the time of operations.

36. A policy for the aerial AA defence of the Republic will be instituted regarding the prohibition of civil and military aviation and the rules of interception for aircraft, including:

a. prohibition of civil and military aviation and requirement for permits by high authorities and publication of relevant regulations;
b. rules for intercepting civil or military aircraft varying the prohibition instructions must be approved by high authorities;
c. until the publication of instructions relating to the rules of interception of delinquent aircraft, the following procedures will apply:
1. interception of aircraft identified as hostile
2. interception of aircraft engaged in actual hostile activity against a defended target or [AA] artillery positions.

Coastal Observation

37. The Coastal Guard will maintain a coastal watch and report on all hostile ships and landing craft in the Port Said and Abu-Kir areas. Reports [of observers] will be directed as follows:

a. from the Port Said area (inclusive) to Ras al-Bar (not inclusive) – to the local commanding officer at Port Said and to Eastern Command;
b. from Ras al-Bar (inclusive) to al-Magdaba (not inclusive) – to the Liberation Army forces in Damiat or Rashid, who will pass on the information to their HQ in Tanta;
c. from al-Magdaba (inclusive) to Abu-Kir – to the officer commanding the defensive sector at Abu-Kir;
d. the reporting procedure from Abu-Kir to Ras al-Tin will be coordinated between the Coastal Guard and Northern Command;
e. the area between Ras al-Tin and al-Makhas is the responsibility of the naval forces. Information will be passed on to the coastal defence room at Ras al-Tin and from there to the joint command;
f. the area from al-Makhas to Sidi Barbar is the responsibility of the Coastal Department. Information will be passed on to the Coastal Police at al-Makhas and from there to the Joint Command;
g. adjacent areas will pass on information to each other according to the situation.

38. The Border Force is in charge of observation between al-Amaria and Marsa Matruh. Information will be passed on to Burj al-Arab and from there to the Joint Command at Alexandria. It [Border Force] is also in charge of the area from Gabat al-Buss (not inclusive) to al-Gardaka (inclusive). Information will be passed on to Eastern Command.

39. Eastern Command maintains a watch between Suez and Gabat al-Buss (inclusive). Information regarding the landing of forces in the Bir Adib area will be passed on to the Eastern Cairo Command.

Air Support

40. *Method of requesting air support for the Alexandria and Cairo Fronts*

    a. *Requests for armed air support*: These requests are to be directed through the operations networks via the operations branches, according to the normal command procedure, to the operations and planning directorate which will pass them to the Combined Operations Centre at al-Zamalik.

    b. *Requests for urgent air support*: These requests are to be directed via the units from the Combined Operations Centre in al-Zamalik through the signal net of the Air Support Officer Company.

    c. *Requests for air patrols in the Alexandria Front*: These requests are to be directed to the air commander in the northern region, who will respond to the request if possible or refer it to the Combined Operations Centre at al-Zamalik.

41. *Method of requesting air support for the Sinai, Canal and Gulf of Aqaba Fronts*

These requests will be directed to the Combined Operations Centre at the Canal.

42. *Bomb Line*

    a. Officers commanding formations (brigades and front commands) will notify the reference points and lines of forward localities to the Combined Operations Centre through the urgent air support net every four hours, or immediately if there is any change in these localities.

    b. The bomb line will be coordinated at the Combined Operations Centres and reported to each [ground] army and air force unit every four hours, or immediately if there is any change in the situation.

    c. The Combined Operations Centre at Eastern Command and the Combined Operations Centre at al-Zamalik will exchange information regarding the bombing line in the two operations areas every four hours, or immediately if there is any change in the situation.

    d. *Times for reporting on the bombing line are*: 0400, 0800, 1200, 1600, 2000, 2400 or any time that the situation dictates.

    e. The bombing line will be reported to the strategic operations centre at the times detailed in paragraph d.

43. *Mutual Land-Air Identification and Determination of Targets*

    a. The Combined Operations Centres will publish instructions to facilitate the mutual identification between land and air, as well as the coded colours and means of determining targets in accordance with the capabilities of the units.

    b. Units, formation and area commands will provide series of coloured marking tapes in accordance with standard procedures.

44. Appendix B, attached, details the air support staff officers for the Alexandria and Cairo fronts [appendix not attached].

Responsibility for Explosion and Demolition

45. Explosion and demolitions in the defensive fronts – [will be carried out] on the authority of the front commanders.

46. Explosive charges will be laid only at the appropriate time.

47. The Army Operations and Plans Directorate should be consulted before carrying out primary demolition activities, but there is no need to do so in the case of final activities that have been postponed.

48. The evacuation, blowing up and destruction of airfields – [will be undertaken] on the authority of the airfield commanders, after consulting their commands (Air Force). The security force at each airfield should be notified in time before demolition orders are issued.

Administration

49. The Quartermaster Branch will issue the necessary administrative orders.

Storage

50. *Food*: Units will hold at least 15 days 'dry' rations at a special rate of supply, according to the state of the stores and as determined by the Quartermaster Branch.

51. *Ammunition*

Areas will hold ammunition in quantities customary on the Eastern Front, on condition that these quantities are reported to the commands and with information to the Quartermaster Branch, which will supply the required quantities to each area.

52. *Fuel*

    a. Units will keep fuel reserves sufficient for a distance [i.e. move] of 200 km;

    b. Areas will keep fuel for the infantry units sufficient for a distance of 400 km in the rear;

    c. Areas will keep fuel for the armoured units sufficient for a distance of 500 km in the rear.

53. *Water*

Distribution will be carried out according to the needs of the areas, with the Quartermaster Branch being informed.

54. *Defensive Materials*

Appendix C, attached, details the defensive materials allocated to the Alexandria and Cairo fronts [appendix not attached].

55. *Medical Procedures and Reduction of Losses*

Manpower Branch will publish its plan regarding supplies, medical arrangements and evacuation of the wounded.

Internal [Signal] Communications

56. *Command Centres*: a. *Eastern Command*: al-Jala Camp in Ismailia; b. *Northern Command*: Bos al-Daka; c. *Western Cairo Command*: Teachers' Cultural Institute, behind the al-Ahram Building in al-Haram St.; d. *Central Cairo Command*: Central [Command] Area camp; e. *Eastern Cairo Command*: 18th Brigade HQ camp at al-Maza; f. *Delta Command*: Eastern Delta – Istirahat Alri at al-Zkazik [apparently a rest home]; Central Delta – Istirahat

Al Ray at Tanta [apparently a rest home]; Western Delta – Science Faculty at Mahram Bek Cairo, 18 Suk al-Tufika St.

57. The Signals Corps will publish orders which will include the requisite signal plan for linking the various fronts to the Army Operations and Plans Directorate in Cairo.

58. A unit from the air support officer company will maintain the signal net for urgent air support.

Director of Army Operations and Plans
Lt. General Abdulla al-Sharqawi

CONTRIBUTORS

Julian Amery is a veteran Conservative M.P. His publications include *Sons of the Eagle* (1948); several volumes in *The Life of Joseph Chamberlain*; *Joseph Chamberlain and Tariff Reform Campaign* (1969); and an autobiography, *Approach March* (1973). He is also a contributor to the *Daily Telegraph*. In the period of the Suez Crisis he was Member of the Round Table Conference on Malta, 1955; Parliamentary Under-Secretary of State and Financial Secretary, War Office 1957–58; Parliamentary Under-Secretary of State, Colonial Office, 1958–60; and a leader of the Suez Group. Since then he has been Secretary of State for Air (1960–62), Minister of Aviation (1962–64), Minister of Housing and Construction (1970–72) and Minister for Foreign and Commonwealth Affairs (1972–74).

Alfred Leroy Atherton is a veteran American diplomat and Director of the Harkness Fellowships of the Commonwealth Fund. He has had extensive experience in the Middle East and has served as Deputy Assistant Secretary of State 1970–74; Assistant Secretary of State 1974–78; Ambassador-at-Large with Special Responsibility for Middle East Peace Negotiations, 1978–79; and Ambassador to Egypt 1979–83. During the period of the Suez crisis he was Second Secretary, US Embassy, Damascus, Syria 1953–56 and Consul at Aleppo, Syria 1957–58.

Shlomo Avineri is the Herbert Samuel Professor of Political Science at the Hebrew University of Jerusalem. A graduate of the Hebrew University of Jerusalem and the London School of Economics, he has taught at Yale, Cornell, the University of California, Australian National University and has been a Fellow at the Woodrow Wilson Centre in Washington D.C. and Director General, Israeli Ministry of Foreign Affairs (1976–77). His publications include *The Social and Political Thoughts of Karl Marx* (1968); *Hegel's Theory of the Modern State* (1972); *The Making of Modern Zionism* (1982); *Moses Hess: Prophet of Communism and Zionism* (1984); *Arlosoroff; An Intellectual Biography* (1989).

391

Yonah Bandmann, Lt. Colonel (Res.), is a Researcher at the Israel Galilee Research Centre for the History of Hagana-Defence Force. During his military service, 1959–80, he served as a researcher on Middle Eastern affairs. His publications include many articles on Egypt and, in particular, on the Egyptian army.

Mordechai Bar-On is a Fellow of the Ben-Gurion Research Centre and Archives. He has published on the IDF and public affairs as well as on the Sinai Campaign of 1956 and the Six-Day War. Before receiving his Ph.D. from the Hebrew University of Jerusalem he served in the IDF, the Jewish Agency and was a Member of the Knesset. His responsibilities included Chief Education Officer, IDF, 1962; Head of the Youth and Hechalutz Department of the Jewish Agency; Member of Knesset, 1984–86. During the Sinai Crisis he was Head of the Office of the Chief of Staff (1956–57).

Yehuda Z. Blum holds the Hersch Lauterpacht chair in international law at the Hebrew University in Jerusalem. His publications include: *Historic Titles in International Law*; (Ed.) *Encyclopedia Hebraica* (1973–); *Secure Boundaries and Middle East Peace* (1971). His legal and diplomatic experience includes Assistant Judge Advocate-General of the IDF 1956–59; Senior Assistant to the Legal Adviser, Ministry of Foreign Affairs, 1962–65; and Permanent Representative to the UN, 1978–84.

Jean-Paul Cointet is Professor of History at the Institut d'Histoire, University of Sorbonne, Paris. Some publications include *La France Libre* (1975); *La France et les Français* (1975–77); *De Gaulle et la Discussion nucléaire* (1984); *Un Camarade en République: Guy Mollet* (1987). He is titular member of the Société d'Histoire Moderne et Contemporaine (Bureau), and of the Association Française des Relations Internationales. He is a frequent contributor to learned journals on contemporary French history.

Galia Golan, Darwin Professor of Soviet and East European Studies, is Chairperson of the Department of Political Science and former head of the Mayrock Centre for the Study of the Soviet Union and Eastern Europe at the Hebrew University of Jerusalem. She is the author of *The Czechoslovak Reform Movement* (1971); *Reform Rule in Czechoslovakia* (1973); *Yom Kippur and After: The Soviet Union and the Middle East Crisis* (1977); *The Soviet Union and the Palestine Liberation Organisation* (1980); and *The*

Soviet Union and National Liberation Movements in the Third World (1988).

Chaim Herzog has served as President of the State of Israel since 1983. Intelligence Officer, IDF 1948–50; Defence Attaché, Israel Embassy, Washington and Ottawa 1950–54; Field Commands 1954–59; Director of Military Intelligence 1959–62; Governor, Administered Territories, 1967; Permanent Representative to the UN 1975–78; Member of Knesset 1981–83. His publications include *Israel's Finest Hour* (1967); *Days of Awe* (1973); *The War of Atonement* (1975); *Who Stands Accused* (1978); *Battles of the Bible* (1978); *The Arab–Israeli Wars* (1982).

André Martin has served in the French army since 1932. At the time of the Suez Crisis he was Brigadier General of the French Air Force and Deputy Chief of Operations at Army Headquarters under the command of General Ely and his deputy General Challe. He was also active in secret negotiations between France and Israel. On account of the organisation of the command he was unable to have any influence on the events in Cyprus. He later reached the rank of Chief of Staff of the Air Force: Grand Croix of the Légion d'honneur.

Elhannan Orren is a military historian, serving as a Lt. Col. (Res.) and Researcher in the Department of Military History GHQ, IDF. His extensive service commenced with the Haganah and the Jewish Infantry Brigade Group, and he is a graduate of the Command and Staff College. He has published extensively on Israeli military history. His books include Ben-Gurion's *Diary of the War of Independence (1947–1949)* (co-editor). During the Sinai Campaign he served in a Divisional Combat Team.

Shimon Peres is a veteran Member of the Knesset and former Prime Minister. He is presently Deputy Prime Minister, Minister of the Treasury and Leader of the Labour Party. His publications include *The Next Step* (1965); *David's Sling* (1970); *From These Men* (1984); and numerous articles in Israeli and foreign publications. During the period of the Sinai Crisis he was Director-General of the Ministry of Defence 1953–59 and actively involved with developing the Israeli–French relationship including the secret discussions at Sèvres.

Yitzhak Rabin, Maj. Gen. (Res.), is Minister of Defence. Past service includes Prime Minister and Leader of the Labour Party

(1974–77). He was previously posted as Ambassador to the US (1968–73). His military career began as a Palmach commander (1943–48). With the IDF he served as Representative at the Rhodes Armistice Negotiations, 1949; Commander-in-Chief of Northern Command 1956–59; Head, Manpower Branch 1959–60; Deputy Chief-of-Staff and Head of General Staff Branch 1960–64; Chief-of-Staff IDF 1964–68. His publications include *The Rabin Memoirs* (1979).

Itamar Rabinovich is Dina and Yona Ettinger Professor of Contemporary Middle Eastern History at Tel Aviv University and Director of that University's Dayan Centre for Middle Eastern and African Studies. His latest books include *The War for Lebanon 1970–85* and *Ethnicity, Pluralism and the State in the Middle East* (co-editor).

Robert Rhodes James is a veteran Conservative M.P. He has published extensively including biographies of *Lord Randolph Churchill* (1959); *Rosebery* (1963); *Churchill: A Study in Failure, 1900–39* (1970); and *Anthony Eden* (1986). During the Sinai Crisis he was Assistant Clerk at the House of Commons, 1955–61. Subsequently he served as Senior Clerk, 1961–64; Fellow of All Souls' College, Oxford, 1965–68, 1979– ; Director, Institute for Study of International Organization, 1968–73; Principal Officer, Executive Office of the Secretary General of the UN, 1973–76; Minister Responsible for Higher Education, 1979–85 and 1986–87; for Higher and Further Education 1987– .

Robert Schulzinger is Professor of History at the University of Colorado, Boulder. He is the author of several books including *American Diplomacy in the Twentieth Century* (1984) and *The Wise Men of Foreign Affairs; the History of the Council on Foreign Relations* (1984). He also served on the staff of the U. S. Senate Committee on Foreign Relations in 1982.

Col. John A. Sellers, MBE has served extensively with the Indian Army and the British army in a variety of posts including India, Burma, Germany, Cyprus and the Middle East. A graduate of the Staff College and the Joint Services Staff College, he was also an instructor at the School of Land–Air Warfare and the National Defence College. He now writes volumes on various aspects of warfare for the British Army's prime source of doctrine, the Army Field Manual. His chief interest is the study of war and military history. He has written a number of case studies for the Services.

Sasson Somekh is the Halmos Professor of Arabic Literature at Tel-Aviv University and has been a Visiting Professor at Princeton University and a Visiting Fellow at St. Antony's College, Oxford. He has published extensively on modern Arabic literature including *The Changing Rhythm: A Study of Najib Mahfuz's Novels* (1973), *Two Versions of Dialogue in the Drama of Mahmud Taymur* (1975), *The Question of Language in Modern Arabic Literature* (1980), and *The Language of Fiction in the Works of Yusuf Idris* (1984).

Moshe Shemesh is a Senior Lecturer in Middle Eastern Studies at the Ben-Gurion University of the Negev and Fellow of the Ben-Gurion Research Centre in Sede Boqer. He received the M.A. (with distinction) in General History from the Hebrew University of Jerusalem in 1977 and a Ph.D from the London School of Economics and Political Science in 1983. In 1988–89 he was a Weidenfeld Visiting Fellow at St. Antony's College, Oxford. His publications include *The Palestinian Entity 1959–74: Arab Politics and the PLO* (1988) and articles on Palestinian Politics and the PLO, the Lebanon Crisis, Egypt and inter-Arab relations.

Selwyn Ilan Troen is the Sam and Anna Lopin Professor of Modern History at Ben-Gurion University of the Negev and the former Director of the Ben-Gurion Research Centre and Archives. He was a Fellow of the Davis Centre for Historical Studies at Princeton University and a Weidenfeld Fellow at St. Antony's College, Oxford. He also held visiting posts at S.U.N.Y. at Stony Brook, Harvard and Columbia. His publications include *The Public and the Schools* (1975) and *St. Louis* (1977). He writes on Israeli social history and his most recent publications include *National Jewish Solidarity in the Modern Period* (co-editor) (1988).

Rechavam Zeevy, Maj. Gen. (Res.), is a member of the Knesset and Chairman of Eretz Israel Museum in Tel-Aviv. He has served as Chief-of-Staff Central Command, 1961–64; Assistant Chief of Operations Division, GHQ, 1964–68; Commander-in-Chief Central Command (1968–73); Adviser on Terrorism to Prime Minister Rabin, 1974–77. At the time of the Suez Crisis he was Chief-of-Staff Southern Command (1955–57).